Praise for the Book

"Indian healthcare is poised for a massive disruption. The sheer diversity of India demands indigenous and creative solutions; Tilak's recognition of this important element is highly appreciated. An important feature of this book is that the idea of management is dealt with in a wholesome manner, with Tilak making sure that he touches upon several facets of management, from leadership to marketing to finance and human resource management".

Prof Viswanath Pingali, *Associate Professor of Economics, Indian Institute of Management, Ahmedabad, India*

"*Management of Healthcare in India: Need for a Paradigm Shift* passionately argues why there is an urgent need for fundamental reforms in our healthcare institutions. Rapidly changing medical practices and information technology require a modern approach to healthcare and management of healthcare institutions. Mr Tilak Shankar is uniquely qualified to discuss these issues as he has vast experience working with healthcare institutions. So he provides multiple examples from Indian hospitals. The book deserves to find a place in all libraries".

Dr V. Mohan, MD., PhD, DSc, *Chairman; Dr. Mohan's Diabetes Specialities Centre and President, Madras Diabetes Research Foundation*

"This book by Mr Tilak Shankar is a compelling and timely work that addresses the urgent need for reform in India's healthcare management. With 16 insightful chapters, including expert contributions on public health, tribal health and AI, the book offers a well-rounded perspective on institutional transformation. I have known Mr Shankar for nearly three decades and have closely observed his expertise in managing healthcare systems across the corporate and public sectors globally. His deep understanding and practical wisdom shine through every page, making this book essential reading for healthcare leaders and policymakers".

Dr Shravan Subramanyam, *MD & Group CEO, BPL Medical Technologies; Former President, Healthcare Federation of India (NATHEALTH)*

Management of Healthcare in India

The book analyses the four key pillars of Indian healthcare – information, management, human resources and financing – to identify major systemic flaws and proposes practical, actionable solutions. It highlights how better resource utilisation can improve patient care, reduce costs and enhance access.

India's complex and multiple healthcare systems have proved incapable of delivering affordable care to its population. Acute funding shortage is one of the reasons for poor health outcomes. Public health, with its vast countrywide network, is hamstrung by a procedure-bound bureaucrac, which does not focus on patients. Private healthcare institutions offer excellent tertiary care on par with global quality standards but excessively focus on profitability. Non-profit healthcare organisations that offer succour to the underprivileged sections of society are faced with perennial funding challenges. India needs a strong public health system, robust non-profit healthcare institutions and high-quality private hospitals. The Indian hospital sector is now an attractive destination for investment. Private equity investments into private hospitals have made superior quality of care with state-of-the-art technology possible.

This book will be of interest to academics and practitioners in the field of medical sociology, history of medicine, health and development studies, healthcare administration and management and South Asian studies.

Tilak Shankar is a commerce graduate from the University of Madras and has a post-graduate diploma from the Indian Institute of Management, Ahmedabad (IIMA). He was a Director with AF Ferguson & Co. and is presently the CEO of Management Solutions. He has carried out more than 300 consulting engagements, including many healthcare organisations.

Management of Healthcare in India

Need for a Paradigm Shift

Edited by Tilak Shankar

Routledge
Taylor & Francis Group
LONDON AND NEW YORK

First published 2026
by Routledge
4 Park Square, Milton Park, Abingdon, Oxon OX14 4RN

and by Routledge
605 Third Avenue, New York, NY 10158

Routledge is an imprint of the Taylor & Francis Group, an informa business

British Library Cataloguing-in-Publication Data
A catalogue record for this book is available from the British Library

ISBN: 978-1-032-77800-6 (hbk)
ISBN: 978-1-041-15995-7 (pbk)
ISBN: 978-1-003-68494-7 (ebk)

DOI: 10.4324/9781003684947

Typeset in Sabon
by Deanta Global Publishing Services, Chennai, India

Contents

Figures

Tables

Contributors

Tilak Shankar is a commerce graduate from Madras University and has a post-graduate diploma from the Indian Institute of Management, Ahmedabad (IIMA). He was a Director with AF Ferguson & Co. and is presently the CEO of Management Solutions. He has carried out more than 300 consulting engagements, including for many healthcare organisations. The organisations included private hospitals, charitable hospitals and international agencies. He has served on the Board of Cancer Institute, Chennai, and the Board of Childs Trust Hospital, Chennai, India. He has assisted many non-government organisations (NGOs). He had served on a commission appointed by the Government of Tamil Nadu on certain administrative reforms.

Sudharshini Subramaniam has completed MD in Community Medicine and a Certificate Course in Health and Family Welfare Management. She is a WHO SEARO Region Research Fellow on 'Strengthening Gender Equity and Intersectionality in Health Policy and Systems Research'. She is currently an associate professor at the Institute of Community Medicine, Madras Medical College, Chennai, India, and works as an Honorary Consultant at Rural Women's Social Education Centre (RUWSEC), Thirukazhukundram, Tamil Nadu, India.

Pritha Venkatachalam holds a master's degree in development management from the London School of Economics and an MBA from the Indian Institute of Management, Bangalore, including an exchange programme at Melbourne Business School. She is a partner and Co-Head, Asia, and Africa at Bridgespan with experience in over 25 countries. She has extensive experience in public health, on strategy, results delivery and operating models.

Shailendra Hegde, MD, DNB, MBA, is a medical doctor with specialisation in public health and preventive medicine from St. John's Medical College and a Master of Business Administration in International Organisations from the University of Geneva, Switzerland. Dr Hegde has over 17 years of experience in leading and delivering clinical services, conducting community-based research and providing academic training in a variety of healthcare institutions, Dr Hegde is well versed in managing large healthcare programmes, managing projects at Jhpiego, Piramal foundation, and has co-authored 45 publications and has implemented Anamaya, focusing on tribal health.

Mala Sarat Chandra has an architecture degree from the University of Cincinnati in Cincinnati, Ohio, and MBA from the University of Pittsburgh in Pittsburgh, Pennsylvania. She has held senior positions in the United States with Microsoft, Motorola, Sun Micro Systems and Tandem Computers, managing large software teams. She has several patents, won awards and has spoken at various fora in different parts of the world. She has developed several consumer products, creating industry-changing software platforms and innovative software platforms.

Foreword

As the landscape of healthcare continues to evolve, the need for a comprehensive understanding of its diverse facets becomes increasingly paramount. In the *Management of Healthcare in India: Need for a Paradigm Shift*, the esteemed authors delve into the intricacies of India's healthcare system, offering profound insights into its public health initiatives, private sector dynamics, the pivotal role of non-profit organisations, and management as the crucial fourth pillar supporting the other three.

In a nation as vast and diverse as India, the challenges within the healthcare sector are multifaceted. The authors, drawing upon their extensive expertise and experiences, navigate through these complexities with precision and clarity. By dissecting public health, private health, non-profit organisations and management, they provide readers with a holistic perspective, shedding light on both the achievements and the hurdles encountered along the way.

Public health stands as the cornerstone of any healthcare system, and its significance cannot be overstated. Public health infrastructure in India is created in a geographically diverse landscape. Through meticulous analysis, the authors elucidate the evolution of public health policies in India, examining their impact on the nation's populace and outlining avenues for further improvement.

In parallel, the exploration of the private healthcare sector uncovers the interplay between quality, accessibility and affordability – an equilibrium that remains elusive yet indispensable. With a keen focus on innovation and best practices, the authors offer valuable insights into leveraging the strengths of the private sector to augment the overall healthcare landscape.

Furthermore, the vital role of non-profit organisations in bridging gaps and addressing underserved communities cannot be overlooked. By highlighting exemplary initiatives and collaborative endeavours, the authors underscore the transformative potential inherent in philanthropic endeavours within the healthcare sphere.

Finally, effective management serves as the linchpin that binds these pillars together, ensuring coherence, efficiency and sustainability. Through case studies and strategic frameworks, the authors elucidate the principles of sound management practices tailored to the nuances of the Indian healthcare context. Incidentally, IIM Bangalore has been successfully running Certification in Healthcare Management for all cadres of healthcare workers to arm them with a better understanding of healthcare delivery and to see the impact their roles have on costs and efficiencies of operations.

India is facing a huge shortage of healthcare workforce. We need policy initiatives to mitigate the shortage as soon as possible. Technology will disrupt the way healthcare is delivered. Clinical and non-clinical decisions will be increasingly based on technology in driving patient safety, improving quality, bringing down costs and enhancing accessibility. India will become the first country in the world to dissociate healthcare from wealth.

As we navigate the complexities of healthcare provision, *Management of Healthcare in India: Need for a Paradigm Shift* serves as an invaluable guidepost, offering actionable insights and fostering a deeper understanding of the intricate ecosystem that underpins the nation's well-being. I commend the authors for their scholarly contribution and trust that this seminal work will inspire meaningful discourse and drive positive change within India's healthcare landscape.

Dr Devi Shetty
Chairman, Narayana Health, Bengaluru

Preface

Medicine and management, to some administrators, appear to be two unrelated disciplines. Nothing can be further from the truth. In a fast-changing medical field, a static medical institution is likely to be left behind by not adapting appropriate management concepts. Some private hospitals have demonstrated how each operational improvement leads to better patient care, cost control and generation of profits. This message that management is a key factor in all hospitals has to get wider currency.

This is not a textbook. The book focuses on the Indian experiences of different hospitals, describes management processes and examines the robustness of institutions to cope with rapid developments. It identifies good practices that should be emulated by all hospitals.

The book was started in the early part of COVID-19 years. Sometime in 2020, I was housebound. No friends could visit us. There was anxiety about the unknown virus, and, at least initially, a scramble to get the COVID vaccination. Perhaps the right time to write a book? The advent of the Internet had made referencing much easier.

I wanted to ensure that the book focused on the practical issues of management, based on my work experience. There is very little theory in this book. In addition to my exposure to the industry, my consulting engagements with government hospitals, charitable hospitals and some corporate hospitals made me realise that each of these institutions is unique. My conversations over the years with medical and management experts highlighted the gap between the application of management techniques and hospital needs. This book attempts to discuss the role of management concepts and techniques for the three major providers of Indian healthcare, namely, public health facilities, charitable and non-profit institutions, and private and corporate hospitals. Our government hospitals, non-profit hospitals and private hospitals each cater to different segments of our population in rural and urban India. We have huge gaps in our ability to meet the health needs of 1.4 billion people. India need not choose any one system of healthcare over the other, since healthcare needs are so large that no one system can adequately meet the need for good quality, affordable care. All the health systems should be robust to adequately tackle the present challenges and emerging future health problems as well. Poor management is a major reason for suboptimal health outcomes in large parts of our ecosystem.

I became acutely aware over the course of my work in the healthcare sector that the state of affairs in different parts of India is far from satisfactory. We have unacceptable levels of infant and maternal mortality, instances of children under the age of five dying prematurely, significant stunting and wasting and tuberculosis deaths. All these numbers are reported year after year by various government agencies with clinical indifference. Government hospitals are always overcrowded and understaffed. The sorry state of our primary healthcare centres and large government teaching hospitals should make anyone sad and angry. Who is responsible for the way in which we treat human beings, our fellow citizens? Exposure to charitable hospitals strengthens your faith in human values, though their struggle for survival is palpable. On the other hand, private equity funds and IPOs have enriched corporate hospitals.

The last few decades have witnessed dramatic changes in our healthcare system. The rapidity of change in medical technology, information technology and new medicines has revolutionised healthcare. There is a very short time gap between the introduction of a new drug in a developed country and its introduction into the large Indian market. Corporate hospitals have grown and obtained national and international quality accreditations. They are also crowded, emphasising the need for tertiary care of a large number of patients.

Our society has become highly fragmented: rural and urban, rich and poor, illiterate and well-informed. Yet diseases don't seem to differentiate. Diabetes affects the rich and poor alike. Poor diabetics cannot afford to take medicines regularly. How do we respond to these various changes?

A modern hospital cannot be run on outdated methods. Our public health system is a good example. The present generation can scarcely believe that some 40 years ago, government hospitals were the primary source of medical care. The decline of government hospitals has been rapid. A visit to a government hospital or a health centre will highlight the fact that there is very little accountability for poor performance.

The central theme of this book is that good management is essential for all sections of our healthcare.

Many of the basic problems that a majority of the hospitals face can be solved by applying the necessary management principles. Problems of long waiting time, non-availability of medicines, poor use of technology, poor use of traditional and social media for patient communication, analysis of data for decision making and ensuring high uptime of medical equipment can be solved by using the applicable techniques that are mostly simple. There are larger issues of strategy, policies and institutional response to changing patient needs.

The book has been enriched by experts who readily agreed to contribute a chapter each. Dr Sudharshini Subramaniam, a practising physician, an associate professor and a passionate advocate of public health, has written a very insightful chapter on public health. Dr Shailendra Hegde, a practicing doctor and community health researcher with vast experience of running large health care programmes, and Pritha Venkatachalam, who has significant experience in strategy and public health with a 25-year stint in a nonprofit organisation, have contributed a chapter on tribal health, a lesser-known subject. All of us have focused largely on the Indian experience. Mala Sarat Chandra, a software industry expert, has contributed a chapter on artificial intelligence.

This is not *yet* another book describing Indian healthcare systems. This is a small attempt to bring about change in our health systems. Everyone has been a patient at some point of time. Experiences of long waiting times and massive hospital bills have brought home to each of us the need for reforms.

Acknowledgements

I have a long list of people to thank for making this book a reality. The seeds of this book were sown by A.R. Parthasarathy, a Partner in RGN Price, a well-known accounting firm in Chennai, India. He suggested that I put my consulting work experience in a book form. He assembled a small team to do some basic research. We went through several drafts of the table of contents. I met with Dr Arjun Rajagopalan, a reputed vascular surgeon and formerly Medical Director of Sundaram Medical Foundation, and asked him whether I should venture into writing a book. He strongly recommended that I start immediately. I also sought advice from Dr V. Mohan, a well-known expert on diabetes and chairman of a large specialty hospital, also in Chennai, India. His enthusiastic response further encouraged me to go ahead.

This book has also gained from the inputs of several specialists. Dr Sudharshini, a passionate advocate of public health, has written an illuminating chapter on public health. Mala Chandra, a software industry expert, brought in her considerable experience in IT and AI to elaborate on the entry of AI into the healthcare sector. Pritha Venkatachalam, expert in public health and strategy, and Dr Shailendra Hegde, a dedicated doctor having a rich experience of running large health care projects, have shared their experience on a unique subject – tribal health. L. Sriram, a finance expert and an old friend K. Venkatakrishnan, a partner with RGN Price, guided me on the finance chapter. K.M. Madhumitha, a young Chartered Accountant, helped me with research on private equity funds. A.V. Ram Mohan educated me on quantitative techniques. This knowledge helped me to examine its applicability in healthcare.

Ashok Anantaram, a marketing expert, readily shared his experience on hospitality and hospital marketing to enrich the chapter on marketing. Pushpa Gopal and Gopal Kalyanakrishnan provided valuable guidance. Our good friend Sanjay Kaul was an inspiration. Raksha Patel readily helped with many secretarial matters.

Venkatesh Krishnamoorthy was a patient and thorough copyeditor who competently nursed my manuscript till it was ready for publication.

My two days at Narayana Health, Bengaluru, were immensely useful. The hospital fixed appointments with their top management and was ready to share any information that I needed for this book. Particular thanks to

Ms J. Sandhya, CFO, who made my visit a memorable one. I was impressed with the single-minded focus on patient welfare and compassion in every staff member I met. The sight of a large number of children who had undergone heart surgery was a moving experience.

I spent several days at Sundaram Medical Foundation and met with a large number of senior staff to appreciate the importance of good management practices in every department. This hospital is a NABH-accredited, non-profit hospital run by the TVS group.

My family stood rock like in supporting this venture. My daughter Sucharita and her husband Satish helped me immensely. Similarly, my son Raghav and his wife Anisha gave many useful tips. My wife Purna was always encouraging the first-time author.

Acronyms

ABNHPS	Ayushman Bharat National Health Protection Scheme
AFHC	adolescent-friendly health clinics
AI	Artificial Intelligence
AI steth	Artificial Intelligence Stethoscope
AIIMS	All India Institute of Medical Sciences
ALOS	average length of stay
ANM	auxiliary midwife
AOA	Articles of Association
ARPOB	average revenue per occupied bed
ASHA	accredited social health activists
AYUSH	Ayurveda, Yoga, Unani, Siddha, Homeopathy
BPO	business process outsourcing
CAG	Comptroller and Audit General
CAGR	compounded annual growth rate
CAP	College of American Pathologists
CDV	customer-derived value
CEO	chief executive officer
CFO	chief finance officer
CGM	continuous glucose monitor
CHC	community healthcare centre
CME	continuing medical education
COPD	chronic obstructive pulmonary disease
CR	Confidential Report
CRM	customer relationship management
CSR	corporate social responsibility
CTO	chief technology officer
CWE	chief wage earner
DNB	Diplomate of National Board
EBITDA	earnings before interest tax depreciation amortisation
EHR	electronic health record
ERP	enterprise resource planning
GDP	gross domestic product
GOI	Government of India
GSDP	gross state domestic product

HFA	Health for All
HLEG	High-Level Expert Group
HMIS	Health Management Information Systems
HR	human resources
HWC	health and wellness centres
IAS	Indian Administrative Service
ICMR	Indian Council of Medical Research
ICU	intensive care unit
IMA	Indian Medical Association
IMR	infant mortality rate
IPO	initial public offer
IT	information technology
JCI	Joint Council International
JD	job description
JSY	Janani Suraksha Yojana
KRA	key result area
LHT	local health traditions
LP	linear programming
MCI	Medical Council of India
MCTS	Maternal Child Health Tracking System
MDG	Millennium Development Goals
MLHCP	mid-level health care providers
MMR	maternal mortality rate
MOA	Memorandum of Association
MOTA	Ministry of Tribal Affairs
MRP	maximum retail price
NABH	National Accreditation Board for Hospitals and Healthcare Providers
NABL	National Accreditation Board for Testing and Calibration Laboratories
NCD	non-communicable diseases
NFHS	National Family Health Survey
NGO	non-government organisation
NHM	National Health Mission
NHP	National Health Policy
NHRM	National Health Rural Mission
NHS	National Health Service
NIRTH	National Institute of Research in Tribal Health
NLEM	National List of Essential Medicines
NLP	natural language processing
PDS	public distribution system
PG	post-graduate
PHC	primary healthcare centre
PMBJP	Pradhan Mantri Bharathiya Janaushadi Pariyojana
PMJAY	Pradhan Mantri Jan Arogya Yojana

PPP	public–private partnership
PRI	panchayati raj institutions
PVTG	particularly vulnerable tribal groups
QOL	quality of life
QR	quick response
RKS	Rogi Kalyan Samiti
ROI	return on investment
RWD	real-world data
SC/ST	Scheduled Caste and Scheduled Tribes
SEC	Socio-Economic Survey
SKU	stock-keeping unit
SOP	standard operating procedure
TPA	third-party administrators
TRI	Tribal Research Institute
UHC	universal health coverage
UNICEF	United Nations Children's Fund
VHSNC	village health sanitation and nutrition committee
WFS	weekly iron and folic acid supplementation
WHO	World Health Organization

1 Introduction

Tilak Shankar

India is one of the world's largest and fastest growing economies. But its public health expenditure is abysmally low at around 2 per cent of the GDP. Clearly, this low level of expenditure is inadequate to provide a decent level of healthcare to the citizens. The per-capita health expenditure, which is a better indicator of health expenditure, varies widely between INR 1,800 and INR 10,000[1] across states based on the respective state's Gross State Domestic Product (GSDP) and its population. A large part of the health expenditure, in the quoted per-capita expenditure figures, is in the form of out-of-pocket expenses incurred by individuals seeking treatment.

In addition, healthcare institutions have to keep pace with the burgeoning needs of the diverse population in India. Both the government and the private sector have a key role to play in providing quality healthcare to the citizens. The public healthcare system needs to reflect a country's economy and development. One of the major weaknesses in India's healthcare systems is poor management of resources – both public health and large parts of the private sector. For example, if public hospitals effectively utilise their existing resources, they would have played a much larger role in providing quality patient-oriented care. India's healthcare needs a paradigm shift.[2] The most populous nation's complex systems – traditional and contemporary medical care – have not been meeting the healthcare needs of the population for several decades. India's health outcomes are unsatisfactory. There are vast imbalances, personal health expenditures are increasing and most health institutions are weak. Patient-oriented, affordable quality care for all citizens or universal healthcare has remained a desirable but distant goal.

The rapidity of external developments demands fundamental reforms in our healthcare institutions. The new paradigms are significant developments in medical technology, robotics, use of information technology including artificial intelligence, path-breaking drug development, use of micronutrients, new treatment protocols, new funding sources and quality accreditations. Each development requires a competent, flexible organisational response from all healthcare institutions. No healthcare institution can survive by merely reacting to external developments. Adequate forecasting systems and strong management processes are required for organisations to adapt, grow

DOI: 10.4324/9781003684947-1

and contribute to patient care. Modern medicine should be matched by modern management.

No institution – public or private – can survive in the twenty-first century with outdated management practices. Many private hospitals have demonstrated the advantages of employing modern management practices for attracting a large quantum of funds, effective patient care and growth and profitability. India is confronted with the twin challenges of coping with traditional illnesses and emerging diseases. Technological developments and modern medical care still demand that disease management and patient orientation should be at the centre of any new approach – be it public or private healthcare. Advancements in medical sciences require innovative, nimble management of resources at the national and state level and in all individual hospitals. The present Indian healthcare system falls considerably short of this demand.

The combined public–private form of healthcare is witnessing a momentous change at present. India is rapidly moving towards a market-driven healthcare system, which is unsuitable for a developing country with a significant proportion of poor population. In public health, large resources – funds, human resources and numbers of patients – are governed by bureaucracy, which is unsuitable for prompt patient-oriented care. The public health system in India has a country-wide network of 200,000 primary health centres, large numbers of staff but hampered by poor funding, medical vacancies and a crushing bureaucracy. Simple managerial improvements at these centres can bring immediate medical relief to millions of underprivileged sections. While funding should be increased, it should be accompanied by empowering the ground-level staff to attend to patient needs at the centres.

This book focuses on the importance of good management of all healthcare institutions, with a specific emphasis on developments in Indian healthcare. This chapter is divided into two sections, with Section I providing an overview of healthcare infrastructure in India and Section II dealing with how the issues confronting healthcare can be addressed.

Section I: Healthcare infrastructure in India

Healthcare in India

At the time of independence and for many decades thereafter, the Indian medical system confronted a slew of health issues such as unacceptable levels of infant and maternal mortality, high fertility rates, leprosy, tuberculosis with a high prevalence, malnutrition, low life expectancy and inadequate health infrastructure.

India witnessed a rapid growth in population – from about 340 million in 1947[3] to about 1,457 million in 2024[4], a four-fold increase, severely affecting our already fragile public health system. India responded to the growing healthcare needs of the population by creating more hospital beds and ramping up the count of doctors, nurses and other staff in the healthcare system. Private hospitals and nursing homes also contributed handsomely to fulfilling the needs of the patients. One-third of the population even now lives in 4,000 cities and towns, and the balance two-thirds live in 650,000 villages.[5]

As already stated, the government expenditure on health, estimated at around 2 per cent of the GDP,[6] is much lower than what has been recommended by the World Health Organization and even lower than many developing countries. In fact, healthcare expenditure as a proportion of GDP has been steadily declining over the years. About two-thirds of the national health expenditure is incurred by states and the balance one-third by the Government of India.[7] While there has been an improvement in several metrics like life expectancy, it is no cause for celebration. On several health indicators, India stays at the bottom of the table. There are huge interstate variations in health outcomes. There are sharp differences between health facilities and the health of the population between rural and urban India. Similarly, there is a significant disparity in health outcomes between Scheduled Castes, Scheduled Tribes and the rest of the population. The inequality in healthcare is only growing.

AYUSH and allopathy

India's healthcare system (Figure 1.1) has a mix of allopathy and a wide range of alternative medicines. The Ayurveda, Yoga and naturopathy, Unani, Siddha and Homeopathy are grouped together and christened AYUSH by the Government of India. At present, allopathy, which also has a long history in India, is one of the major healthcare systems. Each of the traditional systems, over the centuries, has served our population well. Allopathy co-exists with AYUSH in villages and cities.

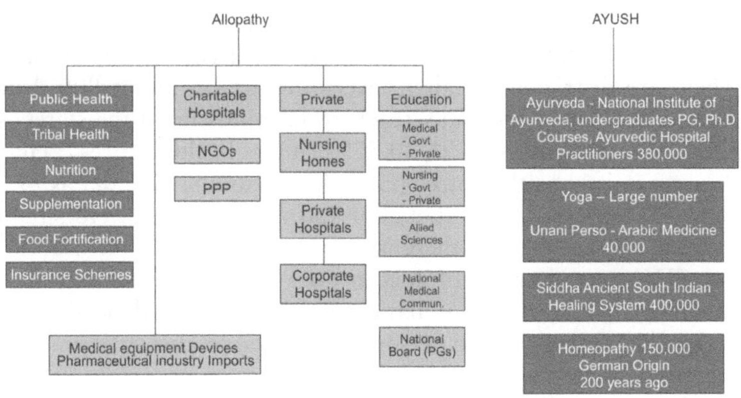

Figure 1.1 India's healthcare system: An overview.

Systems of healthcare

At present, there are three major systems for providing allopathic care in India:

1. Public health system (hospitals, primary health centres, health and nutrition-related programmes of the government)
2. Non-profit or charitable hospitals
3. Private hospitals (for-profit, including corporate hospitals)

In addition, diagnostic centres and retail pharmacies, as part of the larger health ecosystem, respectively catering to the testing needs and dispensing medicine (with online pharmacies delivering medicines home), operate in rural and urban areas. We will briefly discuss the key features of the above three systems.

Public healthcare in India

Healthcare is vested with the states. The Government of India broadly draws the policies and takes care of the funding and monitoring of the implementation of various national health programmes. In addition, it has established national health institutes (for example, the All India Institute of Medical Sciences (AIIMS)). In recent years, the Government of India's health footprint has been growing.

In state governments, the health department is headed by a Health Secretary, who usually belongs to the Indian Administrative Service (IAS). Several medical departments come under the Health Secretary's jurisdiction, such as medical education, rural health, family welfare programmes, preventive medicine, alternative systems of medicine, various heads of department managing health projects and health administration (Figure 1.2). The basic health network consists of sub-centres, primary healthcare centres (PHCs), community health centres (CHCs) and wellness centres.

There is a sanctioned staff strength (many decades ago) at each centre. There are district hospitals in every district (in about 800 districts), and in addition, there are many teaching hospitals in all the states. There were 157,819 sub-centres (SCs), 30,579 primary health centres (PHCs) and 5,951 community health centres (CHCs) functioning in India as of 2021. Of these 156,101 SCs, 25,140 PHCs and 5,481 CHCs were situated in rural areas.[8] In many states, there is an acute shortage of medical doctors; in most CHCs, the shortage of doctors goes up to 80 per cent of the sanctioned strength.[9] The rural population is thus forced to depend on private hospitals, unqualified medical personnel (quacks) or alternative medicine to meet their healthcare needs.

India has an excellent network of 1.3 million anganwadi centres[10] and an additional one million accredited social health activist (ASHA) workers[11]

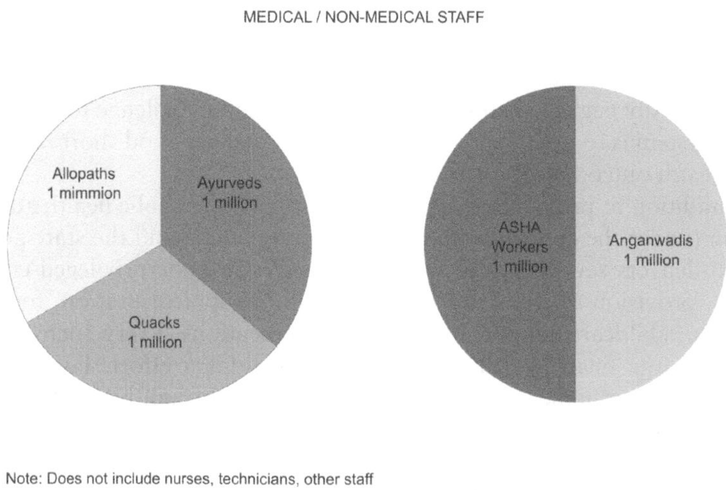

Figure 1.2 India's healthcare system (allopathy).

Source: Natural Medical Communication 2019 data.

providing the 'last-mile coverage'. ASHAs are part-time workers, poorly compensated and not utilised effectively. It is unfortunate that the excellent field network of anganwadis and ASHA workers is wasted by neglect. Anganwadis, which come under the Integrated Child Development Scheme (ICDS), are responsible for the nutrition, health and early education of zero- to six-year-old children. Figure 1.3 shows the public health infrastructure at the village level.

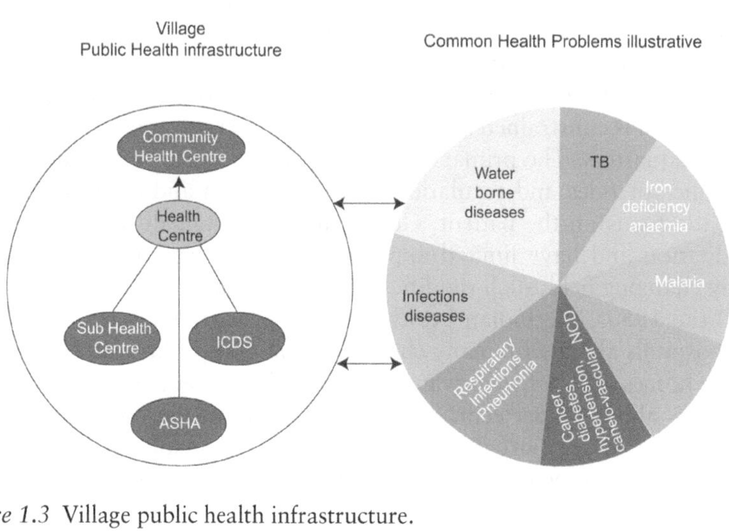

Figure 1.3 Village public health infrastructure.

There are about 150 districts in India where the Scheduled Caste and Scheduled Tribe population makes up more than 20 per cent of the total population.[12] The health needs of the Scheduled Castes and Tribes are unique. They are sadly neglected and segregated. The biggest challenge for the public health system is to use the present network and deliver good short- and long-term health outcomes.

In addition to providing treatment at hospitals, the public health administration (under the control of the Government of India and the state governments) delivers several health welfare measures to underprivileged citizens, that is, provision of free food grains, nutrition supplementation, food fortification, childcare support and similar interventions. Every such measure involves large financial resources apart from human effort. For example, the ICDS programme, one of the largest initiatives jointly funded by the Government of India and states, incurs an expenditure of INR 30,000 crore per annum. This programme includes children from the age of six months to six years, pregnant and lactating mothers, pre-formal education, supplementary nutrition and other programmes.[13]

Food fortification is another major initiative, with 100 per cent funding by the Government of India for rice fortification with iron, folic acid and vitamin B_{12}. Four states – Haryana, Rajasthan, Madhya Pradesh and Maharashtra – are carrying out wheat and rice fortification programmes. Several other commonly consumed items such as salt, tea and maize are also being fortified. The potential benefit far exceeds the cost of such programmes.[14]

Every single programme involves huge expenditure and encompasses multiple states covering a large population in rural, tribal and urban areas. The need for effective management cannot be overemphasised.

India's hospitals present a complex picture. Public health, which is a major provider of both health and medical care at hospitals, catering to the healthcare needs of more than 600 million people, is hobbled with multiple management challenges – low funding, medical staff vacancies, overcrowding, outdated systems and processes and incompetent staffing patterns. Even the facilities available at each government hospital are poorly utilised. The entire public system is constrained by centralised bureaucratic governance from the state headquarters. The primary focus of public healthcare system is on the compliance of rules and regulations, administration and auditing. There is truly little focus on the patient. Government hospitals do not have quality accreditation and have limited appreciation of modern management. In a rapidly changing field, such rigidities are incompatible.

Till the 1980s, the Indian healthcare system was dominated by government hospitals along with many charitable and non-profit institutions, small nursing homes and a few private hospitals. The extent of urbanisation in 1980s was about 18 per cent, hence the majority of the population, which lived in rural or semi-urban areas, was served by small nursing homes in addition to government hospitals. Urbanisation has accelerated in the last four decades.

From the late 1980s, corporate hospitals have started playing a key role in tertiary care, particularly in urban centres. In the last four decades, public hospitals have lost their primacy, resulting in serious implications for society. Our country-wide health network, which should be the 'envy' of any private sector, is sadly under-utilised. The entire public health system is underfunded, bureaucratised, centralised, poorly led and severely understaffed. Severe insufficiency of medical staff is regularly reported, with no signs of any innovative solutions to solve the challenge. The dearth of medical personnel, coupled with shortages of medicines, poor infrastructure and poor hygiene, has a serious impact on health outcomes.

India has an estimated 1.8 million hospital beds, of which about 1.1 million beds are in the private sector, and the remaining 0.7 million beds are with various state governments and under the Government of India.[15] Private sector beds have been steadily growing.

A huge urban–rural divide marks the health infrastructure in the country. An estimated 70 per cent of all hospital beds are in urban areas, with an estimated 1.8 million allopathic doctors who are concentrated in a few states.[16] There is a huge imbalance in the doctor–population ratio between rural and urban areas. There are significant differences in the doctor–population ratio among the various states. Uttar Pradesh, for example, with a population of over 200 million has a doctor–population ratio of 1:18,000.[17]

Private sector healthcare

Private sector, which dominates the healthcare infrastructure in India, is itself undergoing fundamental changes. There are a substantial number of nursing homes, stand-alone laboratories, imaging centres and retail pharmacies in the unorganised sector. These organisations have been playing a key role in providing medical care in rural and urban areas. They are neither run efficiently nor do they provide quality healthcare. These organisations are being absorbed by large hospitals and corporate entities that have substantial funding resources. The future could see a consolidation in the private sector, and only a few brands are likely to serve the healthcare space. The brands could be local, regional or pan-India. Brand management is going to be a major differentiator in the perception of the public.

Private hospitals can be grouped into three classes: Small nursing homes, charitable or non-profit institutions and for-profit hospitals. Charitable or non-profit hospitals, an important segment in providing affordable care, are perennially confronted with financial deficits and require strengthening of their management structure. Small nursing homes providing primary and secondary care are focused only on outpatient care with limited inpatient facilities. Corporate hospitals adopt modern management practices for profit generation and shareholder value creation. It can be concluded that in most of the healthcare organisations, there is a management deficit.

Private hospitals are usually formed as partnerships or sole proprietorships, or as private limited companies. Corporate hospitals are formed as joint stock companies, and many of them are listed on stock exchanges. Since the advent of corporate hospitals in the late 1980s, there have been major changes in the tertiary care system, more specifically in large urban areas. Tertiary care, robotic surgeries, transplants and microsurgeries are among the services provided by corporate hospitals. The corporate sector quickly scaled up its quality of care, obtaining accreditation by international/national quality organisations. The corporate hospitals are profitable, thereby attracting investor funds whose expectations of profits are high.

Non-profit institutions

Non-profit hospitals have been doing yeomen service to meet the healthcare needs of the rural and urban population for over several decades. They have been acting as a bridge between the government and private hospitals. The non-profit hospitals are formed as societies or trusts, governed by a Board of Trustees. Many of them, which are stand-alone institutions, are under financial stress. Some of the well-known hospitals are Christian Medical College and Hospital (Vellore, Tamil Nadu), Arvind Eye Hospital (Madurai, Tamil Nadu), Bombay Hospital and Research Centre (Mumbai) and Gangaram Hospitals (New Delhi), which have been doing outstanding work in different parts of the country.

Non-government organisations

India is fortunate to have a large number of non-government organisations (NGOs)[18] serving people in healthcare, education, food supply, disability care, old poor citizens, in natural calamities and many more. In healthcare, there are hundreds of philanthropic organisations that help cancer survivors, those requiring cataract surgeries and palliative care. Some of the examples of these NGOs are Swasth Foundation, Rural Healthcare Foundation and the Foundation for Mother and Child.

Other private hospitals: Rural and urban

Patients reach out to nursing homes near their residences for primary and secondary care. There are about 70,000 private hospitals in India in rural and urban areas. Very often, patients in rural areas must travel long distances to access healthcare institutions, especially private nursing homes. These nursing homes typically have 20–50 beds and handle primary and secondary care. A general physician, sometimes a gynaecologist, with minimal facilities, including a small delivery room and a pharmacy, are available in a private hospital. Because of their small size, they do not have the minimum number of beds for obtaining quality accreditation. In the case of larger cities and towns, the nursing homes may have more departments such as obstetrics and gynaecology, paediatrics, orthopaedics, an operating theatre, a pharmacy and a laboratory for basic testing.

Private laboratories in rural India present an unflattering picture of outdated technologies, a shortage of trained manpower and test results that may or may not be reliable.[19] Patients have very little choice but to rely on such poor facilities.

Corporate hospitals

Corporate and large private hospitals, including single-specialty hospitals, have gained a reputation for offering quality tertiary care across many cities over the last four decades. High- and middle-income patients choose these hospitals for the level of care and affordability. Even poor patients (thanks to government schemes and the support of private trusts) receive treatment and surgical care in these hospitals. A high quality of treatment and surgical excellence, reinforced by international and national quality accreditations, has been the defining feature of all the corporate hospitals. They attract substantial amounts of funds given their focus on profits. Foreign private equity funds have also invested in some of the corporate hospital chains.

One of the disconcerting features, however, has been the question of medical ethics in these hospitals. The medical fraternity itself expresses the fears, apart from the public. In their book *Healers or Predators? Healthcare Corruption in India*,[20] Samiran Nundy, Sanjay Nagral and Keshav Desiraju have highlighted the instances of corruption in hospitals. Some examples they provide are the incidence of high C-section deliveries, incidence of unnecessary hysterectomies, selling medicines and consumables at maximum retail price (MRP), while the hospital could be buying at discounted prices, and doctors getting a 'referral' fee from the labs for referring patients for investigation. It is believed that generating profit and creating shareholder wealth are the main aims of corporate hospitals. The service motive of serving society does not define their functioning. An investigation by the Competition Commission of India has found excessive profiteering by corporate hospitals.[21]

Health insurance

Health insurance, which plays a key role in covering hospital expenses worldwide, has not played any significant role in India till the year 2000. Both life insurance and general insurance were managed exclusively by public sector corporations for a long time. Health insurance was part of general insurance and did not receive much attention. In the year 2000, the insurance industry was opened up to the private sector. Several new ventures were formed, and there has been a structural change in the insurance sector. Exclusive health insurance companies have also been formed in addition to newer general insurance companies. Since then, there has been a spurt in the health insurance coverage of the general population. In addition to private insurance offered by corporations and individuals, state governments and the Government of India have been providing insurance cover to various sections of the population so that they can be treated in private hospitals also. The treatment cost in private hospitals has been increasing rapidly. Private insurance schemes can at least partly meet hospitalisation bills.

Medical education

Of the 90,000 medical doctors that India produces every year, about half of them earn their degrees from private medical colleges (Figure 1.4).[22] There are an estimated three million nurses working in hospitals and clinics. India lags behind in adhering to the WHO norms in all the above categories – beds and the number of doctors and the number of nurses per 1,000 population. Private colleges have made medical education expensive, and this, in turn, has altered medical ethics among the practitioners. About half the number of MBBS seats are from private medical colleges, and about 20,000 post-graduate medical seats are also from private medical colleges. These graduates pay high fees at private medical colleges (including capitation fees). They do not find it attractive to join government service at a lower salary, postings in rural areas and for other reasons. Also, most practitioners from private medical colleges prefer to work in urban areas with private hospitals.

Quacks in Indian healthcare

According to the Indian Medical Association (IMA), there are more than one million quacks working in India (Figure 1.5). These unqualified persons,

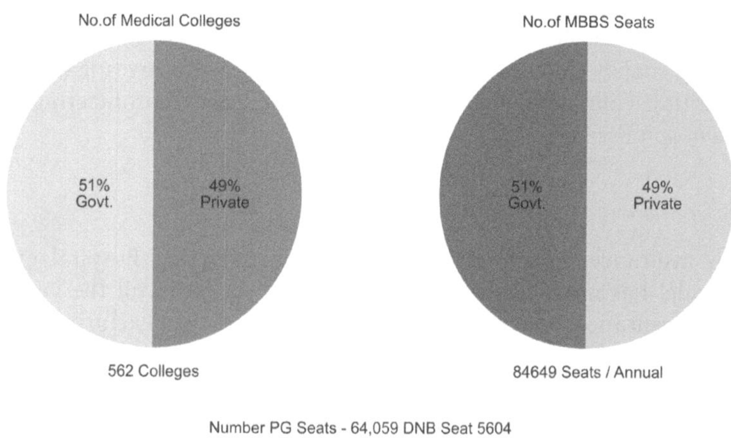

Figure 1.4 Medical education in India.

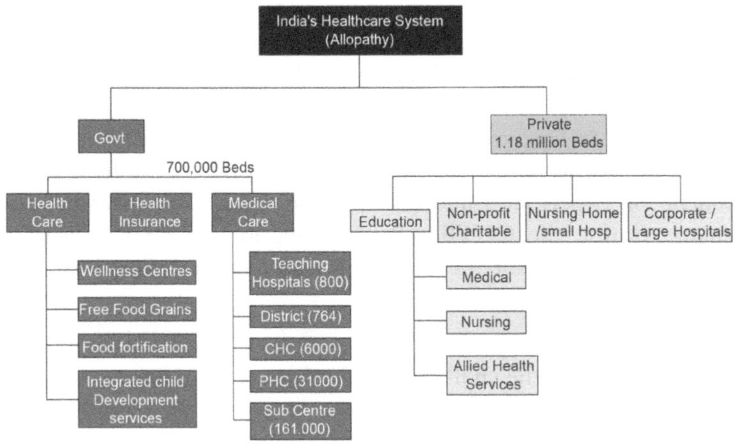

Figure 1.5 Medical and non-medical staff.

posing as medical personnel, treat patients, undertake deliveries, carry out surgeries and do home visits with near impunity. It is rationalised by pointing out that the acute shortage of qualified medical professionals, particularly in rural areas, has resulted in the emergence of a system of quacks. There have been several incidents of disastrous medical outcomes as a result. The IMA has listed various rules and regulations that bar quackery by unqualified persons and restrain them from practising modern medicine.[23]

Diagnostic centres

There are about 100,000 private stand-alone diagnostic laboratories of which only about 2 per cent have quality accreditations.[24] There are about one million stand-alone pharmacies, mostly small ones, in the unorganised sector. They perform a key function by providing flexible working hours and easy access. Many pharmacists in urban and rural areas also prescribe medications themselves! In the next few years, the retail pharmacy sector is likely to be dominated by large private hospitals and other companies.

Recent developments, technology and digitisation

In the last few decades, there have been significant developments in medical technology, with many hospitals introducing advanced technologies (expensive as well as low cost). Several advanced drugs and pharmaceutical products have been introduced. Personalised medicine is slowly replacing the present systems of medication.

Hospitals are moving away from paper-based medical records to real-time computerised systems. Digitisation is already linking all departments in the hospital, helping a seamless transfer of data. As a result, research and teaching are in for revolutionary change in the future. The Government of India is planning an ambitious digital mission linking all government hospitals in the country.

Some corporate hospitals have started introducing artificial intelligence (AI) for diagnosis, which is also helping patients from remote areas to have the benefit of expert consultations. Tele-consultations became popular, particularly during the COVID-19 pandemic and post-COVID-19 phase. Drones are being used for the transportation of vaccines and medicines to remote areas.

Section II: Addressing the challenges of healthcare in India

Concept of a hospital

The concept of a hospital is far different at present as compared to even a few decades ago. Hospitals are now offering preventive health advice, treating patients' various ailments, providing home care aid, helping in rehabilitation post-discharge, keeping health records digitally, assessing quality-of-life post-discharge, supplying medicines at home and doing telephonic/video consultation, in addition to providing many other services. Each of these functions requires good management practices with a focus on patient service and patient retention.

The economic size of a hospital has also undergone changes. Earlier, a 500-bedded hospital was considered optimum. The concept of management 'bandwidth' has also undergone changes. With the advent of information technology (IT), even a 3,000-bedded hospital at an individual location is not considered excessive. In fact, the largest hospital chain has as many as 70 locations with nearly 10,000 beds under its management (Apollo Hospitals in India). Decentralisation and the use of IT have enabled effective control. Ownership and management can be distinct. Many other options of management are constantly emerging, depending on the local needs.

Rapidly changing environment

In the last four decades, since the advent of corporate hospitals, there have been fundamental changes in the healthcare ecosystem in India. Epidemiological developments, advancements in medical technology, information technology embedded in healthcare, urbanisation and rising income levels, development of new drugs including personalised medicine, changing patient expectations, availability of biomarkers and preventive health require that every healthcare institution strives to keep pace with the changes. The most important change has been investment by private equity funds, venture capital funds and hospitals raising funds from stock markets through initial public offers (IPOs).

Are management systems in all our hospitals contemporary? Most of them are not. Let us focus on the largest health provider – the public hospitals. It is an accepted practice world over that public health would have quality accreditation and provide equal quality care to all its citizens. Our healthcare should be benchmarked against the best international standards. However, our public health falls short on most counts. There is a significant rural–urban difference, as well as a North–South India gap in health outcomes. Similarly, there are many districts that are lagging behind in healthcare access.

The changing nature of healthcare

Hospitals have witnessed a sea change in the way they function and are managed over the years, and this can be attributed to the following factors:

- **Size**
  The concept of manageable size of a hospital has undergone fundamental changes.
- **Footfall**
  The number of people visiting government and private hospitals, diagnostic centres and retail pharmacies has increased multifold.
- **Technology**
  Digitisation, artificial intelligence and mobile telephones have redefined the functioning at all levels, including communication.
- **Funding**
  There is a marked increase in funding in the private sector hospitals in contrast to the public healthcare system.
- **Medical equipment**
  Rapid obsolescence of medical equipment requires continuous capital expenditure and skill upgrading of the medical support team.
- **Inclusion and diversity**
  Every healthcare institution has to commit to fostering a diverse and inclusive workplace, free of discrimination and biases.

Patient focus

The purpose of any hospital/clinic or health centre is to provide prompt, quality and affordable care to every single patient. This consists of two parts: Patient interface and the back-office operations. Patient interface includes receiving the patient, waiting time, doctor consultation, admission, diagnostic tests, imaging and pharmacy services. Back-office includes housekeeping, high uptime of all medical equipment, information technology support, access to records, ordering of medicines and consumables, diet services and compliance with all government regulations. Affordable care is possible when all resources are productively employed, costs are controlled and every aspect of the operations is professionally managed. Advancements in medical technology, the potential of information technology and management concepts should be fully utilised for the benefit of the patient community and for the institution itself. Mobile telephony has become ubiquitous, and it can provide cost-effective communication between the hospital and the patient. This is true of both urban and rural areas.

Need for urgency to address healthcare issues

India, with its 1.4 billion population, is confronted with malnutrition, stunting and wasting, infant and maternal mortality, under-five mortality, tuberculosis (TB) deaths and the rapidly increasing incidence of non-communicable diseases – diabetes, cancer, hypertension and respiratory illnesses in rural and urban areas. The government has gathered a large amount of data from hospital records as well as through various surveys. There is a need for quick action on the part of the government, non-profit institutions, private healthcare sector, NGOs and society at large to address major health issues. The shortcomings should be addressed in each of the 800 districts by empowering the local officials to implement local solutions. It is clear that a smaller, empowered organisation structure is more effective in running hospitals.

Management of healthcare institutions

There are broadly two administration/management systems in our healthcare: Bureaucracy (which is responsible for the delivery of the public healthcare system) and private management structure (which runs private healthcare organisations). A private management structure is nimble and flexible and is amenable to change to suit business imperatives. Government departments, both at the state and the Government of India level, follow a bureaucratic form of governance. 'Bureaucracy is a specific form of organisation defined by complexity, division of labour, permanence, professional management, hierarchical coordination and control, strict chain of command and legal authority.[25]

This book does not intend to study the bureaucratic system per se. Instead, the non-suitability of the bureaucratic form of governance for the healthcare sector is clearly emphasised. In a service-oriented hospital sector, there is a need for flexibility and quick response at each location 24/7, which the bureaucratic system is not capable of providing. The private sector, on the other hand, follows a system of management suitable to its aims and the size of its activities.

How does a hospital provide patient-centric, affordable, quality medical care both in government and private institutions? The experience of well-run hospitals in India has proved the need for the application of modern management principles.

What is management?

Management plays a crucial role within every organisation as it encompasses the orchestration of resources to realise specific aims. In simpler terms, management is the systematic procedure of strategising, structuring, guiding and overseeing the endeavours of individuals striving to meet the goals of the organisation. This pivotal function is instrumental in enabling organisations to achieve their goals efficiently. Management functions are not linked to ownership of an organisation: Government or private. In other words, government organisations can use principles of management equally effectively to serve patients.

Evolution of management thoughts

Management thoughts can be traced back to the nineteenth century. Modern theories of scientific management, quality and behavioural theories have enriched our understanding of large organisations. Several hundred management experts have researched various organisations to study organisational dynamics.[26]

Till a few decades ago, the health ecosystem consisted of many nursing homes, non-profit hospitals and government hospitals. Most patients were dependent on these facilities. The scene has changed since the late 1980s. Now, there are many medium to large hospitals dominating urban areas. Many corporate and private hospitals focusing on tertiary care with high-tech medical technology are providing quality care. There is competition among the health providers.

Thanks to the economic liberalisation policies of the government, a large services sector comprising telecom, banking, insurance, retail industries and healthcare sector has come into existence. Information technology has revolutionised all the sectors. Thus, it became even more necessary to run all the organisations on modern lines utilising management principles.

Administrative and management structures of hospitals

The administrative and management structure can be furthermore examined at two levels: (i) macro level, i.e., pan-India or at each state level and (ii) micro level, i.e., at individual hospital or health centre level.

At the national and state level, the governments decide on broad policies, allocate funding and define major initiatives to be taken. The Government of India formulates policies and strategies and launches national missions on rural and urban health, nutrition, digitisation and funds all such national missions. State governments implement all such missions. At each hospital or health centre, medical care is provided. State governments fund and manage the functioning of activities of all hospitals in their state, in addition to other welfare programmes.

A large number of reports are generated on various metrics. As a country, India has progressed on many fronts of healthcare. There are also worrying signs about inequalities, poor outcomes in many populous states and poor management of available resources.

Management principles and techniques can significantly help healthcare institutions, irrespective of whether they are government, non-profit or private. In each of these sectors, there is considerable scope for improving patient service, cost control and staff motivation. Each one of the healthcare providers caters to diverse types of patients whose health needs, affordability and expectations are different. The health insurance industry is already bringing tighter control on hospital bills. Quality accreditation is likely to become a regular feature in large hospitals.

Public health

Management principles, both strategic and operational, should be applied to all public health institutions. The first focus should be the hospital sector, where improved functioning can provide relief to millions of underprivileged patients from rural and urban areas. In fact, small improvements in government hospitals can directly affect the functioning of quacks and small nursing homes.

The basic requirements are that in every government hospital, medical staff should be present, equipment should function, medicines should be available and support services should treat patients compassionately.

As already mentioned, there are 30,579 PHCs and 5,951 CHCs. There are well-defined norms for setting up health centres, including in tribal areas. The People's Archive of India, which reported on Rural Health Statistics 2021–22, reveals

> There were significant gaps in the infrastructure providing specialised care at CHCs, the report reveals. CHCs lacked 83.2 per cent of the required surgeons, 74.2 per cent of the required obstetricians and gynaecologists, 79.1 per cent of physicians and 81.6 per cent of the required paediatricians. 'Overall, there is a shortfall of 79.5% specialists at the CHCs as compared to the requirement for existing CHCs', the report adds.[27]

The first point of contact for a patient is the facility closest to their residence, a PHC. These centres should be managed well to provide quick and quality medical care. Basic management principles of planning, delegation, empowerment, accountability, digitisation, initiative in decision-making and role clarity should be employed at all centres, with patient as the focus. At these locations, *operations management* is the main need.

The main requirement in any hospital is that the patient should be received courteously and promptly. Apart from technical skills, each member should be trained in soft skills. Extensive orientation training is needed for all the staff so that they can appreciate their role in serving the community. CHCs are the major health centres that have beds and a sanctioned medical strength of four specialists. Unfortunately, there are high vacancies in CHCs.

The roles of the medical staff and the administrative staff should be distinct. Health centres should have electricity and water, all medical and non-medical equipment should be in working order round the clock and all essential medicines needed for outpatients and inpatients should always be available. There is a large database of past patient flows, diagnosis-wise and also prescription patterns. It should be easy to plan and stock all requirements. The field staff should be empowered to handle all day-to-day responsibilities.

Equipment maintenance can be outsourced, and the outsourcing agency should be held accountable for keeping the uptime of equipment. Non-core functions, such as laundry, housekeeping and kitchen, may also be outsourced. Districts with high infant mortality, maternal mortality and under-five mortality need to be chosen first for implementation of the new strategy.

STRATEGIC MANAGEMENT

The public health policymakers are required to evolve a robust hospital management plan, whose strategies are based on facts and figures taken from the data collected in the past. There are vast amounts of data available from outpatient records, patient census and field studies. Studies on changing medical technology, information technology and new medicines are easily available.

There are several strategic changes which are essential for public health management based on hospital, community and external data. The main objective is to bring back public health as a primary source of healthcare for all citizens. This would require major initiatives on several fronts involving effective engagement from the state governments.

This strategic initiative can be founded on two main verticals: Medical and managerial. Within each field, there will be multiple sub-specialties. Some of the areas where strategic initiatives are required are listed below.

INSUFFICIENT FUNDING

State funding of health care: Most states are unable to fund revenue and capital expenditure requirements from their overall state revenues. Health expenditure on a per-capita basis is extremely low in states with large populations. The Government of India should evaluate the options of international funding, raising low-cost funds, floating of national/state health bonds, pay wards and public donations. Some government hospitals have created a small number of rooms in which the patient pays a nominal amount, which are called pay wards. While the funds from such pay wards may not be significant, it nevertheless brings in the concept of service. Expenditure should be linked to measurable outcomes monitored by independent agencies. It should be ensured that extra expenditure does not result in wastage or corruption.

SHORTAGE OF MEDICAL DOCTORS

Shortage of medical doctors/specialists in CHCs and shortage of faculty in medical colleges have been perennial problems. In the short term, it may not be possible to augment the number of specialists to the required number. Plans to fill such urgent needs should be evolved. Temporary staff consisting of retired doctors and secondment from charitable and other private institutions should be explored. The Government of India has ambitious plans to digitise the entire medicare system. This exercise should be preceded by simplification of the existing systems, which are paper-based.

Organisation and methods (O&M) studies are a common method in management to simplify processes. Contemporary auditing systems should replace the present auditing systems. Government hospitals are constrained by existing auditing systems in their day-to-day operations.

Urgent implementation of quality accreditation at all centres is necessary. This would require changes in infrastructure, documentation of standard operating procedures (SOPs) and staff training that entails expenditure. Accredited hospitals are also responsible for ensuring adherence to defined metrics.

Non-profit hospitals and corporate hospitals

Non-profit hospitals should also obtain quality accreditation and improve management processes. Their financial viability can be ensured only by utilising the right management concepts. Financial management consists of budgeting integrated with quality procedures, evaluation of capital expenditure, costing systems and professional fund-raising. In addition, modern HR practices on performance appraisals, compensation and leadership development are required to attract and motivate staff.

Corporate hospitals with a pan-India presence employ modern management practices to satisfy their various stakeholders and patients, including foreign patients. Ethical management principles need to guide corporate hospital operations. They should act as responsible corporate citizens, refraining from high profiteering and work towards contributing positively to the community they serve.

Paradigm shifts towards future healthcare

For building a robust health infrastructure in the country, a paradigm shift from the current management practices and systems of operations is needed. This book will focus on specific management concepts that can improve the functioning of hospitals and the healthcare system. Good management systems are the foundation of the industrial sector as well as the service sectors. It is essential that all sectors of the healthcare sector adopt modern management practices in a systematic manner. The following areas need to be exclusively focused upon:

- Strategic management
- Financial management
- Marketing management
- Human resources
- Quality
- Information technology
- Operations research and application of quantitative techniques

Public healthcare

The key strategic challenges for public health systems are as follows:

- Tripling health budgets at the state level and new ways of raising financial resources
- Reforming the administration from the headquarters – from top to bottom
- Strengthening of the foundation of public health, i.e., PHCs and CHCs by enhancing facilities, ensuring availability of staff and digitising; strengthening of the ASHA system and anganwadis; innovative strategies to make PHCs attractive to doctors and medical students and motivating the staff at all levels
- Delegation of operational-level decision-making to the districts; activities need to be fine-tuned depending on the health needs of the local population in each district, with a special focus on tribal health
- Functionally integrating all health-related activities like nutrition, food fortification, social welfare programmes, etc under the health department. Empowering and making staff accountable for results
- Coordinating with local charitable hospitals and NGOs in delivering healthcare
- Replacing the present audit-oriented approach with a patient-focused approach
- Introducing National Accreditation Board for Hospitals and Healthcare Providers (NABH) and National Accreditation Board for Testing and Calibration Laboratories (NABL) accreditations in all healthcare institutions in over a decade

Future of public health

The size of our population, the scale of public health and medical operations in more than 200,000 locations and the size of the budget require effective management and auditing techniques. The public health system has been under great stress for several decades and there is an apprehension that public hospitals may slowly disappear. There have been suggestions that governments should only be a regulator and not a healthcare provider.

Private and non-profit hospitals in future

In the next two decades, private nursing homes are likely to be absorbed by larger hospitals. Similarly, smaller diagnostic laboratories and pharmacies are likely to be absorbed by larger hospitals and companies. There would be a consolidation and emergence of large, organised segments.

Non-profit hospitals have to strike a balance between providing affordable care, while remaining financially viable. They should not be inward-looking and should frequently review their place in the healthcare system. The very existence of the non-profit sector will come under stress.

Corporate hospitals must constantly review their strategies to balance between shareholder expectations and staying ethical.

Summary

India is the most populous nation in the world and is growing. It is also one of the fastest-growing economies. Its complex health and medical needs require the coordinated efforts of government and private institutions. The medical world is rapidly changing, and India should ensure that its outcomes are on par with those achieved in developed countries. Healthcare needs money and management. There should be a coordinated effort to match our economic progress with progress in health.

Organisation of this book

The book is divided into four parts. After this introductory chapter, which provides an overview of the healthcare system in India and remedies for its shortcomings, Part I ('State of play') comprises four chapters. Chapter 2 by Sudharshini Subramaniam on public health and Chapter 3 by Shailendra Kumar Hegde and Pritha Venkatachalam on tribal health focus on the much neglected and underperforming parts of our healthcare system. Both these topics are written by experts in their respective fields. Chapters 4 and 5 are on non-profit healthcare institutions – one on their present state and another a case study on one of the well-managed non-profit institutions, Sundaram Medical Foundation, based in Chennai.

Part II ('Operationalising healthcare') gives a sneak peek into the nuts and bolts of management, largely focused on large and corporate hospitals. They are added to showcase how sound management principles help these hospitals to be run efficiently, stay profitable and attract investments for their growth. In addition, some of the well-known tertiary care hospitals are also known for excellence in patient care that they attract patients from outside

India as well. Chapters 6–9 deal with leadership, management science in healthcare, marketing and human resources, while Chapter 10, written by Mala Sarat Chandra, a software expert, explains how artificial intelligence is transforming healthcare in India. Chapter 11 stresses the importance of quality by focusing on accreditations, and Chapter 12 dwells on the important part played by support functions in a hospital.

Part III ('Financing healthcare in India') deals with the financial management and the funding ecosystem of healthcare institutions in India. While Chapter 14 is concerned with how financial management is important for cost savings and patient care, Chapter 15 explains how private equity (PE) funds and initial public offerings (IPOs) are changing the face of healthcare in India.

Part IV ('Looking to the future') includes two chapters – Chapter 15 on public health reforms, a crucial lever of healthcare to achieve not only universal healthcare but also inclusive healthcare that caters to the poor and underprivileged sections of society. Chapter 16 takes a holistic view of the future trends and how they are likely to alter the healthcare landscape of India.

Notes

1 National Health Accounts, Estimates for India, 2019–20. https://nhsrcindia.org/sites/default/files/2023-04/National%20Health%20Accounts-2019-20.pdf
2 A.M. Al Muammar, Z. Ahmed, and A.M. Aldahmash, 'Paradigm shift in healthcare though technology and patient-centeredness', *International Archives of Public Health and Community Medicine,* 2 (2018): 015, https://doi.org/10.23937/iaphcm-2017/1710015
3 Demographic trends in India, Britannica, https://www.britannica.com/place/India/Agriculture-forestry-and-fishing
4 India population, https://www.worldometers.info/world-population/india-population/
5 Rural and urban population in India from 2018–2021. Statistica. Release date April 2023, https://www.statista.com/statistics/621507/rural-and-urban-population-india/
6 'Health expenditure at 2.1% of GDP in FY 2023: economic survey', *Livemint*, 31 January 2023, https://www.livemint.com/news/india/health-expenditure-at-2-1-of-gdp-in-fy23-economic-survey-11675160463795.html
7 National Health Accounts, Estimates for India, 2019–20, Ministry of Health and Family Welfare, Government of India, https://nhsrcindia.org/sites/default/files/2023-04/National%20Health%20Accounts-2019-20.pdf
8 People's Archives of Rural India, https://ruralindiaonline.org/hi/library/resource/rural-health-statistics-2020-21/
9 '80% shortfall of specialist doctors in CHCs: Health Ministry report', *The Hindu*, 13 January 2023, https://www.thehindu.com/news/national/80-shortfall-of-specialist-doctors-in-chcs-health-ministry-report/article66370205.ece
10 '13.63 lakh Anganwadi Centres (AWCs) of the 14 lakh AWCs sanctioned across the country are operational as on 1 June 2018', Press Information Bureau, https://pib.gov.in/newsite/PrintRelease.aspx?relid=181218#:~:text=13.63%20lakh%20Anganwadi%20Centres%20(AWCs,are%20operational%20as%20on%2001.06

11 Annual ASHA Update, Ministry of Health and Family Welfare, Government of India, https://nhsrcindia.org/sites/default/files/2022-07/Annual%20ASHA%20Update%202020-21.pdf
12 State/UT wise overall population, ST population, percentage of STs in India/State to total population of India/State and percentage of STs in the State to total ST population, https://tribal.nic.in/ST/Statistics8518.pdf
13 ICDS programme in Delhi, https://wcd.delhi.gov.in/wcd/introduction-integrated-child-development-services
14 'Cabinet approves continuation of supply of free Fortified Rice under Pradhan Mantri Garib Kalyan Anna Yojana (PMGKAY) and other welfare schemes from July 2024 to December 2028', Press Release, Ministry of Consumer Affairs, Food and Public Distribution, https://pib.gov.in/PressReleasePage.aspx?PRID=2063447
15 Estimated number of public and private hospital beds across India as of 2019 (in 1,000s), https://www.statista.com/statistics/1128673/india-number-of-public-and-private-hospital-beds-estimated/
16 Rema Nagarajan, 'Skewed distribution of docs a bigger problem than shortage', *Times of India*, 10 September 2018, https://timesofindia.indiatimes.com/india/skewed-distribution-of-docs-a-bigger-problem-than-shortage/articleshow/65697841.cms
17 Yusra Husain, 'Only 1 doctor for 18,000 population in Uttar Pradesh', *Times of India*, 14 December 2018, https://timesofindia.indiatimes.com/city/lucknow/only-1-doctor-for-18000-people-in-uttar-pradesh/articleshow/67085181.cms
18 '10 NGOs which have revolutionised healthcare in India', https://give.do/blog/10-ngos-which-have-revolutionised-healthcare-in-india/
19 'Addressing the gap in diagnostic services in rural India', *Economic Times*, https://health.economictimes.indiatimes.com/news/diagnostics/addressing-the-gap-in-diagnostic-services-in-rural-india/84420975?redirect=1
20 Sanjay Nagpal, Keshav Desiraju, and Samiran Nundy, *Healers or Predators: Healthcare Corruption in India*, Oxford University Press, 2018. This is a very candid book wherein the authors, two practising doctors and a former Union Health Secretary, have expressed their anguish at the exploitation by corporate hospitals.
21 'Max, Fortis, Apollo and other big hospital chains have been overcharging patients: CCI investigation', moneycontrol.com, https://www.moneycontrol.com/news/business/indias-largest-hospital-chains-abused-dominance-through-excessive-pricing-finds-cci-investigation-9219251.html
22 'India has largest number of medical colleges, what about good doctors?', *The Quint*, 25 January 2022, https://www.thequint.com/opinion/india-has-largest-number-of-medical-colleges-what-about-good-doctors#:~:text=Close%20to%2090%2C000%20MBBS%20graduates,colleges%20are%20produced%20every%20year
23 IMA Anti Quackery, https://www.ima-india.org/ima/archive-page-details.php?pid=291
24 List of NABL accredited testing laboratories in India, http://www.labgo.in/nabl-accredited-testing-labs-India
25 Bureaucracy, https://www.britannica.com/topic/bureaucracy
26 Ugo Chuks Okolie and Uzezi Enioyme Oyise, 'The evolution of management: a historical perspective', *Journal of Public Administration, Finance and Law*, 2021, 207–215, https://www.jopafl.com/uploads/issue22/THE_EVOLUTION_OF_MANAGEMENT_A_HISTORICAL_PERSPECTIVE.pdf
27 Rural Health Statistics, 2021–22, https://ruralindiaonline.org/en/library/resource/rural-health-statistics-2021-22/#:~:text=As%20of%20March%2031%2C%202022%2C%20there%20were%206%2C064%20functional%20CHCs,11%2C909%20since%20the%20year%202005

Part I

State of play

2 Public health system in India

Achievements, challenges and the way forward

Sudharshini Subramaniam

Introduction

India's healthcare delivery system is made up of public health system, private healthcare system and a diverse mix of AYUSH (Ayurveda, Yoga and Naturopathy, Unani, Siddha and Homeopathy) systems, co-existing and delivering a variety of healthcare services. There has been a substantial improvement in health status of the population over the years, but there is an evident epidemiological transition with non-communicable diseases predominating the health burden, accompanied by an increasing life expectancy and declining fertility rates. While the aggregate data show that India is progressing in terms of health indicators, the trend is not homogenous across the country. The public health system faces multiple challenges such as poor budgetary allocation for the health sector, several layers of health inequities including gender, caste, class, urban–rural disparities, inadequate access, poor quality of services, overcrowded health facilities, poor investment in primary care, increased investment in secondary and tertiary care, weak research and development, paucity of human resources and corruption. This chapter focuses on the measures to strengthen this system, which include reorienting the public health system to primary care and the active engagement of the private sector in service provision, with the government performing a regulatory role rather than being a healthcare provider. Decentralisation of healthcare planning and task-shifting/sharing in healthcare services (by bringing in community volunteers to the service to support healthcare delivery) would pave the way towards achieving universal healthcare in India. The ultimate goal of such a system would be the attainment of universal health coverage. India's healthcare delivery system is diverse with a well-organised and widespread public health system infrastructure, which fulfils the healthcare needs of about 30 per cent of the poorer sections of society, a large for-profit private healthcare system, offering a wider range of services at a cost, and a diverse mix of AYUSH (Ayurveda, Yoga and Naturopathy, Unani, Siddha and Homeopathy) systems, co-existing and delivering a variety of healthcare services [1, 2]. The public health system is organised in three tiers: The primary, secondary and tertiary healthcare system. This chapter focuses on the public health system of India, covering the history of healthcare planning

DOI: 10.4324/9781003684947-3

and delivery in independent India and the organisation of the public health system with current advances in public healthcare delivery. The limitations of the existing public health system are highlighted, and recommendations for the way forward are provided.

History of healthcare planning and delivery: Building public health infrastructure and expansion of the private healthcare sector

Until 1983, India had no official health policy. Although a policy-driven approach was absent, health planning in the country had started even before independence [2]. In 1946, the Bhore Committee submitted the 'Health Survey and Development Committee' report, which is considered the most comprehensive health plan document in India to date. The Bhore Committee envisaged a National Health Service that should be available to everyone irrespective of their ability to pay. Nearly eight decades later, the Committee's recommendations are yet to come to fruition [3].

In the post-independence years, health planning was built into a part of the Five-Year Plans. While these plans laid emphasis on social sectors like health, education and water supply, investment in these sectors was abysmally poor. In the early 1950s and 1960s, the plans were disease-specific and highly techno-centric. These plans led to the formation of vertical disease-specific programmes like the National Malaria Eradication Programme, and personnel were trained for specific disease control. The funding and supplies for these programmes came from international agencies like the World Health Organization (WHO), United Nations International Children's Fund (UNICEF) and the Rockefeller Foundation. The donors largely drove the policy agenda and budget allocation in the health system [4]. This approach failed to take good health to the people due to its lack of focus in addressing the determinants of these diseases, which were largely social, and its piecemeal approach lacked sustenance. The basic health infrastructure was still not available for large sections of the population. There were inadequacies in healthcare institutions and shortages of human resources for healthcare delivery. The first two Five-Year Plans were disease-specific and target-driven. It was only in the Third Plan that resource allocation was done for primary healthcare as recommended by the Bhore Committee. Heavy emphasis was laid on population control, and close to 50 per cent of central government resources were directed towards family planning programmes. A vertical programme, specific to family planning, was in place, which adopted different strategies like a target-based approach, incentivising family planning behaviours and payment for motivators. The government began to realise the need for primary healthcare to maintain the gains of the disease-specific programme when the country witnessed the resurgence of malaria. In the Fifth Plan, strengthening of public healthcare was done through the Minimum Needs Programme, under which water supply and sanitation were also stressed upon. In the middle of the Fifth Plan, a national emergency was declared (as a fallout of political developments) during which a compulsive and forceful family planning programme was implemented.

On the human resources side, a larger stress was laid on increasing the number of doctors, but little attention was paid to paramedical and nursing staff. Uni-purpose workers who worked in different disease-specific programmes were converted to multipurpose workers as per the Kartar Singh Committee's recommendations [5]. A mere increase in numbers was not translating into getting adequately trained human resources to work in rural areas. The Shrivastav Committee, which was given the task of looking into medical education and support manpower, recommended the creation of a village-based health volunteer cadre called Community Health Workers to rectify the problem of the dearth of human resources in rural areas. This was the first time India started de-professionalising healthcare and started engaging the local community [6].

At the 30th World Health Assembly in 1977, Health for All (HFA) 2000 was set as a social target to be achieved by the governments and the WHO. In the Alma-Atta Declaration (1978), the gross inequities in health between and within countries were declared unacceptable, and to achieve HFA by 2000, primary healthcare was considered the key [7]. The signatory governments were given choices to innovate in implementing primary healthcare in their countries. Public healthcare in India took a giant leap in 1983 when the Parliament endorsed the National Health Policy (NHP), making it the first ever official national health policy, framed 38 years after independence. NHP 1983 had the goal of *providing universal, comprehensive primary healthcare services.* This policy recognised that the urban health infrastructure had expanded while the rural areas did not receive as much attention [8]. The specialised form of medical care was availed of mostly by the elite classes in the urban areas, while the rural areas and the poor were deprived of the benefits of good health and medical services. It was after NHP 1983 that various efforts were made to expand the primary care centres in a phased manner, prioritising rural areas. Rural expansion was accompanied by deprofessionalisation of medicine as health volunteers were introduced, thereby enhancing community participation and calling for the expansion of private sector involvement in providing curative services to reduce the government's burden. The policy also had fixed targets, which were largely demographic in nature. Following NHP 1983, rural areas received attention, and PHC expansion aimed at achieving the target of one PHC per 30,000 population and one sub-centre per 5,000 population. While there were efforts towards expanding the infrastructure for primary health centre, the stumbling blocks were the non-availability of trained manpower, drugs and other resources, and these centres remained underutilised [8]. The neoliberal economic policies and financial structural reforms of 1991 paved the way for the massive expansion of the private sector in healthcare. The goal of providing universal, comprehensive primary healthcare services was far from reachable by 2000. It was in the year 2000 that India announced the National Population

Policy (NPP 2000) and became a signatory to the Millennium Development Goals (MDG) [9].

In the Ninth Plan, NHP 1983 was reviewed in the context of its objectives and goals and to align with the MDG. The need for its reappraisal and reformulation was acknowledged, which led to the NHP 2002. The objective of this policy was to achieve an acceptable standard of good health among the general population of the country. However, this policy did not mention the goal of universal, comprehensive primary healthcare services. The policy urged the need for obtaining meaningful data through health information systems, including national health accounts to plan policies and programmes. While the policy is concerned with regulating and building accountability for the private health sector by introducing statutory licensing and monitoring of minimum standards, it was highly criticised as the policy recommendations largely promoted the private sector. This policy led to an expansion of the privatisation of healthcare as subsidies were offered to private hospitals. The consequence of the expansion of the private health sector was the weakening of the public health system.

The NHP 2002 is the forerunner to the National Rural Health Mission (NRHM), which was launched as a flagship health programme of the government in 2005. The focus of NRHM was pushed to demographic achievements, such as reducing the total fertility rate, infant mortality rate and maternal mortality ratio, which formed the basis for the components of NRHM [10].

The objective of NRHM was universal access to equitable, affordable and quality healthcare service that is accountable and responsive to people's healthcare needs, at the same time working with other sectors to address the wider social determinants of health. NRHM has been viewed as the state-governed holistic intervention in the field of health, planned and executed in a mission mode. The programme was extended till 2017, assuming the significance of NRHM in the improvement of health indicators, in particular the infant mortality rate (IMR) and maternal mortality rate (MMR) and improvement in general health conditions. The Twelfth Five-Year Plan extended NRHM to include the 'urban poor', and the programme was simply renamed National Health Mission (NHM). The cornerstone of NRHM was decentralised planning and enabling states to address their priorities. It introduced the provision of untied funds, public–private partnership, convergence of the health sector and involvement of Panchayati Raj Institutions (PRIs). Other determinants of health (e.g., water, sanitation, education, nutrition, social and gender equality) were also included in the programme to develop a fully functional health system at all levels, right from the village to the district level [11].

The 65th World Health Assembly held in Geneva in 2012 identified universal health coverage (UHC) as a key priority to consolidate all advances in public health. UHC ensures that everyone, everywhere should has access to essential healthcare services without financial hardship. A couple of years earlier, the Planning Commission of India had constituted a High-Level Expert Group in 2010 with a mandate of developing a framework for UHC. Achieving UHC was also the overarching goal of Sustainable Development Goals [12]. The National Health Policy of India 2017, which is in alignment with the SDG, also resonates with the need for UHC and emphasised the expansion of primary healthcare services from selective services to encompass a comprehensive service provision. India was also a signatory member of the Astana Declaration in 2018, which also emphasised the critical role of primary healthcare. Ayushman Bharat, the Government of India's flagship programme on health, was launched in 2018 with two key components: (i) Delivering comprehensive primary healthcare services by setting up Health and Wellness Centres (HWCs) and (ii) Pradhan Mantri Jan Arogya Yojana (PM-JAY), which provided financial protection services to the socially vulnerable and low-income population for availing secondary and tertiary care. Ayushman Bharat aims at ensuring access to healthcare by strengthening public health infrastructure by creating a wide network of health facilities [13].

While the Government of India has laid a larger framework for establishing public health facilities, states are given the flexibility to decide the proportion of facilities depending on the population density, local disease epidemiology, availability of human resources, caseload and other such parameters. In the following sections, we will discuss the public health system in India. We will first describe the building blocks of the health system as elucidated by WHO, namely leadership and governance, health system financing mechanisms, essential drugs and medicines, health information systems, health workforce and health service delivery.

Building blocks of the public health system

Public health service in India is delivered through a three-tiered system comprising the primary, secondary and tertiary care facilities. Primary healthcare is delivered at the community level through the Health Subcentres (HSCs), in which an Auxiliary Nurse Midwife (ANM) handles the day-to-day operations. She is responsible for the primary-level care provided at these centres. Under the Ayushman Bharat scheme, these HSCs have been upgraded to HWCs. Then there are Primary Health Centres (PHCs), each serving a population of about 30,000 people in rural areas. The PHC is headed by a medical officer who guides a team of healthcare providers, including nurses, pharmacists, laboratory technicians, ANMs, health inspectors, health educators and office staff. The PHC caters to the primary healthcare needs of the population, including maternal and child health, treatment of common minor ailments, prevention and control of outbreaks, nutrition, water supply, sanitation, immunisation and contraception services. Under the Ayushman Bharat scheme, many PHCs have also been upgraded to HWCs. Another form of primary healthcare delivery for children and women occurs through the anganwadi programme under the Integrated Child Development Services (ICDS) at the community level. This programme operates from the Anganwadi Centre (AWC) at the community level, where children below six years are provided supplemental nutrition, nutritional monitoring, preschool non-formal education, regular health check-up and referral services. The AWCs serve as the venue for the Village Health Sanitation and Nutrition Day (VHSND), during which the ANMs and anganwadi workers engage in health and nutrition education for pregnant women, lactating mothers and adolescent girls. In the AWCs, immunisation for pregnant women, contraception products and weekly iron and folic acid supplementation (WIFS) for adolescent girls are provided. Through these primary healthcare delivery mechanisms, the outreach of the public health system extends to all the members of the community [14]. Under the erstwhile National Nutrition Mission (also called Poshan Abhiyan), healthcare programming aims to reduce malnutrition among children who receive supplementary nutrition, growth monitoring, micronutrient supplementation, deworming, immunisation and nutrition education through anganwadi centres to combat malnutrition and improve overall health. The other nutrition-related interventions include the Mid-Day Meal scheme, which provides supplementary nutrition to school-going children.

At the secondary level, the health system delivery comprises the taluk and district hospitals and community health centres. In these 50- to 100-bedded hospitals, broad specialty services are provided, including general medicine, general surgery, orthopaedics, trauma care, emergency services, eye care, ear, nose, throat care, child care, specialised obstetric care including emergency caesarean sections, blood transfusion, tubectomy and vasectomy services. The hospitals at the second level of the public healthcare system serve a population of about 1–1.5 lakh people. Specialist doctors, nurses and allied health professionals are available for patients. In addition, X-ray, imaging and laboratory services are also available at the secondary level facilities. They serve as the referral units for patients from the Primary Health Centres [14].

eSanjeevani, the National Telemedicine Service of India, is an ambitious project to achieve UHC. The cloud-based eSanjeevani platform operates in two modes: (i) eSanjeevani AB-HWC (a provider-to-provider telemedicine platform), in which teleconsultation is provided to patients who walk into HWCs, facilitating connection to the doctors and specialists in hubs established in the secondary/tertiary level health facilities or medical colleges and (ii) eSanjeevani OPD (a patient-to-provider telemedicine platform), which empowers citizens to access health services within the confines of their homes through smartphones or laptops [15].

The tertiary care health facilities include the medical college teaching hospitals and specialty and super-specialty health facilities. They have about 500–1,000 beds and offer specialty and super-specialty services. In the referral chain, patients who require specialty and super-specialty services are referred from the secondary health facilities to the tertiary care hospitals.

The healthcare workforce is an essential building block of the healthcare services delivery through the tiered health system described above. India has a low density of health workers per 10,000 population. The health workforce is skewed across the states and also characterised by a conspicuous urban–rural divide. The WHO estimates that India requires at least 1.8 million doctors, nurses and ANMs to achieve the target of 44.5 health workers per 10,000 population [16]. The creation of mid-level healthcare providers (MLHCP) under the Ayushman Bharat scheme has the potential to substantially improve the health human resource availability in the public health system [17]. The recent policy introduced in 2019 has envisaged increasing the intake of medical students in all the existing medical colleges, as well as opening medical colleges in each district of India. This would increase the number of doctors. However, there will still remain a huge human resource crunch due to the shortage of nurses and other allied health professionals. The health budget for 2023 has proposed opening nursing colleges, which is likely to increase the number of nurses available for healthcare service delivery.

The Ministry of Health and Family Welfare has put in place a Health Management Information System (HMIS) to monitor and evaluate the performance of the National Health Mission (NHM). The data obtained from the HMIS has helped the government in identifying target aspirational districts for greater focus, as well as to review the programme implementation plans of individual states. The data available from the HMIS aids evidence-based policymaking. It provides data on service delivery as well as human resources. The health facilities are graded based on data available from the HMIS, and this helps in the allocation of funds and improvement of performance. Digitisation of patient health information in hospitals is being implemented in a phased manner. Digitisation of community health work through m-health and maternal and child health tracking systems (MCTS) is also being implemented in many states [18]. Another initiative by the Government of India is to create a 14-digit unique Ayushman Bharat Health Account Number for each citizen of India to ensure hassle-free linking of healthcare benefits and access to healthcare and records [15]. As digitisation of healthcare information is happening at a rapid phase to ensure security and privacy of data, the Digital Personal Data Protection Bill, 2023 was passed [19].

Access to effective, safe and good quality medicines is a priority need of the public health system in India. To fulfil this objective, India adopted the first National List of Essential Medicine (NLEM) in 1996, which has undergone three revisions since – in 2003, 2015 and 2022 [20]. The essential medicines satisfy the priority healthcare needs of the majority of the population. The drugs that are enlisted in the NLEM are made accessible at an affordable cost and are of good quality. At the same time, the list also ensures the rational use of drugs. There is a separate list for primary, secondary and tertiary level health facilities. The Ministry of Health and Family Welfare also floated the Pradhan Mantri Bharatiya Janaushadi Pariyojana (PMBJP) under the Department of Pharmaceuticals. The main objective of this programme is the provision of good quality generic drugs accessible at affordable prices to all. Under this scheme, dedicated Janaushadi Kendras have been opened all over the country to make low-cost generic medicines accessible to all [21].

Given this policy planning framework and the building blocks of the public health system, it is now important to understand the progress made in public healthcare in India so far.

Health indicators: Where do we stand?

In the 75 years since independence, the healthcare system in India has witnessed a slew of changes, which is reflected in the various health indicators. A few indicators over a period of nearly 35 years is presented in Table 2.1.

Table 2.1 shows that though there has been a substantial improvement in health status over the past 35 years, we are yet to achieve universal health coverage. Figure 2.1 illustrates the distribution of health expenditure across

Table 2.1 Health indicators over a period of nearly 35 years

Indicator	*1990*	*2010–2015*	*2020–2023*
Crude birth rate[a]	36.9/1000	21.8/1000	19.5/1000
Crude death rate[a]	14.9/1000	7.1/1000	6.0/1000
Total fertility rate[b]	4.5	2.2	2.0
Maternal mortality ratio[a]	556/1000000	122/1000000	97/1000000
Infant mortality rate[a]	129/1000	44/1000	28/1000
Life expectancy at birth[a]	49.7 years	69 years	70 years
Children who are stunted[b]	52%	38.4%	35.5%
Children who are underweight[b]	53.4%	35.8%	32.1%
Children who are wasted[b]	17.5%	21%	19.3%
Overweight[b]	–	2.1%	3.4%
Prevalence of anaemia among women aged 15–49 years[b]	–	53.1%	57%
Causes of death – non-communicable diseases[c]	37.9%	61.8%	–
Causes of death – communicable diseases[c]	53.6%	27.5%	–
Causes of death – Injuries[c]	8.5%	10.7%	–
Institutional deliveries[b]	25.5%	78.9%	88.6%
Percentage of the population with safe drinking water from pump/pipe[b]	68.2%	89.9%	95.9%
Percentage of the population with no toilet facility[b]	30.3%	48.4%	70.2%
Fully immunised	35.4%	62%	76.4%
Diabetes prevalence	NA	7.1%	8.9%
Total health expenditure as % of GDP[d]	NA	4% [2014–15]	3.2%

(*Continued*)

Table 2.1 (Continued)

Indicator	*1990*	*2010–2015*	*2020–2023*
Government health expenditure as % of GDP[d]	NA	1.15%	1.28%
Government share as % of total health expenditure[d]	NA	28.6% [2014–15]	40.6%
OOPE share as % of total health expenditure[d]	NA	64.2% [2013–14]	48.2% [2018–19]
Doctor:population ratio	NA	NA	1:834
Nurse:doctor ratio	NA	NA	1.7:1
Shortfall of female health workers in PHC/SC[e]	NA	NA	3.5%
Shortfall of allopathic doctors in PHC[e]	NA	11.9%	3.1%
Shortfall in specialist posts in CHC[e]	NA	81.5%	79.5%
Average population covered by an SC in rural India[e]	NA	5,426	5,691
Average population covered by a PHC in rural India[e]	NA	32,944	36,049
Average population covered by a CHC in rural India[e]	NA	1,54,512	1, 64,027
Shortfall of urban PHCs[e]	NA	–	39.7%
Shortfall of health workers [female] in UPHCs[e]	NA	–	35.5%
Shortfall of specialists in UCHC[e]	NA	–	46.9%

NA: Data not available.
Abbreviations: OOPE, Out-of-pocket expenditure; PHC, public health centre; SC, sub-centre; CHC, community health centre; UPHC, urban public health centre; UCHC, urban community health centre.
[a]Sample Registration System.
[b]National Family Health Survey.
[c]India State-Level Disease Burden Initiative, 1990–2016.
[d]National Health Accounts (2013–14; 2018–19).
[e]Rural Health Statistics 2021–22.

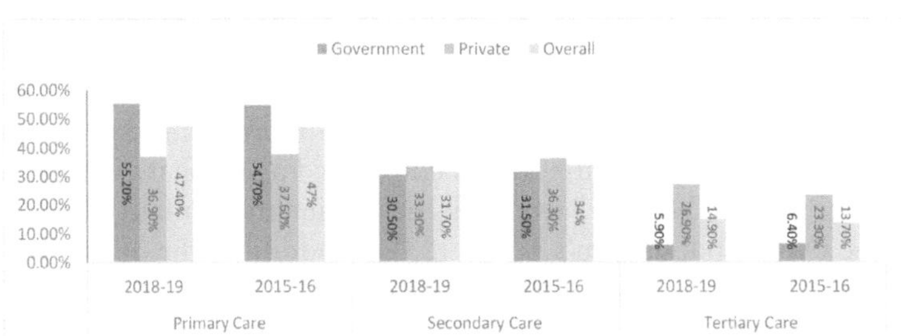

Figure 2.1 Health expenditure by primary, secondary and tertiary care (%).

Source: National Health Accounts 2018–19.

primary, secondary and tertiary care, highlighting the contributions from the government and private sectors for the years 2015–16 and 2018–19. The government plays a crucial role in financing primary health care. On the other hand, tertiary care is largely dependent on private sector funding, highlighting the financial burden on individuals for specialised medical treatments. There is an evident epidemiological transition with non-communicable diseases contributing to a larger proportion of deaths in recent times. Social determinants like poverty, food security, water supply and sanitation have undergone substantial improvements in the past decades, which has resulted in a decline in deaths due to communicable diseases. With increasing life expectancy and declining fertility rates, the proportion of the elderly in India will increase in the coming years. It is estimated that there are nearly 138 million elderly persons in India in 2021, which is further expected to increase by 56 million in 2031 [22]. The elderly population with a higher risk of non-communicable diseases and their complications will contribute to the major disease burden in the country in the future. While there is a shift in the disease epidemiology, the nutritional indicators have not made significant improvements over the years.

In the past four decades, efforts towards task-shifting/sharing in rural healthcare through Community Health Workers (CHWs) by involving health volunteers like Accredited Social Health Activists (ASHA) has been successful. At the same time, a larger investment has been made towards increasing specialist and super-specialist care, which in turn is increasing the overall cost of healthcare. There has been an increase in the proportion of health expenditure on tertiary care, which is contributed largely by the private sector. Another major disparity is the huge shortfall in the input indicators related to urban healthcare delivery.

While the aggregate data reflect that India is progressing in terms of health indicators, it is not homogenous across the country. There are huge differences between states, based on social determinants like gender, caste and class. In the following section, we have used IMR to demonstrate inequity in healthcare achievement in the country.

Infant mortality rate: An example to demonstrate inequity in health

IMR is the number of children who die before attaining the age of one year for every 1,000 live births in the year. It is an important marker of the overall health status of the country and is considered a surrogate marker for the population's health because the various determinants of infant mortality also affect the overall population's health [23]. In addition, the health system of a country can only be as good as its protection of the most vulnerable in the country. So, if newborns and infants, the most vulnerable, are protected, then the health system is probably functioning well. The estimated IMR in India as per the Sample Registration System 2020 is 28/1,000 live births, which means India has achieved the target that was fixed in the National Health Policy 2017 [24]. There has been a definite improvement in IMR over the

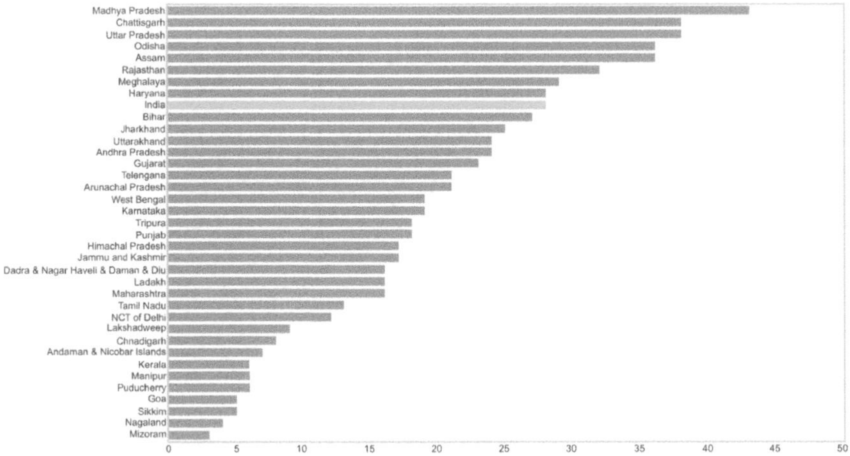

Figure 2.2 State-wise infant mortality rate in India 2020.

Source: Sample Registration System Bulletin 2020 [24].

years from 129/1,000 live births in 1979 to 28/1,000 live births in 2020 [24]. The IMR is not uniform across the country. As for every indicator, for this parameter too, there are several Indias within India. There are disparities in the IMR between states, and the rate of decline is also different across states.

The data (Figures 2.2 and 2.3) show that there has been an improvement in IMR in all the states but at a slower rate. IMR in India declined by nine points between 2015 and 2020, dropping from 37/1,000 in 2015 to 28/1,000 in 2020. The data also reveals enormous differences between the states, with Mizoram having an IMR comparable to that of high-income group countries and IMR in Madhya Pradesh (43/1,000 live births) is similar to that in low-income group countries. The rate of decline in IMR has also not been uniform across states, with the states having poor IMR showing a slower

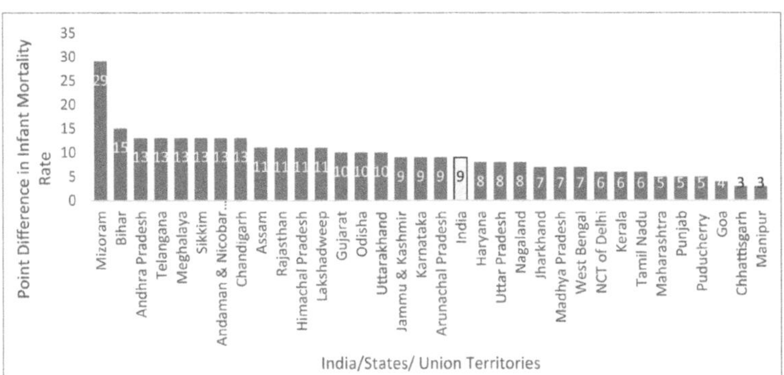

Figure 2.3 Point decline in infant mortality rate between 2015 and 2020.

Source: Sample Registration System Bulletin 2020 [24].

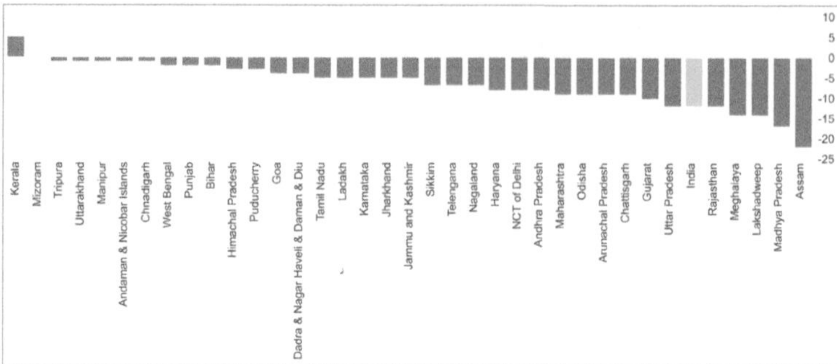

Figure 2.4 Urban–rural difference in IMR in 2020.

Source: Sample Registration System Bulletin 2020 [24].

decline. For example, Madhya Pradesh with the highest IMR had only a seven-point decline in IMR over five years, whereas Mizoram with the lowest IMR had the maximum improvement with 29-point decline in five years.

The IMR is not only different across states but is also based on rural–urban locality, gender, caste and class.

There is a 12-point difference between rural and urban regions at the national level (Figure 2.4). The urban regions in all the states had a better IMR compared to their rural counterparts, with Kerala and Mizoram being exceptions. Mizoram had no rural–urban difference, and urban Kerala had a higher urban IMR compared to rural Kerala. There was no gender difference in IMR at the national level (Figure 2.5). However, the IMR continued to be higher among infant girls than boys in 18 states. On the other hand, IMR among boys was higher in 10 states, with the highest difference noted in Himachal Pradesh. A secondary data analysis done in rural North India noted that infant girls had a higher risk of dying than boys during the post-neonatal period across all socio-demographic and economic strata.

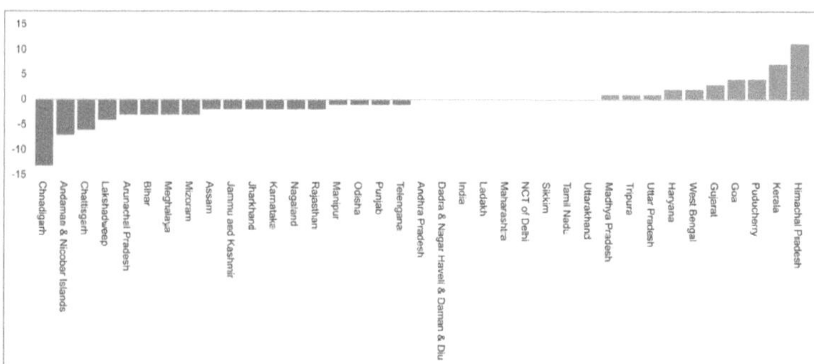

Figure 2.5 Gender difference in IMR in 2020.

Source: Sample Registration System Bulletin 2020 [24].

IMR has demonstrated the existence of inequity, with the most vulnerable group at higher risk than those who are not so vulnerable. A similar pattern is also observed in other key indicators like the maternal mortality ratio or life expectancy, for example. Such inequity highlights the gap in public healthcare delivery system, whose primary purpose is to cater to the vulnerable sections of the population. Therefore, it is imperative that steps are taken to ensure universal health coverage in India. There are several important challenges in the public health system, which stand in the way of achieving universal health coverage. The following section will address some of these challenges.

Challenges faced by the public health system

The public health system in India faces many challenges including poor budgetary allocation for the health sector, several layers of health inequities including gender, caste, class, urban–rural disparities, inadequate access, poor quality of services, overcrowded health facilities, poor investment in primary care, increased investment in secondary and tertiary care, weak research and development, paucity of human resources and corruption.

Poor and skewed budgetary allocation to the health sector

The government spending on health was 1.9 per cent of the GDP in the year 2023–24, which is lower than 2.5 per cent outlined in the National Health Policy 2017 [25]. The tax-funded public outpatient healthcare utilisation in the country is only about 30 per cent. The remaining 70 per cent of outpatient healthcare is accessed by people through the private sector, with out-of-pocket payments. The total health expenditure is roughly about 3–4 per cent of the GDP, with a major chunk of the expenditure happening through the out-of-pocket mode. Government revenue accounted for less than 35 per cent of the total health expenditure, and the proportion of the government revenue allocated to primary healthcare is less than 50 per cent. Even in the budget that is allocated to the public health sector, a large proportion is given to the Ayushman Bharat state-sponsored health insurance scheme for secondary and tertiary level inpatient healthcare. The funding for the NHM, which largely focuses on primary healthcare, is consistently lower than the proportion for inpatient care. This poor and skewed budgetary allocation to health substantially weakens the public health system and primary care [26].

Health inequities due to social determinants

Several social determinants of health such as gender, caste, class, disability, sexual orientation, geographical location and urban/rural residence have a strong influence on access to public health facilities and services. These health inequities stand in the way of achieving universal health coverage. Some of these inequities are inherent within the health system. The health workers come from the same society and therefore perpetuate the social norms and biases. For example, a health worker may bring her notions of caste and caste superiority into the workplace and engage in discrimination on the basis of caste in the hospital. These are inter-personal issues. Apart from them, there are also systemic factors that worsen these inequities, including inaccessible health facilities, lack of awareness of the special needs of the vulnerable people and poor preparedness of healthcare providers to be responsive to their needs, and poor planning of health service delivery to address these social inequities [27].

Poor quality of services

The introduction of the Janani Suraksha Yojana (JSY) scheme, a conditional cash transfer scheme for women who deliver in public health facilities in 2005, led to an increase in institutional deliveries. However, this did not translate immediately into a reduction in newborn or maternal mortality. The reason for this was the poor quality of health services in the public health facilities. Good quality healthcare is one which is safe, effective, patient-centric, efficient, timely and equitable [28]. Lack of adequate human resources, poor commitment of the healthcare providers and other systemic reasons lead to poor quality of services. Often, private healthcare providers are more responsive and patient-centred compared to the providers in public health facilities, leading to reduced trust among people in public healthcare providers. This is the main reason why most of the healthcare provision in India is from the private health sector, posing a great challenge to the public health system. Quality controls, such as accreditations like the National Accreditation Board for Hospitals and Healthcare Providers (NABH), exhibit robust and comprehensive standards. Therefore, it is crucial to encourage their widespread adoption. While private hospitals and laboratories are mandated to obtain such accreditations for empanelment with various insurance schemes, government agencies do not have a similar mandate. However, prioritising the quality of care has become a focal point of the National Health Policy for optimising resource utilisation, enhancing health outcomes and ensuring client satisfaction. Several initiatives have been undertaken to monitor service quality in the public health system. These include the LaQshya initiative for improving labour room quality, MusQan to ensure the provision of child-friendly services and the Kayakalp Award Scheme aimed at enhancing cleanliness, hygiene, waste management and infection control practices in public healthcare facilities. Additionally, a quality certification programme has been implemented for public health facilities, with the goal of recognising high-performing facilities and enhancing the credibility of public hospitals in the community. This programme involves assessing hospitals against the National Quality Assurance Standards [29].

Overcrowded public health facilities

Most public health facilities in India are overcrowded, leading to high patient waiting times. There is also a shortage of healthcare providers, which further worsens the waiting time for patients in the outpatient clinics. The crowd in the public health facilities reduces the amount of time available per patient for the healthcare provider. This leads to poor quality of healthcare. The reduced time available per patient leads to increased errors and, therefore, unsafe care. The overcrowding in the health facilities is also the main reason for the lack of cleanliness and proper sanitation in these facilities. This leads to health facilities themselves becoming sites for disease transmission [30].

Weak investment in health systems and policy research

There is an urgent need to increase investment in health systems research. This will help move India towards the goal of achieving universal health coverage. The quantum of research done on health systems is slowly increasing. Health system research, to a large extent, is narrowly focused on health service delivery, health information, medical technology and vaccines, human resources for health and health governance. However, not much research is done in the areas of healthcare financing models. Most of the research on health systems and policy emerges from only four states in India. There has not been a single paper originating from the North-East. Health system research is essential for implementing evidence-based policies and to ensure accountability of the health system to the community. Therefore, the weakness of health systems research is a major impediment to the public health system in India [31].

Corruption

Corruption in the public health system is a major challenge to achieving UHC. Pilferage of public hospital drugs, medicine, devices and products leads to resource depletion. Some doctors employed in public health facilities are seen to engage in private practice and refer their patients from public hospitals to their private facilities with the intention of realising income outside their jobs. Unofficial payments and bribes demanded by the hospital staff lead to an unnecessary increase in out-of-pocket expenditure for the patients, defeating the purpose of public healthcare delivery [32]. On the other hand, in the private health system, there is unregulated practice of 'cuts' and commissions and its heavy nexus with the pharmaceutical industry, leading to severe conflicts of interest. Addressing these challenges is essential to improving the public health system performance.

Way forward: Strengthening the public healthcare system in India

Reorienting the public health system to primary care

Most successful healthcare models that have achieved UHC have focused on primary healthcare. This is because strong primary healthcare logically reduces the need for investments in secondary and tertiary care. Therefore, the public health system in India must re-direct its focus on comprehensive primary healthcare. The Ayushman Bharat National Health Protection Scheme (AB-NHPS) has a component of HWC, which provides comprehensive primary healthcare [33]. This must be strengthened. At present, there is a skewed distribution of budgetary allocation that favours secondary and tertiary healthcare. This must be reworked, and more emphasis should be laid on comprehensive primary healthcare.

Engaging with the private sector

The private sector has an important role to play in the healthcare delivery mechanism. The private sector, including the non-profit and non-governmental organisations, has the capacity to reach out to the remotest corners of the country. They have a presence among the people within the community, even where the public health system has not been able to reach. This not only involves the private doctors but also the unregistered private medical practitioners. The private health sector is not adequately regulated. There are no measures to ensure the implementation of standard treatment guidelines. There are no mandatory registration and accreditation requirements. Therefore, strict implementation of the Clinical Establishments Act and accreditation of health facilities must be done to ensure that the private sector is regulated. Private providers must be actively engaged in the delivery of national health programmes, including tuberculosis elimination, leprosy elimination and non-communicable disease control programmes [34]. There must be areas where the private and public sectors should collaborate in the delivery of healthcare services.

The government must take up the role of a regulator rather than a provider

Despite 75 years in its relentless role as a public health service provider, the government has not been able to move close to UHC. This might be the right opportunity to move towards a more regulatory role and move away from being a provider. The Ayushman Bharat and other state-level health insurance schemes can empanel more private sector hospitals, and the state can take the role of governance, financing and regulation. This will ensure that the largest provider, the private system, is regulated adequately.

Decentralisation of healthcare planning

Some states have a strong local self-governance system in the form of a solid Panchayati Raj body. Healthcare planning must be decentralised at the level of the Panchayat bodies. The NHM has several measures to ensure community engagement in health planning, including the Village Health Sanitation and Nutrition Committee (VHSNC) and the Rogi Kalyan Samitis (RKS). Such decentralisation can ensure adequate community engagement and locally responsive and relevant health planning [35].

Task-shifting/sharing in healthcare

An urgent need to ensure universal health coverage is to demystify healthcare. ASHAs, ANMs and anganwadi workers (AWWs) are extremely important human resources in the primary healthcare infrastructure as they are the most accessible point of contact for the community. Primary healthcare must be inclusive (not just reliant on medical professionals), simplified and made available at the community level, delivered by these frontline health workers. The work of these frontline workers must be respected, and they must be adequately compensated.

Conclusion

The goal of any health system is to ensure well-being and welfare of its people. The public health system attempts to achieve these goals in a welfare mode as a duty of the state towards its people. The original model of public healthcare provision is slowly becoming less popular globally, in favour of publicly funded health financing systems. The public health system in India should gradually make this shift and become a regulator and use alternate financing mechanisms for public healthcare delivery. The ultimate goal of such a system would be the attainment of universal health coverage.

References

1. Chaturvedi S, Porter J, Pillai GKG, Abraham L, Shankar D, Patwardhan B. India and its pluralistic health system – a new philosophy for Universal Health Coverage. *The Lancet Regional Health – Southeast Asia*. 2023;10:100136.
2. Abhiyan JS. Health system in India: Crisis and alternatives. *Towards the National Health Assembly II, Booklet*. 2006; 2.
3. Duggal R. Bhore committee (1946) and its relevance today. *The Indian Journal of Pediatrics*. 1991;58:395–406.
4. Duggal R. Health planning in India. *India Health: A Reference Document*. 2002;4356.
5. Joseph SK, Kuragayala P. Capacity building as an intervention for human resource challenges in health care sector. *International Journal of Interdisciplinary Research and Innovations*. 2018;6(3):31.

6. Perry HB, Zulliger R, Rogers MM. Community health workers in low-, middle-, and high-income countries: An overview of their history, recent evolution, and current effectiveness. *Annual Review of Public Health*. 2014;35:399–421.
7. Chan M. Return to Alma-Atta. *The Lancet*. 2008;372(9642):865–866.
8. Duggal R. Historical review of health policy making. *Review of Healthcare in India*. 2005;21:e40.
9. Srinivasan K. Population concern before Independence. In *Indian Horizons*, Kejariwal OP (ed.). New Delhi: Indian Council for Cultural Relations, 2000.
10. Dhingra B, Dutta AK. National rural health mission. *The Indian Journal of Pediatrics*. 2011;78:1520–1526.
11. Ghosh A, Ghosh R. Maternal health care in India: A reflection of 10 years of National Health Mission on the Indian maternal health scenario. *Sexual and Reproductive Healthcare*. 2020;25:100530.
12. Zodpey S, Farooqui HH. Universal health coverage in India: Progress achieved and the way forward. *Indian Journal of Medical Research*. 2018;147(4):327.
13. Lahariya C. 'Ayushman Bharat' program and universal health coverage in India. *Indian Pediatrics*. 2018;55(6):495–506.
14. Modi I. Health care delivery system: India. In: *The Wiley Blackwell Encyclopedia of Health, Illness, Behavior, and Society*. 2014. p. 816–823.
15. ABHA | ABDM [Internet]. (cited 18 December 2023). Available from: https://abha.abdm.gov.in/abha/v3/
16. Hazarika I. Health workforce in India: Assessment of availability, production and distribution. *WHO South East Asia Journal of Public Health*. 2013;2(2):106–112.
17. Desai S, Bishnoi RK, Punjot P. Community health officer: The concept of mid-level health care providers. *International Journal of Community Medicine and Public Health*. 2020;7(4):1610.
18. Ramani KV. A management information system to plan and monitor the delivery of health-care services in government hospitals in India. *Journal of Health Organization Management*. 2004;18(2–3):207–220.
19. The Digital Personal Data Protection Bill, 2023 (Internet). (cited 11 February 2025). Available from: https://prsindia.org/billtrack/digital-personal-data-protection-bill-2023
20. Manikandan S, Gitanjali B. National list of essential medicines of India: The way forward. *Journal of Postgraduate Medicine*. 2012;58(1):68.
21. Mukherjee K. A cost analysis of the Jan Aushadhi scheme in India. *International Journal of Health Policy Management*. 2017;6(5):253.
22. Senior Citizens – status in India | Social Welfare (Internet) (cited 11 February 2025). Available from: https://socialwelfare.vikaspedia.in/viewcontent/social-welfare/senior-citizens-welfare/senior-citizens-status-in-india?lgn=en
23. Reidpath DD, Allotey P. Infant mortality rate as an indicator of population health. *Journal of Epidemiology and Community Health (1978)*. 2003;57(5):344–346.
24. General R. SRS bulletin sample registration system. *Office of the Registrar General, India*. 2021;54(1):1–9.
25. Press Release. Press Information Bureau (Internet) (cited 2025 11 February). Available from: https://pib.gov.in/PressReleasePage.aspx?PRID=2034937
26. Bhatia M, Singh DP. Health sector allocation in India's budget (2021–2022): A trick or treat? *The International Journal of Community and Social Development*. 2021;3(2):177–180.
27. Subramanian SV, Ackerson LK, Subramanyam MA, Sivaramakrishnan K. Health inequalities in India: The axes of stratification. *The Brown Journal of World Affairs*. 2008;14(2):127–138.
28. Mohanan M, Hay K, Mor N. Quality of health care in India: Challenges, priorities, and the road ahead. *Health Affairs*. 2016;35(10):1753–1758.

29. Quality Assurance Framework | National Health Systems Resource Centre [Internet]. (cited 27 December 2023). Available from: https://qps.nhsrcindia.org/quality-assurance-framework
30. Bhattacharyya S, Issac A, Rajbangshi P, Srivastava A, Avan BI. 'Neither we are satisfied nor they' – users and provider's perspective: A qualitative study of maternity care in secondary level public health facilities, Uttar Pradesh, India. *BMC Health Service Research*. 2015;15(1):1–13.
31. Dandona L, Katoch VM, Dandona R. Research to achieve health care for all in India. *The Lancet*. 2011;377(9771):1055–1057.
32. Sachan D. Tackling corruption in Indian medicine. *The Lancet*. 2013;382(9905):e23–e24.
33. Lahariya C. Health and wellness centers to strengthen primary health care in India: Concept, progress and ways forward. *The Indian Journal of Pediatrics*. 2020;87(11):916–929.
34. Chakravarthi I. Regulation of private health care providers in India: Current status, future directions. *Indian Journal of Public Administration*. 2018;64(4):587–598.
35. Kumar V, Mishra AJ. Healthcare under the Panchayati Raj Institutions (PRIs) in a decentralised health system: Experiences from Hardoi district of India. *Leadership in Health Services*. 2016;29(2):151–167.

3 Tribal healthcare in India

In need of reforms

Shailendra Kumar B. Hegde and Pritha Venkatachalam

Introduction to the tribal populations of India

The original inhabitants, indigenous to the land, were its first residents before the arrival of migrant populations from other parts of the world. The word 'Adivasis' (meaning original inhabitants) is derived from Sanskrit. It can be assumed these people would have inalienable rights over the land or wield significant influence over society and polity. Unfortunately, the truth couldn't have been further away from this. Adivasis have not only been denied such rights and privileges, but they have also been reduced to a political constituency or a marginalised segment of our society. They have been 'othered' and treated differently from the mainstream society. There is limited respect for their way of life and a lack of understanding of their social and political structures. This reality is reflected in the development indicators of the Adivasi communities.

Most Adivasi communities are classified as Scheduled Tribes (STs) in the Constitution of India. Article 342 of the Constitution defines Scheduled Tribes as follows:

> The President of India, may with respect to any State or Union Territory and where it is a State, after consultation with the Governor thereof by public notification, specify the tribes or tribal communities or parts of or groups within tribes or tribal communities which shall for the purpose of this Constitution be deemed to be Scheduled Tribes in relation to that State or Union Territory, as the case may be.

The list of Scheduled Tribes differs from state to state, which often creates confusion. An inexhaustive list of Scheduled Tribes in various states and union territories is provided in Table 3.1.

The decline in the development indicators of the ST communities started during the colonial era, when the colonial administration, without adequate thought, decided to notify them all as criminals. These communities had put up the most strenuous resistance to the imperial retaliation during the First War of Indian Independence. As they had native knowledge about the vagaries of the vast Indian jungles where they resided, the tribes are believed to

DOI: 10.4324/9781003684947-4

Table 3.1 An inexhaustive list of Scheduled Tribes distributed by states and union territories

S. No.	*State/union territory*	*Scheduled Tribes*
1.	Andaman and Nicobar	Oraons, Onges, Sentinelese, Shompens, Jarawa
2.	Andhra Pradesh	Andh, Bhil, Bhaghata, Chenchus, Dabba-Yerukala, Dhulia, Gadabas, Gond, Goundu, Jatapus, Kammara, Kattunayakan, Kolam, Manna Dhora, Nakkala, Pardhan, Rona, Savaras, Sadhu-Andh, Sugalis, Thoti
3.	Arunachal Pradesh	Abor, Apatanis, Galo, Monpa, Singpho, Sherdukpen
4.	Assam	Chakma, Chutiya, Dimasa, Gangte, Garos, Hajong Khasis
5.	Bihar	Asur, Baiga, Birjia, Birhor, Chero, Gonds, Parhaiya, Santhals, Savar
6.	Chhattisgarh	Agariya, Bhattra, Bhaina, Biar, Khond, Mawasi, Nagasia
7.	Goa	Dhodia, Dubia, Naikda, Siddi, Varli
8.	Gujarat	Bamcha, Barda, Bhil, Charan, Dhodia, Paradhi, Patelia, Gamta
9.	Himachal Pradesh	Gaddis, Gujjars, Khas, Lahaulas, Lamba, Pangwala, Swangal
10.	Jammu and Kashmir	Bakarwal, Balti, Beda, Gaddi, Garra, Mon, Purigpa, Sippi
11.	Jharkhand	Bhumji, Birhors, Gonds, Khaira, Mundas, Santhals, Savar
12.	Karnataka	Adiyan, Barda, Bhil, Gond, Iruliga, Koraga, Patelia, Yerava
13.	Kerala	Aarayan, Arandan, Eranvallan, Kurumbas, Malai, Uralis
14.	Madhya Pradesh	Baigas, Bharia, Bhils, Birhors, Gonds, Katkari, Kharia, Kol, Khond, Murias
15.	Maharashtra	Bhaina, Bhunjia, Dhodia, Katkari, Khond, Rathawa, Warlis
16.	Manipur	Aimol, Angami, Chiru, Kuki, Maram, Monsang, Paite, Purum, Thadou
17.	Meghalaya	Chakma, Garos, Hajong, Jaintias, Khasis, Lakher, Pawai, Raba
18.	Mizoram	Chakma, Dimasa, Khasi, Kuki, Lakher, Pawai, Raba, Synteng
19.	Nagaland	Angami, Garo, Kachari, Kuki, Mikir, Nagas, Sema
20.	Odisha	Gadaba, Ghara, Kharia, Khond, Matya, Oraons, Rajuar, Santhals
21.	Rajasthan	Bhils, Damaria, Dhanka, Meenas (Minas), Patelia, Sahariya
22.	Sikkim	Bhutia, Khas, Lepchas
23.	Tamil Nadu	Adiyan, Aranadan, Eravallan, Irular, Kadar, Kanikar, Kotas, Todas
24.	Telangana	Chenchus
25.	Tripura	Bhil, Bhutia, Chaimal, Chakma, Halam, Khasia, Lushai, Mizel, Namte
26.	Uttarakhand	Bhotias, Buksa, Jannsari, Khas, Raji, Tharu
27.	Uttar Pradesh	Bhotias, Buksa, Jaunsari, Kol, Raji, Tharu
28.	West Bengal	Asur, Khond, Hajong, Ho, Parhaiya, Rabha, Santhals, Savar

have descended from the forests at crucial points to launch strident attacks against the British-controlled armed forces. The reaction of the British to these brazen acts of defiance and counterattack was the Criminal Tribes Act of 1871, which deemed the people belonging to these tribes and sub-tribes as criminals, who could therefore be subjected to police action. They could therefore no longer live as they had hitherto lived – roaming freely in the forests, living off the produce and having their own social practices and political structures of leadership. They were also often confined to settlement camps under the harsh rules of the administration. This kind of segregation and isolation was alien to an inherently nomadic and non-pastoral population that had historically enjoyed a reasonable level of independence even when they were controlled by the princely states.

The treatment of tribals as secondary citizens continued until India gained independence. In independent India, laws were enacted to decriminalise the population. In fact, special treatment was accorded to the Adivasis by way of a differentiated and decentralised political and administrative structure under the Indian Constitution. Since then, laws such as the Panchayat (Extension to the Scheduled Areas) Act, 1996, and the Forest Act, 2007, have also been enacted by the Indian state in recognition of the need for their greater participation in their own governance and rights over the forests.

However, as history has shown us repeatedly, societal change does not occur with the mere passing of laws, especially when unjust or hegemonic structures need to be dismantled. Sadly, the marginalisation of ST communities continues to this day. They continue to be deprived of access to forests, and due to 'development' creep, the tribal peoples are also afflicted by lifestyle diseases such as hypertension, diabetes and mental illness, in addition to the diseases that traditionally affect them.

The tribal population in India is made up of many tribes and sub-tribes, and they are disparate and large in number; yet, as insensitive as it can be, they are often treated as a singular, homogenous population. To make matters worse, they are measured by a lens that is alien to them and by legacy systems that have historically sought to diminish them. Hence, the popular discourse on tribal peoples' health is still dominated by health indicators as prescribed in the Western medical system, and we have not cared to understand what makes them unique genetically; for example, why are they able to be highly functional despite low levels of haemoglobin? We do not know adequately yet. Developing an understanding of these features, coupled with enabling them to adopt their own unique health and wellness practices, may well be the secret to better health outcomes for the tribal peoples.

The way a country takes care of its most vulnerable people speaks volumes of its development. With an objective of providing a more focused approach towards the integrated socioeconomic development of the Scheduled Tribes in a coordinated and planned manner, an independent Ministry of Tribal Affairs (MoTA) was set up in 1999 by bifurcating the Ministry of Social Justice and Empowerment. It is the nodal ministry responsible for overall policy planning and coordination of programmes for the development of tribal people. However, the sectoral programmes and schemes for the development of these communities, as well as their coordination, fall under the ambit of the concerned ministries. These are intended to support and supplement the efforts, primarily of other union ministries, the state governments and partly of voluntary organisations via financial assistance and to fill critical gaps within the institutions and programmes serving tribal people.

Tribal peoples constitute 8.6 per cent of the total population of India, with a total of 104 million people and growing at a rate that is faster than the rest of the population (the decadal population growth rate of STs between 2001 and 2011 stood at ~24 per cent against ~18 per cent of the entire population).[1] Madhya Pradesh has the largest ST population (15 million), followed by Maharashtra (10 million), Odisha (9 million) and Rajasthan (9 million). In fact, more than two-thirds of India's ST population lives in the seven states of Madhya Pradesh, Chhattisgarh, Jharkhand, Odisha, Maharashtra, Gujarat and Rajasthan (Figure 3.1).

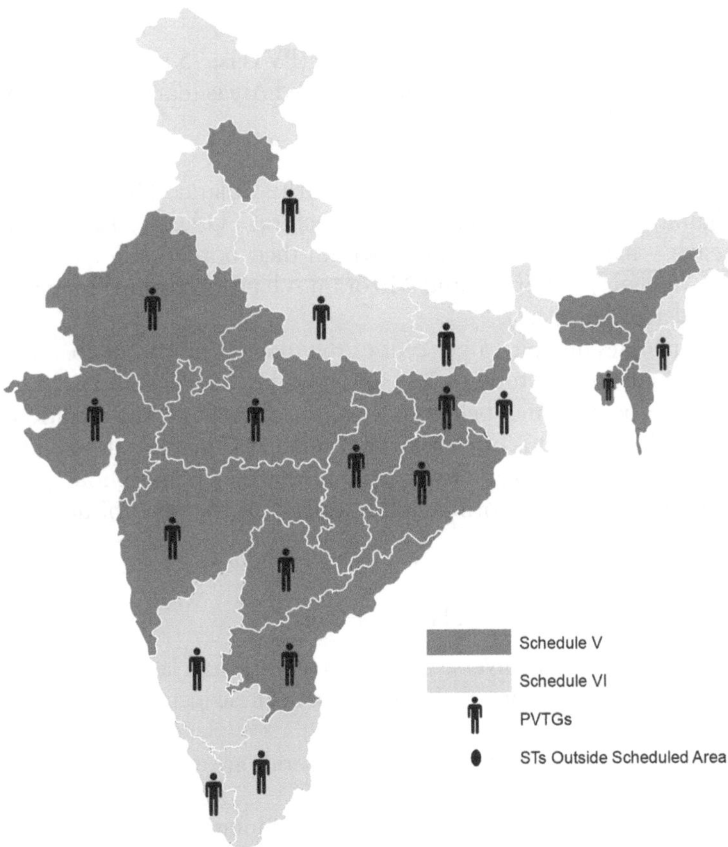

Figure 3.1 State-wise tribal population.

Note:

1. *Percentage within each state refers to the proportion of India's tribal population residing in that state. For example, 15 per cent of India's tribal population resides in Madhya Pradesh.*
2. *The ST population of the new state of Andhra Pradesh is derived from the difference of the population between undivided Andhra Pradesh as per Census 2011 and the new state of Telangana.*
3. *Meghalaya and Assam are in the North-East of India.*

The expert committee on tribal health jointly constituted in 2013 by the Ministry of Health and Family Welfare and Ministry of Tribal Affairs[2] (MoTA), Government of India, categorises tribal peoples as:

1. Tribal communities living in Schedule V areas, tribal-dominated blocks and districts
2. Tribal communities of North-East India and those living in Schedule VI areas in that region
3. Particularly Vulnerable Tribal Groups (PVTGs; 75 tribes/subgroups)
4. Tribal people living outside the Scheduled Areas (data on this segment is hardly available)

Ten states – Andhra Pradesh, Chhattisgarh, Gujarat, Himachal Pradesh, Jharkhand, Madhya Pradesh, Maharashtra, Odisha, Rajasthan and Telangana – have Schedule V areas within their border, while four states – Assam, Meghalaya, Tripura and Mizoram – have Schedule VI areas within their borders (Figure 3.2).

Tribal peoples inhabit 15 per cent of the total geographical area of India.[3] The MoTA identifies a total of 705 unique tribes in India[4] and each of these tribes has its own distinct belief systems, social customs and traditions with an overall identity that is often semi-independent from the national identity.[5] While popular culture has mostly painted a rather homogenous picture of tribal communities, they form a solid bedrock of the spirit of diversity that defines India as a nation.

Distribution of the tribal population of India

Despite being extremely diverse in terms of culture and language, tribal communities share some common characteristics. These include the following:

- Most tribal communities reside in rural areas and often in forest habitations.
- There is relative egalitarianism in the community.
- There is an absence of complex political structures, and the communities are marked by strong kinship bonds.

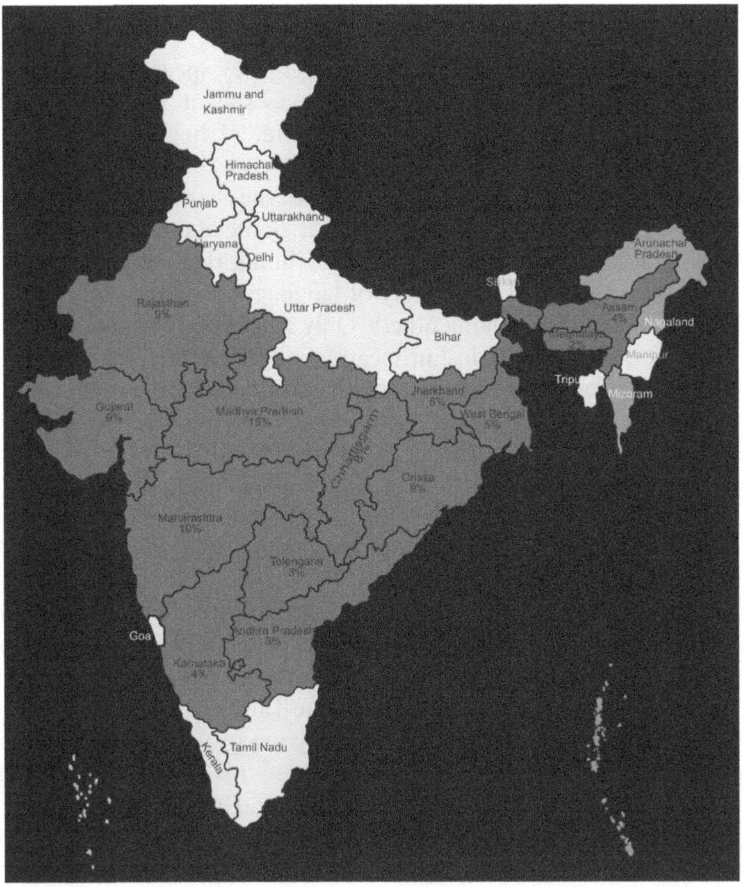

Figure 3.2 Distribution of tribal peoples across India.

However, thousands of years of socio-cultural evolution and co-existence, in addition to their distinctness, have also yielded various similarities not only among tribal communities but also between tribal and non-tribal communities in India.

The similarities among various tribal communities are often observed to be higher when they have lived in proximity to each other for a long time. Anthropologist B.S. Guha provided a basic theoretical system of three zones for the classification of tribal communities in India based on their geographical distribution: (i) North and North-eastern zone, (ii) Central zone and (iii) Southern zone. It is often observed that Gonds, Mundas and Santhals who predominantly reside across various states in the central zone of India share some elements of similarity. To a certain extent, the tribal communities living in the North-Eastern states of the country share some similarities.

Linguistic landscape of the tribal peoples of India

Tribal peoples have a rich linguistic heritage. They speak 461 different languages out of a total of 780 unique languages spoken in India.[6] The tribal languages of India are divided into four different linguistic families, such as Indo-European, Dravidian, Austro-Asiatic and the Tibeto-Burman subfamily of the Sino-Tibetan languages. Most of the central Indian tribes speak either Dravidian or Austro-Asiatic languages. Some of the major tribes speaking Dravidian language are the Gond, the Khond, the Koya, the Oraon and the Toda. The Austro-Asiatic family of languages is spoken by the Santhal, the Munda and the Ho, among others. Only a few tribal groups, like the Bhil and the Halbi, speak the Indo-European family of languages.[7]

Generally, two main linguistic sub-families exist in North-East India among the tribal population: Austro-Asiatic group and Tibeto-Burman Group. Khasi is the only group belonging to Austro-Asiatic group in this region, whereas the Tibeto-Burman family is widespread and adopted by the Adi, Apatani, Boro, Chutia, Deuri, Garo, Hajong, Kuki, Maran, Mech, Rabha and Tripuri tribes. The other groups are the Tai groups and the Indo-Aryan speakers.[8]

Languages of tribal groups inhabiting the southern zone primarily originate from the Dravidian language group. For example, Irulas, one of the prominent tribes of the southern zone, speak the Irula language, an independent Dravidian language belonging to the Tamil–Malayalam subgroup of south Dravidian languages. Muduga tribe living in the Attapadi region also speak a language that shows clear semblance with the Dravidian language group, while being distinct from the major and more popular Dravidian languages such as Kannada, Tamil or Malayalam. N. Rajendran, who was the first to study the language spoken by Muduga community, presented a detailed argument regarding the distinct features of their language.[9]

Festivals and rituals

The practices of ceremonial exchange among tribal peoples show how marriage alliances and other social ties are central to the meaning and the strategies of relationships among clans and kin groups. However, the ongoing exchanges that form and renew alliances are not restricted to marriage but rather provide the template for a wide range of events that may involve various sorts of relationships as well as death. Rituals represent the cosmic order as well as the agricultural cycle and the taboos associated with it.[10] They are often connected with traditional economic activities such as foraging, hunting or agriculture. Here, the exchanges are believed to be happening between humans and others such as nature. This template that guides and defines various relationships is rooted in the philosophy of animism. Animism is understood as a subjective relationship with other sentient beings and has been reformulated as a relational ontology.[11]

Various foraging rituals, for example, include not only human relatives but also non-human relatives, rock ancestors and grandparents' deities and other non-human persons.[12] This very template of exchange between human and other sentient beings informs the common practice of various forms of sacrifices performed as part of most rituals. Sacrifices of pigs, goats, chicken or something of value to the community are commonly observed. The faith is that in exchange of the sacrifices made, the earth goddess or ancestors or a particular deity, depending on the context of the ritual, will protect their harvests from wild animals or an insect infestation, or they will provide boon to the community with timely monsoon, good harvest or successful hunt or heal their diseases and pain or bless them with a healthy and prosperous life.

For example, Sohrai (Soharae), the winter harvest festival, is the most important festival for the Santhals who live in Chhattisgarh, Jharkhand and West Bengal. On the first day, rituals and sacrifice of hens are conducted by the village priest (*naike*) in an open space as an invocation of their gods (Bongas). After a feast of rice boiled with the hen, the village headman (*manjhi*) officially announces the beginning of the festival. The second day focuses on invoking blessings from Bongas at the household level. The cattle are sent to graze early in the morning, while in their absence, the women clean and decorate their huts and prepare food following ceremonial guidelines, which is later served as 'prasad'. Upon return, the cattle are warmly welcomed and their horns anointed with oil and vermillion. Garlands made by strewing paddy strands are tied across their foreheads. Earthen lamps are lit in the cattle sheds in the evening. The next day is devoted to worshipping the cattle sheds followed by various games and recreational activities involving the cattle. After two more days of various rituals, the village headman (*manjhi*) formally closes the festival celebration.[13] The other important festivals celebrated by Santhals are Baha, Maghsin, Eroksin and Karam. Similarly, the Mundas, who live in Bihar, Chhattisgarh, Odisha and West Bengal, also observe different agricultural festivals, like Garam Dharam, Maghe Parav, Sarhul and Halchar. Each of these festivals either involves animal sacrifice or offerings (also an act of sacrifice) of grains and other valuable materials.

The facilitator of rituals and festivals (priests, *shamans* or monks): A key influencer in tribal communities

Priests, *shamans* or monks mediate between deities and the lay community. Priesthood is sometimes linked to a certain territory; among the Tiwa in the borderland between Assam and Meghalaya, each of the six original villages is assigned to a priest who wields supreme authority in customary matters. Among most tribal groups of central India, two types of priesthood are encountered. The village priests, called *dihuri*, *baiga* or *naeke*, oversee the agricultural rituals. The second type of priest is often considered a *shaman*, a medium or a healer and is called *ojha*, *guniar* or *mati*.[10] The names of both types of priests vary depending on the community's linguistic context. In the

North-East, sacred specialists may belong to both genders and have overlapping roles rather than a clear division of labour. Some communities, like that of the Konyak Naga, have female *shamans*, mainly differing from male *shamans* in that the latter perform sacrifices, while the female ritual specialists do not generally spill blood. The healing praxis implies negotiating with the spirits associated with the landscape for the release of the sick person's entrapped soul.[13]

Social structure

The social structure of tribal communities is primarily patrilineal and/or patrilocal with a few exceptions such as Garo and Khasi tribes in Meghalaya. Most of the tribal communities have local governance systems that they have followed traditionally to address the internal disputes, facilitate marriages and other exchanges within the community, ensuring that the community members abide by their traditions. The Munda tribe follows the *parha* system, where the community is headed by Pahan (the village head), and has a structure very similar to Gram Sabha but headed by elderly male members of the community. Santhals have followed the *manjhi–pargana* system as their traditional local governance mechanism and continue to abide by the system for a significant share of governance-related issues. The village headman is elected for certain communities in certain geographies, while for many communities, it is a hereditary role. Many tribes in the North-East refer to their head of community or village as king in their respective languages.

Karbi tribes who dwell across the states of Assam and Arunachal Pradesh have a traditional parliament known as 'Pinpomar' and the parliament selects *Lingdokpo* or king of the community. The *Lingdokpo* continues to have a prestigious status in the community and plays a significant role in the governance aspects of the Karbi tribe.[14]

Mostly, the tribes of central India are monogamous, but the practice of polygamy is also occasionally present and is not frowned upon. The practice of *sororate* (refers to the custom where a man marries the sister of his deceased wife, or a sister of his wife if she is barren, to ensure the continuation of the family line) and *levirate* (refers to the custom where a man is obliged to marry his brother's widow) is socially accepted. The tribal communities of central India follow tribe endogamy and clan exogamy and because of this practice, the marriage within the clan is strictly prohibited and members of the clan are considered brothers and sisters.[7] A similar practice is found among some of the tribes from the North-East. For example, among the Wancho community clan, endogamy is prohibited.[15]

While similarities exist, as we delve deeper into the tribal life and culture, the diversity and differences start to appear. We can find a rigid patriarchal and monogamous societal structure in certain tribes, while some other tribes embrace the tradition of eloping before marriage to explore physical and emotional compatibility. While a higher rate of work participation of women of a particular tribal community may come across as an indicator of gender equality, deeper research can unveil a disproportionate load of labour among the women in that community. In addition, an element of influence of the colonial regime and non-tribal communities impacted a section of tribal people in India, which is often referred to as a process of 'acculturation'. There is also evidence suggesting negative impacts on the tribal people's nutritional status because of reduced diversity in their food and their rising dependence on the public distribution system (PDS), which was initially not designed considering regional and local food habits. This design flaw in the early versions of PDS can be attributed to our tendency to focus on or capitalise on the similarities and ignore the diversity that makes a community and their needs significantly different from another community. While we shall continue to categorise various aspects of tribal communities for the ease of our understanding, there is a persistent need for all of us to embrace a more micro-lens that offers us with a detailed and clear understanding of the fascinating and diverse cultural landscapes of tribal communities in India.

Sociodemographic profile and the health and nutrition status of tribal peoples across India

The National Health Policy 2017 has acknowledged that the challenges faced by the tribal communities are geographical and infrastructural and calls for situation-specific reforms in health service delivery. To carry out situation-specific reforms, we need disaggregated data at the block and district levels. However, we do not have tribe-specific data to understand the health and nutrition status of tribal people, at any level. At the national level, broadly, the health and nutrition indicators of tribal people vis-à-vis national average have been computed through multiple data sources (Table 3.2).

The Tribal Health Compendium leverages data from the National Family Health Survey, round 4 (NFHS-4) and provides the best data to understand the health status of the tribal populations.[16] Here we present an overview of the household characteristics, socio-demographics and health and nutrition status of the tribal populations synthesised from the Tribal Health Compendium.

Overall, when compared to ST households, a higher proportion of non-ST households had electricity (non-ST: 88.9 per cent; ST: 82 per cent), an improved source of drinking water (non-ST: 90.8 per cent; ST: 82.2 per cent), access to an improved sanitation facility (non-ST: 50.8 per cent; ST: 27.4 per cent), used clean fuel for cooking (non-ST: 46.5 per cent; ST: 19.2 per cent) and had water and soap (or detergent) at hand-washing place (non-ST: 62.4 per cent; ST: 40.2 per cent). A higher proportion of ST households (63.8 per cent) did not have a toilet facility when compared to non-ST households (36.1 per cent). Literacy, especially female literacy, has been identified as an important determinant of the health and nutrition status of a family and community. There is a 16.1 per cent difference in the literacy rates of tribal

Table 3.2 Comparing health indicators for the Scheduled Tribes population with all-India data[a]

Parameter	*India*	*Scheduled Tribes*	*SDG 3 targets*
Maternal mortality (per 100,000 live births)	130	260	70
Proportion of pregnant women that are anaemic (%)	50	57	24
Proportion of under-five children that are stunted (%)	38	44	21
Under-five mortality (per 1,000 live births)	50	57	11
Malaria (cases per 100,000 population)	89	334	0
Tuberculosis (cases per 100,000 population)	138	703	0

[a]Multiple Data Sources: SDG India Index, Baseline Report, 2018 – NITI Aayog; NFHS (4) 2015–16; National Nutrition Strategy, Government of India, NITI Aayog; Tribal Health in India, Report of the Expert Committee on Tribal Health (2018); Thomas BE, Adinarayanan S, Manogaran C, Swaminathan S. Pulmonary tuberculosis among tribals in India: A systematic review and meta-analysis. *Indian Journal of Medical Research* 2015;141(5):614–23; Malaria NBVDCP data.

(53.9 per cent) and non-tribal women (70.0 per cent), while there is a 9.4 per cent difference in the literacy rates of tribal (77.2 per cent) and non-tribal men (86.6 per cent).

Antenatal check-ups and consumption of iron and folic acid are essential for the health of the mother and the foetus during pregnancy. When compared to ST mothers, a higher proportion of non-ST mothers received antenatal check-up in the first trimester (non-ST: 70.6 per cent; ST: 66.6 per cent), and they also made four antenatal care visits during their pregnancy (non-ST: 51.9 per cent; ST: 45.4 per cent). Given the status of the above two indicators, as expected, a higher proportion of non-ST mothers received full antenatal care (21.6 per cent) and consumed iron and folic acid tablets for 100 days or more during their pregnancy (30.8 per cent) when compared to their ST counterparts (16.1 per cent and 26.3 per cent, respectively). Although both the ST and non-ST mothers are not doing well on all the above four indicators, the ST mothers are worse off.

There was 11.4 per cent difference in the institutional delivery rates between ST (68.6 per cent) and non-ST women (80.2 per cent). This translates into a large difference in the maternal mortality rates between the two groups.

Policymakers and public health experts consider the birth weight of the newborn as one of the key markers of not just the health system of the state but also the prevailing socioeconomic status. Malnutrition among the under-fives affects their cognition, learning ability and lifelong earnings. A high level of malnutrition shows high deprivation in terms of economic and social freedom in society. Overall, a higher proportion of ST children were born with low birth weight (20.6 per cent) when compared to non-ST children (17.9 per cent).

The prevalence of stunting, severe wasting and underweight among ST children (43.5 per cent, 10.1 per cent and 44.6 per cent, respectively) was higher compared to non-ST children (37.8 per cent, 7.1 per cent and 34.6 per cent, respectively). Across India, ST women were more undernourished (31.2 per cent) when compared to non-ST women (22.0 per cent). The prevalence of anaemia among ST children (6–59 months) and pregnant and non-pregnant ST women was higher when compared to their non-ST counterparts.

These data lead us to understand the relative differences between the ST and non-ST populations across India. Unsurprisingly, the ST population fared poorly in all the health and nutrition indicators across India.

The only exception is in non-communicable diseases, where the prevalence of high blood sugar levels was lower among both ST men and women when compared to non-ST men and women. Although the prevalence of high blood pressure levels was slightly higher among both ST men and women, when compared to their non-ST counterparts, these differences are not significant.

If India intends to achieve its Sustainable Development Goal (SDG) targets, 'inclusion' of tribal peoples in the development agenda is important, thereby leading to improvement in their health and nutrition status and that of India.

Health infrastructure in tribal areas

Health infrastructure in tribal areas has traditionally been deficient on multiple aspects. Based on our population norms as a country vis-à-vis the actual status in tribal areas, the deficit continues, despite the best efforts of the government to bridge the gap (see Table 3.3). As of 31 March 2021, there were a total of 26,351 Sub-Centres (SC), 3,966 Primary Health Centres (PHC) and 975 Community Health Centres (CHC) in the tribal areas of the country as against a requirement of 33,507 SCs, 5,015 PHCs and 1,245 CHCs. This amounts to a deficit of 8,503 SCs (25.4 per cent), 1,464 PHCs (29.2 per cent) and 347 CHCs (27.8 per cent) in the tribal areas of India.

However, what is most concerning is the deficiency of human health workforce across the tribal areas of the country (Table 3.4). While we are doing well with respect to the frontline staff at SCs and PHCs (auxiliary nurse midwives (ANMs) and doctors), there is a deficit of over 50 per cent with respect to male health workers (54.01 per cent) and health assistants (63.68 per cent) (Table 3.5). This means that the stress on the existing staff at SCs and PHCs is very high, which in turn may lead to poor quality of services. Across tribal areas of the country, there is an 81.69 per cent deficit of specialists (comprising surgeons, gynaecologists, paediatricians and physicians) at the CHCs. This is a matter of huge concern because without the availability of specialists at the CHCs, it is extremely difficult to provide high-quality healthcare

Table 3.3 Comparing household characteristics and health and nutrition indicators of tribal and non-tribal people across India

Indicators	*ST population*	*Non-ST population*
Household characteristics		
Households with electricity (%)	82.0	88.9
Households with an improved drinking water source (%)	82.2	90.8
Households using improved sanitation facility (%)	27.4	50.8
Households with no toilet facility (%)	63.8	36.1
Households using clean fuel for cooking (%)	19.2	46.5
Households with the presence of water and soap or detergent at handwashing place	40.2	62.4
Literacy rates		
Literacy rates – women	53.9	70.0
Literacy rates – men	77.2	86.6
Family planning		
Households using any family planning method	48.6	54.1
Maternity care		
Mothers who had antenatal check-up in the first trimester (%)	66.6	70.6
Mothers who had at least four antenatal care visits (%)	45.4	51.9
Mothers who had full antenatal care (%)	16.1	21.6
Mothers who consumed iron and folic acid for ≥100 days during pregnancy	26.3	30.8
Institutional delivery rate	68.6	80.2
Nutritional status of under-five children		
Children with low birth weight (%)	20.6	17.9
Stunted (height-for-age) (%)	43.5	37.8
Severely wasted (weight-for-height) (%)	10.1	7.1
Underweight (weight-for-age)	44.6	34.6
Children (6–23 months) receiving adequate diet (%)	8.9	9.7
Women with BMI below normal (<18.5 kg/m^2) (%)	31.2	22.0
Anaemia among children and women		
Children aged 6–59 months that are anaemic (%)	63.5	58
Pregnant women that are anaemic (<11.0 g/dl) (%)	57.6	49.5
Non-pregnant women aged 15–49 years that are anaemic (<12.0 g/dl) (%)	59.1	52.4
Prevalence of hypertension and diabetes mellitus among adults aged 15–49 years		
Women with high blood sugar levels	7.1	8.7
Men with high blood sugar levels	9.4	12.1
Women with high blood pressure levels	9.4	8.9
Men with high blood pressure levels	13.9	13.4

Notes: High blood sugar level: >140 mg/dl; High blood pressure: systolic >140 mmHg and/or diastolic >90 mmHg).

Table 3.4 Comparing population norms for health facilities in tribal areas with the current status

Health facility	*Norms for tribal areas (population covered)*	*Current status in tribal areas (2021)*
One Sub-Centre	3,000 people	3,839 people
One Primary Health Centre	20,000 people	25,507 people
One Community Health Centre	80,000 people	1,03,756 people

United Nations Development Program. *Enhancing Effectiveness of Tribal Development Programs: Results*. UNDP India; 2024. Available from: https://www.undp.org/india/publications/enhancing-effectiveness-tribal-development-programmes-results-2024#:~:text=India%20is%20home%20to%20around,the%20country's%20total%20population%20(approx.

Table 3.5 Current status of health human workforce in tribal areas of India (as of 31 March 2021)

Positions	*Required as per population norms*	*Shortfall in numbers*	*Shortfall in percentage (%)*
Auxiliary nurse midwife at Sub-Centres	26,351	852	3.23
Auxiliary nurse midwife at Primary Health Centres	3966	724	18.26
Male health worker at Sub-Centres	26,351	14,233	54.01
Health assistants (male and female) at Primary Health Centres	7932	5051	63.68
Doctors at Primary Health Centres	3966	340	8.57
Surgeons at Community Health Centres	975	800	82.05
Obstetrician and Gynaecologist at Community Health Centres	975	769	78.87
Physicians at Community Health Centres	975	837	85.85
Paediatricians at Community Health Centres	975	851	87.28
Total specialists at Community Health Centres	3900	3186	81.69
General duty medical officers at Community Health Centres	1950	69	3.54
Nursing staff at Primary Health Centres	3966	607	15.31
Nursing staff at Community Health Centres	6825	349	5.11

United Nations Development Program. *Enhancing Effectiveness of Tribal Development Programs: Results*. UNDP India; 2024. Available from: https://www.undp.org/india/publications/enhancing-effectiveness-tribal-development-programmes-results-2024#:~:text=India%20is%20home%20to%20around,the%20country's%20total%20population%20(approx.

services. This pushes tribal people to either seek healthcare at higher centres or in private facilities, both of which lead to a high out-of-pocket expenditure. It also creates an unfavourable perception about the public health system in the minds of tribal people, negatively affecting their health-seeking behaviour, in the form of more and more tribal people turning to tribal healers, pharmacies and quacks for their healthcare needs, which often worsens their health.

There are a multitude of reasons for this deficit in health workforce, especially specialists. These range from tribal peoples living in hilly and forested areas, lack of roads and other means of transport, low and patchy network connectivity to low scope for professional interaction or growth for the health professionals, poor educational opportunities for their children and potential social isolation. All these factors have deeply and negatively impacted the relationship between tribal people and the health system.

In most tribal areas of India, the proliferation of qualified private healthcare providers is minimal with very few practitioners practicing medicine in these areas. This, coupled with deficiencies in the public healthcare system, pushes the tribal people to depend heavily on tribal traditional healers.

Traditional tribal healers and their healing practices

The traditional systems of medicine in India include the regulated group of systems, namely ayurveda, yoga, unani, siddha and homoeopathy (codified under the acronym AYUSH) and those that are unregulated traditional systems which are non-codified and grouped under 'local health traditions' (LHTs).[17] These LHTs have an articulated theoretical framework and clinical traditions with a diverse range of preventive and therapeutic modalities.[18] Some may also have a recorded '*materia medica*' in the local language.

A traditional tribal healer does not have formal medical training but is considered by the local community as being competent to provide healthcare using animal, plant and mineral substances and certain other techniques based on the social, cultural and religious background as well as the knowledge, attitudes and beliefs that are prevalent in the community regarding physical, mental and social well-being and the causation of the disease and disability.[19] The healer lives within the community, enjoys a huge amount of support and goodwill and influences the health-seeking behaviours of the local community.

Traditional healing practices are widely prevalent across India and more so in central India.[20] Accessing healthcare within the tribal community is determined by many factors, including but not limited to the credibility of the healer, cultural identities, individual health status, beliefs and understanding of the disease. Supernatural beliefs such as bad luck, reverse bad luck, magic, poisoning and ancestral problems also determine how to access traditional healthcare.[21] Tribal population relies largely on traditional medicine for almost all their healthcare needs including primary healthcare services due to their trust in the healer, low cost, cultural beliefs and practices and also trust deficit in the allopathic government system of medicine. Other reasons for tribal populations consulting traditional healers include their belief in the wrath of Gods causing ill health, inability to disclose certain problems to the modern medical practitioner, side effects of drugs and incurability of certain diseases by modern medicine, supernatural forces and belief that diseases were the repercussion for their sins and medicines only work if their deities permit it.[22]

Singh et al. reported that traditional healing is the first source of healthcare service in rural India, and the use of this form of healing for short-term morbidity is higher among tribal people when compared to other caste groups.[20] Bhat et al. reported that patients visit traditional healers for conditions such as body pain, stomach disorders, fractures, jaundice, kidney stones, skin diseases, gynaecological problems, burns and cancers as well.[23]

A tribal healer learns the art of healing from an accomplished traditional tribal healer, in the *guru–shishya* (master–student) tradition, with the *shishya* spending a considerable amount of time working under the shadow of a guru. The knowledge is transferred from the guru to his *shishya* almost entirely orally without any written text. The traditional tribal healing knowledge has been generated by communities over centuries using components of the ecosystem that are locally available and accessible.[24] There are different kinds of traditional tribal healers. They can be informally classified based on methods of treatment into those who

(a) Use herbs to treat their patients
(b) Use herbs and faith (which includes mantras and certain rituals)
(c) Use only belief systems (*andh-shraddha*) and tantric rituals
(d) Carry out animal sacrifices and occult practices

Also, among the traditional tribal healers, there could be specialisations with some healers only focusing on fractures, poisonings or jaundice.

Some authors have also reported that traditional tribal healing systems are not organised and streamlined in an evidence-based manner but are practised as an assortment of natural medicine, superstition and religious belief.[25] Although multiple studies have been conducted across India focusing on the traditional healing practices and perceptions of the community on folk medicine, the focus has mostly been on ethnobotanical aspects of the herbal drugs that are used in the clinical management of the diseases[20,25,26,27,28,29,30,31] and not on the perspectives and practices of traditional healers on health, disease management and the health system itself.[23] According to the World Health Organization (WHO), the quantity and quality of safety and efficacy data on traditional medicines are not sufficient to meet the criteria needed to support their use worldwide.[32] However, this position seems to be changing rapidly, as recently the WHO, in partnership with the Government of India, has established the Global Centre for Traditional Medicine in India with the aim of maximising the potential of traditional medicines through modern science and technology.[33]

Most importantly, tribal peoples believe in tribal healers, tribal medicines and their practices. Hence, an exploration of this tribal knowledge and practices is essential for upholding the system and inclusive development of the tribal communities. Efforts are ongoing for proper conservation, validation and documentation necessary for the promotion and development of tribal medicine and tribal healing practices.

Why focus on tribal peoples' health and nutrition?

If the health and nutrition status of tribal peoples is not improved, there is a high risk that India will fail to achieve the targets of SDG 2 and SDG 3 by 2030. Without an explicit focus on the unique challenges faced in delivering healthcare services to its tribal population, India runs the risk of excluding and further marginalising them as well as undermining its efforts to reach SDG 2 on hunger and SDG 3 on health and well-being.[34] Even though tribal people constitute only 8.6 per cent of India's population, they contribute disproportionately to the negative health and nutrition outcomes. Therefore, we need to allocate resources disproportionately to improve the health and nutrition status of the tribal people. There is adequate evidence to show that laws, programmes and interventions designed to benefit the most vulnerable groups such as the differently abled or people of colour, often end up benefiting all of society, across the world.[35] This 'curb-cut effect', which describes how addressing disadvantages or exclusions experienced by one group of people, creates an environment that enables everyone to participate and contribute fully. We believe that when this effect is applied to tribal communities, it will have a similar impact on the overall health and nutrition status of India, and hence it is important to focus on the 8.6 per cent tribal population of India.

General principles of working with tribal peoples

It is important to understand that a few general principles are to be followed with care across public systems, especially the health systems to enable better engagement between tribal peoples and public systems.

Dignity and sensitivity to address discrimination

There exists no satisfactory definition of the term 'tribe' anywhere.[36] Anthropologists and others have fallen back on listing group characteristics to identify people as 'tribals'. But often these lists themselves serve better to illustrate the prejudices and presumptions of the compilers, than to make any, but a very tenuous, and sometimes even arbitrary, delineation between tribal peoples and non-tribal peoples.[37] This trend is visible in almost all the attempts to identify and define tribal groups across the globe. The issue is not limited to the scope of academic discourse or administrative definition. In the authors' experience, they have witnessed instances where practitioners from both the public and private sectors used terms like 'backward', 'primitive', unhygienic' and 'unaware', clearly in a derogatory connotation. In one of the instances, the authors even witnessed that members of tribal communities were lacking knowledge and intelligence as they did not speak the language of the majority there. We need to attempt to consciously understand the prejudices that we carry with us due to our lack of knowledge and awareness about the rich cultural heritage of tribal communities. The distance between the caregivers and tribal communities can be addressed as more and more efforts are put to inculcate the basic values of treating people with dignity irrespective of their ethnicity or class or gender identity. Jan Swasthya Sahyog Hospital in Bilaspur, the SEWA Rural Hospital in Jhagadiya, Basic Health Care Services in Rajasthan, SEARCH Hospital in Gadchiroli and many other organisations across India have shown how members of tribal communities seek care actively once they learn about places where they are treated in a dignified and sensitive manner.

A participatory approach for improved health equity and outcome

A participatory approach is a cost-effective way to extend a healthcare system to the geographical and social periphery of a country; communities that begin to understand their health status objectively rather than fatalistically may decide to take a series of preventive measures; communities that invest labour, time, money and materials in health-promoting activities are more committed to the use and maintenance of the things they produce, such as water supplies; health education is most effective in the context of village activities; and community health workers, if they are well-chosen, have the confidence of the people.[38] Ekjut, a non-profit organisation working with tribal communities in Chakradharpur in Jharkhand, proved the effectiveness of community participation not only to address the issues of discrimination and oppression but also to improve health outcomes. A participatory learning and action cycle with 244 women's groups was implemented in 18 intervention clusters covering an estimated population of 1,14,141. Participatory interventions with community groups can influence maternal and child health outcomes, if key intervention characteristics are preserved and tailored to local contexts.

Challenging the deficit discourse to address stereotypes

'Deficit discourse' refers to discourse that represents people or groups in terms of deficiency – absence or lack or failure. It particularly denotes a discourse that narrowly situates responsibility for problems with the affected individuals or communities, overlooking the larger socioeconomic structures in which they are embedded. It is implicated with race-based stereotypes, and there is evidence that it is a barrier to improving health outcomes.[39] When we design an intervention for marginalised peoples, such as tribal communities, we often find the use of language indicating something they lack instead of something that they have been robbed of systematically over time. We say that *we need to address the lack of awareness* instead of saying the *system's (public and private) incapability to ensure dissemination of knowledge in a contextual manner that can be easily accessed and absorbed needs to be addressed*. By doing so, we shy away from the pieces of evidence that clearly show how tribal communities in India have been systematically oppressed, especially starting from the British colonial time.

Breaking free from 'othering'

Othering is a phenomenon in which some individuals or groups are defined and labelled as not fitting in within the norms of a social group. It is an effect that influences how people perceive and treat those who are viewed as being part of the in-group versus those who are seen as being part of the out-group. Othering also involves attributing negative characteristics to people or groups that differentiate them from the perceived normative social group. It is an 'us vs. them' way of thinking about human connections and relationships. This process essentially involves looking at others and saying, 'they are not like me' or 'they are not one of us'.[40] Othering is often heavily informed by in-group and out-group biases. These biases normalise and rationalise our desire to be respectful to people who we consider to be like us while discriminating against people we consider as 'other'. Othering explains how peoples from tea tribes (tribal members from the central Indian belt who were forcefully moved to the North-Eastern states of India as labourers in tea gardens) are often more marginalised than tribal communities who form a majority in North-Eastern states. Othering can be addressed mostly by investing in interventions that help members from different communities engage with each other, exchange knowledge and experiences and connect over commonalities and understanding that diverse cultures can co-exist in harmony when we intend to and put our efforts towards a collaborative living.

Transforming healthcare service delivery in tribal areas

The expert committee on tribal health[2] recommended the creation of a functional, universal and sustainable system of healthcare for tribal people by 2022. The committee also recommends changes in the population norms for tribal areas with tribal health and wellness centre being at the centre of health service delivery. This has obviously not happened for various reasons. However, it is never too late to start, and a beginning can be made by paying extra attention to those areas where a large proportion of people belong to tribal communities, such as the 177 'tribal' districts identified by MoTA (where at least 25 per cent of the total population are tribal people) and focus on creating a functional, universal and sustainable system of healthcare keeping in mind the needs of the tribal people.

This can only be achieved by building a robust primary healthcare system keeping in mind the principles, such as dignity, sensitivity, equity, participatory approach, positive discourse, and avoiding 'othering'. Investing in and developing a sensitive health human workforce to deliver healthcare services will go a long way in delivering high-quality service.

It is also important to ensure that in the medium to long term, a larger proportion of tribal people themselves are involved in the delivery of healthcare services in proportion to the population of that area. For example, if the proportion of the tribal population in the Bastar district of Chhattisgarh is 65.93 per cent, then a high proportion of the health human workforce across all levels in Bastar must belong to tribal communities. But this cannot happen overnight. And hence, we must start investing in people and processes in tribal districts like Bastar right now, to achieve this, over time.

This system should be complemented by a strong data management system that can help the health human workforce, administrators and bureaucrats take evidence-based decisions in real time. To ensure that data are of high quality, there is a need to invest in technology at all levels. Technology has the power to help tribal peoples leapfrog the challenges and transform their lives. And hence the use of technology cannot be limited to data but must extend to all aspects of healthcare delivery, including preventive care, point-of-care services, diagnostics, tele-consultations, referral and follow-up, procurement, supply chain and so on. The volume of data coming in from these digital devices and processes coupled with advancements in artificial intelligence and machine learning, if leveraged appropriately, can open an entirely new chapter in positively transforming the health and nutrition status of tribal peoples of India.

Investment in research to better understand the 'tribal' way of life can generate insights that can be leveraged not only to provide a more customised package of services to tribal peoples but also to the non-tribal people. The National Institute of Research in Tribal Health (NIRTH), Jabalpur, under the Indian Council of Medical Research (ICMR), Department of Health Research, Ministry of Health and Family Welfare, Government of India, is the only publicly funded organisation dedicated to research on the health of tribal peoples of the country. The Tribal Research Institute (TRI) at the state level is the research body of the MoTA. The core responsibility of TRI is to act as a body of knowledge and research as a think-tank for tribal development and preservation of tribal cultural heritage, providing inputs to states for evidence-based planning and appropriate legislations, capacity building of tribal people and persons and institutions associated with tribal affairs and dissemination of information and creation of awareness. There are 26 TRIs supported by MoTA. There is a need to strengthen these institutes. Firstly, research from these institutes must inform policy and practice across the tribal regions. Secondly, there is a need to create a common forum for better coordination and convergence. It is also important to partner with local tribal organisations not only to enhance the value and quality of research but also to build better rapport with the tribal communities, making the research outputs and outcomes more authentic.

For the systems to work effectively and efficiently, it is imperative that there is '*communitisation*' of healthcare services. The National Rural Health Mission defines 'communitisation' as a process of institutionalising and scaling up of community-led action for health. It is important to engage with tribal community members through various existing or new formal or informal networks and co-opt them in the process of healthcare service delivery as well as governance. These networks could be those of tribal youth, tribal women's self-help groups, tribal healers, local tribal leaders and any other local groups that may be influential. These tribal community members can then be involved in governing the system and services as well, thereby building a strong connect between the community and the health system. The destination for *communitisation* would be complete ownership of the health system and health services by the community.

Neither the government nor the community can, by themselves, solve the problems of tribal health in India. There is a need for convergence and collaborative action. There is a need to bring local tribal communities, government, implementers, researchers, funders, technologists and the private sector together at multiple levels, to bring about systemic and scaled health impact.

Transformative improvements in tribal health outcomes will be complex and extremely challenging to achieve. But India no longer has the luxury of continuing to wait and watch as hundreds of thousands of its tribal people suffer and die from preventable causes.

Conclusion

Tribal peoples form a large and significant part of India's population. They face numerous challenges, and their health and nutrition indicators are poor. It is the responsibility of the state as well as the communities themselves to improve the health and nutrition status. There is a need to focus on strengthening the delivery of primary care services to tribal peoples while keeping in mind a host of principles, including dignity, sensitivity and community participation.

Notes

1 Census of India 2011. *Delhi: Office of the Registrar General and Census Commissioner*. Ministry of Home Affairs, Government of India; 2011. Available from: https://censusindia.gov.in/census.website/data/census-tables

2 Expert Committee on Tribal Health. *Tribal Health in India: Bridging Gaps and a Roadmap for Future. Ministry of Health and Family Welfare.* Government

of India; Ministry of Tribal Affairs, Government of India. New Delhi (India), Ministry of Health and Family Welfare, India; 2018. Available from: http://www.tribalhealthreport.in/full-report/

3 United Nations Development Program. *Enhancing Effectiveness of Tribal Development Programs: Results*. UNDP India; 2024. Available from: https://www.undp.org/india/publications/enhancing-effectiveness-tribal-development-programmes-results-2024#:~:text=India%20is%20home%20to%20around,the%20country's%20total%20population%20(approx.

4 Ministry of Tribal Affairs, Government of India. *State and Union Territory-wise list of Scheduled Tribes in India*. Available from: http://www.tribalhealthreport.in/full-report/

5 Bodhi SR, Jojo B. *The Problematics of Tribal Integration: Voices from India's Alternative Centers*. Hyderabad: The Shared Mirror Publishing House; 2019. Available from: http://www.ticijournals.org/wp-content/uploads/2019/07/The-Problematics-of-Tribal-IntegrationVoices-from-Indias-Alternative-Centers.pdf

6 Das AK. Documenting the tribal and indigenous languages of India, *Journal of Scientometric Research* 2024;13(3):935–6. Available from: http://dx.doi.org/10.5530/jscires.20040868

7 Tripathi B, Mohanta BK. *Tribes of Central India: An Overview in Recent Research on the Tribes of Central India*. New Delhi: Aayu Publications; 2016. Available from: https://www.academia.edu/27637249/Tribes_of_Central_India_An_Overview

8 Chaudhuri S. Landscaping tribal culture: Towards A cultural landscape approach in North-East India. *International Journal of Research and Scientific Innovation*. 2022;9(3):59–63. Available from: https://www.rsisinternational.org/journals/ijrsi/digital-library/volume-9-issue-3/59-63.pdf

9 Saranya S, Jisha NS. *Sociocultural and Linguistic Divergence, and Uniqueness among Irula and Muduga Communities in Attapadi: A Comparative Study*. School of Indian Languages, University of Kerala. International Seminar; 2021. Available from: https://www.academia.edu/49093863/Irula_and_Muduga_Tribes_in_Attappady_Sociocultural_and_Linguistic_study

10 General introduction. In Carrin MM et al., eds, *Brill's Encyclopaedia of the Religions of the Indigenous People of South Asia*. Handbook of Oriental Studies series. Section 2: South Asia, Vol. 36. Leiden, Netherlands: Brill Academic Publishers, 2021.

11 Bird-David N. 'Animism' revisited: Personhood, environment, and relational epistemology. *Current Anthropology* 1999;40s:S67–91. Available from: https://www.academia.edu/19548365/Bird_David_N_1999_Animism_revisited_Personhood_environment_and_relational_epistemology_Current_Anthropology_40s_S67_S91

12 Fortier J. The ethnography of South Asian foragers. *Annual Review of Anthropology* 2009;38:99–114. Available from: https://anthro.du.ac.in/e-resources2020/rpm/The%20Ethnography%20of%20South%20Asian%20Foragers.pdf

13 Choudhury IR. Sohrai – A festival of harvest and art, November 2015. Available from: https://indroyc.com/2015/11/11/sohrai-unique-festival-of-jharkhand/#:~:text=Sohrai%20is%20a%20winter%20harvest%20festival%20and%20one,or%20Kali%20puja%2C%20in%20the%20month%20of%20October-November.

14 Introduction – Tribes and Culture: Karbi Anglong District. Government of Assam, India. Available from: https://karbianglong.gov.in/information-services/tirbes-and-culture

15 Wancho History. *Central Institute of Indian Languages*, Mysuru: Department of Higher Education Ministry of Education Government of India. Available from: http://lisindia.ciil.org/Wancho/Wancho_Hist.html

16 International Institute for Population Sciences (IIPS) and Piramal Swasthya Management and Research Institute (PSMRI) 2020. District Factsheets: Health

and Nutrition Indicators for the Tribal and Non-Tribal Population, 2015–16: Compendium Hyderabad: PSMRI.
17 Lambert H. Medical pluralism and medical marginality: Bone doctors and the selective legitimation of therapeutic expertise in India. *Social Science and Medicine* 2012;74:1029–36. https://doi.org/10.1016/j.socscimed.2011.12.024
18 Singh A, Madhavan H. Determinants of use of traditional healing in India: Evidence from a nationally representative survey. Indian Institute of Technology, Mumbai, India. Azim Premji University, Bangalore, India. Presented at the Association of America Annual Conference, 2016. Available from: https://www.researchgate.net/publication/301363174_Determinants_of_use_of_traditional_healing_for_minor_and_major_morbidities_in_India_evidence_from_a_nationally_representative_survey#fullTextFileContent
19 Singh A, Madhavan H. Traditional vs. non-traditional healing for minor and major morbidities in India: Uses, cost and quality comparisons. *Tropical Medicine and International Health* 2015;20(9):1223–38. Available from: https://doi.org/10.1111/tmi.12540
20 Rai R, Nath V. Use of medicinal plants by traditional herbal healers in central India. Division of Biodiversity and Sustainable Management Tropical Forest Research Institute, Jabalpur. *Indian Forester*, March 2005, pp. 463–8. (Accessed on 3 April 2025). Available from: https://www.indianforester.co.in/index.php/indianforester/article/viewFile/1721/1609
21 Ao M. Health outcome measures and determinants of using indigenous medicine in a pluralistic healthcare in Nagaland, Northeast India. *Clinical Epidemiology and Global Health* 2020;8(1):205–10. DOI: 10.1016/j.cegh.2019.07.002
22 Venkatramana P, Latheef SAA. Health seeking behavior among tribes of India. *Studies of Tribes and Tribals* 2019;17(1–2):1–7. DOI: 10.31901/24566799.2019/17.1-2.413
23 Bhat S, Naik AC, Kholkute SD. Attitudes and beliefs of patients of non-codified traditional medicine in Belagavi region. *International Journal of Research – Granthaalayah* 2018;6(1). DOI: 10.29121/granthaalayah.v6.i1.2018.1629
24 Shankar R, Deb S, Sharma B. Historical note: Traditional healing practices in North East India. *Indian Journal of History of Science* 2015;50(2). DOI:10.16943/ijhs/2015/v50i2/48242
25 Sonowal CJ, Purujit P. Tradition vs transition: Acceptance of health care systems among the Santhals of Orissa. *Studies on Ethno-Medicine* 2007;1(2):135–46. DOI: 10.1080/09735070.2007.11886306
26 Subin AJ. Use, prevalence and people's attitude towards traditional medicine in outpatient department setting of a tertiary care hospital in Northeast India. *Indian Journal of Pharmacy Practice* 2021;14(2):135–9. DOI: 10.5530/ijopp.14.2.25
27 Shankar R, Lavekar GS, Deb S, Sharma BK. Traditional healing practice and folk medicines used by Mishing community of North East India. *Journal of Ayurveda and Integrated Medicine* 2012;3(3):124–9. DOI: 10.4103/0975-9476.100171. https://www.researchgate.net/publication/232814049_Traditional_healing_practice_and_folk_medicines_used_by_Mishing_community_of_North_East_India
28 Bora D, Mehmud S, Das KK, Medhi H. Report on folklore medicinal plants used for female health care in Assam (India). *International Journal of Herbal Medicine* 2016;4(6):4–13. Available from: https://www.florajournal.com/archives/?year=2016&vol=4&issue=6&part=A&ArticleId=322
29 Sahoo G, Wani AM, Satpathy B, Sandeep R. Traditional medicinal plants of Odisha. *Research and Reviews: A Journal of Pharmacognosy* 2020;7(3):7–10. Available from: https://pharmajournals.stmjournals.in/index.php/RRJoPC/article/view/905

30 Sahu CR, Nayak RK, Dhal NK. Traditional herbal remedies for various diseases used by tribals of Boudh district, Odisha, India for sustainable development. *International Journal of Herbal Medicine* 2013;1(1): 12–20. Available from: https://www.florajournal.com/archives/?year=2013&vol=1&issue=1&part=A&ArticleId=4
31 Pattanaik C, Reddy SC, Das R, Reddy MP. Traditional medicinal practices among the tribal people of Malkangiri district, Orissa, India. *Natural Product Radiance* 2007;6(5):430–5. Available from: https://www.researchgate.net/publication/258911781_Traditional_Medicinal_Practices_among_the_tribal_people_of_Malkangiri_district_Orissa_India
32 Telles S, Pathak S, Singh N, Balkrishna A. Research on traditional medicine: What has been done, the difficulties, and possible solutions. *Evidence Based Complementary and Alternate Medicine* 2014;495635. Available from: https://www.hindawi.com/journals/ecam/2014/495635/
33 WHO establishes the Global Centre for Traditional Medicine in India. Geneva. March 2022. Available from: https://www.who.int/news/item/25-03-2022-who-establishes-the-global-centre-for-traditional-medicine-in-india
34 Hegde SKB, Venkatachalam P. Are India's healthcare goals inclusive of tribal peoples? *India Development Review*, February 2020. Available from: https://idronline.org/are-indias-healthcare-goals-inclusive-of-tribal-peoples/
35 Blackwell AG. The curb-cut effect. *Stanford Social Innovation Review* 2016;15(1):28–33. DOI: 10.48558/YVMS-CC96
36 Fuchs S. *The Aboriginal Tribes of India*. New Delhi: Macmillan India; 1974, p. 24.
37 Heredia RC, Srivastava R. *Tribal Identity and Minority Status: Tha Kathkari Nomads in Transition*. New Delhi: Concept Publishing; 1994, ch. 1, p. 12.
38 MacCormack CP. Community participation in primary health care. *Tropical Doctor* 1983;13(2):51–4. DOI: 10.1177/004947558301300202
39 Fogarty W, Bulloch H, McDonnell S, Davis M. Deficit discourse and indigenous health: How narrative framings of Aboriginal and Torres Strait Islander people are reproduced in policy. The Lowitja Institute and National Centre for Indigenous Studies. The Australian National University. 2018. Available from: https://www.lowitja.org.au/wp-content/uploads/2023/05/deficit-discourse.pdf
40 Cherry K. How othering contributes to discrimination and prejudice: The psychology behind us vs. them. Podcast. Available from: https://www.verywellmind.com/what-is-othering-5084425

4 Non-profit hospitals

A challenging future

Tilak Shankar

Introduction

Philanthropy aimed at social or community welfare is integral to all cultures. In India, philanthropy manifests in many ways. Several philanthropic institutions have been functioning for decades, engaged in the cause of education and healthcare and other forms of social assistance, such as Alcoholics Anonymous, shelters for abandoned babies, legal help for women in distress and providing assistance of all kinds during times of natural calamities and wars. Alcoholism is a major social problem affecting millions of families, particularly women. So, organisations treating such patients serve an important cause. Cutting across faiths, munificent individuals or community organisations have set up hospitals for the benefit of not only their own communities but also for the general population that needs access to healthcare. Some have also established laboratories and pharmacies. These institutions can be seen in almost all parts of India. There are several examples of faith-based hospitals providing succour to all other faiths as well. Christian, Jain and Hindu hospitals and missionaries provide treatment to all faiths. Much before corporate social responsibility became mandated by law, many industrial groups had created foundations to set up and manage hospitals around their key facilities or in towns that had poor healthcare facilities. Individuals who have excelled in the medical profession, either after retirement from government service or after a busy professional practice in India or abroad, have set up hospitals in their field of expertise. In later years, the hospitals have grown, expanded to related fields of medical and nursing education, translational research and community work.

Private healthcare in India

There are an estimated 43,000 private healthcare institutions in India with 1.18 million beds (2024 data).[1] Private institutions can be broadly classified based on the number of beds – small nursing homes, medium-sized and large hospitals, as well as based on specialisation, that is, primary, secondary and tertiary care hospitals. In addition to medical care, they provide education in related fields and translational research.[2]

DOI: 10.4324/9781003684947-5

Charitable and non-profit hospitals come under the private hospitals category along with for-profit nursing homes and hospitals. A separate estimate of the number of charitable and non-profit healthcare institutions is not readily available. Nursing homes (20–50 beds) predominate in the for-profit category, making up about two-thirds of the number of private healthcare facilities. The remaining one-third comprises medium and large private hospitals, specialising in secondary and tertiary care.

A charitable and non-profit hospital typically has about 250 beds, but a bigger hospital may have up to 3,000 beds in a single location. Many of these institutions also offer graduate and post-graduate medical degrees, nursing and allied medical sciences education, diploma courses and continuing education programmes.

For-profit nursing homes usually have multiple ownership forms. They may be proprietor-run, formed by a partnership between individuals or registered as private limited companies. Medium and large non-profit hospitals are run by trusts or societies, foundations or as Section 8 companies. Section 8 of the Companies Act, 2013, relates to the incorporation of companies with charitable or non-profit objectives (discussed in detail later).

Nursing homes or small hospitals have a bed strength of about 20–50 beds, providing both primary and secondary care. According to Dr Nikhil Datar, a well-known gynaecologist from Mumbai, 'nursing homes are miniature hospitals with the advantages of access, personalised service and cost, and they are a vital part in a vast country such as ours'. The demand for such medical facilities supports this view.[3] It can be assumed that they will continue to survive, perhaps in a different avatar.

The non-profit or charitable hospitals could be run by faith-based groups, managed by philanthropists or run by medical doctors. The larger institutions run medical, nursing and allied health sciences and hospital administration programmes. Some of them have been functioning for over a century in rural and urban areas (see Figure 4.1) for various forms of non-profit hospitals.

India is home to a rich practice of traditional medicine, and there are several well-known traditional medical centres, some even in the form of large hospitals, in existence for many years. But this book focuses only on allopathic institutions as they are most visible and readily sought after by the general population.

Motives for setting up hospitals

Charitable or non-profit institutions operate in diverse fields – ophthalmology, obstetrics and gynaecology, paediatrics, oncology and general medicine. They can be found in a major city, a town or a tribal district. Founders might have multiple reasons for setting up a hospital. Anecdotally, it is learnt that a philanthropist or a doctor might have been moved by the suffering of an expectant mother, or a person going blind due to cataract or a young person dying due to a heart attack.

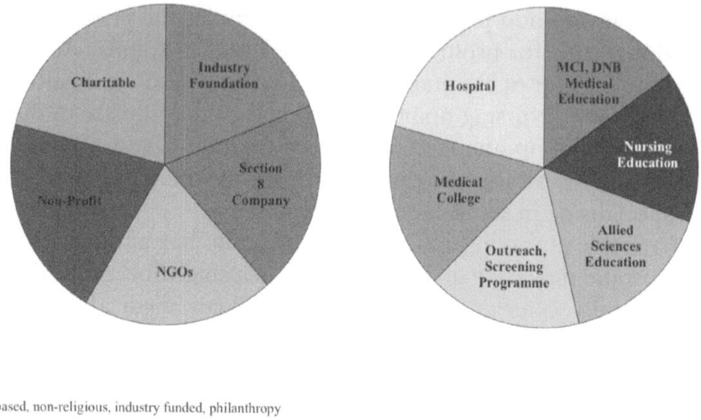

Figure 4.1 Non-profit institutions in India.

Dr Ida Scudder[4] set up CMC Vellore in the year 1900. Dr Scudder, a missionary, was moved by the plight of expectant women in rural Tamil Nadu. It is now a hospital with more than 3,000 beds, running a large number of teaching courses in medicine, nursing and all other allied sciences. Dr Gullapalli Rao witnessed a number of Indians with preventable blindness and set up an eye hospital to help them overcome blindness.[5] The L.V. Prasad Eye Institute, established in Hyderabad, has now spread to Telangana and Andhra Pradesh. Dr Pratap Reddy saw a young industrialist dying of a heart attack and started Apollo Hospitals to cater to the tertiary care needs of people.[6] These are a few examples of an adverse and impactful event prompting a medical professional to start hospitals.

Mother and child healthcare appears to be the most powerful reason. Non-government organisations (NGOs) perform various supporting services to help patients and hospitals. There are thousands of such NGOs doing yeomen services in rural areas and cities. Collectively, hospitals and NGOs are a critical link in our healthcare system. The common thread is compassion for the suffering of a fellow human being.

Common attributes

Charitable institutions share many common attributes:

- Providing affordable care and free medical care to the underprivileged sections of society, middle-income groups, the scheduled castes and tribal populations.
- Offering medical, nursing and allied sciences education at affordable costs (Figure 4.1); these institutions inculcate a sense of free service to

all the students, compassion for poor patients, treating common illnesses and inculcating ethical values.

- Providing good medical care in rural and remote areas, which minimises the need for these people to travel to large cities. Hence, many hospitals are established in small towns, tribal areas and places where many underprivileged people live.

Importance of non-profit healthcare institutions

Charitable and non-profit institutions fulfil a crucial healthcare need by offering quality secondary and tertiary medical care at affordable costs to underprivileged and middle-class patients. In terms of cost, facilities and level of care, they lie between government hospitals and private hospitals. They also contribute to human resource development through their various education services, organising screening camps, following up patients requiring further treatment, offering continuing medical education (CME) and carrying out translational research on many ailments. The author has been impressed by the multiplier effect of such CME programmes on fellow professionals. Their importance should be measured both quantitatively (number of patients) as well as qualitatively (level of care and illness that can be treated in these facilities).

Management structure of non-profit hospitals

Non-profit institutions – both single-speciality and multi-speciality hospitals – function in rural as well as in urban areas. The management structures vary depending on their size, number of locations from where they function and leadership styles. If it's a faith-based institution, members of the community will be represented on the Board. If it is part of an industrial group, Board members will be from the companies along with other members. If it's a stand-alone institution, then the founder along with select members of the public will be on the Board of Trustees.

Difference between charitable and non-profit institutions

A charitable institution would provide free inpatient/outpatient treatment based on socio-economic considerations. The percentage of free care would vary depending on the institution. A non-profit or not-for-profit may not provide free care or only a small proportion of free patients. Both are service-oriented without profit motives, do not have shareholders (except Section 8 companies) and surplus from operations, if any, is retained in the institution itself. These institutions may be registered as a society, a trust, a foundation or a non-profit organisation under Section 8 of the Indian Companies Act, 2013 (also known as Section 8 companies). By normal definition and understanding, any institution which keeps all its surplus within the organisation without distributing any surplus to its owners/shareholders is a non-profit institution.

Section 8 company

A Section 8 company can be formed for promoting commerce, art, science, sports, education, research, social welfare, religion, charity, protection of the environment or any such other purpose. Such a company must apply its profits, if any, or other income to the promotion of its goals and not pay any dividend to its members. The company may be incorporated with or without a share capital. In terms of its benefits, Section 8 companies are also eligible to be registered as charitable institutions for the purpose of getting exemption under the Income Tax Act, like a trust or a society.

Charitable purposes include relief for the poor, education, yoga, medical relief, the advancement of any other object of public utility, preservation of the environment (including watersheds, forests and wildlife) and preservation of monuments or places or objects of artistic or historic interest. Public charitable trusts, by definition, must be created for the benefit of the public.

Societies may be registered for charitable purposes. If the institution is a trust or a society, then it is bound by its Trust Deed, and if it is a company, by its Memorandum of Association (MOA) and Articles of Association (AOA). We will use the term non-profit institutions for both non-profit and charitable institutions henceforth in this chapter.

Categories of non-profit hospitals

Numerous hospitals are run by faith-based institutions, where patients are treated without discrimination. Christian faith-based organisations run more than 1,000 hospitals in India with 60,000 beds, offering medical care, medical and non-medical teaching programmes, outreach programmes and rural hospitals.[7] Some of them have a global reputation for their medical and research work. Ramakrishna Mission runs 14 hospitals, 131 dispensaries and 87 mobile units in various parts of the country, including many backward regions of the country.[8]

Many communities run regional institutions. Religious institutions like the Tirumala Tirupati Devasthanam and Sathya Sai institutes and Hindu Mission and communities like the Jain community and Islamic organisations run hospitals, dispensaries and laboratories offering services at highly subsidised rates. There are several independent non-profit institutions that run hospitals, both multi-specialty and single specialty, in various parts of the country for several decades. Large industry foundations set up by industrial conglomerates like the Tata group, Birla group, Reliance group, Infosys, TVS, Murugappa group and Vedanta have been operating hospitals for several decades as non-profit institutions. Rotary International, Lions Club and Freemasons also provide assistance in healthcare projects. These organisations raise funds for a wide range of charitable work including healthcare. Funds could be donated to non-profit hospitals, for free surgeries, organising blood donation camps, free spectacles, low-vision aids and, in addition, for buildings, beds and wheelchairs. The Rotary International also operates hospitals, for example, Rotary hospitals in Chennai.[9]

Bhagwan Mahavir Jain Hospital,[10] Amar Jain Hospital[11] and BP Jain Hospital[12] provide outstanding service. Gurudwara Bangla Sahib Hospitals and Al Ameen Charitable Hospitals also operate in the non-profit mode for the benefit of the general population.

In the field of ophthalmology, there are many outstanding examples – Sankara Nethralaya, Aravind Eye Hospital, L.V. Prasad Institute, Sankara Hospitals, Dr Shroff Eye Hospital (New Delhi), Eye Q Eye Hospitals and Indira Gandhi Eye Hospitals – that are run as non-profit organisations. These hospitals have been doing outstanding work in the eradication of 'preventable blindness' in the country, along with the national institutes of ophthalmology. All of them provide free cataract surgery and have been treating various other eye ailments for several decades. The services include bringing poor patients from their villages for treatment and dropping them back after treatment. In fact, the model followed by these institutions has been commended by authors in various books and articles. Dr Vijay Govindarajan and Dr Ravi Ramamurti, in their book titled *Reverse Innovation in Healthcare,*[13] have commended the examples of Indian ophthalmic hospitals doing innovative work in the management of their hospitals. They have recommended that US hospitals should learn from these experiences, hence the title of their book *Reverse Innovation*. Dr C.K. Prahalad, in his path-breaking book *The Fortune at the Bottom of the Pyramid*,[14] has brilliantly explained as to why poor people are also a key market for all goods and services, including healthcare. Both authors have highlighted key management aspects of Indian hospitals – such as high productivity of staff, use of appropriate technology, cost control, patient-friendly features in their hospitals, and combining entrepreneurial features with bold innovation as features as key success factors for their organisations. It is essential that more such institutions are formed in all parts of India.

The non-profit ophthalmic organisations receive donations and provide tax benefits to the donors. Some are also registered to receive foreign donations under the Foreign Contribution Regulation Act (FCRA). In many cases, the state government provides these organisations land free of cost or at a concessional rate, requiring them to provide free or subsidised care in return.

A distinctive feature of non-profit hospitals lies in their medical and nursing education protocols, which are designed to treat the most common ailments. Private hospitals, on the other hand, train their medical post-graduate students largely in secondary and tertiary care. Many non-profit institutions also provide tertiary care.

Another distinctive characteristic of non-profit institutions is that they do not focus on revenue. Dr V. Shanta, the former chairperson of the Cancer

Institute in Chennai, with whom this author has had several interactions, exemplified this ethos by saying, 'No patient is denied treatment because they cannot afford it'. This institution, which is over 60 years old, works actively by partnering with the Tamil Nadu government. This institution exemplifies compassion, provides high-quality tertiary care, offers the highest medical degrees in oncology without a capitation fee, treats paediatric cases with innovative strategies, undertakes high-quality research and offers extensive screening programmes.

Despite their significant contributions, a key challenge for all these institutions is financial survival. The operating deficits pose a serious managerial challenge.

Board of Trustees

Non-profit institutions are registered as a society or a public trust. They are required to have a Board of Trustees/Governors – ranging from 10 to 15 trustees. The Boards are accountable to all the stakeholders, including governments, patients, employees and society. Some members of the operating management team could also serve on the Board of Trustees. The roles of the independent or non-executive members of the Board and full-time management members are distinct. Ultimately, the Board is responsible for ensuring compliance with various regulations. The trustees of non-profit or directors of a company have legal liabilities.[15,16]

In the experience of the author, corporate hospitals have a strong management team, which ensures effective control of operations. Therefore, the Board can focus on long-term planning, expansion, succession planning, future funding and formulating major policy changes. However, in non-profit hospitals, the management systems may not be strong, and the entire organisation would be preoccupied with day-to-day pressures (with exceptions).

Composition of the Board of Trustees

The Board may include representatives from the medical fraternity, management experts, industrialists, philanthropists, social workers, lawyers, bankers, and in some cases, ex-officio nominees from the state government or the Government of India.

The Board can play a proactive role in financial management, fundraising and succession planning. In actual practice, many non-profits find it difficult to attract suitable members to join as trustees and actively contribute to the management of the organisation. The composition of the Board is important because the donors, government, and other stakeholders depend on a strong Board to run the organisation effectively.

Important roles of Board members and trustees

It is essential that various members perform specific roles in governance. The roles of each member may be divided into two broad verticals: Medical and managerial. Quality accreditations recommend specific role for each Board member. It may be desirable to have a well-balanced Board of Trustees.

- A senior medical professional from outside the hospital can bring an external perspective of medical developments.
- Finance, legal, banking, IT, marketing and HR functions in a hospital can significantly benefit from outside expertise.
- The efficient management practices, including financial prudence, strategic management, modern internal audit and entrepreneurship, can be provided by experts on the Board.
- Fund-raising is a key function of the trustees and suitable personnel can be included on the Board.

In the experience of the author, Board members require two key qualities: Ability to spend adequate time and a desire to learn about the functioning of a hospital. An industrialist, a banker or a lawyer should appreciate the nuances of a hospital. For example, a decision on major equipment replacement, determining the retirement age for doctors or discontinuing some activities should not be taken only based on financial considerations. There should be no corporatisation of non-profits.

Challenges facing non-profit organisations

Attracting the right individuals to serve on the Board of Trustees of such institutions has been a challenging task for most institutions. A trustee needs to develop a deep understanding of the ethos, the value systems and nuances of a medical institution. The composition of the Board plays a key role in deciding the quality of governance and management of the overall organisation. Members should spend quality time guiding the institution on all overall good management practices, particularly financial self-sufficiency, and not merely attending board meetings. There should be a mix of young and experienced professionals to serve on the Board.

The Chairperson of the Board of Trustees is also the head of the organisation, playing a critical role. Very often, the founder would play this role. Sometimes, a senior member who is acceptable to most Board members could be elected as the Chairperson. The main requirement for this role is leadership and guiding the organisation through good and bad times. Identifying the right Chairperson becomes crucial in the absence of the founder.

Many hospitals are run by entrepreneurial-minded doctors who do not realise that good management is essential to run a modern healthcare institution. A modern non-profit hospital needs to provide free and affordable care, modernise medical and other equipment and pay competitive salaries to staff. These objectives are possible only if noble intentions are matched by the effective use of resources and the availability of adequate finances. Most charitable hospitals have about 300-plus beds in secondary and tertiary care. If they are faith-based, some donations from that community can be expected. If they are stand-alone institutions, then they have to manage their own finances.

Sustaining non-profit hospitals

Three major steps are required to strengthen non-profits:

- Non-profits themselves have to strengthen their internal management processes to meet the external challenges.
- Governments should take steps to strengthen non-profit healthcare sector.
- Greater involvement of society.

Besides the bigger picture efforts, the sustenance of the non-profit healthcare institutions can be discussed in two parts:

- Ways in which governments can help such institutions
- Ways in which the institutions can help themselves

Our healthcare system will be significantly poorer without a robust non-profit healthcare sector. The contribution of single-specialty and multi-specialty hospitals in rural and urban areas over many decades requires strengthening both financially and managerially. The quantum of aid would vary depending on the nature of the institution.

Strengthening internal organisation

Three areas are chosen in this chapter to discuss specific management challenges – finance, marketing HR and IT. In addition, Board members should contribute their perspectives on relevant external developments – technological, patient profile, and competition.

Financial management

Non-profit hospitals are funded in a variety of ways – by faith-based institutions, industrial foundations, philanthropists, bank finance and others. Once the hospital comes into existence, funds are required to meet the operational expenses as well as to meet capital expenditure. If there is an adequate quantum of income to meet all the expenses – from patients and other sources, for example, government grants and donations – then the financial position of that organisation is said to be comfortable. Capital expenditure forms the single largest item and can be incurred only when adequate funds are available. However, in reality, most hospitals experience operational deficits for two reasons: The cost of treating free patients and subsiding a significant portion of the paying patients. Normally, even the paying patients would be charged much less than other private hospitals. Hence there are operational deficits. Different managements – faith-based, industry-funded or stand-alone institutions – are equally impacted by this deficit. When there are persistent annual operational deficits, the main funders would critically examine the extent of financial support that they can provide. They would expect the Board and the management to implement necessary operational improvements on the path to financial self-sufficiency. In other words, managements cannot depend only on donations for meeting operational deficits.

Non-profit hospitals, as a matter of policy, fix their patient charges lower than other private hospitals, since profit-making is not their objective. There are no owners who expect returns on investment or resort to borrowings. The cost of treatment is a crucial deciding factor for middle-income groups and non-profit hospitals, with their affordable cost and quality care, would be ideally suited for such groups of patients. This is a large group. Even otherwise, some of the well-known hospitals are sought after by all sections of the population because of their popularity in their specialty or because of the quality of care.

Sustainable financial model

A central concern for all non-profit institutions revolves around establishing a sustainable financial model. The major sources of revenue are as follows:

- Paying patients
- Interest income from corpus funds
- Government grants
- Donations – foreign donations, corporate social responsibility (CSR) funds, individual donations
- Other miscellaneous funds

Income from inpatients comes from their hospitalisation charges, laboratory tests, investigation charges and medicines. Tariff determination is a dynamic process – in some departments, it could be once a year, and in some others, once in six months. Departments such as laboratories have high variable costs, relatively low investment and provide high profit margins. Pharmacy also generates high margins. Most private hospitals focus on several metrics such as case mix, average length of stay, average revenue per occupied room and margins from different categories of rooms. However, non-profits measure performance by traditional metrics such as number of free care and patient-oriented parameters rather than by financial metrics. The management should examine every one of these variables and how to increase revenues. This process should not result in fixing targets for doctors and departments and pressuring them to meet revenue goals. Doctors should focus on the medical needs of each patient and not on commercial aspects. It can be argued that the objectives of the management percolate to the staff. When one of the main objectives of a hospital is profit-making, then there would be pressures on the doctors to generate revenue and technology could be employed to attract and retain paying patients, while providing high-quality patient care. In the case of non-profits, the focus would be on providing 'no-frills' patient care, frugality in operations and maintaining free patient and paying patient mix.

Secondary and tertiary care

The crucial variable is whether the hospital is a secondary care or a tertiary care hospital, each characterised by entirely different cost structures. The proportion of free care/subsidised care is dependent on this variable. In the case of tertiary care, the proportion of free-cum-subsidised patients would be significantly lower compared to primary or secondary treatment.

The extent of free-cum-subsidised care for outpatients and inpatients could vary depending on the specialty of the hospital, the extent of cross-subsidy by paying patients, government aid and donations. In the case of an ophthalmic hospital, the cost of a cataract surgery or a paediatric hospital treating an appendectomy are both much lower than a cancer hospital treating blood cancer or providing an expensive bone marrow transplant. Therefore, both the proportion of free cases and the number of patients would vastly vary between hospitals. Many ophthalmic hospitals provide free cataract surgeries up to 40–50 per cent of their total inpatients, while a tertiary care facility would have a maximum of 20–25 per cent of inpatients.

In some cases, charitable work is measured not merely by the number of patients but by the financial costs involved in such work. Many non-profit institutions also provide undergraduate and post-graduate medical education without any capitation fees. They would incur costs for such subsidies. Additionally, these institutions organise screening camps, run mobile vans and conduct patient education programmes in villages, which add up to their expenses. Normally, after screening, if the patient needs further treatment, they also provide free treatment.

Noble goals should be supported by strong management processes. A simple costing system is necessary to arrive at the cost of providing many services. Even when the hospital tariff is not linked to actual costs, it helps

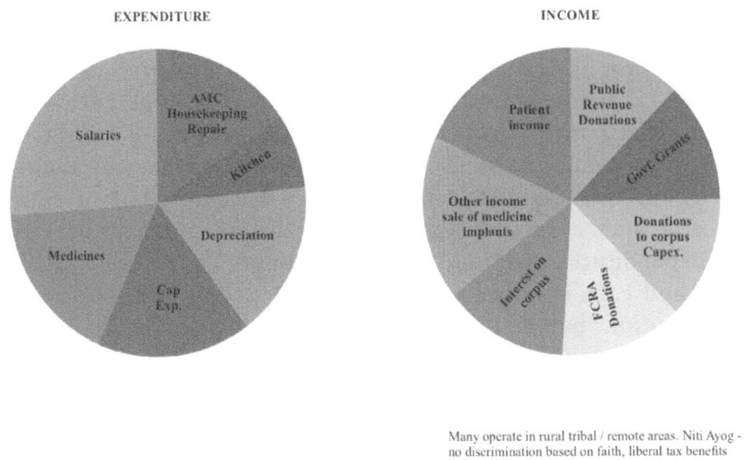

Figure 4.2 Non-profit hospital finances.

in assessing the profit margin of various services. A pie chart of income and expenditure in non-profit hospitals is shown in Figure 4.2.

Evaluation of capital expenditure

Cost data is required for determining viability of capital expenditure. Apart from cost data, capital expenditure should be evaluated based on projected utilisation of expensive medical equipment. Budgeting systems should be based on metrics available from quality systems, even if the hospital has no formal quality accreditation. The finances of every hospital are dependent on various activities carried out by different departments.

Patient charges

Patient charges should be constantly benchmarked against comparable non-profit and other private hospitals. Patient charges are normally categorised based on room category – dormitory, shared rooms, non-air-conditioned rooms and air-conditioned rooms. It is essential that non-profits fix lower charges to attract paying patients, for example, room rent, X-ray charges, CT scan charges and consultation fees. Paying patients would expect creature comforts such as air-conditioned rooms, food and low waiting times, and therefore they can be charged higher. A non-profit has to provide such differentiation.

All major items of revenue, including laboratory charges, imaging and total cost for major treatments, should be periodically compared and revisions effected. This exercise, unfortunately, is not given much importance.

Fund-raising

A key function in all charitable or non-profit institutions should be fund-raising. These organisations engage in different practices for raising funds. In a faith-based or industry-funded institution, the Board and Management would normally present their performance, their funding needs and intended use of funds. If they are a stand-alone entity, the Board of Trustees are responsible for fund-raising to meet the deficits, fund capital expenditures and build a corpus. Donors have different causes to support, and each institution should make a strong pitch to the donors. Some institutions handle this function internally, with the Board members playing a key role in approaching past and new donors. Some employ a professional agency who would have a database of donors and make presentations to them.

There are several causes that appeal to the donors – children, cataract, cancer, free food to patients and free medicines. In addition, donors contribute based on the work done by the hospital and reputation of the trustees. Most importantly, large donors who make contributions for a specific objective expect the hospital to utilise the fund *only* for that purpose. Some donors may expect regular reports on the use of funds. Government grants also require specific accountability. Some donors may donate for a new building, a ward or a single bed. Some of them aim for tax benefits, and small donors may not expect any tax benefit. Fund-raising organisations usually will have access to donor databases and recommend to each hospital strategies to present an appropriate appeal. It is essential that every non-profit institution supplements their efforts by engaging professional fund-raising organisations for soliciting funds annually.

Human resources management

The main strength of a non-profit hospital is its staff members – doctors, nurses and other allied department staff members. The take-home pay of doctors, whether they are paid salaries or offered 'fee-for-service' compensation, is normally much lower than their counterparts in a for-profit private hospital. Other staff members are also paid relatively low salaries. In such situations, management should find methods to motivate every staff member.

Doctors in non-profits are not allowed private practice outside the institution. Management believes that if the doctors are allowed to do so, their attention would be diverted from free-cum-subsidised hospital patients. Service is the motivation for staff members working in such institutions. It should be noted that staff salaries, even at low salary levels, are still the single most important cost in hospital operations – as much as 50 per cent of the total expenditure.

Staff motivation

It has been generally noted that monetary compensation is not the key motivating factor for employees to work in an organisation. There are others, such as job satisfaction, opportunities for research, and, importantly, no targets to generate revenue. Some of the senior doctors the author spoke to emphasised these aspects for choosing to work in a non-profit hospital rather than a corporate hospital.

Boards and managements should not be complacent about their staff members. Innovative HR methods should be employed to involve all senior staff in the management of the hospitals. Regular communication between the Board and the staff members is needed to determine future directions for the institution, challenges ahead and plans for growth. Participatory management is known to provide immense benefits. Unfortunately, such initiatives are rarely taken.

Social marketing

Large sections of India's population are ignorant about diseases, the importance of hygiene and the implications of not paying heed to warning signals. There is an urgent need to educate the public (in rural and urban areas) about diabetes, iron-deficiency anaemia, tuberculosis and adult and child vaccinations. Social marketing consists of two parts: Creating health awareness and sales efforts for improving patient flow. Marketing should be an important function in non-profit hospitals. It is necessary to attract paying patients to subsidise the other patients. There is a mistaken opinion that marketing is needed only for corporate and private hospitals.

Sales effort would include efforts to attract paying patients by meeting insurance companies, negotiating rates with them, meeting corporates, meeting large companies and factories for health check-ups for employees and families and visiting senior citizen homes. Very often, this function is not carried out effectively. Each hospital should focus on not only the current patients but also on new potential segments. Geriatric patients are emerging as one of the important segments in healthcare and are likely to grow to a very significant number in the future.

As regards marketing, non-profit hospitals need to develop effective websites. Attention needs to be paid to website design and ease of its navigation, as well as patient education, in addition to activities such as organising webinars in local languages, meeting corporates regularly, carrying out patient satisfaction studies and improving patient services undertaken like any other private hospital. Non-profit hospitals must compete with other non-profit and private hospitals to attract paying patients. Hence, marketing efforts are essential. Unfortunately, many non-profits are 'inward looking' and ignore external developments.

Paying patients are choosy

Non-profit hospitals cater to a mix of free-cum-subsidised patients and paying patients, including middle-income patients seeking affordable treatment. Attracting high-income patients to cross-subsidise free patients has always posed a challenge. Such patients do not like to mix with free patients, even as outpatients. Preferences for accommodation, food and nursing care also vary, requiring specific arrangements. Paying patients would be willing to pay for air-conditioned single rooms. Even in corporate hospitals, there is segregation among distinct categories of single rooms, and a differentiation between rich and super-rich or VIP patients is made. In every hospital, including corporate hospitals, room preference defines the class distinction. Non-profit hospitals need to pay attention to specific features to attract paying patients, aiming for operational surplus. They should be provided distinct categories of rooms, separate waiting areas and priority in many services, including nursing.

Hospital information technology (IT)

Information technology is no longer mere data processing to eliminate paperwork. Hospitals require online information about patient condition, lab reports and scan images while treating inpatients. Realising the significance of technological developments, the Government of India has launched an ambitious plan to digitise all health centres and hospitals in the country. Non-profits are beginning to realise the potential of an integrated computerised system, also known as enterprise resource planning (ERP). In fact, additional tools such as data analytics, use of mobile technology for delivering healthcare,[17] are transforming health delivery, streamlining processes and reducing operational costs. Hospitals are using WhatsApp groups to connect all departments with doctors, laboratories and imaging centres. This has revolutionised communication. No hospital can be left behind.

Patient information should be available on each desktop of the doctor and nurse and in the laboratory, or on tablets or mobile phones on a real-time basis. The entire medical team can take quick action as required. It improves efficiencies throughout the hospital. Other tools like data analysis and AI can help dig deep into vast databases. Patient communication is made simpler, thus improving patient satisfaction. Research and teaching have hugely benefited from IT tools.

IT is beginning to differentiate hospitals from each other. Non-profit hospitals hesitate to invest in IT because of the cost of software, human resource requirements and the necessity of revamping the entire management processes. IT is emerging as a key differentiator in hospitals. Investment in IT is no different from investment in medical equipment.

Government and society initiatives

The Government of India and all state governments have been helping non-profits and NGOs. In the context of healthcare moving towards a market-driven system, there is a need to provide greater assistance – direct and indirect. There is a compelling need for opinion leaders to strengthen non-profits in multiple ways.

NITI Aayog report on charitable hospitals

The NITI Aayog report of October 2021[18] emphasises the diversity of hospitals – faith-based, community-based, co-operative, trust hospitals and hospitals managed by foundations. Faith-based healthcare institutions affiliated to Hindu, Christian, Muslim or Sikh faiths have silently served the society in villages, tribal areas and cities for decades. While their work may not grab headlines or media attention, it is important to recognise and strengthen their contribution.

The NITI Aayog report is based on a sample survey of not-for-profit hospitals and recommends government support for such institutions. It has proposed several added benefits:

- 100 per cent tax exemption under Section 80G of the Income Tax Act to the donors.
- Provision of grant-in-aid like the Gujarat government system, wherein up to 75 per cent of the expenses are reimbursed to the hospital.
- Granting of unencumbered land to charitable hospitals.
- Provision of low-cost working capital to non-profit hospitals, since there are delays in the settlement of bills by the government. (The author would instead suggest a revolving fund so that when the fund amount is spent, it can be topped up automatically. This will ensure that in case of delays in reimbursement by the government, the hospitals do not experience cash flow challenges.)

Non-profit hospitals, whether functioning as multi-specialty hospitals, or single-specialty hospitals, take the initiative and actively take part in working with public health. In the field of ophthalmology, some hospitals have obtained national and international recognition for their service-minded delivery, research, teaching and continuing medical education programmes. These institutions serve as role models for not only other ophthalmic hospitals but also for all multi-specialty hospitals worldwide as role models.

Both the Government of India and the respective state governments need to examine the capital expenditure requirements of the non-profit institutions and provide annual grants. This process should be decentralised to districts with clear guidelines and accountability. Regular consultation with non-profits, government representatives and local communities is necessary to suitably address the community's local medical needs. The government could identify three or four urgent health issues in each district and provide aid to the respective non-profit hospitals in those areas. Similarly, the existing resources, such as accredited social health activist (ASHA) workers and anganwadi workers, should be allowed to work with non-profits also.

If governments can align government funding with society's priorities for each district, the charitable hospitals can function better. Many charitable hospitals have supportive facilities like a CT scan, MRI, paediatric high-frequency ventilators and new operating theatres. If the government and non-profit hospitals decide to collaborate on making this a common facility for patients coming to either hospital, it becomes a win–win situation. Collaboration in terms of co-usage of equipment, mutual funding and sharing facilities will help patients and the hospital administration by splitting the costs.

Operational collaboration is equally important. In many primary health centres (PHCs) or community health centres (CHCs), there is an acute shortage of surgeons, paediatricians, neonatologists, ophthalmologists or anaesthetists. Non-profit hospitals can help PHCs or CHCs that face acute staff shortages. Private hospitals can be roped in for tele-consultation. Non-profits and NGOs should collaborate with the government in mutually beneficial programmes like food fortification, combating acute malnutrition and following up adults or children for immunisation. Inter-linkages of computerised systems of government and non-profit hospitals are essential to achieve operational coordination. The rigid boundaries between government facilities and private hospitals should be breached, ensuring that the objective is the patient and not profit-making.

Achieving collaboration with the government can work effectively only if there is a change in the mindset – both on the part of government staff and the non-profit institutions. While initial challenges and frictions may arise, the larger goal justifies navigating through these transitional phases. Leadership in both organisations should work together.

Society's involvement

Civic society should be more involved in helping non-profits. People should serve on Boards, volunteer in various activities, donate funds and provide their expert help free of cost.

It is essential that such partnerships between the government and private sector should not be based on gains for the private sector, as cautioned by Sujata Rao, former Health Secretary, Government of India.[19] The aim of the private sector should be to provide service to the public health system, not to profit covertly from such initiatives.

It is imperative to formulate well-designed strategies tailored to each state and indeed to each district. The strategies should find specific areas where the government, non-profit hospitals and NGOs in each district outline clear deliverable periods. Metrics for assessing the impact of these initiatives should be set up at the outset. There should be independent measurements to evaluate the impact of the new initiatives. The vitality of charitable institutions is crucial for our country's health.

Both the state governments and the Government of India should explore avenues to align these institutions' plans with the state government's health goals. Collaborative efforts should aim to enhance community healthcare, fostering cooperation and a shared service-oriented spirit. Both the government systems and non-profit hospitals should work towards a common cause of improving the healthcare of the community. The collaboration between the government and non-government organisations is not an idealistic solution. Our health needs are so large that an obvious solution may be considered idealistic. The proposed digitisation plan by the Government of India should ease the coordination of patient treatment between the government and non-profit hospitals.

It is necessary to include only quality-accredited institutions in the proposed plans, ensuring that all such institutions obtain the necessary quality accreditations, such as National Accreditation Board for Hospitals and Healthcare Providers (NABH) and National Accreditation Board for Testing and Calibration Laboratories (NABL). The quality of care should not be compromised for free and subsidised medical care. Institutions working in tribal areas and areas where the underprivileged live should be prioritised.

Key criteria

The key criteria for helping non-profit institutions may be as follows:

1. Track the record of the institution in terms of the quantum of charitable work done by each of them over, say, the last five years.
2. Work done in rural and tribal areas should be given special weightage.
3. Study of audited accounts to examine the quantum of free work done in monetary terms.
4. The governments should take into account the membership of the Board of governors or trustees. The government authority, for example, officials from the health department, should meet with key trustees to understand their ethos, management structure and finances.
5. The government authorities should study the institutions' five-year plan and explore how government aid would help them achieve their long-term goals.
6. Quality accreditation – governments should insist on a plan for getting accreditations from charitable institutions. The accreditations should include NABH for the hospital and NABL for their laboratories.
7. The institutions should be encouraged to suggest innovative programmes, which have a long-term and/or short-term impact on the target population.

8. Government aid should include research and teaching programmes and screening programmes.

Programme-based aid from the government to the non-profit institutions

Non-profit hospitals, based on their specialisation, may provide services such as cataract surgery, heart surgeries, dialysis for kidney patients or cancer treatment. For instance, the Government of India has been reimbursing non-profit ophthalmological hospitals at the rate of INR 2,000 per surgery. Similarly, the Government of India provides a one-time grant of INR 75 lakh to set up operating theatres for performing cataract surgery in hilly areas. However, the actual cost of each surgery or procedure or treatment, even at the lowest, would surpass the reimbursement amount. The meagre reimbursement would mean that the hospital must depend on donations or cross-subsidisation by paying patients, thereby limiting extent of free work. The reimbursements by the government should consider the amounts at least equivalent to amounts reimbursed under the Ayushman Bharat insurance schemes.

Larger role beyond treatment

The role of hospitals should extend beyond treating patients and discharging them. There is a need to ensure that the quality of life of the patient improves post-treatment. For instance, cancer patients should receive a follow-up for at least five years. But most of the hospitals, being overcrowded, lack the resources for comprehensive follow-up. For example, in the case of paediatric cancer patients from underprivileged families, the family would not be able to provide adequate nutrition to the patient post-discharge. It is important for the sponsors to fulfil this requirement for the well-being of the child and indeed the society.

Paediatric cases

In recent decades, child morbidity and mortality rates have decreased in many Indian states, which is a cause of concern. Innovative approaches are needed at the district level to address issues like stunting, wasting and malnutrition. A collaborative effort involving government hospitals, non-profit hospitals, private practitioners and private hospitals is essential to tackle each major public health problem.

Consider paediatric cancers. According to Dr R. Venkatraman, a senior oncologist, 'it is estimated that the incidence of cancer in the age group 0–19 years of age is at 75,000 new cases a year, with only half being diagnosed'. The survival rate is likely to be extremely low. This major public health issue requires an urgent and coordinated response for finding solutions. For example, in hospitals, especially where children are treated, the medical protocol should be supplemented by appropriate nutrition. On discharge, many of the patients go back to their normal diet due to poverty. The government, in consultation with non-government organisations (NGOs) and non-profit institutions, should implement a programme where supplementary nutrition is supplied to every such child at the doorstep. The task is huge but should be carried out with active collaboration between ICDS centres, anganwadis, non-profit institutions and the civic society. The non-profit hospitals have a key role to perform in this context. They should set up a budget for such post-discharge follow-up.

District-specific plans

The Government of India, based on medical outcomes, should shortlist about 100 districts out of the total 800-plus districts in India, where the health needs and health outcomes require urgent intervention. This can be the first phase. The focus should be on combating infant mortality rate (IMR), maternal mortality rate (MMR), tuberculosis (TB), low immunisation of infants, diabetes, iron-deficiency anaemia, stunting and wasting.

The state governments should consult with non-profit hospitals and NGOs and work out an action plan for each of the above major health challenges for a five-year period. The district collectors should be involved in this exercise. There is an urgent need for an alternative approach. At present, each of these players functions in separate silos with very little communication among themselves. There is a need for a consultative approach among each of the key players towards planning for the health needs of each district and tackling the issues, both in the short term and the long term.

Government systems and private hospitals would find it difficult to work with each other. There could be turf wars, and each entity is afraid of being taken over by the private sector. Therefore, it may be prudent to start with clearly earmarked areas of operation for each of the stakeholders. The non-profit institutions can offer to pay the ASHA workers directly or through the government. The computerised systems of all the non-profit hospitals concerned should be synchronised with the government systems. The Government of India is at present working on a digital health mission where the systems of the government hospitals themselves are planned to be integrated.

Skill development

There are substantial gaps in skill development training in large cities and the rest of the country. The gaps are not only among medical doctors but also among nursing staff and different allied specialties. It is recommended that large private hospitals extend support and partner with state governments to plan an annual calendar of skill development programmes for government hospitals, small nursing homes and non-profit institutions. These training programmes could be made a mandatory requirement as part of the continuing medical education programme, in which skill development for a prescribed number of days per employee per year is stipulated.

Conclusion

Non-profit institutions play a pivotal role in our healthcare systems, providing a crucial link in medical care, medical education and community service. The future of non-profit institutions should not be left to market forces. If done, many of them might not survive. It is the duty of the government and society to ensure that various measures are initiated to strengthen non-profit institutions and NGOs. It is imperative that both the government and the society should support these institutions. Collaboration between government hospitals and non-profits is essential in addressing health challenges. A symbiotic relationship between government and non-profits can lead to improved healthcare and a more inclusive healthcare system.

Notes

1 'Private healthcare in India: Boons and banes', Expressions, Institut Montaigne, https://www.institutmontaigne.org/en/expressions/private-healthcare-india-boons-and-banes
2 'Estimated number of public and private hospitals across India in 2019', *Statistica*, https://www.statista.com/statistics/1128425/india-number-of-public-and-private-hospitals-estimated/
3 'Dear nursing homes: Here's how to stay alive', *Healthcare Executive*, https://www.healthcareexecutive.in/blog/2018/11/22/dear-nursing-homes-heres-how-to-stay-alive#:~:text=with%20a%20population%20of%20more,provide%20secondary%20and%20tertiary%20care
4 Ida Scudder, https://ourdailybread.org/dr-ida-scudder/
5 L.V. Prasad Eye Institute, https://www.lvpei.org/
6 Apollo Hospitals, https://www.apollohospitals.com/company-overview/the-apollo-story
7 'Over 1000 Christian hospitals available for Covid treatment', *Money Control*, 26 March 2020, https://www.moneycontrol.com/news/trends/health-trends/over-1000-christian-hospitals-across-india-available-for-covid-19-treatment-5077671.html
8 'Activities 2023–24: medical work', Belur Math, Ramakrishna Math and Ramakrishna Mission, https://media.belurmath.org/activities-2023-24-medical-work-13485/
9 Ambattur Rotary Charitable Trust (ARCT), https://www.arctchennai.com/home
10 Bhagwan Mahaveer Jain Hospital Group, https://www.bmjh.org/
11 Amar Jain Hospital, https://whchospital.com/pages/about
12 B.P. Jain Hospital, https://bpjainhospital.in/
13 Vijay Govindarajan and Ravi Ramamurti, *Reverse Innovation in Healthcare*, Harvard Business Review Press, 2018.
14 C.K. Prahalad, *The Fortune at the Bottom of the Pyramid*, Wharton School of Publishing, 2005.
15 'Rights, duties and liabilities of trustees', *Law Bhoomi*, https://lawbhoomi.com/rights-duties-and-liabilities-of-trustees/

16 Liabilities of directors under Companies Act, 2013, https://www.icsi.edu/media/filer_public/50/1a/501a2e51-3ace-426e-98fb-22889403a947/liabilities_of_directors_under_companies_act_2013-final.pdf
17 'Delivering healthcare over cell phone', *Apollo Hospitals*, https://www.apollohospitals.com/la/corporate/apollo-in-the-news/delivering-health-care-over-cell-phone/
18 'Study on the not-for-hospital model in India', *NITI Aayog*, https://www.niti.gov.in/sites/default/files/2023-03/Study-on-Not-for-Profit-Hospital-model-in-India.pdf
19 'Commercialisation of health services can be a recipe for disaster, says Sujatha Rao', *The Hindu*, 21 September 2024, https://www.thehindu.com/sci-tech/science/commercialising-health-services-can-be-a-recipe-for-disaster/article68664340.ece

5 Sundaram Medical Foundation

A case study

Tilak Shankar

Sundaram Medical Foundation (SMF) was established in 1990 by Dr S. Rangarajan and Sundaram Finance Ltd, a company part of the prestigious TVS group, an automobile conglomerate based in Chennai, the capital of Tamil Nadu. Dr Rangarajan, who qualified as a chartered accountant, also completed MBA and went on to become a physician. He defied his family tradition of joining the business to pursue his passion of serving others. SMF was formed as a charitable trust with a vision of establishing 'a hospital, providing quality health care, which is cost-effective and community-centred, in an environment which is clean, caring and responsive to the needs of the patient'. After Dr Rangarajan's demise in 1997, his family took over the overall governance of the hospital, helped by a professional management team, and Dr Rangarajan Memorial Hospital was also added to the hospital's name. SMF began its operations in 1990 with a modest bed strength of 50 beds, progressively growing in size and becoming well known in the community for its excellence in care. By 2021, it had over 220 beds with activities spread around the main hospital in Anna Nagar, an outpatient centre in Mogappair, a smaller facility in a nearby area, and a separate outpatient facility. During this period, SMF had developed over 40 specialties in medicine with a strong focus on obstetrics and gynaecology, paediatrics, general medicine, general surgery and orthopaedics and emergency medicine.

SMF serves the needs of patients in a prominent neighbourhood of Anna Nagar in Chennai. Anna Nagar is a popular residential locality, close to a large industrial area. Most of the inpatients and outpatients come from suburbs located within a 30 km radius. The hospital presently serves about 15,000 inpatients and over 300,000 outpatients per annum. The average length of stay (ALOS), an important metric for a hospital, is about five bed days per patient. The bed occupancy is about 80 per cent, going up to 100 per cent frequently.

The hospital directly employs about 600 staff at various levels and another 300 as contract staff who provide outsourced services. Outsourcing of non-core areas has helped to focus on medical care. Most of the doctors are either visiting or in-house consultants who work exclusively with the Foundation.

DOI: 10.4324/9781003684947-6

In addition, there are accredited medical consultants who are pre-registered to admit their patients under the care of the hospital's consultants.

Vision of the SMF founder

The vision of SMF was set at the time of its founding:

- To provide cost-effective medical treatment in chosen areas, providing 'affordable medical care'
- To provide high-quality medicare through sound medical and management processes
- To function as a community-centred hospital
- To provide post-graduate level and DNB programmes in many disciplines and publish in peer-reviewed international medical journals
- To strictly follow procedures as per the relevant national certifications and remain fully certified
- To focus on preventive health practices in the community

While these core objectives have remained constant, there have been modifications in the last 25 years. The trustees pointed out how in the later years, multiple changes have impacted the definition of the hospital: 'The concept of community hospital itself has undergone many changes due to newer patient expectations and medical needs, developments in medical technology and information technology, demographic changes in the neighbouring areas and medical insurance.' As a result, SMF has added newer departments, installed an MRI facility and opened a large outpatient unit as well.

Organisation structure

SMF is a public charitable trust headed by a Board of Trustees comprising two executive trustees and nine independent trustees. One of the trustees looks after community work and marketing. The Board of Trustees provides broad policy guidelines, approves budgets, initiates major actions towards expansion and ensures compliance with all aspects, ensuring general alignment of the operations of SMF with its vision.

The day-to-day activities of the hospital are carried out by the following team:

- Trustee and Medical Director who is responsible for all technical/medical aspects
- Trustee and Director – Administration, who is responsible for finance, personnel and day-to-day hospital administration
- Trustee – community work and marketing
- All medical and administrative teams work under the leadership of the executive trustees.

Role of the medical director

The medical director, a busy surgeon, coordinates all the major medical departments. Besides his professional role as a surgeon, he is responsible for nursing, laboratory, radiology and all support departments such as operating theatres, physiotherapy and pharmacy. Medical departments consist of several specialised disciplines such as obstetrics and gynaecology (OBG), general medicine, plastic surgery, general surgery and orthopaedics made up of highly qualified professionals in their respective areas. Junior doctors and post-graduate students (DNB) provide support to the senior staff.

The medical director is responsible for ensuring that all necessary support facilities, such as operating theatres, consulting rooms, laboratories, nursing staff and medicines, are efficiently managed. The medical director is also responsible for the recruitment and addition of appropriate consultants, planning and procurement of medical equipment and ensuring that all professional needs of medical consultants are met and coordinates teaching, publications and research work. Many committees have been formed to assist the medical director. The processes are guided by the National Accreditation Board for Hospitals and Healthcare Providers (NABH) protocols.

Long-term planning

The medical director has an important role in envisioning the long-term directions of the institution. All medical institutions face the challenge of staying up-to-date in medical and information technology, keeping pace with the fast-changing medical technology. The medical director's role encompasses operational and strategic planning with a vision for the future.

Role of director – administration

Hospital administration occupies a critical role in the overall management of the hospital. The director – administration looks after HR, finance and accounts, IT, patient relations – inpatients and outpatients, support services such as canteen, security and housekeeping, procurement of capital equipment and procurement of drugs (in coordination with medical departments), engineering services such as civil, electrical and bio-medical services. Some of the services, such as security, canteen and housekeeping, are outsourced. Several metrics are utilised to monitor various administrative services, both in-house as well as outsourced services. However, the primary role of director – administration is not merely routine monitoring of administrative activities, which are carried out in routine operations, but also includes formulating the future directions for the institution, growth in capacity, upgradation of IT services and use of emerging technologies and administrative processes wherever possible.

Reviews and coordination

SMF has 24 committees to review and coordinate the activities of the hospital. A few of the key committees are as follows:

- Morbidity and mortality committee
- Ethics committee
- Grievances committee
- Infection control committee
- Nursing committee
- Patient relations committee – focusing on both outpatients and inpatients
- Pharmacy committee
- Quality improvement committee.

Quality is coordinated by a full-time senior professional to study computerised data of all departments. Regular meetings are held to discuss various deviations from standards in these meetings and corrective actions are initiated.

All the major committees are headed by one of the directors as appropriate. In addition, the Board of Trustees meet once a quarter to review performance, deliberate on key issues and the explore the scope for improvement.

Pharmacy committee

The work of this committee is added to highlight its significance. Medicines are a major part of patient bills. Hence, it is essential that cost controls are effectively employed. An effective pharmacy review committee has been functioning since the hospital's inception, monitoring all the drugs prescribed by its medical teams; the committee evaluates the generic equivalents of all drugs prescribed, taking into account factors such as the profile of the patients and suitability of drugs, which is approved by the review committee. The use of antibiotics is an important part of this review. In India, prescription of antibiotics, including self-prescription by the patients themselves, is common, leading to drug resistance later. Many studies[1] have highlighted the excessive use of antibiotics for inpatients in Indian hospitals. It is, therefore, incumbent on each hospital to install systems for monitoring the prescription of antibiotics.

Twin leadership structure

Leadership is the single most important factor in the evolution, growth and sustenance of any institution. When the visionary founder Dr S Rangarajan passed away a short time after the hospital started functioning, it was necessary to ensure that his successors continued his work. It was at this time the idea of a twin leadership was born. Dr Arjun Rajagopalan, an eminent vascular surgeon who was associated with Dr Rangarajan in the planning stage of SMF, was appointed as the medical director. S. Ravindran was appointed as director – administration. Both Dr Rajagopalan and Ravindran were also appointed as trustees. These two leaders together ensured that the morale of the entire team was kept high during the transition, recruited medical and administrative personnel, initiated teaching courses and guided the expansion of the hospital. They also introduced systems and procedures and commenced work on hospital-wide computerisation. Working in tandem, they put the hospital on a strong footing for more than 15 years. In the meantime, the next set of leaders was ready. Dr P.V. Jaishankar, an eminent orthopaedic surgeon, was appointed as medical director and T.N.P. Durai as director – administration. They also joined the Board as Trustees. Dr Vijayabharati Rangarajan was appointed as a trustee, and she took up various community activities and also marketing.

A modern hospital requires both medical and management skills. A dual leadership can work when there is mutual respect, communication and a process of joint decision making. SMF is a good example of both medical and management teams working for a common purpose.

Growing medical specialisation

The medical director pointed out that SMF has largely remained a primary and secondary care hospital since its inception. Obstetrics and gynaecology, paediatrics, general medicine, general surgery and orthopaedics continue to be the main focus areas. However, with the changing epidemiological profile of the urban population, other specialities had become necessary. As a teaching hospital, SMF had to ensure the availability of emerging technologies and medical specialisation to the aspiring students. In paediatrics, for example, paediatric cardiology, neurology, nephrology, radiology and robotics were added. The hospital also developed specialisation in hand surgery, thigh surgery and hip replacement eventually. As the hospital grew, developing skills in new specialties, improving treatment efficiency and cutting down operating costs were achieved. The hospital all along kept its singular focus on responding to patient needs. Recently, a magnetic resonance imaging (MRI) facility has been added to imaging services.

Affordable healthcare in practice

Affordable care is systematically built on selection of key components of cost. Some of the areas are:

- Case mix
- Bed configuration
- Use of built-up space
- Control of the costs of medicines
- Optimal utilisation of all equipment
- Control on wastages and review of internal processes

The cost of hospitalisation is the total amount incurred by a patient from the time of admission till discharge. The patient or their family members decide on a particular hospital based on its reputation, perceived competence of doctors and the cost of treatment. There is a distinct preference for affordable care, with proximity to home becoming an added consideration. It is essential that the patient knows the total charges prior to admission.

The cost of inpatient charges is dependent on

- Inpatient care: Bed and room composition and tariff
- Doctor consultation charges
- Length of stay of patients, based on the treatment protocol
- Practice of ethical medicine
- Tariffs charged for various services – inpatient and outpatient
- Rates charged to the patients for medicines and consumables
- Cost control by effective utilisation of medical equipment and operating theatre

Despite the government hospitals providing free medical care, for various reasons, many middle-income patients prefer to be treated in private hospitals. When the capital cost of the project and subsequent capital expenditure are funded by the industrial group in the case of SMF, the need for generating funds from the hospital or through external funds does not arise, as the hospital is an industry-managed non-profit organisation.

Ethics of care at SMF: A distinguishing feature

Good ethical practices form the cornerstone of providing affordable care to patients. Doctors at the hospitals do not ask for unnecessary procedures, tests or second opinions that yield no additional information. Every doctor that the author met at SMF mentioned this aspect.

There are many doctors who practice only at the SMF hospital, devoting all their time to working there. Many visiting consultants prefer to practice at SMF because of the ethical practices being followed. Once a year, the committee reviews the complete list of medicines prescribed for various factors, such as chemical composition of both generic and branded medicines, as well as their prices, and recommends a final list of medicines. This process ensures that expensive drugs are not recommended when there are cheaper alternatives.

Hospital consumables are the other important item affecting the cost of treatment. These are items such as gloves, masks, personal protective equipment (PPE), syringes, cleaning chemicals and so on. As there is no maximum retail price (MRP) on many of these items, some hospitals inflate their usage and prices of such consumables. SMF follows the practice of purchase price plus administrative charges.

Management practices at SMF: Focus on operational excellence and keeping costs minimal

Good systems and procedures are essential for providing affordable care. Sound management practices include quality accreditation, budgetary control, effective information systems, well-defined organisation structure, cost control, formal policy guidelines, metrics for evaluation, accountability of staff and systematic performance reviews by senior management.

Bed composition and tariff

Every hospital carefully plans the configuration of its beds and room facilities. Corporate hospitals keep a higher percentage of high-end rooms with a minimal number of general ward beds. In some of the non-profit hospitals, the number of general ward beds could be 50 per cent or more.

At SMF, deluxe rooms constitute 10 per cent of the total bed strength. The daily tariff in 2021 varied from INR 3,000 for a bed in the general ward to INR 6,650 for an air-conditioned single room, taking into account the profile of the patients. In a corporate hospital, the room charges are much higher with multiple special categories such as single, deluxe, executive deluxe and suites.

At SMF, at the time of admission, as per the NABH requirements, the patient or their attendant should be informed about the total cost of hospitalisation. Room tariffs usually do not constitute a major part of the patient's bill, even though there is a perception that a high room tariff is synonymous with high overall charges. The average revenue per occupied room (ARPOB) in corporate hospitals ranges from INR 60,000 to INR 75,000 per day, a figure keenly watched by investors. There are no such pressures in a non-profit hospital.

At the time of admission, a social worker meets the family members and assesses if the patient needs a discount. After due evaluation, a discount of 10–30 per cent is offered to the patient. About 15 per cent of inpatients and 30 per cent of outpatients are treated free of charge at SMF.

Similarly, registration charges are fixed at moderate levels – INR 250 for an outpatient consultation and INR 450 for an inpatient visit. In a corporate hospital in Chennai, specialist consultation charges range from INR 1,000 to INR 1,500. Laboratory charges, MRI and radiology charges are periodically compared with those charged in other non-profit hospitals to ensure that all SMF charges are reasonable.

Average length of stay (ALOS)

ALOS is an important factor in minimising the overall cost of hospitalisation. It is a useful metric to understand how effectively the hospital is able to utilise its beds, discharging current patients and admitting new patients. There are differences in ALOS in tertiary and secondary care hospitals. Departments such as general medicine, general surgery and obstetrics and gynaecology (OBG) admit many patients for different medical needs. On average, the ALOS for the SMF hospital is four or five days per patient. This average, according to the medical director, is being systematically brought down by various medical and administrative measures to improve affordability as well as to treat more patients and minimising the likelihood of hospital-acquired infections. Purely from a commercial point of view, the income from a new patient is at its highest in the first few days of admission and sharply reduces thereafter. SMF also offers home care to all patients who need such attention, including doctor visits.

Measures of patient satisfaction

SMF focuses on patient satisfaction through:

- Hassle-free admissions and discharge procedures
- Minimal paperwork at every stage of treatment
- Efficient housekeeping
- Great inter-departmental coordination among areas like laboratories, radiology, blood bank and so on

The hospital functions like a well-oiled machine, at the same time showing compassion in dealing with patients and their attendants.

Capital expenditure evaluation and utilisation

SMF is frugal in replacing old or in procuring new equipment. According to the medical director, all medical departments follow a systematic and transparent system for procurement, replacement and new equipment every year. At a meeting, all medical departmental heads discuss their individual requests. Replacement requests are discussed where the department concerned explains the need for replacement, utilisation of the equipment, revenue generated and operating costs with supporting data. Similarly, new equipment details are presented for discussion. Thereafter, the group consolidates the final list for discussion with the director – administration. Often, the Board of Trustees may ask the team to include some advanced equipment, which may not have been proposed by the medical group but is essential for the future.

Utilisation of key equipment

SMF does not focus or require high utilisation of equipment, as it can lead to undesirable practices. On the other hand, the review process ensures that investments are productive without pressuring the doctors or fixing targets for doctors. SMF regularly reviews the actual utilisation of all major medical equipment. The hospital provides for depreciation as a part of the commercial accounting system. Such periodic reviews with department heads ensure the requests for new equipment are always aligned with expected utilisation. It is possible to be efficient without commercial focus.

Quality control

Renowned quality guru Edwards Deming has defined quality as 'predictable degree of uniformity and dependability of outcomes relevant to customer needs at low cost'. A good quality control system brings down the operating costs. SMF is accredited by leading quality organisations in India, such as the National Accreditation Board for Hospitals and Healthcare Providers (NABH), the National Accreditation Board for Testing and Calibration Laboratories (NABL) and the International Organization for Standardization (ISO). These accreditations reflect the importance given by the top management to ensure the quality of medicare. The accreditations bring about a discipline in collating, analysing and taking action on various healthcare metrics. Many medium-sized hospitals (around 250 beds) consider it a luxury to get NABH accreditation. This is a short-sighted approach.

Role of metrics in quality evaluation

The NABH stipulates 35 metrics, which not only measure quality but also the accountability for quality as linked to specific departments; for example, metrics specific to nursing, operating theatres and infection control are measured and reported. At SMF, there is a portal from which relevant data is available to every decision maker, containing all quality-related data for the month, as well as past trends. A senior team member heads the quality movement, and every department has a quality champion to provide ongoing support.

Achieving medical outcomes through quality processes

The vision document of SMF refers to 'medical outcomes'. In SMF, the five major departments for admission are obstetrics and gynaecology, paediatrics, general medicine, general surgery and orthopaedics. All medical outcomes in each of these five departments are evaluated every quarter; further, the quality data is discussed in the grand hospital rounds with all senior medical staff. The mortality and morbidity committee also analyses the medical outcomes in different departments, and necessary steps are undertaken.

Importance of accreditation

Accreditations by NABH and NABL are awarded by independent agencies after a scrutiny of infrastructure, staffing, processes and outcomes. There is a mistaken impression that certification by NABH and NABL is expensive, the cost of which many not-for-profit hospitals cannot afford. This is not true. SMF has demonstrated that quality is essential for every hospital since it deals with human lives.

Best practices in organising patients

Outpatients

The author spent two half-days at the Outpatient (OP) Centre, on busy mornings, in the year 2023. The hospital handles about 700–1,000 patients a day, in a separate building, ten kilometres from the hospital building. There are over 100 doctors attending patients at the OP Centre on a given day, utilising dozens of cubicles for patient consultation. In addition, there are clearly demarcated areas with signages for each department in all the three floors of the OP Centre. There are also separate areas for MRI, X-ray, pathology laboratories, audiology and physiotherapy, arranged department-wise for the use of outpatients. The location of each facility on different floors is based on expected patient traffic on a typical day.

Doctor availability in the OP Centre for each day of the week is meticulously planned. All changes in doctors' schedules are communicated in advance, ensuring patient satisfaction. The OP facilitation department has nearly 50 staff members working in multiple shifts from 8 a.m. to 8 p.m., six days a week. All the doctor appointments are centralised, as is the despatch of consultation reports, in person or by email.

When a new patient registers, an outpatient number is given, which acts as a link. When a patient is asked by the consultant to take lab tests, for example, a bar code is generated, which ensures that the blood samples are correctly correlated with each patient as per NABL requirements. A small number of walk-in patients who are not registered as hospital patients also come to the OP Centre for specialised needs such as lab tests, physiotherapy and MRI. SMF is planning to widely market its services for non-hospital patients as well. During the period of study in 2023, the OP Centre also monitors the waiting times of patients. It had been found that the waiting time is high – two to three hours. The Centre is actively evaluating methods by which the waiting time can be minimised.

The manager in charge of the OP Centre organises training programmes to ensure that all employees understand their roles and are helpful to patients. In addition, there are frequent sensitivity programmes for employees and a well-designed performance appraisal system to align employees with patient satisfaction.

Inpatients

The hospital has 176 beds in its main campus at Shanti Colony, Anna Nagar, and 36 beds in Mogappair. Nearly 70 beds are for varying levels of intensive care patients, including children. A combination of paper-based and automated systems registers the patient with a unique medical records (MR) number.

There are 35 staff members in this department responsible for registration, admission, cashless insurance facilitation, coordination on all insurance claims, monitoring of patient needs in the wards, complaints handling and discharge procedures. This department also handles the processing of bills, the collection of advances from patients and evaluating concessions required through social workers. As per NABH requirements, all necessary records are maintained in paper and digitised formats.

Efficiency improvement methods

ALOS requires the management of a number of discrete processes, as shown below:

- The cause for admission (elective, emergency, accident cases), age of the patient, medical condition, time of admission (day or night)
- Ensuring smooth coordination between admissions, operating theatres/labour room, availability of required doctors, anaesthetist, nurses, laboratories and imaging
- Ensuring availability of drugs and medicines, consumables, in the theatres and in stores, which are vital for patient care
- IT plays a key role in ensuring seamless connectivity between all departments – transfer of data, both on the medical as well as on the administrative side

Modern management offers a number of techniques and principles for improving efficiency and hence patient satisfaction. Several industrial engineering techniques and organisation and method studies, and workflow analyses greatly enhance organisational effectiveness. The adage 'what is measured is managed' is effectively utilised at SMF.

Information technology has become a great differentiator in healthcare. The extensive use of mobile telephony, wireless internet, hand-held devices, tablets and artificial intelligence has become cost-effective in offering a range of options. SMF has been constantly working on these options, optimising its processes in the hospital.

The inpatient department also handles patient complaints. As the manager explains with a smile, 'none of the patients have complaints about our doctors, but they do complain about housekeeping, food etc.'

Finance and Accounts

Finance and Accounts is headed by a deputy general manager. As a registered private trust, SMF follows an accrual system of accounting, even though many non-profit institutions follow a cash-based accounting system. The accounting software is an integral part of the enterprise resource planning (ERP) already implemented across all departments in SMF. Therefore, all basic inputs for the accounting system flow from other computerised subsystems such as billing, payroll and materials.

Budgeting

In January of every year, detailed budgets are prepared for all departments, which is finally consolidated into a hospital-wide annual business plan. These budgets take into account the number of patients, category-wise bed usage, proposed tariff revisions, level of outpatient activity, various items of costs and their increases, income and expenditure from key service departments such as laboratory, pharmacy, diagnostics and so on.

Capital expenditure

Capital expenditure budgets are undertaken in collaboration with the medical director and director – administration. All major capital items are evaluated for return on investment (ROI) and projected utilisation. Priority is given to replacement items. Typically, the expectation is that in three years the investment will be recovered. The total amount of capital expenditure is linked to the depreciation of the previous year plus surplus from operations. Occasionally, the Board decides on big-ticket capital items for strategic reasons and funds them.

Management reporting

There is a monthly finance and operations review by the top management, followed by a Board-level review. All financial aspects of SMF's operations and their linkages to physical actions are discussed. Such reviews result in identifying the actions to be taken to improve performance.

The finance department also studies departmental revenues with particular reference to payment patterns of patients for all major revenue-earning departments. It also tries to initiate measures for changing the payment mix. For example, if the number of patients utilising the insurance facilities is considered low, then corrective measures are initiated. The top revenue-earning departments, such as OBG, paediatrics, general medicine, general surgery and orthopaedics, are closely monitored. Similarly, the conversion rate of outpatients into inpatients, if abnormal, is brought to the attention of the top management.

The hospital does not have a formal cost accounting system, a typical omission among hospitals. Hospitals normally tend to benchmark their tariff, salary structure and other operating cost elements with other comparable hospitals in the local areas.

Information technology (IT)

SMF has had excellent IT systems for over two decades. The interlinked system has more than 40 modules, covering all inpatient and outpatient departments. The systems are developed on a Java platform with a facility for users to develop simple queries themselves.

A patient app has also been developed. Tele-consulting had become popular during the COVID-19 pandemic. The hospital is also examining the use of artificial intelligence (AI). Other development works are also under way, such as form to text, two-factor authentication and online OP booking.

Human Resources

The Employee Handbook of the hospital starts with the motto, 'Let us all work together towards our vision'. Given to all new employees, it spells out all aspects of employment such as attendance, leave rules, loan schemes, canteen facilities, employee rights and responsibilities, patient rights and responsibilities, performance appraisals, disciplinary action and training programmes. A formal induction of all new employees is an important first step. The professionalism of the institution with a formal welcome of all new employees leaves a deep first impression.

Staff strength

SMF employs about 600 staff members directly and another 300 persons through various contractors. Thus, it has a bed-to-staff ratio of 1:4.5, which is broadly in line with comparable hospitals. The contract employees are involved in departments like housekeeping, security, canteen and as ambulance drivers. About 50 per cent of the direct employees are nurses.

The hospital has several schemes and committees, such as suggestion schemes, sexual harassment committee and grievance redressal committee. The non-management staff and the contract staff are unionised. The SMF management enters into an agreement with these unions every four years.

Pivotal role of HR

The HR plays a pivotal role and is not treated as administrative department. Changes in medical technology, information technology, competition from other hospitals, changing patient expectations and cost pressures, all require a nimble workforce. Skill levels of nurses, administrative staff, medical staff and technicians need constant upgradation in line with emerging practices. In the words of one of the hospital consultants, 'the duty nurse has to respond to the needs of a patient at 2 a.m., take quick action, and all the while maintain her composure'. She has to be motivated and professional in discharging her duty at all times.

Apart from nurses, a number of DNB students who are medical graduates doing their post-graduation work also serve as frontline workers.

Medical doctors

The hospital employs a small number of full-time doctors on its payroll, some doctors as registrars and junior consultants. Some specialists work as consultants, on a 'fee-for-service' model. Their remuneration is directly linked to the number of patients treated, either as outpatients or inpatients. They are further classified into doctors who practice only at SMF, visiting consultants and accredited consultants who may also practice elsewhere. In addition, the post-graduate students doing DNB courses are paid stipends as per DNB guidelines.

The HR plays only a facilitating role, leaving the technical medical component of work to the medical team.

Recruitment

Based on the request from various departments, HR initiates the search process. Since the largest number of recruitment requests is from the nursing department, various nursing colleges are contacted. The newly recruited staff go through induction programmes at a separate training centre. The hospital has also specified a number of training days per annum per person.

Salary structure

Salary scales are broadly divided into management and other staff. All the jobs are stratified into a number of grades. There are many loyal staffers and, hence, due weightage is given to the number of years of service in their pay. There is a grade equivalence table, which slots various jobs in the hospital as a means of comparing different skills for equivalent pay. The hospital provides several employee-friendly allowances and benefits. These include dearness allowance, special basic, house rent allowance, conveyance allowance, washing allowance, functional allowance, education allowance, special allowance, risk allowance, leave travel allowance and ad hoc allowance. Subsidised meals are provided. Employees and their families get subsidised medical care at the hospital. Medicines for employees and their families are also provided at a discount.

Nurses

This group forms the largest number of staff members in the hospital, with over 300 nurses in various skill categories. The allocation of nurses to the various departments, such as intensive care unit (ICU), neonatal intensive care (NICU), wards and operating theatres, are as per NABH requirements. The nursing department is headed by a senior person.

Other staff

The hospital employs technicians in laboratories, phlebotomists, attenders, assistants, staff in inpatient and outpatient departments, HR, IT, engineering services and finance and accounts.

Performance appraisal system

The performance appraisal system for staff takes into account various factors such as job knowledge, performance, ability and aptitude, dependability and attendance. In the case of management staff, factors such as planning, initiative, creativity and leadership are added in the appraisal form. These factors are mostly qualitative. Perhaps it may be advisable to link the metrics which are measured in the NABH system with the employee appraisal systems.

The annual appraisal is done for all employees by their immediate superiors and reviewed by a senior. Appraisal details are discussed with the employees concerned, and their views are recorded in the appraisal form. The idea is to enable all employees to improve their performance through thoughtful feedback.

Increments

Based on an acceptable rating in the final appraisal, the staff member is given one increment. In the case of outstanding performance, the employee would be eligible for a double increment.

Performance-based pay

In the case of management staff, there is also a performance-based pay. The main factors for assessing the performance pay for managers are the following:

- Contribution of the staff member, taking into account factors such as crisis management, initiative and steady performance, in the last three years
- Value to the hospital, which would include leadership qualities, potential to assume additional responsibilities and team work

Based on the above factors the quantum of performance pay could reach up to 100 per cent of the base pay.

Promotions from within

As a policy towards increasing employee motivation, the management attaches emphasis on internal promotions for meritorious staff. Only in exceptional cases does the hospital recruit laterally from outside. As a result, many senior positions are headed by staff who have been with the organisation for many years. The management believes that it encourages synchronisation of the SMF ethos among all staff members.

Job rotation

The management believes in rotating staff through transfers across departments for gaining a wider exposure. Many staff members who hold senior positions in the hospital have been transferred from administrative roles to positions in patient relations, IT and quality management. Likewise, many medical staff have been given additional responsibilities such as teaching, community work, administration and quality management. Such conscious attempts at job rotation help the employee gain a good understanding of how other functions operate, widening the perspective of managers and doctors.

HR challenges

Retention of staff is a major concern for all hospitals, and SMF is no exception. Attrition, particularly among junior levels of nurses, is a major challenge. The nursing department has multiple levels of supervision and support to junior nurses to ensure constant mentoring and communication with them.

Providing affordable healthcare requires strict control on human resource costs. This would require control on the number of staff required in each department in relation to the workload, particularly in the context of increasing levels of computerisation. The other challenge is upgrading skill level in all areas, in both medical and non-medical departments.

External environment and the future of SMF

Chennai has long been considered the 'medical capital' of India. Several medical colleges and private hospitals produce a large number of trained medical graduates and allied health sciences professionals. Since 1990, several large tertiary care hospitals have come up in different parts of the city, some of which are corporate hospitals. There are 59 private/corporate hospitals in Chennai.[2] In addition, there are many single-specialty hospitals and several not-for-profit hospitals, which attract patients from all over the country and overseas as well. There are several hundred NABH-accredited hospitals in Chennai.[3]

The future plans of SMF have to be examined in the context of the environment for growth in Chennai, as well as how far SMF has come in fulfilling the founder's vision. The hospital has completed a quarter century of being a model hospital in providing affordable healthcare for the community. Its comprehensive range of services are much sought after by the community. Factors like growth in inpatients and outpatients over the years and high rates of bed occupancy have validated the relevance of the SMF model of healthcare. The hospital is a one-location facility, with no specific plans to move to other locations.

Management by growth

Management theory differentiates between management of growth and management *by* growth, pointing out that both strategies are important. A steadily growing organisation opens up opportunities for growth, both professional and personal, for its employees. Whenever town hall meetings are conducted by large organisations, one of the predictable questions from employees is about the future plans of the organisation. Growth creates environment opportunities for innovation, provides challenges for younger employees and improves the competitive atmosphere within the organisation. In many institutions, growth is top-management-driven. This, of course, ensures that the Board is constantly looking for new growth areas and planning the requirements for funds and qualified staff to manage growth. Thus, a balance between career aspirations of the staff combined with top management vision provides an impetus for growth. However, in the case of non-profit hospitals, they are constrained by funds, and hence, their approach to future planning would be different. Unless they raise large donations or have a clear plan to grow any major growth may not fructify.

Growth options for SMF

- The SMF template can be readily replicated in many new locations by providing its proven know-how to other hospitals. The transfer of know-how can be made available to like-minded institutions or new groups who wish to benefit from such expertise and whose value systems match with that of SMF.
- Alternately, SMF itself can grow in several geographical locations of the country, while expanding its present facility.
- The professional aspirations of senior medical staff should play a key part in planning for the future, in expanding medical specialisation, which in turn would meet the aspirations of junior staff. All departments would want to plan for a minimum number of beds for their specialty

and acquire contemporary technology for their needs both requiring large investments.

- One of the challenges is the shortage and high turnover of nurses. Some hospitals overcome this hurdle by starting their own nursing colleges. This, of course, is a strategic decision for SMF, requiring permissions from various authorities and investments in land, buildings and faculty. However, a nursing school does not automatically guarantee that the nursing shortage would be solved. However, the experience of many hospitals suggests that it is one of the ways of recruiting nurses.
- As a teaching institution, SMF provides advanced training to their DNB students in the use of the state-of-art medical technologies. This would require regular upgradation, which in turn would require the hospital to grow from their present strength and constantly invest in modern technology. The hospital's recent investment in MRI is one example of responding to such growth needs.
- Competition also would force every hospital to modernise, grow and be responsive to the community's changing needs.
- Apart from medical technologies, investments would also be needed for upgradation of IT, network infrastructure and other facilities like ambulance services.

The SMF Board of Trustees is considering several short- and medium-term options. The OP Centre is an example of providing the same medical expertise available at the main hospital in another location. Likewise, 'Mother and Child' is a core area, which can provide immediate growth opportunities for obstetrics and gynaecology, and many sub-specialisations in paediatrics, which are already key areas of practice.

Conclusion

The SMF case study illustrates many distinctive features, some of which are as follows:

- Sundaram Finance Limited, which has set up a hospital, has been supporting it for more than three decades and funding both operational deficits and capital expenditures. The top management of the group has been closely involved in the overall policymaking and operations review every month.
- Strong management processes have been the foundation of the hospital. The dual leadership style has been working effectively. The basic character, that is, primary and secondary, has remained the same, while it has been nimble to adapt to external changes.
- A medium-sized hospital catering to middle-income groups also requires patient-oriented processes, quality accreditation and contemporary information technology to be a respected hospital. This is a good model.

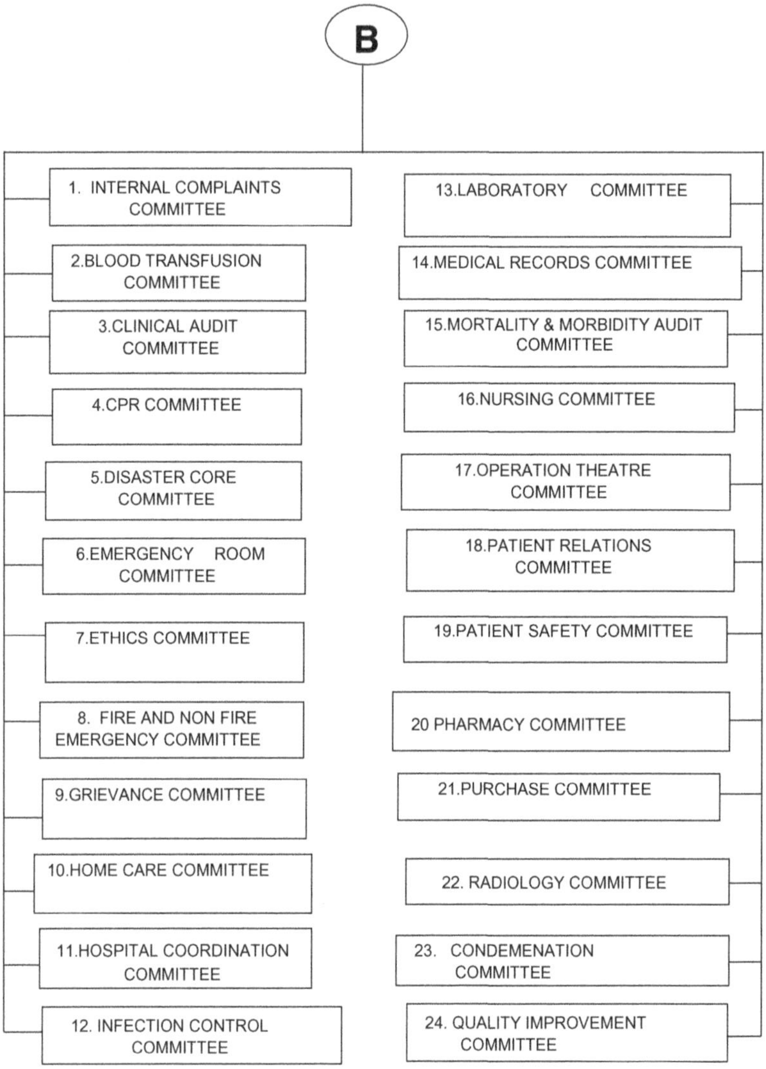

Various committees in Sundaram Medical Foundation as part of the hospital operations.

Notes

1 Daphne Clarance, 'How antibiotic misuse is creating a health emergency in India', *India Today*, 7 October 2024, https://www.indiatoday.in/health/story/how-antibiotic-misuse-is-creating-a-health-emergency-in-india-2612415-2024-10-07
2 Private hospitals in Chennai, Scribd, https://www.scribd.com/document/528613871/Private-Hospitals-in-Chennai#:~:text=Hospitals%20in%20Chennai-,This%20document%20lists%2059%20private%20hospitals%20in%20Chennai%2C%20India.,phone%20number%20for%20each%20hospital.
3 NABH hospitals in Chennai, Quality Health for You, https://www.qualityhealth.in/nabh_hospitals_chennai

Part II

Operationalising healthcare in India

6 Leadership in healthcare

Tilak Shankar

Introduction

India's healthcare system consisted of public hospitals, many nursing homes and a few charitable hospitals to start with, until the private healthcare system scaled up exponentially. The government took on the burden of healthcare by providing treatment for major illnesses and there were times when major surgeries were performed only in government hospitals before modern private hospitals came into existence. Independent doctors ran private clinics to attend to small illnesses, and nursing homes were a few and far in between. Some inspired individuals started private organisations – for example, the Cancer Institute and Voluntary Health Services, both in Chennai – with the vision of providing quality healthcare at an affordable cost without commercial interest.

Some specialists, trained abroad, wanted to bring a change in the way healthcare was provided in the country by adding a layer of quality. They set up large private hospitals, which eventually evolved to become chains of hospitals (for example, Apollo Hospitals) across cities, providing innovative healthcare services for treating basic illnesses to highly complicated ones through a combination of skilled doctors and cutting-edge techniques, with the aid of technology.

Government spending on healthcare is 1.9 per cent of the GDP in 2023–24, according to the Economic Survey 2023–24.[1] Out-of-pocket expenditure constituted 48.2 per cent of the total health expenditure, going by the National Health Accounts report for 2018–19. The report further added that the private sector constitutes 58 per cent of the hospitals in the country, 29 per cent of beds in hospitals and 81 per cent of doctors. According to the National Family Health Survey-3, the private medical sector is the primary source of healthcare for 70 per cent of the households in urban areas and 63 per cent of the households in rural areas.

Private medical care consists of various providers, ranging from small nursing homes to major players operating a chain. In the last two decades, multiple insurance companies offer insurance cover for patients undergoing treatment in health facilities (to the extent of covering the entire health expenses during the hospital stay), and private laboratories have evolved

DOI: 10.4324/9781003684947-8

with facilities to perform various kinds of medical tests for patients. In addition, imaging centres offer imaging services, including procedures such as magnetic resonance imaging (MRI), X-rays, computed tomographic (CT) scans and a range of radiology services.

In addition, the pharmaceutical and vaccine industries have grown to the extent that India could be called the pharmacist to the world. Startups and established companies have brought in fresh energy by developing various products and services, hardware, medical software, data analytics, and AI, thereby providing innovative solutions to multiple health problems.

Evolution of healthcare organisations in India

Setting up and managing hospitals or nursing homes requires unique skills. Being responsive to the changing needs of the community is the responsibility of the leaders. It is the leaders who invest their energies in formulating suitable strategies to prepare the organisation to meet various challenges. India's emergence as a healthcare destination owes in no small measure to the excellent leadership of institutions in providing quality healthcare. Before discussing leadership, it is important to understand the landscape in which the leaders are operating.

Difficult environment in the 1980s

In general, business leadership had to cope with dramatic changes in the Indian economic environment in the last five decades. The healthcare industry was no exception.

The emergence of new corporate healthcare organisations should be appreciated in the context of the ecosystem prevailing during the 1980s. Fund-raising was exceedingly difficult as banks charged prohibitive interest rates on borrowings. Similarly, the interest charges on debentures were high. Import of medical equipment was very cumbersome due to licensing restrictions, and import duties further escalated the project costs. The Indian medical equipment industry was still in its infancy. The health insurance industry was exceedingly small, managed by government insurance companies. Capital markets were underdeveloped, and new capital issues were non-existent. The country grappled with a foreign currency crisis in the early 1990s. The environment was challenging for all industries, including the healthcare sector.

During this arduous period, charitable hospitals faced numerous difficulties, such as raising funds, seeking donors and sponsors and encouraging trustees to join new trusts. Starting a new venture was very challenging. Leadership in the 1980s demanded the ability to navigate red tape, constantly expect new bottlenecks and wait for the right time to start a new venture. There were no formal quality accreditation standards for hospitals.

Changes due to liberalisation of the economy

The liberalisation of the Indian economy in 1991 ushered in a tectonic shift in how businesses operated. The stifling licensing requirements were gradually relaxed, and foreign investment was facilitated due to changes in government policies. Stock markets became active, and raising funds was progressively easier. In the healthcare industry, large private hospitals enlarged their scope of operations and began expanding into other cities. Private practitioners who ran small home clinics started referring their patients to large hospitals. Single-doctor consultation slowly went out of vogue, and specialist consultations for different ailments became the norm. Diseases also grew in complexity, necessitating a careful approach by specialists. Health facilities rapidly grew to treat various complex ailments, concomitantly incorporating quality standards into their operations. Accreditation by a national health agency became the new benchmark for the standard of care provided by hospitals. Many illnesses that required foreign travel for treatment became available in India, and Indian cities became sought after for medical tourism.

The health ecosystem at present

Urban population in India went up by nearly 100 million in the decade between 2013 and 2023.[2] The population growth was also accompanied by an increase in non-communicable diseases (NCDs), particularly diabetes, cancer, cardiovascular diseases and respiratory illnesses that require early detection and timely treatment. Currently, all major private hospitals have 10–12 centres of excellence with highly qualified and experienced specialist doctors and sophisticated medical equipment for the diagnosis and treatment of various illnesses. Hospitals can no longer treat patients as an amorphous group. Patients are more aware of their rights and have multiple treatment options. Underprivileged sections, under the government insurance schemes, are being treated in private hospitals. Tertiary care, which encompasses coronary bypass surgeries, multi-modal treatment of cancer and paediatric cancers, transplants of liver, heart, kidney, hand, lung and regenerative medicine, is being offered in most of the major hospitals in India at present.

Skilled manpower

Modern hospitals employ highly qualified, young and ambitious staff who have plenty of job opportunities. Corporate hospitals cater to upper-income and middle-income groups. All categories of hospitals – government, charitable or for-profit – will have to be cognisant of the rapidly changing environment.

The idea of treatment is changing and so is healthcare leadership

Treatment no longer begins and ends with hospitalisation. Prevention of complications (e.g., diabetes, cardiac problems), post-discharge nutrition, physiotherapy, rehabilitation, and improvement of the quality of life are essential features of complete care. Medical technology, IT and AI, personalised medicine and biomarkers are revolutionising healthcare.

If there is one single factor responsible for the success or failure of any institution, it is the top leadership. It can be argued that the success or failure of an organisation is attributable to teamwork, and the leadership merely guides them. Lack of proper guidance in such a scenario leads to setbacks at the firm level. In this chapter, we delve into the pivotal role that leadership plays in deciding the success or failure of any organisation.

Types of healthcare facilities in India

In healthcare, four broad streams of hospitals that require different types of leadership can be identified:

- Corporate hospitals
- Non-profit hospitals
- Small hospitals or nursing homes and start-ups
- Government hospitals

The skills needed and the challenges of leadership for each group are completely different. How thousands of healthcare organisations that fall into the above-mentioned categories cope with the pace of change and how leadership plays a role needs to be evaluated. It is essential that leadership understands the patient profile, their affordability and the extent of insurance cover.

Over the last few decades, there appears to be a clear segmentation of patients for different categories of nursing homes, government hospitals and private hospitals. For outpatient visits, the location of the hospital/clinic appears important. For other types of elective treatment, distances, inconvenience or cost do not appear to be limiting factors.

Corporate hospitals

Leadership in corporate hospitals is no longer restricted to medicine; it also involves managing modern technologies, countering competition, raising large funds, utilising sudden inflow of funds, meeting the requirements of private equity, venture capital funds, rewarding investors, all the time providing high-quality patient service. Many corporate hospitals do not have a fund deficit, thanks to private equity funding and initial public offers (IPOs). There have been major changes such as the following:

- Medical technology and information technology (IT) have become a differentiator. WhatsApp has become an effective tool for communication with patients.
- Use of information technology has gone beyond digitisation. Artificial intelligence, data analytics, and AI are routinely employed. Personalised and precision medicine are becoming common.
- Finance and marketing functions have become highly sophisticated.

In a corporate environment, leadership's primary role has now become strategic. Leadership must constantly focus on de-risking their business. They cannot merely depend only on hospital bed income.

Non-profit hospitals

In non-profit hospitals, the leadership's involvement is no longer merely operations-related, but the leadership team must constantly reassess their institution's role in society. Their working models must be critically examined, and their fundamental beliefs must be constantly reassessed.

Government hospitals

Government hospitals cater to the needs of socio-economically weaker sections of the society in India. But the operation efficiency of these hospitals is not up to the mark. There is a need for a new leadership in the government hospitals. Every aspect of the functioning of public health needs to be significantly reformed. The present model and pace are not working either to the benefit of patients or to the system itself.

Nursing homes

Nursing homes/small hospitals are typically facilities that have 20–50 beds, providing primary and secondary care in small towns and also in urban areas, usually doctor-owned and managed. Leadership and day-to-day management are combined in one or a small group of members. Personal medical care by the owners is a special feature of the nursing homes. Decisions on investment, specialisation and obtaining quality accreditations are usually decided based on affordability of each expenditure.

Start-ups

There are an estimated 8,000–10,000 medical start-ups in India, which are registered with the Department for Promotion of Industry and Internal Trade (DPIIT). These startups are promoted and managed by professionals and provide various medical products and services – online provision of medicines and wellness services, nutrition advisory services, innovative diagnostic kits, continuous glucose monitoring devices, online access to gyms, artificial intelligence and many others. Leadership of such start-ups are usually based on the skills of the founders, their entrepreneurial skills, ability to see a business opportunity and perseverance in the face of successive disappointments.

Leadership

What do leaders do?

There has been a constant debate about whether leaders are born or shaped by circumstances. There are many examples to prove both theories – both in the business sector as well as in the healthcare sector. Leadership is largely a personal trait. Some have inherited leadership positions; others are self-made leaders.

Some create new institutions, while some manage an existing institution and develop them further. Self-made leaders may not start with a large capital, but that does not dampen their enthusiasm. In healthcare, many of the leaders are outstanding medical professionals. They are not satisfied merely with a successful professional practice. They have a vision that they extend far beyond their professional achievements. They may face multiple challenges but are not deterred by failures.

Types of leaders

In *How to Lead,*[3] Rubinstein outlines key attributes for a leader, which can be applied across all institutions. The key attributes can be summarised as 'luck, desire to succeed, pursuit of something unique and new, hard work, persistence, ability to keep learning, integrity and responding to crises'. These attributes transcend industries.

Leadership expresses itself in different forms: Visionary leaders, institution builders, crisis managers and status-quo leaders. Later in this chapter, we have illustrated these qualities with a few examples. In every institution, leaders play a role consistent with the lifecycle of that organisation.

A visionary leader explores new paths, displaying a bold entrepreneurial spirit. They could confront successes and failures in their journey but are steadfast in their goal. Where the leaders are also the founders (institution builders), they display a combination of entrepreneurship, courage in the face of adversity and a burning desire to succeed. A status-quo leader does not wish to make many drastic changes and is comfortable with predictable outcomes. Some organisations can benefit from such leadership. Till the 1990s, most organisations in India were functioning in this mode. The operating environment did not encourage innovation.

If an institution has been in business for several years, it calls for a different kind of leadership. A 'manager-leader' may need to stabilise and manage their activities. An institution facing crises needs leadership qualities of a different kind.

In other words, the qualities required of leadership are dependent on the situation, as well as the environment in which the organisation is functioning. In a rapidly changing environment, the need for leadership keeps changing.

No single type of leadership is inherently superior to other types. Adapting to the needs of the organisation and the environment at a given point of time is the hallmark of a good leader.

Leaders from within

It is believed that leaders should always come from within the organisation as they adhere to the traditions of the founders and the organisation's vision and also foster staff loyalty. It is believed that such leaders will also be acceptable to all the staff and represent continuity (a comforting thought to many insiders).

However, this tradition could lead to inbreeding, thereby hindering fresh thinking. While internal leaders might give the impression of continuity and stability, in the context of a rapidly changing environment, such an approach may not be desirable. The Board, while looking for internal talent, should simultaneously begin the search for suitable external candidates. The main aim is to identify key competency gaps in the organisation and find a leader who can fill the gaps. We have heard the argument from the old timers, 'we have not done this in the last thirty years'. This is a self-fulfilling prophecy.

Uniqueness of the healthcare sector

The healthcare industry, as a service-oriented industry, should focus on patients 24/7. Hospitals deal not only with the patients but also with their anxious relatives. Hence, the staff members should be sensitised and ensure they give confidence to patients and their relatives. The profile of the patient depends on the nature of hospital – government hospital, charitable hospital or a large private hospital.

Leadership should emphasise the importance of compassion on the part of the staff who serve every patient and their attendants. When dealing with underprivileged patients, extra caution is needed to ensure that patients are treated with compassion. Such patients do not expect 'creature' comforts but want compassionate care. The kindness and care towards patients apply universally – in government, charitable and corporate hospitals.

The primary challenge to the leadership lies in inspiring the staff to treat patients with care and dignity. Monetary rewards and fear of punishment will motivate staff temporarily. Leaders must set a personal example and encourage all the senior doctors to be compassionate in dealing with colleagues and patients. The author has seen the chairperson doing rounds, talking to patients, chatting with staff members and sitting with them in the dining hall in many hospitals. This should not be a mere cosmetic exercise. On the other hand, there are hospitals where neither the chairperson nor senior management are rarely seen in the hospital premises, except in the boardrooms. Leaders cannot go merely by 'sanitised' presentations by senior management, without a *feel* for ground-level reality.

The government organisation is bound by rules and regulations and often prioritises procedures and audit rules, rather than patients. Despite these constraints, exceptional leaders and some Indian Administrative Service (IAS) officers have proved their leadership qualities and entrepreneurial acumen and a deep understanding of key medical issues. These leaders not only focus on the issues under discussion but also appreciate the larger healthcare picture. However, such leaders are exceptions, with many officers opting for a short stay in the health department, content to bide their time till their next posting.

Leadership in healthcare

A study of leaders in Indian healthcare reflects a wide spectrum of men and women who faced multiple adversities on their path on the way to creating world-class institutions. Some have formed corporate hospitals; some have set up charitable institutions, while a few others have created non-government organisations (NGOs). Most of them are medical professionals whose institutions are built on their medical expertise. All of them have identified unique needs in society and started a healthcare organisation to address them. This is an important requirement for any venture to succeed.

Leaders and institutions in healthcare in India

'Mighty oaks from little acorns grow' goes a proverb. All great medical institutions start from humble beginnings. The founder of the institution may be in the limelight in the first few years. Thereafter, the institution becomes bigger than the founder. Many leaders have made outstanding contributions. According to Dr Nigam, a senior surgeon from New Delhi, 'leadership requires foresight and perseverance'.

Leadership can take different forms depending on the personality of the leader and their professional interest. Some leaders are innovative in their clinical practice, some buy hospitals and expand, some expand their educational programmes, some focus on research and publications, while others diversify into related areas of business. Some leaders do all of the above. The characteristics often align with what Rubinstein described so eloquently in his book.

Vision

The founding members of an institution broadly define the purpose of the institution, and their successors may revise the vision from time to time. Some leaders have a clear idea of their long-term goals, working diligently on their goals. However, in some cases, there may not be any grand strategies at the initial stages.

Dr Prathap C. Reddy formed the first corporate hospital in India – the Apollo Hospitals group – in 1983 in Chennai, which has grown significantly in the last four decades. While the concept of a corporate hospital was unknown in the 1980s, it was a revolutionary idea, and Dr Reddy had to face several challenges, including scepticism about his idea. 'How can you make profit from illness?' was the common question. However, Dr Reddy was able to convince the investors about his business model, and today Apollo has become a global brand. Dr Reddy created a team of doctors, appointed highly qualified professionals to the Board of Directors and pursued his vision relentlessly in the face of several difficulties. Diversifications into retail pharmacies, medical software and health insurance business came much later. He was able to envisage a clear need among the community for high-quality tertiary care across India. Leadership qualities of Dr Reddy included institution building, fund-raising, creating many firsts in medical care and diversification into allied businesses and continuous growth.

Dr K.S. Sanjeevi founded the Voluntary Health Services (VHS) in Chennai in 1958 as a charitable institution. At the outset, he envisioned universal health insurance, where the public would pay a small premium to take health insurance. He set up a chain of private health centres, similar to those of the public health system of the government, where primary and secondary care were provided. He also set up a tertiary centre in Chennai called the Voluntary Health Services (VHS). In addition, Dr Sanjeevi set up a division for conducting scientific research on Ayurvedic and Homeopathic medicines. VHS is now a multi-specialty teaching hospital with 465 beds, catering to the middle and underprivileged sections. Dr Sanjeevi started VHS after retiring from government service with very limited funds. Many of his ideas were revolutionary at that time – health insurance, 'hub-and spoke model', with tertiary care facilities at the main hospital, developing a health record system for follow-up. All these ideas were implemented nearly 75 years ago.

Dr Devi Shetty,[4] an outstanding heart surgeon, founded Narayana Health in 2000 in Bengaluru and has built a nation-wide network of multi-specialty hospitals following strict ethical principles. He has built a corporate hospital with a conscience. His hospital has recently also launched a health insurance company. Dr Devi Shetty is not only a busy heart surgeon, but he is also closely involved in the use of IT in healthcare, has built a large IT team and is also the Chairman of the Board of Governors of the Indian Institute of Management (IIM) Bangalore, emphasising the importance of management in healthcare.

Eminent ophthalmologists – Dr S.S. Badrinath (Sankara Nethralaya), Dr G. Venkataswamy (Aravind Eye hospitals), Dr Gullapalli Rao (L.V. Prasad Eye Institute), Dr Mahipal Sachdeva (Centre for Sight), Dr Sorabji Shroff (Dr. Shroff Charity Eye Hospital) and Dr Harsh Bhattacharjee (Sankardev Eye Hospital, Assam) – have created world-class ophthalmic institutions which cater to all sections of the society. Each of these institutions is unique in its organisational structure, financing of operations and high percentage of the extent of free work. They have been providing high-quality ophthalmic care to thousands of poor patients and have also brought in innovation in their fields. They have contributed to human development by creating thousands of doctors, nurses and other technical staff. They have not been constrained by their modest financial resources in carrying out free/subsidised work. Institutions reflect the personality of the founder/leader, and if the successors carry forward the legacy, without taking into account changing medical practices and the needs of patients. The long-term survival depends on its ability to adapt to external changes.

Dr V. Mohan established Dr. Mohan's Diabetes Speciality Hospitals in 1996 in Chennai, following the footsteps of his father, Dr M. Viswanathan, a diabetes pioneer. He emphasised his leadership style in his interactions with the author: 'to build a team, delegate all routine tasks and monitor based on variations'. He stresses the importance of instilling confidence in the team members, encouraging them to bring only important matters to him. He practices management by exception. His compassionate leadership approach ensures loyalty and key staff are treated with respect, with an emphasis on providing a growth plan. He cites examples of many senior staff members who have grown with the institution over the last three decades. Dr Mohan has the unique distinction of not only being an outstanding clinician but has also extensively published over 1,000 peer-reviewed articles. He also organised an exhibition, 30 years ago, which attracted over 200,000 visitors. Public awareness through exhibitions was a new idea at that time. Dr Mohan's institution has been doing world-class research on genetics. In other words, leadership can take diverse forms depending on specialisation and the vision of different leaders.

Leadership styles

Autocratic leadership

Different leadership styles exist, and there is a school of thought that autocratic leadership is best suited for all sectors, including healthcare. It is believed that the Indian psyche is rooted in a feudal culture and is accustomed to strong leaders. This school believes that leaders should be unpredictable and decisive, demanding implicit obedience. The staff should fear the leader. The proponents of this theory assert that strict discipline and fear among the staff ensure unity of command.

On the other hand, there have been instances of strong leaders leaving behind a string of failures, weakened organisations and no successors. Organisations have disappeared altogether for various other reasons, including poor leadership.

Democratic leadership

There is another school that believes that a more democratic form of leadership is superior since consultation and staff participation strengthen the organisation. In such situations, a more relaxed atmosphere prevails, and employees are motivated to perform well. This leadership style is viewed as more suitable for a service industry like healthcare.

In many organisations, where the leader acts as the 'first among equals', allows staff members to freely express their views in various discussions. In these discussions, a range of opinions emerge.

Resistance to change

One noticeable challenge in many organisations is the resistance to change, whether they are covert or overt. Leaders recognise the necessity of adapting to a rapidly changing environment and the consequences of lagging behind. Some of the senior staff may wish to follow *precedence* and are not ready for any innovative ideas. This not only slows down the progress of the institution, but it demotivates large numbers of youngsters.

Divide and rule

The author has come across many instances where the leader chooses to 'divide and rule' as a strategy for dominance. Such leaders will stage-manage important meetings, where they will obtain the concurrence from a group of senior members to support his or her view, before any meeting, so that opposition is silenced. Such leaders are weak and are unsure of their own position and seek prior support so that they can hold on to their positions. Such weak leadership is harmful to the organisation. Inevitably, the successors tend to be like their predecessors, perpetuating leadership styles.

Sycophancy

A common occurrence is the presence of sycophants at various levels. Some leaders like to surround themselves with unquestioning supporters. Even if the Board or the management consists of people with different views, they usually defer to the leader on major decisions. The danger arises when the leaders perceive themselves as infallible, leading to the harmful 'echo chamber effect'. Sycophants, in the meantime, benefit with their proximity to the leader, but the long-term impact is detrimental to the institution. The health of any organisation is dependent on encouraging dissent and diverse viewpoints, which will contribute to the quality of overall decision-making.

Primacy of organisation

Boards should prioritise the organisation's interest as the primary concern for the future and not give in to the opposition. Even in the face of resistance, the Board must communicate the need for change, sending a strong message by making organisational changes. Board members should have one-on-one discussions with the senior staff and explain the need for change. Unfortunately, most Board members avoid such proactive actions. They prefer a 'soft option' over a 'hard' choice.

The National Accreditation Board for Hospitals (NABH) explicitly assigns responsibility for succession planning to the Board of Trustees. It is essential for the Board to articulate a comprehensive plan, applying cases where gaps exist in the organisation and initiate such changes. This is a customary practice in all industries to have a clear plan for finding future leaders.

Expiry date

Leadership is not a perpetual role, and many leaders are hesitant to find a successor in their lifetime, often choosing to keep control or assume titles such as 'emeritus leaders' but in effect continuing their leadership roles for many more years. However, regardless of their contribution as founders or leaders, there is an 'expiry date' beyond which his/her continuation does not help the institution. Recognising that each institution needs distinctive styles of leadership at various stages of its life cycle, orderly succession should be planned many years in advance. When the succession is orderly, it helps the growth of the institution. The process of succession should start well in advance of the leader stepping down a few years before the leader hands over charge. Developing leadership at the department level is another step in grooming orderly transition throughout the organisation. The Board has a key responsibility in this regard, but unfortunately the board members shy away from this task.

Leadership qualities

Entrepreneurial leadership

Many leaders are entrepreneurs. In the case of private or corporate hospitals, this attribute is a *sine qua non*. These leaders are 'driven' in their quest for excellence, market leadership, creation of shareholder value and technological leadership. They would also have a good understanding, almost a sixth sense, of the patients' needs.

There are leaders from the non-profit sector who are equally entrepreneurial. A leader of a charitable institution made a major investment decision even though many of the staffers were against this investment. Another leader, also from a charitable organisation, decided to commit to a major programme, which needed a substantial expenditure, without consulting the other Board members. Some decisions can prove to be right or wrong.

Mentoring role

Many leaders, particularly in private or corporate hospitals, recall the role of their own seniors, who mentored them into becoming leaders. Mentors normally identify talent, provide opportunities for their mentees, help the mentees directly and indirectly and groom them for future leadership positions. These mentees may be considered as favourites of the boss and could turn to be the envy of their colleagues. If the mentee overtakes someone more senior, it is likely to cause discontent. The mentee will be given opportunities early in his/her career, given job rotations and will experience accelerated growth. Some of the mentees may come out in flying colours, as leaders. Some may not.

Communication

Communication skills are paramount for leaders. Effective communication need not be based solely on oratorical skills or their felicity in writing. Simple, direct, *believable* communication is crucial.

In today's diverse media landscape, including traditional outlets and various social media platforms, leaders employ different communication channels, such as small group sessions, town hall meetings, newsletters and press briefings.

The image of the leader is often synonymous with the organisation itself, and some leaders cultivate a 'larger than life' image. Successors may thus face challenges, requiring time and effort to build credibility and acceptance.

Institution builders

Leadership requires the ability to handle failures and disappointments with equanimity. Some doctors could have easily chosen to be content with their practice, earning money, and enjoying a good reputation. However, they opt to embark on building an institution entailing risks, investing their personal reputation and finances. Establishing an institution involves recruiting senior staff, setting up systems, dealing with architects and builders, obtaining government permissions, importing medical equipment and working with a team of lawyers, bankers, accountants and other co-investors. A medical doctor may not always be equipped to handle these interactions.

At every juncture, setbacks may occur. Bankers may ask for additional collateral, key doctors may not join, there could be land acquisition challenges and other unexpected developments that could jeopardise progress. Financial problems may surface once the hospital is functional. Competing institutions may resort to unethical practices, or there could be legislative changes affecting the new hospital. At every stage, the founders may have self-doubts about the wisdom of having invested time and resources in the venture.

Hard work

A crucial attribute of effective leadership is the willingness to put in long hours, typically 12–14 hours every day of the year, sacrificing holidays and family life for the sake of the institution. Even in the face of disappointments, leaders keep a single-minded focus.

Value systems

The value systems of the leader play a significant role in shaping the institution. Some leaders prioritise quality, patient satisfaction and moral values over monetary aspects. Those leaders insist on ethical practices in every aspect of the institution. It could be in the purchase of equipment, utilisation of funds, dealing with employees, suppliers and honesty in patient billing. Such leaders will not accept even the slightest deviation from these high-value systems. These values percolate to the entire organisation.

Focus percolates

The focus and priorities of the leaders quickly start percolating at various levels of management. For example, in the case of Dr Mohan's hospitals, the importance given to research publications is clearly noticeable. In the case of Narayana Health, Dr Devi Shetty takes a personal interest in using information technology in patient care as well as in constantly upgrading technology. The IT team spoke of several examples of how Dr Shetty used to explain the medical departments' requirements to the technology team. The late Dr V. Shanta, former chairperson of the Cancer Institute, at every meeting, would bring the discussion back to compassion for the underprivileged patients.

Grace under pressure

Leadership is severely tested during crises such as fire, strikes, key resignations and big challenges like the one posed by the COVID-19 pandemic. One of the corporate hospitals had a big fire in which many patients lost their lives. Some Board members were arrested, and the other members had to go through protracted legal challenges. In another hospital, unions went on strike for months, and the hospital had to be closed for several months.

In another hospital, senior doctors resigned *en masse* and this had a major impact on some of the departments. The morale of the entire organisation suffered as a result.

COVID-19 created a huge problem for all hospitals globally. Patient census dropped, staff members fell ill and there was a problem of acute shortage of staff. Many of the charitable hospitals and some corporate hospitals could not pay the salaries of the staff regularly during this period.

Each adversity brings out the best in leadership. A sharp drop in the number of patients and the fall in revenues require prompt action and swift resource mobilisation, which in turn needs strategising through consultations with some senior staff and select Board members. The leadership should ensure that there is no despondency among the staff, and decisions should be communicated quickly. Leadership should always communicate to the staff a sense of confidence in their ability to handle every crisis.

How to develop leaders

Performance appraisal systems offer insights into the strengths and weaknesses of an individual. Performance trends over a period provide valuable data. Some organisations implement a system of job rotation for promising leaders, sponsor them for external training programmes and put in place feedback mechanisms, all of which contribute to leadership development. Progressively, the senior management should transfer the individual to important segments of the organisation so that they can perform independently.

What makes a successful leader?

There is no ready-made formula. A good leader should be an attentive listener. They should focus on the larger picture, while delegating routine responsibilities to other members, who may be more competent for those tasks. Even in the face of failure, the leader should not be despondent. The leader should always be looking out for opportunities to expand, building new partnerships and seeking the recruitment of new talent. A good leader should be forgiving and should not be vindictive.

A CEO shared with the author, 'I will hire someone smarter than me if it will help my company.' A skilled leader builds consensus, even if there are conflicting viewpoints among the team members. The leader should always put the interest of the institution before their personal preferences. In matters of ethics, he/she should never compromise. Similarly, a good leader understands that short-term advantage is transient. The leader should always opt for the longer-term benefit.

In the book *In Search of Excellence*, the authors Tom J. Peters and Robert H. Waterman Jr state: 'A good leader is one who has created more leaders in his/her lifetime rather than many admiring followers.' A good leader should have the willingness to walk away from his/her own creation happily.

The legendary leaders

India has been fortunate to have many legends in diverse fields of healthcare. The author presents case studies of three leaders, with whom the author had the privilege of working with: Dr V. Shanta of the Cancer Institute (WIA), Dr S.S. Badrinath of Sankara Nethralaya and Dr Sai Lakshmi Balijepally, founder of Ekam Foundation, who have left a legacy in healthcare. Another influential leader is Keshav Desiraju, former Union Health Secretary, Government of India, who set an outstanding example of leadership in government with his remarkable foresight, vision and honesty. Mr Desiraju was an outstanding bureaucrat, led many initiatives such as legislation for tobacco control, palliative care, legislation for disability and mental health. The author knew Mr Desiraju personally. He was a man of integrity, spoke his mind and was very clear about the importance of government hospitals. But unfortunately, he passed away young.[5]

Two are institution builders, the other has founded an NGO and the fourth was from the government.

Dr S.S. Badrinath, Sankara Nethralaya, Chennai

Dr Badrinath was an epitome of what Jim Collins calls servant leadership in his book *Good to Great*.[6] Servant leaders simply put the institution above self.

Some leaders leave an impression, even on strangers. The then Chairperson of a large charitable hospital, Dr S.S. Badrinath, was one. The author had an opportunity for several personal interactions with him. He was easy to get along with, warm and full of wit and wisdom with no airs whatsoever. As a young surgeon, after completing his post-graduation in the United States, he decided to return to India to serve the underprivileged section of the country. He started practice and wanting to do much more, set up a charitable hospital, Sankara Nethralaya, in 1978.

Despite limited opportunities and rigid government regulations in the 1970s, the young surgeon brought together a group of like-minded doctors to start a modest ophthalmic hospital, which soon grew to become a landmark destination for eye care in the country. In the year 2023–24, the hospital chain handled 1.1 million outpatients and carried out 60,000 surgeries, which included 30 percent free surgeries. In addition, the hospitals trained Diplomate National Board (DNB) graduates, provided continuous medical programmes to practising ophthalmologists, trained optometrists, offered mobile clinic services and tele-ophthalmology services.

Many of the alumni have set up similar hospitals in various parts of the country. Extensive work on both fundamental and translational research is being carried out. Dr Badrinath's humility, teamwork, unobstructed vision, entrepreneurship and ethics have shaped the success of this institution. He sought the help of NGOs in bringing underprivileged patients to the hospital.

He ensured that the hospital kept the highest quality standards in outcomes. He would address even junior staffers by their name.

This doctor never seemed depressed by failures. At the same time, he would never take any credit for many of his accomplishments. 'It is my team which did the work', he would insist. He was a workaholic. A true Gandhian, he took only a modest salary and very often would return a part of even this to the hospital. Dr Badrinath passed away in 2023. Dr Badrinath was not only an outstanding ophthalmologist but a great institution builder. Sankara Nethralaya is now world-renowned for the high quality of work, teaching programmes in ophthalmology, optometry, allied sciences, charity work and screening programmes. As a person, he was humble, approachable and encouraged research. The author interacted with this legend on many occasions and always admired the leadership qualities of this brilliant ophthalmologist.

Dr Sailakshmi Baljepally, Ekam Foundation[7]

Dr. Sailakshmi Baljepally, a qualified paediatrician, is an unusual medical practitioner. She observed, 'Working in government hospitals, it was depressing to see children suffering for lack of simple medicines or consumable items. In the private hospital, it was heart-rending to observe children being turned away, because the parents could not afford the cost of the treatment.' So, driven by a burning desire to bring about a change, she set up an NGO, Ekam (meaning oneness) in 2009. She decided to adopt a four-pronged approach.

- Focus on mothers and children from underprivileged sections of society, particularly those being treated at government hospitals.
- Train government hospital nurses in paediatric nursing, including neonatal care.
- Aid state government hospitals by repair and maintenance of all medical equipment and dramatically increasing their uptime.
- Provide financial aid to parents whose children require treatment in private hospitals by raising funds. Dr Sailakshmi also raised funds from well-wishers to fund such activities.

The first pilot projects with a government hospital proved successful. Uptime of medical equipment went up from a low of 20 per cent to a high of 90 per cent within a year. Several thousand nurses were hired with Ekam's help. The trained nurses were able to handle complex cases thanks to Ekam's training. The state government, which asked for pilot projects on a trial basis, decided to take help from Ekam for the entire state.

In this short span of 15 years, Ekam helped over a million mothers and children in eight states. Some of the work involved working in Naxalite areas. Ekam has also worked on sustainable development work, organising screening camps to ascertain the medical problems of children.

Dr Sailakshmi sought help from other paediatricians, gynaecologists, management experts, social workers and public health specialists to create this unique NGO, staying in the background and handling successes and failures with equanimity.

Dr Sailakshmi embodies the dictum of 'selfless service' in her personal life as well. Her selflessness came through in a radiant smile whenever a child was saved, thanks to Ekam's intervention. She expertly navigated the challenge of working with the state government's bureaucracy. Despite facing delays by some governments in clearing Ekam's bills, Dr Sailakshmi never gave up hope and was vindicated in the end. Besides working with government hospitals, Ekam also networked with various private hospitals, securing concessional treatment for underprivileged children. Dr Sailakshmi persuaded her doctor friends working in the United States to donate to Ekam. At present, Ekam-US excels in mobilising volunteer support and provides financial support for various projects in different states in India. Dr Sailakshmi was a reluctant leader. Her great joy was saving one more child from disease. Honours meant very little. Dr Sailakshmi passed away in January 2024 at a young age of 49.

Dr V. Shanta, The Cancer Institute (WIA), Chennai[8]

Dr V. Shanta is renowned for putting cancer care on the map of South India. She was the Director of the Cancer Institute, Chennai, and later became its chairperson. She worked tirelessly for seven decades. She lived in a modest facility within the hospital itself.

Dr Shanta worked with two visionaries, Dr Muthulakshmi Reddy, who founded the Institute, and Dr S. Krishnamurthi, the former's son who led the Institute after Dr Reddy's demise. In 2022, the hospital had a 500-bed facility in two locations in Chennai, treating poor patients – adults and children. The focus areas of this institute are:

- Providing modern multimodal cancer care
- Offering the highest level of medical education programmes (M.Ch., DM, MD in Radiology) free of cost with no capitation fees
- Undertaking basic and translational research
- Creating awareness that 'cancer is curable' among the population, organising screening programmes and campaigns on tobacco cessation

The author had the privilege of working with Dr Shanta as a member of the governing body of the Institute. Dr Shanta's commitment to the management process was clear as she would consistently be the first to arrive at meetings, always well prepared, taking notes and following up with the other staff afterwards.

She was equally adept at communicating with a poor patient from a village or with the Prime Minister of India. She displayed compassion for the patients, particularly towards paediatric patients. Dr Shanta ensured that all patients, including patients who were provided treatment free of cost, were provided excellent nutrition at the hospital, particularly children, offering interesting food that they would relish. 'Spare no expense', she would say.

She encouraged NGOs to set up boarding facilities near the hospital for parents during follow-up visits. During the COVID crisis, when the hospital needed funds, she made a public appeal for donations, which was met with an overwhelming response. Her credibility was high, and citizens felt that they had a duty to help the institution. She also ensured that all the staff were paid their full salary during this period.

Dr Shanta worked with the Government of Tamil Nadu and contributed significantly to setting up a cancer registry for the entire state of Tamil Nadu in collaboration with the government. The hospital data could be used for policymaking. The Institute has conducted screening camps with mobile vans donated by sponsors.

She was a great teacher, an institution builder and a visionary. The Government of India, recognising her contribution to cancer care, awarded her the second highest civilian award, Padma Vibhushan, in 2016.

According to Dr V. Varalakshmi, a senior staffer at Cancer Institute, 'Dr. Shanta believed that the doctor–patient relationship is a sacred one. The doctor should approach the patient as a human being, not as a case'. She added, 'Dr Shanta practised what she believed and lived these beliefs all her life – hard work, discipline, treating patients and service to humanity as obligations to society.' She ensured that the highest standards of ethics were followed in her Institution. She passed away in 2022, at the age of 95, leaving behind an enduring legacy.

Common factors

Are there common characteristics among the leaders described above?

The above exemplify leaders from charitable organisations who have painstakingly built their institutions, brick by brick. While acknowledging that three instances may be too few for meaningful generalisation, these leaders embody the finest attributes of leadership.

The first common factor is the simplicity in their personal lives, as well as frugality practised in managing their organisations. Acquiring wealth seems to have been inconsequential. The institution was an extension of their personal value system.

The second common factor is that all three legendary leaders were strategic thinkers, at the same time, deeply involved in routine matters. Many conventional management theories would preach that leaders should delegate. These leaders balanced strategic vision with hands-on involvement in day-to-day operations.

The third factor centres around compassion for the poor. A shared desire to alleviate the sufferings of the poor in practical terms reflected in all the hospital operations. Honours seemed to sit very lightly on their shoulders.

Future leaders

Inspired by Mahatma Gandhi, leaders of the past often reflected the values of simplicity and selflessness. However, in contemporary times, the influence of the Mahatma has diminished, and societal values have undergone fundamental changes in the last five decades. Thus, the future healthcare leaders are likely to have different value systems both in their personal lives and for their institutions.

This book underscores the importance of effective leadership across all healthcare segments, including public health, charitable health and others like NGOs, medical devices, pharmaceuticals and health insurance. The new generation of leaders, particularly the millennials, often appear drawn to material accomplishments, prioritising luxury goods and financial rewards.

The shifting paradigm is undeniable. It is interesting to note that a small number of young professionals are also choosing paths aligned to more meaningful values. Some opt for organic farming; others move to teach in villages and some doctors dedicate their Sundays to organising health camps. Their silent but significant contributions to society deserve wider recognition in traditional and social media.

The success of corporate hospitals proves the crucial need for high-quality tertiary care. This sector has attracted substantial funds from the public and private equity funds, highlighting that hospitals can be profitable under the guidance of their leaders.

APPENDIX

Private healthcare facilities in India

To showcase the robustness of the private sector healthcare in India, a few of the corporate or private hospitals, founded in the last 25 years or so, are listed here. All of them started modestly and expanded over a few years, from one city to multiple cities. All of them offer educational programmes – Diplomate of National Board (DNB), nursing, allied sciences and other specialities in medicine.

Many have created multiple- speciality hospitals with centres of excellence within each hospital. Quality accreditations – national and international – have ensured the maintenance of consistent quality across locations. Some of them have provided free care, organised screening camps and have provided treatment for underprivileged citizens. Specialists in a certain area might start a hospital in their field of expertise, and over a period of time, would have diversified into other departments to offer multi-specialty hospital facilities to the patients. A few have remained as a single-specialty hospital. The examples are drawn from both charitable and for-profit hospitals.

Sir Gangaram Hospital, New Delhi

New Delhi has several healthcare institutions. Sir Gangaram Hospitals, an 80-year-old institution, is a tertiary care hospital with 575 beds, having 47 specialties and running 100 specialty clinics. Out of the available beds, 20 percent of the beds are free beds. It trains doctors and conducts DNB courses in 42 specialties and super specialties, in addition to running a nursing school, carrying out research and publishing peer-reviewed papers.

https://sgrh.com/

Medanta Group of Hospitals

Medanta Group of Hospitals was founded by an eminent surgeon, Dr Naresh Trehan, in the year 2009. In a brief period, this group has set up another four hospitals in North India with a total bed strength of 3,300 beds. It has created centres of excellence in six major disciplines, including cardiology, oncology and neurosciences.

Dr. Lalpath Labs

Dr Lalpath Labs, founded in the year 1949, has grown rapidly over the last eight decades. It now has a domestic network of 280 labs, pan-India operations, 36 National Accreditation Board for Testing and Calibration Laboratories (NABL)-accredited labs. They provided service to 28 million patients in the year 2023–24, generating a revenue of INR 2,300 crore and a profit after tax of INR 362 crore. Its rapid growth, focus on quality, profitability and technology upgradation have been the hallmarks of the institution.

https://www.lalpathlabs.com/

P.D. Hinduja Hospitals

P.D. Hinduja Hospitals, Mumbai, founded in the year 1951, has 520 beds providing tertiary care. It aids needy patients, and the Hinduja family donates to the hospital. The hospital offers DNB courses in 26 specialties, has a college of nursing and offers several allied courses. It has 12 mobile units, which provide medical aid to tribal districts in Maharashtra. It has several national and international teaching and research affiliations.

https://www.hindujahospital.com/

Max Healthcare

Max Healthcare is a New Delhi-headquartered corporate hospital chain with operations in six states with 20 facilities, 4,300 beds and 27,000 employees. It also has a home-care business and laboratories under its brand name. Mr Abhay Soi is the Chairman and Managing Director of this hospital.

https://www.maxhealthcare.in/

Shalby Hospitals

This hospital was founded in 1994 in Ahmedabad by Dr Vikram Shah and has now expanded to 10 multi-specialty hospitals with a bed strength of over 2000. The growth has been organic as well as through acquisitions.

https://www.shalby.org/

Asian Institute of Gastroenterology, Hyderabad (AIG)

AIG is a private limited company founded 25 years ago. It is rated as one of the top 17 hospitals in this field, with an 800-bed strength providing care for gastro, liver, cardiac, transplant and other related services. It runs a DNB course in medical and surgical gastroenterology and PhD programmes. It runs a mobile unit in Andhra Pradesh to perform investigations at the doorstep of poor patients.

Apollo Hospitals group, Chennai

Apollo Hospitals, the first corporate hospital in India, established in 1983 in Chennai, is the largest network with over 10,000 beds. The group runs 73 hospitals, 700 clinics, 2,300 diagnostic centres, and 6,000 pharmacies. It covers 23 clinical areas of excellence. It offers DNB courses in 13 locations in India for 525 seats and, in addition, it also offers nursing, paramedical and management courses.

Narayana Health (NH), Bengaluru

NH, which was founded in the year 2000, has at present 23 hospitals and seven heart centres, pharmacies and diagnostic centres. It has 30 centres of excellence and has one of the most advanced IT systems. Recently, it has diversified into health insurance.

Conclusion

Leadership in the coming decades is likely to be different, requiring multiple skills. In addition to competencies of the past, other new demands would be imposed by the environment. Medical technology, information technology,

AI, new drugs, new medical protocols, nutrition research and investor expectations are likely to dominate healthcare. Leadership will have to ensure the focus of the institution is always on the human angle – the patient.

Notes

1 'As told to Parliament (August 9, 2024): Government health expenditure stood at 1.9 per cent of GDP in 2023–24', *DownToEarth*, 12 August 2024, https://www.downtoearth.org.in/governance/as-told-to-parliament-august-9-2024-government-health-expenditure-stood-at-19-of-gdp-in-2023-24
2 'India Urban population 1960–2024', https://www.macrotrends.net/global-metrics/countries/IND/india/urban-population
3 David M. Rubinstein, *How to Lead*, Simon & Schuster, 2020.
4 Dr Devi Prasad Shetty, 'India Cardiac Society', https://www.narayanahealth.org/c/bangalore/cardiac-surgery-adult/dr-devi-prasad-shetty
5 'Remembering Keshav Desiraju', https://cmhlp.org/remembering-keshav-desiraju-1955-2021/
6 Jim Collins, *Good to Great: Why Some Companies Make the Leap...and Others Don't*, Harper Business, 2001.
7 Ekam Foundation, undated, https://ekam.ngo/
8 Adyar Cancer Institute, Chennai, 2023, https://cancerinstitutewia.in/

7 Management science in healthcare

Tilak Shankar

Introduction

Management science is an interdisciplinary field that can be used to solve complex business problems and improve decision-making using scientific methods. For hospital operations, management science becomes an indispensable tool to manage patient care and ensure efficiency in operations. Quantitative methods, drawn from operations research, statistical analysis and simulation theories, are applied depending upon the problem to be solved. These methods find applications both at macro level, i.e., at a state or at a national level, as well as at micro levels, i.e., a single hospital. At the macro level, many national programmes, such as the Pulse Polio Campaign, follow-up of tuberculosis patients through Directly Observed Therapy Short-Courses (DOTS) or vaccination of pregnant women and newborns, require large resources, coordination among various departments and involve a large number of patients. These programmes require extensive planning and coordination of a large number of activities. For example, the polio campaign requires procurement of polio drops in large numbers, figuring out logistics from the place of manufacture to the districts where they are needed, the number of nurses, availability of consumables, availability of cold storage facilities and mobilising beneficiaries. In other words, it requires detailed planning to make the whole operation cost-effective. The pulse polio campaign covers 735 districts in India, providing polio drops to 15 crore children. This programme is conducted once a year, involving thousands of beneficiaries, a large number of government staff and volunteers on a single day.[1] Likewise, DOTS programme is expected to cover 24 lakh TB patients.[2]

All national programmes require coordination of hundreds of staff members across states and need to be conducted efficiently with tight cost control. Management techniques prove useful for the conduct of these very large programmes with IT support, data analytics and AI.

Problems requiring the application of optimisation techniques

Cost control

One of the management challenges is to minimise transportation costs and avoid wastages. Nation-wide Pulse Polio Campaign is a good example, where

DOI: 10.4324/9781003684947-9

resources are required to mobilise a large number of children, planning for polio drops, transportation and the number of nurses required require efficient planning and execution. Management techniques can help achieve this goal in an efficient manner. The nation-wide COVID-19 vaccination programme, to combat the spread of COVID-19, required administering around one billion doses of the vaccine throughout the country, at various rural and urban health centres and private hospitals. The vaccine, manufactured at two locations in India, had to be distributed to the centres across the country for administration to the public. The vaccines had to be transported by air, road and other modes to thousands of cold storage facilities. Similarly, the availability of medical oxygen during the COVID-19 pandemic was in short supply, and the available resources had to be efficiently distributed across the country. Here again, the supply points were few (apart from own oxygen generation by hospitals), and the requirement depended on the patients who needed oxygen at various hospitals in the country.

A linear programming (LP) model run on a real-time computer system could have played a significant role in optimising supply points and meeting the demands from multiple locations in the country. The non-availability of oxygen led to health crises and loss of lives, which could have been avoided.

Pharmacy procurement

Many states have a centralised pharmacy procurement and distribution system with a vast array of pharmaceutical items and consumables to be procured, stored and distributed to thousands of medical colleges and hospitals, district hospitals and primary health centres. A real-time computer-based LP model can ensure the availability of medicines throughout the public health system.

Quantitative techniques

The classification of quantitative techniques is presented in Figure 7.1.

Management science offers many practical quantitative techniques to address many operational issues of all categories of hospitals. These techniques can be classified into three streams: (i) Mathematical, (ii) Statistical and (iii) Programming. The programming techniques are discussed in this chapter. Programming techniques have been used very effectively in many hospitals. They are also an essential quality improvement tool.

The healthcare industry presents numerous problem areas where quantitative mathematical models can be readily applied. Each interaction of the patient with the hospital requires coordinated efforts of doctors, utilisation of modern testing and treatment procedures, availability of medicines and consumables, hospital space, beds and nursing stations. Large hospital systems offer significant opportunities for applying quantitative models due to the abundance of data. Even small hospitals have data requiring the use of

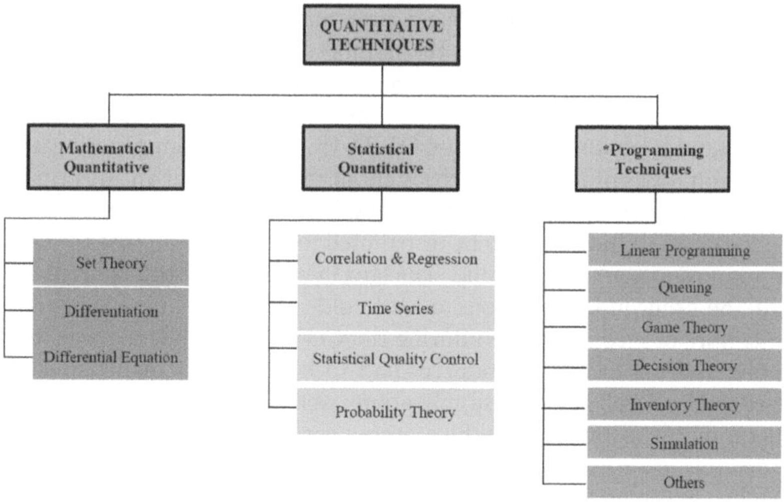

Figure 7.1 Classification of quantitative techniques.

Source: Prof. Reyazuddin (2020). Classification of quantitative technique, lecture notes of quantitative techniques, docsity, https://www.docsity.com/en/docs/classification-of-quantitative-technique/8795459/

mathematical models, but their data sets are simpler and less complex equations would be needed. Outputs from mathematical models need to be moderated by carefully considering the model, which will solve a real-life hospital need.

The application of management theories in general, particularly quantitative applications, require an intuitive understanding of the environment. For example, patients from rural areas may not be familiar with the registration processes or automated systems. Patients coming from distant locations might reach the hospitals early in the day, prepared to spend the entire day waiting for treatment. Patients at corporate hospitals do not wish to wait for an extended period. In other words, any queuing model needs to be tailored to the patient's behaviour.

Queuing theory

This technique focuses on reducing patient waiting time. Patients may wait at multiple counters, for example, in as many as 10 or 12 counters, during a single visit, for example, at the registration counter, laboratory, doctor consultation, payment counters and pharmacy. Queuing theory provides a practical solution.

Basic model of queuing theory

Any queuing study requires the collection of past data such as the arrival pattern of patients at various times of the day, new and review patients, number of doctors and their arrival pattern, number of doctor consultation cubicles/rooms, number of registration counters, number of imaging facilities and so on. Where the study requires more recent data, it has to be collected. The data can reveal the difficulties that outpatients experience during each visit. Based on the data, queuing theory can be applied to find potential solutions and the cost of any major change. The main objective is to minimise the waiting time of the patient and change the systems to be patient-centric. The study may reveal the need for changing doctors' time and number of doctors at various times of the day, automating/simplifying procedures, increasing the number of pharmacies and introducing signages and minimising distance between locations. In other words, the objective is to align the hospital systems based on patient inflow. In reality, the hospital's convenience appears to be a predominant factor.

Queuing studies

Queues can take the form of a physical line or token numbers, files or applications. Therefore, any group of people, documents or applications arranged in order of their arrival or receipt, helping in an orderly service using the first-come-first-served rules is a 'queue'. The rate of arrival and how quickly they get serviced are the two determinants of a queue. Queuing models are also commonly referred to as waiting line models.

Typical queuing applications

The queuing pattern differs significantly between government hospitals and private/corporate hospitals. The government hospital, for example, a teaching hospital in a city, could have 10,000–12,000 outpatients in a day for its 30–40 clinical departments. Appointment systems are not effective in government hospitals due to a variety of reasons. New patients must register with the necessary documentation. Review patients would wait directly at the concerned departments. Absence of signages and distant location or departments/facilities, frequent delays in labs, repair of imaging equipment and absence of medicines in the pharmacy further add to the waiting times. Patients and their attenders may spend the entire day at the hospital to be examined by the doctor for a few minutes. Senior doctors may arrive late for the outpatient consultation. Without fundamental changes, the current situation is unlikely to improve significantly.

Large corporate hospitals

In a multi-specialty corporate hospital, an appointment system is normally used for patient appointments. This appointment system works with other measures to synchronise the number of patients with doctors, nurses, ensuring high uptime of all equipment and distributing patients to multiple clinics or within the main hospital itself.

Payment systems, over the years, have also been streamlined at different counters. In spite of such systems in private hospitals, there can be queue build-ups. Doctors may suddenly leave outpatient area to attend to emergencies. The queuing system has to factor in all the possibilities.

Terms used in queuing theory

The main terms used in queuing include the following.

- *Arrival rate*: Patients, documents, or applications arrive randomly, independent of each another. The arrival pattern is often modelled by a Poisson distribution, that is, how they arrive: For example, within an hour, there would be no arrivals for long minutes, many arrivals in the next minute and so on. The mean arrival rate is called the arrival rate.
- *Service rate*: The time it takes to attend to each patient and document in the service centre determines the service rate of a queue. Service times vary at different counters, that is, registration counter, doctor consultation and payments counter are typically assumed to follow an exponential probability distribution.
- *Queue discipline*: In most circumstances, waiting lines are prioritised on a 'first-come-first-served' (FCFS) discipline. However, other disciplines or priorities also exist, such as emergency admissions or senior citizens.

There is a need to constantly review all the processes and simplify/automate the workflow.

- *Steady state versus transient state*: The queuing system is said to be in a transient mode, becoming stable only when the arrival rates and service rates become steady or achieve normal levels. Here also, they follow Poisson and exponential probability distribution, respectively.

Single channel or multiple channels

The manner in which customers/patients get served at a service point, depending on the number of incoming customers and the ability to serve them within an acceptable span of time is important. In many hospitals, the number of

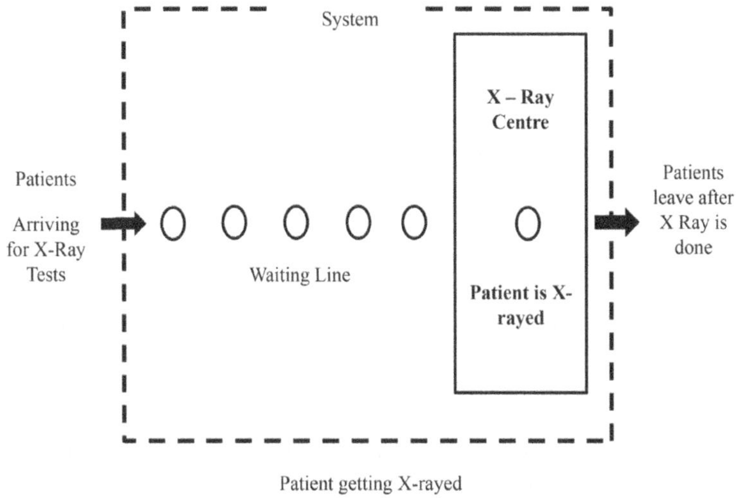

Figure 7.2 Single-channel waiting line.

appropriate specialists is a limiting factor. Arriving patients wait in a single line and may be processed through one service channel or by multiple channels, as shown in Figures 7.2 and 7.3.

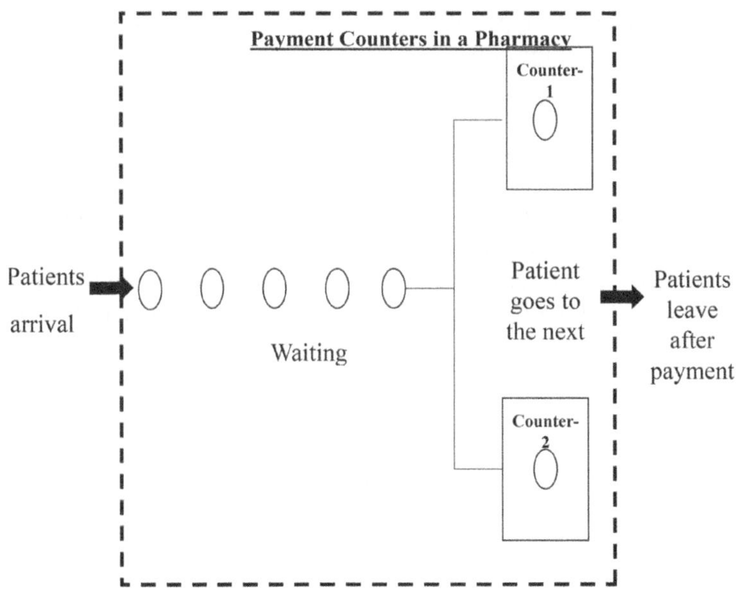

Figure 7.3 Multiple/two-channel waiting line.

Performance characteristics

Queue performance can be assessed through various parameters, providing insights into the efficiency and effectiveness of the system.

- The average number of patients waiting in the line: This includes the average number in the queue plus the average number being served.
- The average time a patient spends in the system: This includes the average waiting time plus the average service time.

Additionally, there are other crucial performance factors like the probability of zero patients waiting for service (P_0), or the probability of someone arriving who must wait for service (P_w) and the probability of x number of units already in the system (P_x).

Collectively, these performance factors guide hospital administrators in deciding the number of service points, single or multiple channels and how to speed up service. If the average waiting time is long, the average number of patients is high or if the number of patients waiting is high, the healthcare system should reduce queue lengths or service time or increase the number of channels.

Performance factors

In Table 7.1, ready-made formulae are provided for calculating performance parameters for various types of queues, offering a practical tool without delving into mathematical proofs.

Notes

1. In multiple-channel models, the arrival rate is applicable to the system, while the service rate is applicable to each channel. The number of channels (k) has to be considered.
2. Probability of zero patients is pre-calculated and can readily be obtained from a table for different numbers of channels. These values serve as valuable references.
3. *How to improve waiting line operations:*

After determining the values of queue performance factors, the hospital administrator must work on the following:

- *Reducing average waiting time*: Minimising the waiting times as close to zero as possible is the primary objective.

Table 7.1 Performance parameters of a queue

SI. No.	*Parameters*	*Single channel*	*Multiple channel*
1	The arrival rate (mean of arrivals per unit time)	λ	λ (for the system)
2	The service rate (mean of number of services per unit time)	N	N (for each channel)
3	Number of channels	1	K
4	The probability that no units are in the system (P_0)	$1 - \lambda/N$	$\dfrac{1}{\sum_{n=0}^{k-1}\frac{\left(\frac{\lambda}{N}\right)^n}{n!}+\frac{\left(\frac{\lambda}{N}\right)^n}{k!}\left(\frac{KN}{KN-\lambda}\right)}$
5	The average number of units in the queue (L_q)	λ^2 $N(N - \lambda)$	$(\lambda/N)k\lambda N \times P_0$ $(k-1)!(KN-\lambda)^2$
6	The average number of units in the system (L)	$L_q + \lambda/N$	$L_q + \lambda/N$
7	The average time a unit spends in the queue (W_q)	L_q/λ	L_q/λ
8	The average time a unit spends in the system	$W_q + 1/N$	$W_q + 1/N$
9	The probability that an arriving unit has to wait for service (P_w)	λ/N	$1/K!\left(\frac{\lambda}{N}\right)k\left(\frac{KN}{KN-\text{»}}\right)P_0$
10	The probability of 'N' units in the system (P_n)	$(\lambda/N)n \times P_0$	$(\lambda/N)n \times P_0/N!$ for $n \leq k$ $(\lambda/N)n/K!-K(n-K)/N! \times P_0$ for $n \geq k$

Reducing average service times or improve service rates by

- Increasing the number of service channels or counters
- Automating the process
- Encouraging patients to use the internet to provide details even before arriving at the hospital
- Utilising the waiting time of the patients for educational purposes such as screening video programmes on the importance of hygiene, symptoms of different ailments and nutritional advice. While patients wait in these areas, a social worker can collect data about the patients for statistical purposes.
- *Communication on waiting times*: Mobile phones can be effectively used for communicating waiting times to patients, or some hospitals may use a public address system.

Cost–benefit analysis

Even though the hospital administrator would plan to minimise the waiting times, they have to balance it with the cost of employing more doctors (if available) and additional support staff. Broadly speaking, the economics of a queue can be described as:

Total cost = Waiting cost + Cost of service

where

Waiting cost per period = Waiting cost per patient × number of patients in the system

and

Cost of service = Cost of service per time period for each channel multiplied by the number of channels (Figure 7.4).

All hospitals should make use of data available about the number of patients arriving at the hospital at different times of the day, different days

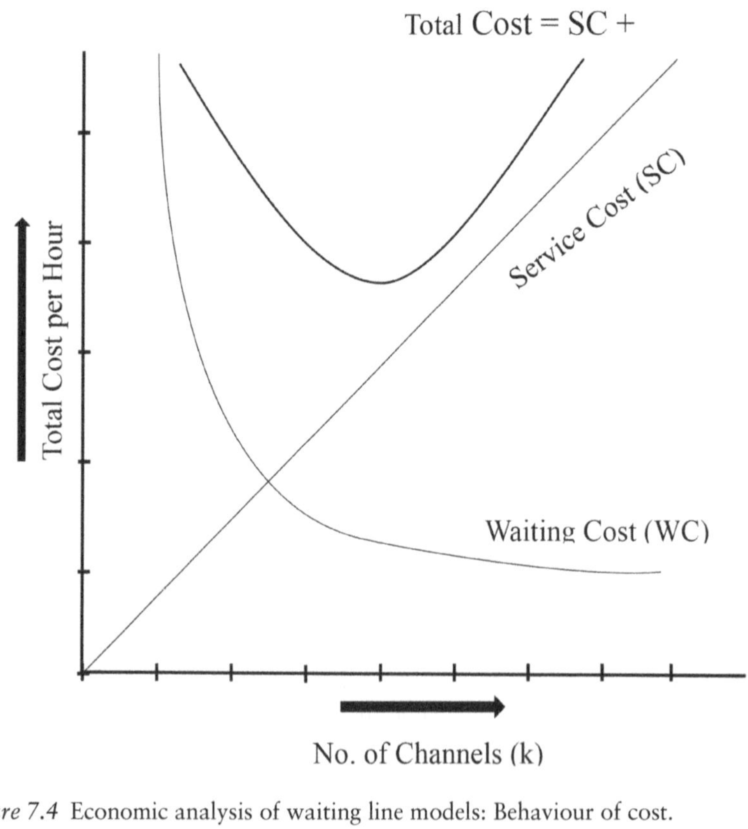

Figure 7.4 Economic analysis of waiting line models: Behaviour of cost.

of the week, the number of pharmacy prescriptions, the number of lab tests and so on. The hospital should also change the staff's shift timings to suit the arrival pattern of the patients.

Social factors

For the management of queues in Indian hospitals, the characteristics of patients have to be considered. Some of them discussed below:

Patient behaviour

- Patients may arrive in the early hours of the day, resulting in long waiting times. If they are from outstation locations, their arrivals could be bunched up with the morning train/flight timings. Hence, queues build up.
- Many rural patients in government and non-profit hospitals are either illiterate or do not know the local language, resulting in confusion about the exact location of the needed facility and doctors' names for their treatment; this results in patients wandering around in the hospital corridors.
- Many patients wait because they are unsure of their turn. So, when they go for a bio-break or for a cup of coffee, they may end up missing their turn. This results in loud announcements on the public address system or the doctors' assistants shouting the patient's name, making for a noisy environment.
- There could be a sharp increase or decrease in the number of outpatients, depending on the day of the week. For example, some patients do not prefer appointments on a particular day of the week or certain time of the day. On festival days, there may be fewer patients.

Hospital processes

In numerous hospitals, particularly government hospitals, there are inherent challenges such as extensive paperwork, overcrowding, shortage of doctors and poor working conditions of medical equipment. In these settings, the waiting time is neither measured nor given much importance.

Infrastructure planning in hospitals

In some hospitals or departments, inadequate facilities add to the discomfiture of patients. Challenges such as equipment down-time, shortage of attenders and inadequate number of doctors further exacerbate the problem. Lack of clear signages exacerbates the waiting problem. The payment counters may be far away from service areas such as laboratories or diagnostic centres. In addition, long distances between various medical departments also result in delays.

Simplification of long waiting times should also take into account various infrastructure-related factors. For example, waiting areas in some large hospitals are often ill-equipped to handle the peak load of patients, resulting in patients and attendants having to sit on the floor, in corridors and near public areas and even wait outdoors. Inadequate male and female toilets required for the projected number of patients and their relatives are a common issue. Organisation and method studies (O&M studies) can systematically eliminate repetitive paper and procedures in various OP areas. Modern technology, including kiosks and mobile phones, offers simple solutions. In this context, the Government of India's initiative to seamlessly connect all government and private hospitals for sharing medical records should potentially mitigate the waiting problems.

Top management should prioritise cutting down patients' waiting time by undertaking studies on patients' behaviour, hospital processes, the number of doctors and both medical and patient convenience-related factors. A seamless flow of patient health information is essential, ensuring compassionate treatment regardless of their economic status.

Queuing theory extends beyond textbooks. Both the patient and the management should not resign to waiting as an inevitable fact. The responsibility lies clearly on the management to measure the waiting times and to monitor improvements adhering to the standards set under National Accreditation Board for Hospitals and Healthcare Providers (NABH).

Capacity planning

There are a wide range of operations research tools, including proprietary software, that can be employed for scientific methods of planning for the capacity of the hospital.[3]

Resources like doctors, nurses and paramedical attendants, facilities like operation theatres and testing facilities have a finite capacity. Medical equipment are obtained based on the estimation of the number of patients. Mathematical models estimate the number of patients, procedures and service times, preventing the creation of unnecessary excess capacity or poor utilisation of available facilities. It is possible that the number of patients could be higher or lower.

Hospital inventory management models

Inventory control models refer to stocking and reordering policies of all hospital supplies, medicines and surgical consumables. Mathematical models can help in scientific determination of consumption, delivery lead times and stock-outs.

Inventory management, often considered a 'back office' function, holds importance for every hospital. Materials used in a large hospital can be categorised under two broad main groups:

- Capital items such as medical equipment, non-medical equipment and a variety of infrastructure-related items.
- Revenue items such as drugs and medicines, consumables, spares and housekeeping items.

Within a hospital's operating costs, material consumption ranks as the second most important expense item after salaries. Effective management of inventory requires the deployment of a senior qualified specialist to head this function. Given the numerous commercial aspects influencing material costs, relying on medical professionals is not practical.

Procurement and inventory management includes:

- Technical description of items to be procured, encompassing chemical composition of drugs, dosages, generic and branded items, spare parts and mechanical items.
- Commercial aspects involving the selection of suppliers, price negotiation, terms of payment, advances to be paid, order quantities and safety stocks.

The entire material management function holds a crucial place in the overall management of a hospital.

Inventory control

Running a large general hospital is akin to managing a manufacturing enterprise or a network of retail outlets for consumer products. In the context of healthcare, service providers must stock broad groups including:

- Medical and pharmaceutical supplies for direct departments
- Surgical items, orthopaedic, cardiac and other implants and consumables used during patient treatments
- Maintenance spares for various equipment
- Housekeeping consumables
- Hospital stationery or other office items

A good healthcare facility should provide distinct stores for pharma, surgical items stores and housekeeping stores.

Classification of inventory

Management of inventory involves dealing with a number of unique items and the sheer volume can be several thousand items in each store. Each stored item, called Stock-Keeping Unit (SKU), is assigned a code for identification within relevant stores. The number of SKUs handled by a store, or a functioning healthcare centre, significantly determines the size, complexity and the comprehensiveness of the inventory management system.

Two widely used methods for classifying numerous SKUs are:

- *ABC analysis*: SKUs are categorised based on their unit values or consumption pattern in descending order. The 80–20 rule often applies with 80 per cent of the cumulative value or consumption accounted for by 20 per cent of SKUs. A and B classes, constituting about 95 per cent, receive distinct management attention.
- *VED analysis*: This is acronym for vital, essential and desirable classification of parts. Vital are life-saving items or crucial for the functioning of critical medical equipment, particularly useful in managing the inventory of maintenance spares, and is extensively employed in spare parts management systems.

The items can be cross classified, allowing simultaneous use of both A, B, C and VED analyses.

Order quantity

The administrator faces the challenge of maintaining a balance between stock availability and high inventory levels and ordering items when needed, which is impractical, since suppliers need lead times for delivery. A finite cost is attached to placing each purchase order and the expiry date for most of the medicines. The main challenge here is to seek an economic order quantity (EOQ) for every SKU in the system, as an optimum balance. (Figures 7.5 and 7.6)

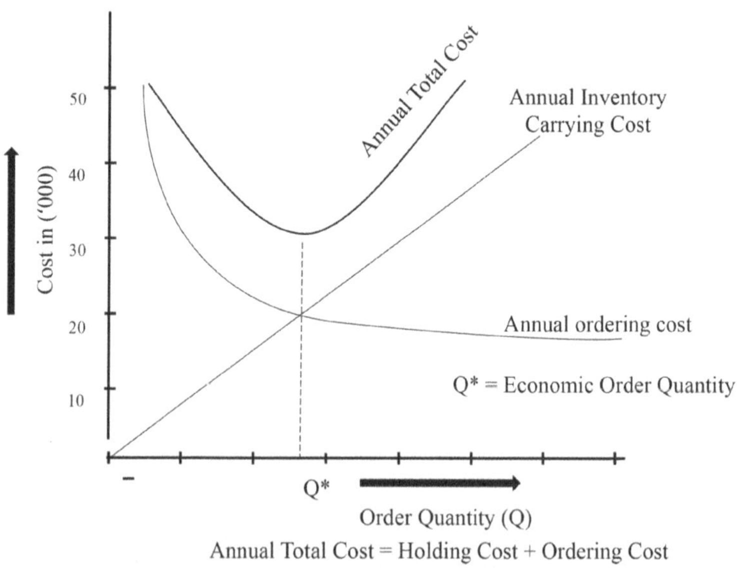

Figure 7.5 Annual holding and ordering cost for pharma item.

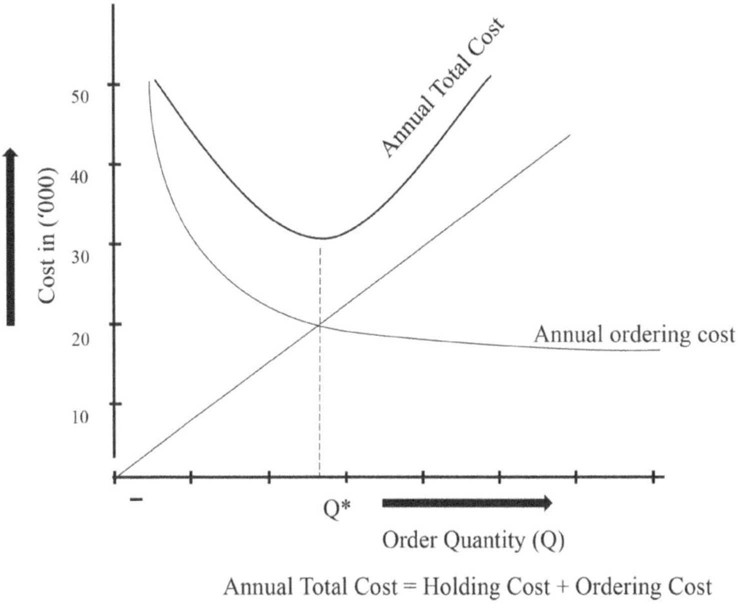

Figure 7.6 Annual holding and ordering cost for pharma items.

Lead times and safety stock

Vendors require lead time between receiving a purchase order and shipping the quantity to the store, and the transit times and processing time have to be built in. Lead time is critical for material planners, as they need to consider the lead times involved for each item in the store and for each supplier.

In scenarios with finite and predictable lead times and consumption rates, there is no need to plan for a *safety stock*. However, during the COVID-19 pandemic, when there was an acute shortage of some drugs, hospitals with surplus stock supplied items directly to other hospitals.

Practical rules

The main steps are as follows:

1. Classify the store items according to their logical groupings, such as pharma, surgical items, maintenance spares for various equipment, housekeeping supplies and so on.
2. Classify each SKU in the ABC or VED or any other logical groups as appropriate.
3. Determine order quantities, safety stocks and ordering intervals based on practical approximations of theoretical values of EOQ, variations in lead times and consumption patterns and past experience in supplies.

4. Adopt a *perpetual inventory model* for all A class items and V class items, where the system automatically releases an order to reach pre-determined levels.

For B and C items, and E and D pre-determined items, adopt a *periodic inventory model* where the system scans the stock levels and releases an order equivalent to the difference between the ceiling stock level pre-determined for such items, minus the stock on hand.

Some advanced concepts in inventory management

Some examples of alternative approaches features are discussed below:

- *Vendor-managed inventory* (VMI): Vendors are treated as an integral part of the supply chain, allowing them access to the inventory levels. Vendors initiate the supply process and reordering points, creating a seamless and mutually beneficial process.
- *Vendor-managed stores (VMS)*: Vendors manage customers' physical stores for specialised items by placing their inventory in the user's premises.

Supply chain challenges in healthcare

There are several challenging aspects of managing material as indicated below:

- Drugs and medicines, for example, involve ordering and stocking a huge variety of branded and generic drugs of varied strengths from different manufacturers. There is a constant demand for procurement of new drugs. Some hospitals have a committee to rationalise drugs which can be prescribed. In some hospitals, branded drugs are not stored.
- Billing software must ensure compliance with maximum retail price (MRP) or at a price lower than the MRP.
- Consumables of a wide range of items, such as gloves, masks, gowns, syringes, kits for laboratories and medical oxygen, also require special attention. The pricing varies from one hospital to another.
- Proprietary spare parts for all electronic equipment should be available to ensure that key medical equipment is in working order at all times.

Managerial aspects of supply chain

Managing materials poses several challenges, as outlined below:

- A careful study should focus on cost optimisation in all the areas of drugs, consumables, spare parts and other 'A' category items. There are some hospitals where the drugs prescribed by doctors are evaluated, and expensive and branded items are substituted with more economical options.

- Another key area is annual maintenance contracts (AMCs). Technical skills and commercial skills are required to get the best deals for the hospital. Medical, purchase and finance departments should be involved.

Many hospitals these days have adopted ERP systems with a focus on tracking purchases, consumption and stock levels. This is a dynamic exercise since material flow and their consumption take place throughout the day. A careful study, prior to computerisation, will enhance its utility to all the users.

- Online computerised systems will track individual items dispensed to various patients, ensure they are billed at the maximum retail price (MRP), adjust their stock levels and depending on the reorder point and raise new purchase orders.
- *Metrics for materials department*: It is important that the accountability parameters for the department head are well defined. It should be ensured that items sent to operating theatres, sub-stores and subsequent billing to patients are tracked for every single item.

Aggregate planning models

An integrated healthcare provider can be viewed as a combination of several facilities, equipment and other resources, which together provide a range of healthcare services to a population living within a defined area. Hence the term aggregate planning model.

In the context of a large hospital, the aggregate planning model captures the following aspects:

- Revenue streams from various facilities
- Costs involved in providing services under various heads
- Investments needed to install, grow and modernise the facilities
- Impact of implementing emerging medical technologies in terms of costs and effectiveness

The study of the results from aggregate models would allow the administrator to view the hospital holistically to identifying those areas for direct future resources and those which may require reductions for overall effectiveness. In these models, the aggregate cost or revenue values over multiple items distinguishing them from each individual line items.

Applying aggregate planning models

In a real-life example, a large healthcare provider deals with the following variables:

- The number and capacity of various medical specialties
- Specific capacities in each specialty, which cover the following:
  - In-patient care, outpatient care, the number of hospital beds, patient wards, number the of consultation rooms, the number and specialty of various medical and paramedical personnel
  - The number of patients requiring different treatments, morbidity rates and the incidence of various illnesses in the served population
  - Revenue generation from major causes of admission such as cardiology and oncology
  - Costs associated with providing services to patients including inpatient care, tests, surgery and radiation. The costs may include operating costs, such as salaries, medical consumables used, costs of operating equipment and all other costs, both fixed and variable, associated with running a facility.
- *Revenue models*: Mapping relationships between volumes and billing rates or costs or consumption rates
- Investments needed to maintain facilities and to build or install new ones, when their usage exceeds expansion
- Specialised skills needed to run such a sophisticated medical facility in terms of medical consultants, surgeons, paramedical staff and others and the costs in their recruitment and training

These models provide insights into the hospital's operation over several years, highlighting specific areas which need attention.

Aggregate planning is done using spreadsheets, or real-time computer planning models must be created for each hospital. This spreadsheet exercise captures volumes, cost lines, usage rates and facility capacities based in past data and realistic assumptions.

Six Sigma models in quality management

Six Sigma techniques are utilised in modern hospitals to meet quality management accreditations. Six Sigma methods involve applying numerical analysis to interpret results and improve quality performance using mathematical models.

What is Six Sigma?

Six Sigma is a series involving statistical analyses with large samples on variance from mean values. Standard statistical analyses are used in many situations where errors from the standard can occur. However, in the context of modern quality movement, the term Six Sigma conveys much more than the traditional standard deviation methods: Six Sigma has now become a general term to denote scientific or mathematical way of analysing operational quality performance in a variety of situations, including hospitals.

Each one of these techniques is required for any modern hospital which has quality accreditations. The quality metric can be built of the findings of the techniques.

Moving from quality manuals to Six Sigma

Many hospitals with quality management accreditations have formal manuals and procedures for all activities in the hospital. Accreditations mandate strict measurement of quality and periodic improvements. Joint Council International (JCI), NABH, College of American Pathologists (CAP) and National Accreditation Board for Testing and Calibration Laboratories (NABL) require a quality manual that spells out in clear terms the process steps and procedures involved in all processes, both major and minor.

Four aspects of Six Sigma

Six Sigma methods complement the existing quality parameters. In its core, Six Sigma has the following four aspects which cover its application:

1. Preventing errors before they occur
2. Solving problems using relevant quantitative methods
3. Detecting problems even while activities are in progress
4. Managing change in the organisation as a result of introducing Six Sigma methods and observing the response

Six Sigma is used in manufacturing, software development and healthcare industries. In hospitals, quality still means producing error-free outcomes, reducing re-admissions and reducing major and minor treatment errors. Therefore, the focus at all times is examining the root causes of repetitive mistakes in a hospital.

Typically, there are many types of errors in a hospital, some of which are highlighted below:

- Errors in diagnosis or delayed diagnosis
- Wrong medication
- Incorrect details entered during admission, leading to errors in the patient's record
- Errors in therapy or treatment, including delays
- Prescribed nursing standards not followed
- Proper medical treatment protocols not followed

- Administrative errors during discharge
- Wrong billing statements

Mortality and morbidity audits point out the end results and recommend corrective actions to be taken. A quick review of these errors typically occurring in hospitals will reveal that such mistakes are very amenable to be measured and corrective actions taken.

Poka Yoke *and error prevention*

Poka yoke (the Japanese term meaning proofing mistakes) is a common method for preventing errors.

Common *poka yoke* methods include:

- Immediate confirmation of verbal orders (particularly relevant in the Indian hospital context, where typically instructions are commonly issued by the senior doctors orally)
- Emphasising the importance of clear, written orders or online prescriptions for medicines and treatment
- Training all staff, through constant repetition and periodic drills. In some hospitals, instructions are displayed prominently on the walls of the respective facility
- Implementing interlocking systems and use of colour-coded keys to prevent mistakes: Ensuring right corridor doors and medicine cabinets are accessed
- Using kits containing all treatment aids for typical procedures to prevent omissions
- Proper patient/sample identification using bar codes/QR codes

These applications extend to various aspects such as improving building designs, methods for preventing the medication errors and workflow to minimise bottlenecks. Analysing bottlenecks, both upstream and downstream of a chosen process, their impact on the process performance in terms of physical capacity limits, and deciding where to place a bottleneck, are all part of the *kanban* methods. *Kanban* is a Japanese term to visualise workflow in a process, expect possible bottlenecks, methods for solving bottlenecks and optimising the entire process.

Problem-solving approaches

In Six Sigma, understanding causes is crucial for minimising errors. Two diagrammatic tools for problem analysis are:

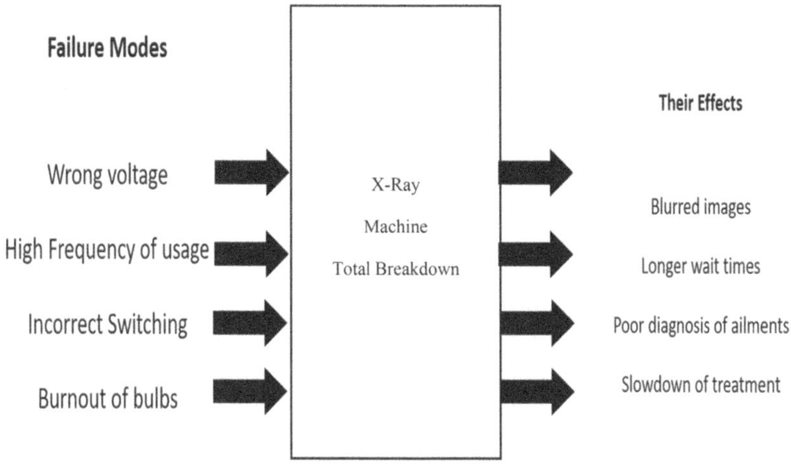

Figure 7.7 Failure modes and effects analysis.

- Failure modes and effects analysis (FMEA), which as the name implies, matches the various ways failures can occur against the effects of such failures leading to failures (Figure 7.7).
- Fishbone diagrams, also known as Ishikawa diagrams, trace the effect of failures such as long delays to intermediate process steps, illustrating errors in these steps culminating in a major failure. Cascading effects of many underlying causes, all of which lead to a big catastrophic failure in the end, are clearly depicted in fishbone diagrams (Figure 7.8).

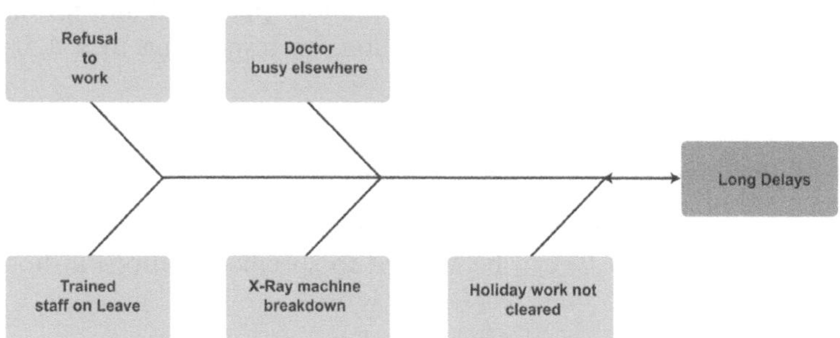

Figure 7.8 Fishbone diagram.

Management actions and problem detection

Management's response to problem analysis methods involves identifying practical solutions, testing their effectiveness and long-term monitoring of newly implemented policies and assess their effectiveness.

Problem identification

In a large hospital, various employees engage in millions of clinical and administrative processes steps every year offering several opportunities for errors. The Six Sigma approach is fundamental in assessing if processes meet the standards. For example, such as X-ray procedure, patients' admission system or a heart bypass surgery are the focus. The first spells out the 'yield', which is the ratio of the number of 'everything done right first time' to the total number of patients going through the process. The negative version of yield indicates the error rate in the system. The second factor is the *system performance time* defined as the total time lapse between the start and completion of the process: Like the patient admission–discharge time or a bill payment process involving medical insurance.

Systematically, tracking the yields and performance times of numerous process events over one year helps derive two key ingredients of Six Sigma:

1. The 'average' values of yields and performance times across different processes
2. The 'standard deviation (sigma)' in these processes indicating departures of values from the average

At one Sigma level, nearly 160 out of 1,000 events would lie outside acceptable rates, at two Sigma levels 23 out of 1,000 and at three Sigma levels one out of 1,000 are in error or non-conformance or rejections. High-performing organisations measure the errors in per million (ppm) and aim for an error rate of three to four errors in one million, corresponding to a 4.5 to 6.0 Sigma level of performance.

Practical applications of Six Sigma in hospitals

The concept of setting process limit set at Six Sigma and process control limit at 4.5 Sigma (Figure 7.9) can be applied to specific situations in hospitals, including:

- Tracking errors in pharmacy order execution
- Addressing variations in medication times from prescribed limits
- Managing waiting times in the CT scan
- Controlling infection rates

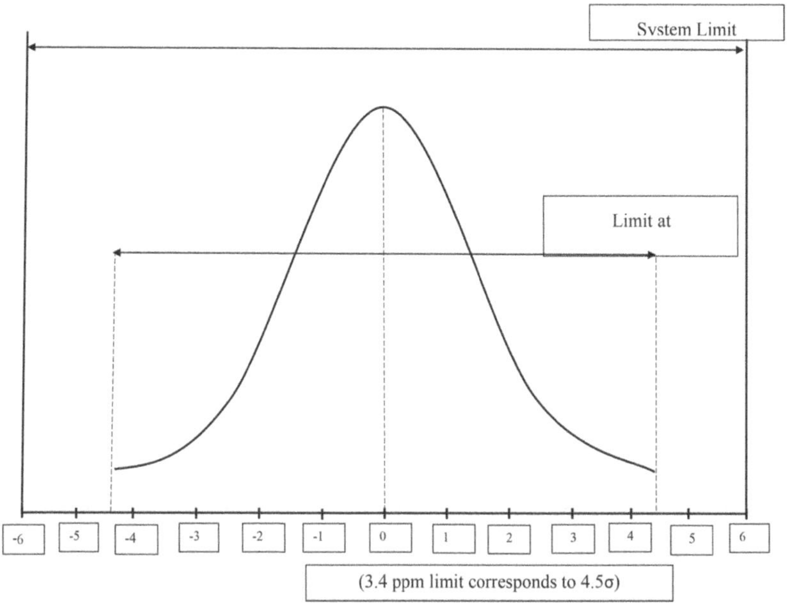

Figure 7.9 Normal distribution with system limits.

The hospital should strategically select departments that impact morbidity and mortality, actively track errors, assign responsibility and ensure continuous improvements. As evident, the upper and lower control limits are set within the three Sigma levels on either side of the average (Figure 7.10). Tracking process performance using such process control charts helps the management identify areas where their processes are going wrong and to initiate remedial steps to bring them to alignment. In some instances, the management may establish new benchmarks for yield or performance data, requiring innovative methods for execution.

Dealing with sparse data sets

The methods discussed so far are readily applicable wherever the process provides numerous data points. In such cases, the average and standard deviation values may not reflect the actual process parameters, and they need to be examined in the context of 'confidence intervals'. The focus is not on reaching the 'right' answer but in knowing how close the right answer is to accuracy. Statistical methods like t-values for average and chi-square test for standard deviation are applied for various confidence levels.

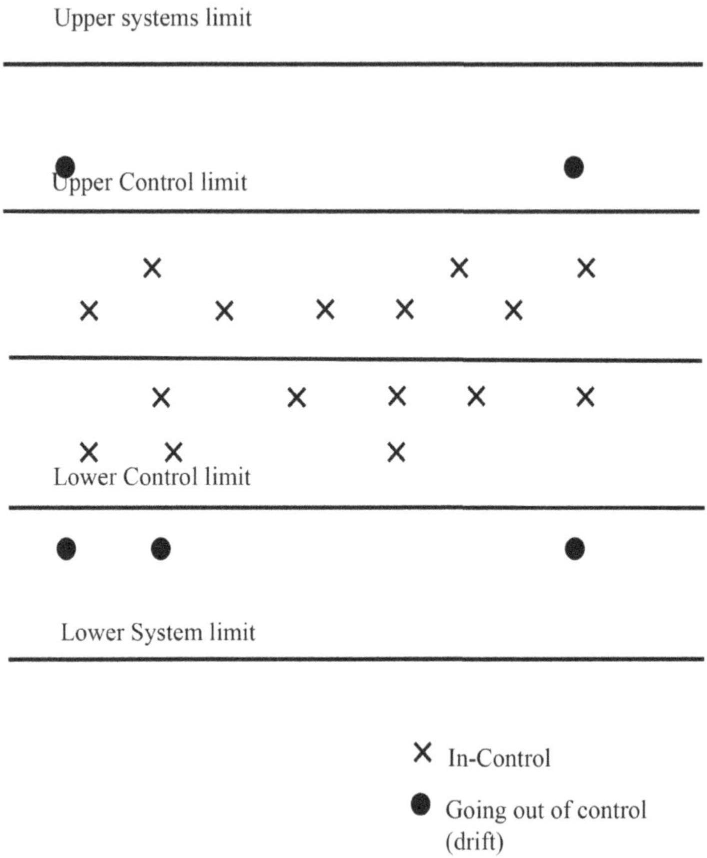

Figure 7.10 Typical process control tracking charts.

More advanced concepts

The Six Sigma methods include the following:

- *Repeatability* and *reproducibility*: Evaluating outcomes by the same employee teams at different times of day or with different employee teams.
- *Analysis of variance:* Variance can be used to track the relationship between two variables using regression analysis or even visual examination of how the points are distributed on a graph. Such variance analysis would be useful to analyse, for example, how day shift and night shift performance differs, or variations between summer and winter time data.
- *Managing change:* Six Sigma methods necessitate significant changes in the process. While small changes can be initiated through methods like

quality circles, larger initiatives such as 'zero defect days' and the incorporation of the suggestion box require a structured approach.

Hospital management can conduct formalised trials to gather data on outcomes, educating staff before deciding on larger changes.

The Six Sigma approach represents a family of quantitative and logical methods that enables a hospital to enhance its error-free performance techniques. Techniques like the *poka yoke* and *kanban* methods seek to prevent errors and align the workforce to established standards. The use of average, upper and lower process limits and control charts enable the management to maintain good processes.[4]

Simulation models

When managers confront significant decisions with potential long-term and substantial implications, the uncertainty surrounding outcomes can be daunting. Simulation is a process where the practical aspects of decision-making are mathematically approximated. The test involves testing various values for 'inputs' and provides a summary of 'outputs' or likely results. Figure 7.11 is a simple approximation of a simulation model.

'Inputs' can be divided into two, namely:

- *Controllable inputs*, where operational decision options available. For example, the number of counters in a service centre or location of a facility are the decisions or inputs that rest within the control of the hospital.

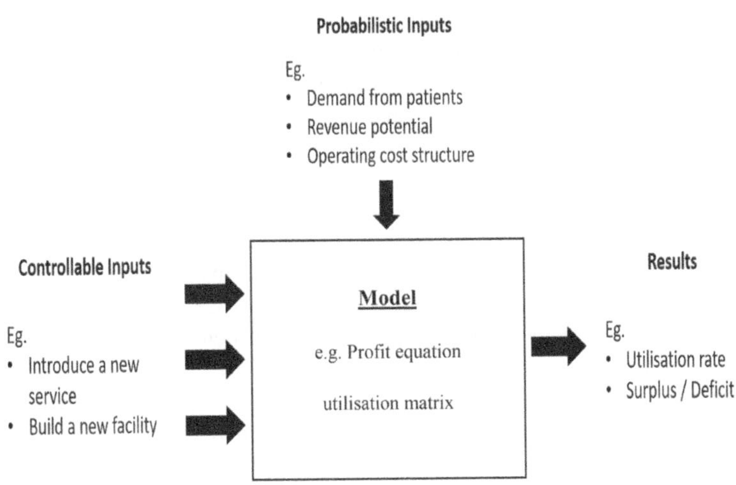

Figure 7.11 Representation of a simulation model.

- *Probabilistic inputs* are factors or circumstances which are randomly generated and outside anyone's control. These inputs occur in the environment in which the simulation experiment is taking place.
- *Project feasibility*: The viability of a project can be assessed by a simulation model.

A simulation model is the close approximation of how these inputs, controllable and probabilistic, interact with the processing system to produce outcomes or results. As it can be seen, by varying the controllable inputs in a number of ways, the performance of the processes can be simulated. When these results are studied later, it would lead to well-thought-out decision.

Use of computer models

Relatively simple simulation exercises, where only a few inputs and variables are involved, can be done by standard spreadsheets; nowadays, spreadsheets offer simulation add-ons, which enable users to programme a simulation model by themselves. When the model moves away from simple to more complex simulations, involving more variables and complicated logic of the underlying processes, computer simulation packages are employed. There are special-purpose simulation packages available, such as GPSS, SIMSCRIPT, SLAM and Arena, which have ready-made features like built-in simulation clocks, means of generating probabilistic inputs to a chosen curve and tables for collecting and analysis.[5] Evidently, these packages would require the user to have some prior exposure and training in their use.

Simulation as an exercise enables the healthcare administrator to reconfirm or gain confidence in the decisions made using mathematical approximations of the real-world processes. Understanding the probable distribution patterns of various inputs, and selecting the right simulation tool, spreadsheets versus computer packages, are the key to utilising the models. Finally, the cost of using these models, particularly the time involved in studying the data needs, and a close familiarity with the operating conditions determine how usefully they can be employed.

Conclusion

This chapter illustrates the potential of multiple management science techniques that can be used, powered by software tools, to address many operational problems. The techniques are merely instruments; the principles behind them are more important. The objective of the techniques is to improve patient care (reduce waiting time of patients, for example), minimise errors by staff, as well as allocate resources more efficiently. It is important that the key learnings from each such study should result in specific actions.[6]

Notes

1 Pulse polio immunisation, National Health Mission, https://nhm.gov.in/index1.php?lang=1&level=3&sublinkid=945&lid=343
2 India TB report 2020. National Tuberculosis Elimination Programme, annual report. Central TB Division, Ministry of Health and Family Welfare, https://tbcindia.mohfw.gov.in/wp-content/uploads/2023/05/India-TB-Report-2020.pdf
3 Humphreys P, Spratt B, Tarivedi M, et al. An overview of hospital capacity planning and optimisation. Healthcare (Basel) 2022;10(5):826. https://pmc.ncbi.nlm.nih.gov/articles/PMC9140785/
4 For more details on Six Sigma, see R. Barry, A.C. Mucko and C.E. Brubaker (2002). *The Six Sigma Book for Healthcare: Improving Outcomes by Reducing Errors* (ACHE Management series). Hospital Administration Press.
5 Simulation models, August 2023. https://www.softwaresuggest.com/simulation-software
6 Further topics on management science and more elucidation of topics covered here are dealt with in more detail in R.K. Martin, J.D. Camm, T.A. Williams, D.R. Anderson and D.J. Sweeney (2013). *Quantitative Methods for Business*, 12th edition, Cengage Learning. This is a highly useful reference book on applying quantitative models in management, where definitions, examples and methods are clearly presented.

8 Marketing

Tilak Shankar

Introduction

In the last four decades, marketing has gained increasing prominence in corporate hospitals, which have grown enormously across the country during this period. Particularly, in the last two decades, the healthcare sector has seen increased investor activity in the form of private equity investments, new investments and listing on the stock market, which have led to acquisitions and mergers and formation of new chains of hospitals. The hospitals are under a heightened pressure for growth and profitability, especially the ones that have attracted investments.

Hospitals have come to devise a structured marketing approach for attracting patients. The principles of market segmentation, differentiation, positioning, developing brand equity and seven Ps are employed as part of their marketing efforts. The role of market research in assessing the potential for hospital services in various geographies as well as in evaluating the effectiveness of various marketing strategies from time to time has become a normal part of operating a hospital business. The marketing approach adopted by hospitals is no different from marketing of any other product or service. The term marketing also includes selling since sales and marketing are a continuum. Marketing is built on innovative strategies and making full use of a variety of tools that are available.

Rapid growth of corporate hospitals

About 50 large corporate hospital chains operate in India at present, with each chain having a presence in various cities and some chains operating multiple hospitals in the same city. The rapid growth in large private hospitals can be attributed to fund availability, demand for quality medical care, urbanisation and entrepreneurial spirit. For example, Apollo Hospitals, the largest of the hospital chains in the country, has 70 hospitals in various cities, some operating under the franchisee model.[1] In Chennai alone, there are 11 Apollo Hospitals in different parts of the city. Max Healthcare operates seven hospitals in Delhi. Due to increasing competition, each hospital chain faces the need to effectively market its capabilities to the patient and doctor

DOI: 10.4324/9781003684947-10

community. The hospital's unique offerings and the skills of various specialists are highlighted in the marketing campaign of the hospitals. Marketing, of course, plays only a supporting role.

The marketing department of a tertiary care hospital typically focuses on three aspects:

- Creating health awareness among the community and establishing brand equity for the hospital
- Building relationships with physicians, smaller hospitals, insurance companies as well as with patients
- Employing cost-effective media channels for communication

Marketing efforts should intelligently leverage internal and external databases, insights from medical experts and experience of other industries such as consumers and the pharmaceutical sector.

The primary objective of marketing is to create awareness among the community about the importance of quick action by patients and families in case of an illness, a heart attack (rush to hospital within the golden hour) or a stroke. There is an increasing awareness, regarding non-communicable diseases (NCD) such as diabetes, cancer, respiratory illness, hypertension and obesity control.

The marketing function broadly refers to a combination of both *sales* and *marketing*. Sales involves the interactions of hospitals with referring doctors and nursing homes, corporates, insurance companies and third-party administrators (TPAs), nursing homes, large residential colonies, senior citizen homes and international patients. Marketing involves brand management, market research, product and services management, marketing strategies, pricing, market segmentation and long-term plans. The latter is typically considered a staff function, while sales is termed as a line function.

In this chapter, the focus is on the following:

- Market potential and marketing strategies
- Market research
- Organisation structure
- Branding, brand equity and logo
- Traditional and social media mix
- Segmentation
- Website as a marketing tool
- Sales

Market potential

In the last four decades, corporate hospitals have targeted patients in large cities and towns as their potential market based on the ability to pay. Economists define this phenomenon as 'demand backed up by purchasing power'.[2] Market potential is assessed at two stages: To determine the location of a new hospital and estimate annual revenues.

Location of corporate hospitals

India has nearly 50 cities with a population of more than one million each and another 50 cities with more than 500,000 each.[3] Cities with more than one million population together account for 115 million people (2011 census), while those with 50,000 population make up another 50–60 million people. Rapid urbanisation and the growth of cities create opportunities for private hospitals. Demography defines the potential market, which is further refined by socioeconomic classification (SEC) groupings, that is, upper-income and middle-income families. The upper-income group is defined as A1, A2 and B1, and the middle-income group is defined as B2 and C1.[4] In practice, tertiary care is sought across all socioeconomic strata.

The market potential also varies based on whether hospitals are single-specialty (ophthalmology, oncology, gastroenterology, obstetrics and gynaecology, paediatrics, orthopaedics) or multi-specialty. A larger chain of hospitals has multiple facilities in the same city, strategically distributed according to demographic considerations. Cardiology, oncology, orthopaedics and transplants are some of the major revenue-generating departments, which draw patients from across the country.

A combination of sales and marketing strategies is deployed to meet the top line (sales), keeping in mind the investor expectations (Figure 8.1). Sales teams focus on key patient groups. Health insurance is beginning to play a

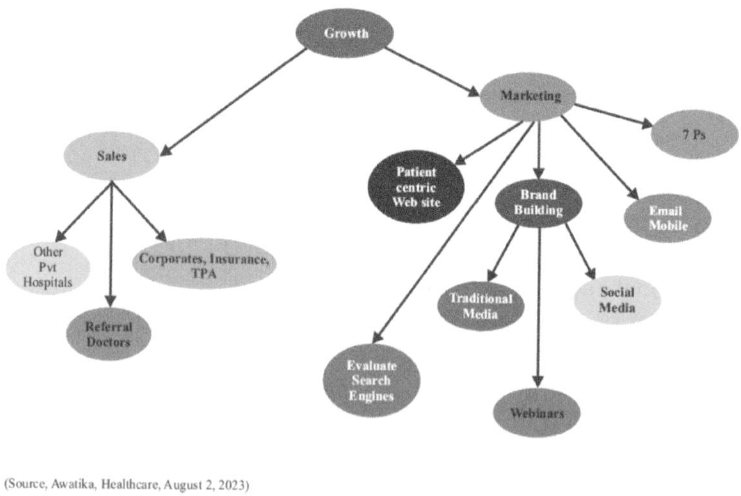

Figure 8.1 Corporate hospitals: Sales and marketing strategies.

key part. There are insurance companies that offer insurance cover up to INR 2 crore per annum per person. Similarly, corporates provide their employees and families with group insurance or self-insurance facilities. Hence, the hospital's sales team regularly meets with the corporates. The sales team also regularly meets doctors and nursing homes that refer patients to their facilities. Referral doctors play a crucial role since the decision to go to a particular hospital or consult a specialist is primarily suggested by them. In addition, there are a large number of walk-in patients based on recommendations from friends and relatives. They might travel long distances to consult a specialist or be treated in a particular tertiary care hospital, even if a similar facility is available in their cities. The 'catchment' areas are no longer restricted to geography. Word-of-mouth continues to play an important part.

The marketing team leverages the brand equity of the hospital and uses webinars for patient education (e.g., diabetes, strokes, infertility) constantly evaluate various marketing tools for their effectiveness. Each step ultimately should result in additional patients over a period of time.

Socioeconomic classification[5]

The socioeconomic stratifications are essentially drawn from consumer product companies for market segmentation (Figure 8.2). The socioeconomic (SEC) grouping helps in a sharp delineation of the potential market. Hospitals plan their sales and marketing strategies taking into the profile of the relevant population, need for setting up new hospitals, clinics, pharmacies and labs. Sales and marketing efforts have to be quite focused to avoid wastage of efforts.

URBAN				RURAL		
Education	**Classification**			**Education**	**Type of Housing (Pucca, Semi Pucca, Kutcha)**	
Skilled workers	E_2	B_2		Illiterate to SSC / HSC	R2	R4
Shop Owners	D	(A_2)		Some college degree	(R_1)	R_2 to R_3
Entrepreneurs and self-employed professionals	C-D	(A_1)		PG	(R_1)	R_2 to R_3
Supervisors	D	(A_2)		Prof. Degree	(R1)	R_2 R_3
Senior Officers & above	B_1	(A_1)				

( ) Cited groups potential patients for Corporate Hospital
(Source : Prana Gupta, PPMS, Nov.8, 2021)

Figure 8.2 Socioeconomic classification and corporate hospitals.

Consumer markets

Traditionally, in the consumer markets, urban Indian households are classified based on two parameters: Education and occupation. The chief wage earner's (CWE) education status and occupation are taken into consideration while segmenting them into seven groups, that is, from A1 to E2. According to this classification, A1, A2 and B1 are considered upper-income groups and B2 and C1 are considered middle-income groups. Private hospitals can focus on the higher and middle-income groups, as a majority of their patients are from these groups.

However, a small section of the population is admitted as inpatients, even from lower-income groups, which Ashok Anantaram, a leading marketing expert, calls customer-derived value (CDV). Since families consider life to be more valuable than the treatment costs, they will admit the patient to a corporate hospital. They may borrow or sell some property to fund the hospitalisation cost. In other words, income grouping alone may not be the only potential market segment.

Marketing strategy

The marketing strategy usually aligns with the overall corporate strategy, converting the Board of Directors' directives into actionable marketing and sales plans. The strategy depends on the management's perceptions of external opportunities and internal strengths. External opportunities could be influenced by geography, epidemiology and psychographic classification. These groupings are dynamic. Internal strengths comprise the reputation of the hospital doctors, availability of expensive modern medical equipment, nursing care, ambience and most importantly, emergency medical care.

Core competencies

Some hospitals prefer to stay local or regional, while others expand nationally. Most hospitals focus on the 10–12 'centres of excellence' in their marketing messages, aimed at major cities with potential local markets. The first hospital or the parent hospital usually remains the primary headquarters of the company.

Market research

Every hospital aims for growth and the Board of Directors plans for expansion within a specific state or region or across multiple cities in India. The decision-making process involves studying the characteristics of each potential market in the targeted market. Sometimes, the Board might take a priori decision to enter a city, prompting the marketing department to conduct a market research study to evaluate the size of the market and competition.

The management can choose to conduct the study internally or hire an external agency. If an external agency is selected, then the agency would be briefed. The agency utilises both secondary data and also undertakes primary research for its evaluation. Secondary data encompasses various demographic factors such as the population growth over the last two decades, age profile of the population, number of industries, size of various towns and cities and the number of hospitals and nursing homes. Clusters with rapid population growth could be potential locations for the hospital. The agency gathers details of medium and large-sized hospitals, their specialisation, bed capacities, major doctors and estimated occupancy rates. Other relevant details are the number of diagnostic centres, laboratories, number of retail pharmacies, number of registered medical practitioners, number of private and government medical colleges, nursing colleges and allied medical science institutions. Other information, such as the number of hotels, tariffs and distances of medical facilities from the hotel, will also be collected. The agency may conduct interviews with some well-known medical professionals, discuss with real estate agents on new buildings and explore the potential rental or sale of large buildings.

The agency presents the findings and its recommendations regarding the market potential, following which the board conducts a financial feasibility study. Internal data are used in the evaluation, including the size of the hospital, medical departments, required equipment and building costs in conjunction with the market survey findings. The decision to establish a new hospital or day-care centres is contingent on factors such as market potential, financial feasibility, as well as strategic considerations.

Market intelligence

It is essential that the management is kept informed about developments that could have an impact on their hospital. Specialist doctors moving from one hospital to another hospital, tariff changes, introduction of new expensive equipment by competition. It is necessary to keep an ear close to the ground. Single-specialty hospitals like those focusing on ophthalmology, oncology, liver diseases and orthopaedics might choose to 'stick to their knitting'. In such cases, considerations will include whether to start a greenfield facility or to acquire an existing hospital in the same discipline.

Corporate and local marketing organisation

The rapid expansion of hospitals in many cities has necessitated the establishment of corporate departments, including marketing. The first major hospital within the group serves as the corporate office, focusing on planning, budgeting and policymaking. Major decisions concerning the website, logo, promotional themes and sales and marketing budgets would be centralised. Major campaigns designed by the corporate headquarters would be implemented with local inputs. Individual local hospitals may be owned by the parent company or could be operated by franchisees. If it is franchisee ownership, there would be consultation between the corporate department and the franchisee.

Factors influencing marketing in a hospital

Income projections

There are multiple aspects which form part of the budgeting process. Some of the key aspects such estimation of patients (new and follow-up) tariff for various services, case mix and income projections.

Annual income projections are a collaborative effort involving medical departments, finance and marketing. Factors considered would include bed occupancy, average revenue per occupied bed (ARPOB), revenue from day-care, revenue from major admission categories, income per patient from new and follow-up patients, the number of major and minor surgeries, income from diagnostic laboratories and income from pharmacy. The average length of stay (ALOS) has progressively declined over the years, necessitating the hospital to attract a larger number of patients progressively.

Sales strategies should also consider generating additional revenue from support services like imaging and pharmacies. Non-hospital patients would also be targeted for this purpose. In recent years, day-care surgeries, treatment, and outpatient consultation and tele-consultations have become important income segments. Some of these services can also be created as sub-brands or even formed as separate companies. Marketing plays a crucial role in monitoring footfalls from each segment while developing strategies.

Number of patients

Each bed requires 80–90 inpatients per year at 100 per cent occupancy, assuming four to five days of ALOS. The Apollo Group of Hospitals had 460,000 admissions and 68,30,000 outpatients in 2021–22.[6] As Dr Devi Shetty, Chairman of Narayana Health, emphasises, 'We generate millions of data every day. We need to analyse and evolve data-based strategies'.[7] Marketing considerations focus on profitable areas. Laboratories and pharmacies, for example, are very profitable.

Quarterly results

Listed companies must report their quarterly results, leading to pressure throughout the system to track performance daily. The top management typically tracks daily income from each of the hospitals. In tertiary hospitals, cardiology, oncology and orthopaedics contribute significantly to revenues with approximately 40 per cent of the revenues contributed by cardiology and oncology. Revenues from these departments are closely monitored. Daily reports on utilisation of major equipment, including major operating theatres, CATH labs, radiology and other investigations, provide key insights to the management on the overall revenue generation of the hospital. Marketing strategies need to address both major departments and utilisation of all its key facilities to ensure effective management.

Tariffs

Recommendations for tariff revisions are typically made by marketing in consultation with finance and medical departments. The tariff structures are influenced by charges in comparable hospitals. In recent years, insurance companies have been actively involved in negotiating overall tariffs for inpatients for different diseases.

Each big corporate hospital typically offers 10–12 different categories of rooms, ranging from general wards to super deluxe rooms, depending on the projected demand. Room tariff for a single room varies from INR 10,000 per day going upto INR 42,000 for a super deluxe room. The Apollo Hospitals chain, which operates over 70 hospitals in multiple cities in India, has differential room tariffs depending on many factors. In fact, within the city, there could be differences in the tariff depending on the location of the hospital. The categorisation is a reflection of the class distinctions and the 'ability-to-pay'. Room tariffs also vary significantly from one city to another within the same hospital chain. Periodic reviews by the marketing department consider occupancy levels and pricing in comparable hospitals and may lead to both tariff revisions and changes in room configuration. It is believed that charges for services, for example, laboratory tests or imaging, may be linked to room categorisation.

Hub and spoke model

Many hospitals adopt a 'hub and spoke' model where clinics are strategically placed in major residential areas. The 'spokes', that is, the clinics will feed the 'hub' – the main hospital. The marketing department would explore residential areas, recognising the importance of outpatients as a feeder for hospital admissions. Typically, the number of outpatients is 10–15 times the number of inpatients.

Other considerations for marketing

Corporate hospitals primarily focus on tertiary care medical services but may offer other services, such as maternal delivery, packaged as a 'comfort' experience. Departments like obstetrics and gynaecology, child immunisation, neonatology, paediatric ICU and infertility are crucial for footfalls and revenue generation (for example, Fortis Healthcare offers obstetrics and gynaecology services, Apollo group has infertility and children's hospitals and Rainbow Hospitals operate children's hospitals).

In the initial years, marketing used to be focused on 'star' doctors. However, in recent times, these 'stars' have been moving from one hospital to another, necessitating the creation of an independent hospital identity. Brand building, service differentiation, hospital ambience and availability of expensive medical equipment are integral parts of the marketing campaigns. These are strategies to build loyalty of the patient towards the hospital.

The chairman of a large corporate hospital once likened marketing a hospital to marketing a star hotel with the patient (customer) as the central objective. Bed occupancy, similar to room occupancy in a hotel, is vital for a hospital's success.

Market segmentation

Hospital marketers categorise the market into various segments, such as geographic, demographic, epidemiological, income groups and psychographic. Segmentation should be 'measurable, substantial. actionable, differentiated'.[8] Hospital records, sample studies and conference presentations provide a wealth of data, highlighting clear regional differences in cardiac diseases, metabolic disorders, chronic obstructive pulmonary disease (COPD) and obesity.[9] Many are chronic diseases. Segmentation helps marketers to understand the importance of various segments.

Data sources

Epidemiological data from hospital records, health check-ups and pharmacy prescriptions assist in targeting specific campaigns for diseases, such as diabetes, impaired glucose tolerance, hypertension, childhood obesity, asthma and heart attacks, in certain cities and in some age groups.

Geriatric population

Demographic classification is another useful segmentation based on age profile. The number of people who are older than 65 years was about 134 million in 2021.[10] This group suffers from several age-related illnesses. The life span has been steadily increasing over the last few decades, bringing in its wake more diseases, including mental health disorders. The government of Kerala has already initiated many senior citizen-specific healthcare programmes. Many senior citizens' homes have sprung up in cities. Sales effort can be focused on these homes, the hospital can organise health check-ups, provide emergency transportation and provide a 'doctor-on-call' facility. Hospitals can work with insurance companies in designing insurance policies that are applicable to senior citizens, inclusion of pre-existing illnesses and relaxation of upper age limits. Recently, one insurance company – CARE insurance company – has introduced a policy with no upper age limit. Exclusive hospitals (specialising in geriatric care) or departments for senior citizens (geriatrics department) focusing on the elderly patients have come up in recent times (e.g., Geri Care Hospital, CARE Hospitals, Sir H.N. Reliance Foundation Hospital and Research Centre, St. John's, Manipal). The exclusive geriatric hospitals are very few in number but growing. However, the larger hospitals have separate departments for senior citizens that have special room arrangements, multi-disciplinary approaches, home doctor visits, nursing care, home visits for blood tests and many other services.

Psychographic segments

Some consumer product companies (e.g., Proctor & Gamble) have devised new marketing models to target customers based on their psychographic profiles (Figure 8.3). PatientBond, an American company, integrates a proprietary psychographic model with a machine learning model to identify healthcare customers' values. The company has adapted the P&G model to healthcare. This segmentation model helps in leveraging communication via email, SMS and personal calls.[11]

It is believed that this approach helps in more effective targeting of patients based on various data from hospital records, patients with chronic diseases, senior citizens, mental health patients and choosing appropriate media. This segmentation can be applied to categorise patients, communicate with selected groups, influence behaviour, help in adherence to diet, exercise and changes in lifestyle. The ethics of this approach, however, is debatable.

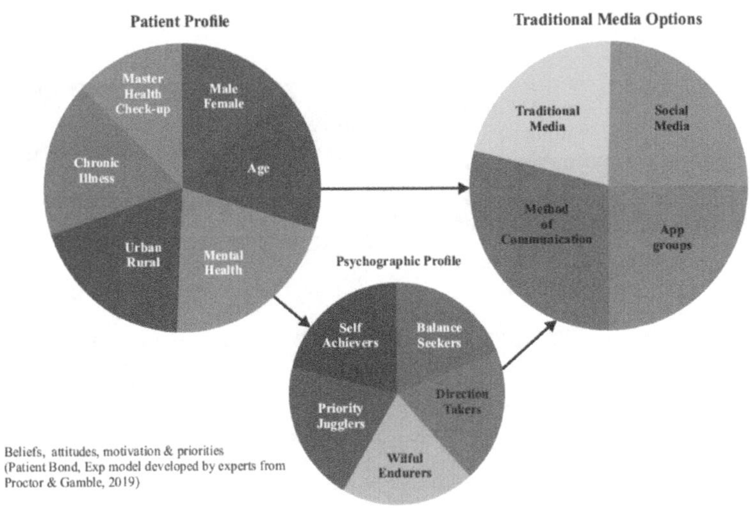

Figure 8.3 Psychographic segments.

Upper-income groups form a significant portion of private hospital patients, and marketing programmes can be tailored using psychographic profiling data. Psychographic segmentation has been described as a grouping of customers based on their goals, beliefs, challenges, interests, likes, dislikes and personality traits.[12] This grouping can be used to categorise patients, communicate to the selected groups and influence behaviour. The objective is also to prevent complications at a future date by encouraging regular follow-up, based on psychographic categorisation. A large section of the patients would be from the upper-income group. Purchases of a product or service are determined by the buyer based on various psychographic factors such as lifestyle, social status and personality type. A large number of luxury products, such as perfumes, luxury cars and travels, are also marketed based on psychographic profiling.[13] Social media companies (Figure 8.4) are able to collect specific data of the target population based on their algorithms. Segmentation refers to the power of social media in reaching out to specific groups, or even individuals to market products.[14]

Psychographic segmentation by hospitals for marketing[15,16]

Psychographic segmentation helps private hospitals to target patient groups based on their psychological profile, their underlying motivations, fears and preferences. For many chronic diseases, for example, diabetes, hypertension and endocrine abnormalities, the psychological profile is a useful marketing tool.

Internet users 213 million (759 million)	**Mobile Internet users - 130 million (1 billion)**
Smart phone users 51 million (175 million)	**Mobile subscribers 900 million**
***Facebook* users 115 million (315 million)**	***Twitter* users 77 million**
Linked in users 23 (100 million)	***Google* plus users 20 million**
***YouTube* users 55 million (467 million)**	***Pinterest* users 8 million (67 million)**

(Updated 2023 figures)
(Source: Greeshma M. India to have 184 mobile Internet - International Business Time Jan 2, 2014)

Figure 8.4 Social media: A goldmine.

Social media

The widespread use of the Internet, along with ubiquitous mobile phones and smartphones, has led to the young and old age groups making extensive use of social media. Since 2014, the use of social media has grown exponentially. Marketers have realised that there is a gold mine in social media in reaching out to customers (Figure 8.4). These media are also facilitating the marketing departments to reach out to specific targeted groups. For example, YouTube has become an extremely popular medium for patient education programmes and Q&A programmes. Twitter (now X) is extensively preferred for posting complaints, which usually gets high visibility. Hospitals pay attention to user complaints on Twitter.

WhatsApp is being employed for physicians to communicate with patients and the other medical professionals within the hospital. Many companies have apps for diet management.

In his book, Nir Eyal[17] describes his 'hooked model' where people get hooked to certain pain killers, food items, Diet Coke and the use of Amazon and become regular users of those services or products. Marketers can use the profiling data along with the health needs of various income categories to 'market' their programmes and media selection. In the case of diabetes, the medical team can work with patients on better diet compliance based on psychographic profiles. The choice of media can be made based on psychographic profiling of young professionals. Apps are available for disorders such as bipolar disorders.[18] Some hospitals utilise WhatsApp to build patient communication.

Underprivileged sections

Some corporate hospitals extend their services to underprivileged patients through various government insurance schemes. For instance, Narayana Health, Bengaluru, is known to admit a significant number of patients in their various hospitals under the government insurance schemes. These individuals may not be technologically savvy and may not be comfortable speaking in English, emphasising the need for management to consider the unique needs of different groups. Hence, marketing needs to be sensitive to different types of patient profiles.

Doctor referrals

Doctor referrals play a crucial role in hospital admissions. Referring doctors may suggest a specific doctor or a hospital, by providing a referral letter. The patient ultimately makes the final decision, considering the hospital, the cost of treatment and whether to undergo the treatment at all. Marketing maintains a database of the referring doctor and keeps close communication with all the referring doctors.

Sales

The corporate marketing department prepares an annual sales plan based on admission patterns, ALOS and detailed operational metrics. Hospital income budgets consider various aspects such as average revenue per occupied room, admissions to centres of excellence and revenue from the intensive care unit (ICU), operating theatres, laboratory, diagnostic centres and outpatient consultations and tests. Tariff revisions and benchmarking against comparable hospitals are crucial considerations. Sales department would regularly call on corporate HR departments, public sector companies, nursing homes and insurance companies for 'selling' the hospital and its services and obtain feedback on patients admitted so far.

Organised sector employees

Employees in the organised sector – both public and private sectors – and their families represent a significant patient group. Tata Consultancy Services (TCS), a software company, for example, employs over 500,000 employees. They are likely to offer corporate health schemes to the employees. Normally, the corporate health schemes will include employees' dependent children and parents. Both private sector and public sector companies and organisations, including the Indian Railways (another large employer), offer hospitalisation for serving and retired employees in corporate hospitals, where required. An estimated 30 million employees plus their families are potential patients in the organised sector.[19] All public sector employees and retired employees and their families are permitted to be treated at corporate hospitals through specially designed insurance schemes.

Regular meetings with the company's HR, inclusion in hospital groups and feedback from discharged patients help strengthen ties with the corporates. Attractive terms are offered by hospitals to large companies in coordination with insurance companies.

The pharmaceutical industry employs a sophisticated system to determine the call frequency of medical representative visits based on the popularity of the doctor, who are categorised as A, B and C depending on their popularity. Data from retail pharmacies (from syndicated databases) are correlated with doctor prescriptions. Diagnostic laboratories have gone public in recent years and are actively engaged in aggressive sales campaigns offering substantial discounts to attract customers.

Marketing organisation

Figure 8.5 describes the typical marketing organisation structure of a corporate hospital. Many hospital chains have a regional or a national footprint. They operate in large cities and in competitive markets.

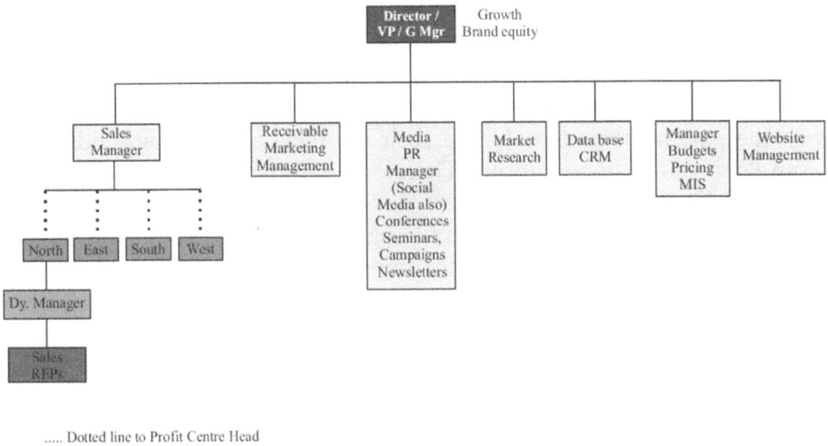

Figure 8.5 Marketing organisation.

Seven Ps of marketing

Four or seven Ps of marketing mix

Jerome McCarthy's original ideas of the four Ps of marketing mix have withstood the test of time.[20] Over the last six decades, including the Internet age, the four Ps have expanded to seven Ps (Figure 8.6).[21] McCarthy outlined the four Ps – product/service, price, place and promotion. The three latter additions were people, processes and physical evidence. We will briefly discuss each of the seven Ps, their concepts and applicability to the healthcare industry. The Joint Commission International (JCI) and the National Accreditation Board for Hospitals and Healthcare Providers (NABH) accredited hospitals have clear guidelines on measurement of quality of each of the seven Ps, a useful framework for critically evaluating the marketing mix in hospitals.

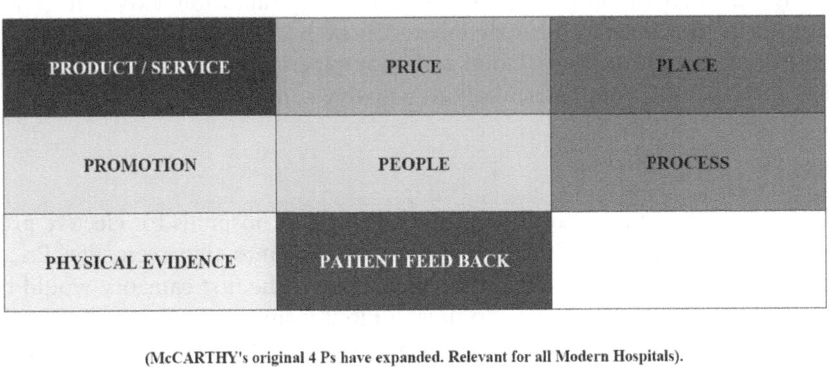

Figure 8.6 7Ps of marketing of hospitals.

The seven Ps provide a useful framework in service-oriented industries to understand the various elements that help in customer or patient satisfaction. Service is intangible and, therefore, it should be packaged. The main objective is to build loyalty to the brand and to cultivate a long-term relationship with the patient, their friends and their families. Each hospital adapts the seven Ps to suit local conditions. Therefore, within the same hospital chain, there could be regional differences.

A study by an expert group, examining two hospitals, namely Apollo and CARE hospitals, has highlighted the importance of the seven Ps – product/service, price, place, promotion, processes, people and physical evidence in the marketing mix of hospitals.[22] In their paper, the authors have highlighted the utility of the 7P concept.

Product/service

Hospitals, being a part of the service industry, provide a range of services to inpatients, outpatients, day-care and home care services, supply of medicines to residences and wellness services. The patient's expectations for each service vary. For example, for emergency admissions, response time, ambulance arrivals, ICU admission, efficiency and the speed at which the patients are admitted to the hospital's ICU and how quickly treatment begins become very important. NABH has eight chapters on emergency departments, including access and medication.[23] Many hospitals offer 24/7 emergency care with highly trained staff and senior doctors. The reputation of a hospital is dependent on its emergency services. It is necessary to constantly improve the emergency services.

In addition, the tertiary care hospital highlights its achievements through difficult, complex surgeries – transplantation of liver, heart, kidney, lungs and hand. Emergency heart surgeries and handling heart attacks, strokes, high-risk pregnancies and paediatric ICU require promptness with an alert and experienced staff. It is a subtle marketing communication.

In the internet and social media age, hospitalisation experiences are quickly communicated through Twitter (now X), WhatsApp and Instagram almost on a real-time basis. Good and poor experiences are shared. Hospitals have to pay attention, particularly to negative comments.

Price

Pricing plays an important role in the selection of hospitals for elective procedures and surgeries. Pricing may be classified into two segments: Price-sensitive segment and price-indifferent segment. The first category would be middle-class patients, those who have limited insurance cover or those who will pay the hospital bills themselves or retired government employees who are covered by government medical schemes. The second category would be those who have a high insurance cover, upper-income, private-sector employees. Depending on the category, pricing would play a decisive role in the selection of a particular hospital.

In the case of stand-alone laboratories, they offer package discounts, senior citizen discounts or other add-ons. Similarly, many retail pharmacies offer discounts and home delivery to regular patients. In all such cases, prices are a key determinant.

From the hospital's point of view, pricing should be balanced with revenue maximisation objectives of the hospital. Patients make a choice based on brand name, word-of-mouth recommendations. These advantages may neutralise the disadvantages of high pricing. Some sections of society automatically opt for corporate hospitals, while lower-income groups may prefer government and non-profit hospitals. Pricing involves various dimensions, viz., differential pricing (discounts for members), package pricing and pricing for various elements of service like the room rent, ICU, surgery charges and charges for equipment use.

Pricing of various services is based on what other hospitals charge and certain premium is added for the brand name of each hospital. Outpatient consultation charges in a corporate hospital may range from INR 800 to INR 2,000 or even more per consultation, depending on the city. Room charges vary. Some hospitals publish their charges on their website. In recent times, due to demands from patients, hospitals have introduced fixed prices for surgeries, which are widely publicised. Pricing is an important but not an overriding factor for the selection of hospitals by patients.

Place and physical location

Place refers to a large number of factors – proximity, ease of access and ambience within the hospital premises. The concept of place is rapidly undergoing changes. Tertiary hospitals get patients from different parts of the country and international patients as well. Tele-consultation has also become popular. Hence, proximity is not a major factor for those patients. On the other hand, proximity is important for local patients for OP visits.

Many hospitals, therefore, have established multiple OP clinics with labs, imaging and physiotherapy services. A well-located hospital remains advantageous even in twenty-first-century India. The ease with which the patient can reach the hospital, particularly in emergencies, contributes to its trust and reputation.

Within the hospital, the ambience, seating, décor, child-friendly facilities, disabled-friendly access, uniform of the staff, clean toilets and wheelchairs make a visible impression on patients.

The Christian Medical College (CMC) Hospital, a 3,000-bed hospital, which is over 100 years old, in Vellore in Tamil Nadu (120 km from Chennai) is an exception to this trend. Vellore is a small town with limited hotel facilities, but CMC is constantly crowded with patients from across the country. While location is an important aspect of marketing, other factors can neutralise the disadvantages of location. Location is important for government hospitals as well.

Promotion

Promotion is carried out by the healthcare industry through traditional media and social media. The message and choice of media is important. In the present times, even the younger population gets ailments such as by heart attacks, diabetes, obesity and hence their healthcare needs have become important. Thus, the challenge lies in choosing appropriate media depending on the age groups. There are extensive studies on media-watching habits of different age groups. Webinars, screening camps, TV shows, podcasts and YouTube shows have been effective in creating awareness among the patient population in general.

People

Staff, regardless of their role and seniority, interact with patients. Every individual who engages with the patient, or helps the family member, serves as an ambassador. Even seemingly minor aspects, such as uniforms, play a significant role. For example, a doctor's coat carrying the emblem of the hospital and name conveys the brand name in subtle ways. Nurses' uniforms also act as another avenue for brand visibility. Soft skill training and bed-side manner play an important part.

It is essential that all the staff members associate themselves with the core values of the hospital. The staff are trained to treat poor patients with compassion. In case of many private hospitals, even though there may not be differences in medical care, there would be significant differences in creature comforts and staff attention. Internal branding or selling the brand to all staff means instilling the vision, mission and beliefs among them in dealing with patients. Medical care is delivered by the nurse who is with the patient, by the doctor who is sympathetic, attentive and gives every patient hope. Staff of charitable hospitals are trained to treat poor patients with compassion – whether the patient has come for a cataract surgery, cancer treatment or a road accident victim. Some corporate hospitals treat VIPs differently. Value systems of the management are reflected in the way their staff treat patients.

Even seemingly unrelated roles, like a uniformed housekeeper and hospital reception staff, contribute to the overall patient experience. Reception staff, as the face of the hospital, are required to possess knowledge about the location of various departments, guide the patient effectively and be familiar with the routine aspects and medical terminology. Given the diverse patient profile, it is essential that the staff be multilingual.

Telephone

Despite the ubiquitous presence of mobile phones, landlines remain a vital part of patient interface. The first-time patient often contacts the hospital's landline. The telephone operator should be familiar with commonly spoken languages, answer the calls promptly and courteously and effectively forward the call. Telephone operators and front office staff should be trained for the job, as they play a part in marketing the hospital. In an era where hospitals have automated their phone system, email communication and WhatsApp messages, it is important to provide human touch to the patients. There are kiosks at the hospital entrance to fix appointments. While kiosks offer cost savings, many patients prefer human interactions. In the future, it is possible that robots could replace human beings with AI-driven systems. Many doctors believe that the human touch itself cures patients. Most senior citizens prefer human response rather than machine interaction. Human beings are social animals, so concern from the hospital staff enhances hospital experience. Hospitals have to strike a balance between efficiency and being sensitive to patient preferences.

Processes

Well-run hospitals would have standard operating procedures (SOP), covering all routine aspects of the hospital's functions as well as handling emergencies, for example, fire accidents, like a well-oiled machine. Efficient internal processes enhance patient experience. Ashok Anantaram, the marketing expert quoted previously, says, 'Every single touch point with the patient should be studied, and the processes should be systematically improved. Registration of new patients, fixing appointments with doctors, or additional tests to be carried, billing, discharge of patients should be systematised'. However, even in accredited hospitals, the discharge process is still cumbersome, with patients having to wait for several hours after the doctor has discharged the patient.

Accreditation standards, such as the JCI and the NABH, require all processes to be documented and regularly reviewed, with quantification and measurability of activities. The standards require that there should be demonstrable annual improvements in patient service. Even non-accredited hospitals should align their processes for quality improvement to enhance patient satisfaction. Streamlining paperwork in emergency admissions or facilitating insurance pre-approvals for elective surgeries are examples. On discharge, the final bill should be settled, and the patient should be given a discharge summary. Internal processes should focus on patient satisfaction. All processes should be examined from the point of the patient and not what is convenient to the hospital. A balance between automated processes and human touch would serve as an effective marketing tool.

Physical evidence and signages

The overall layout of the hospital, as well as areas frequented by patients, also plays a key role in marketing. Every part of the hospital – outpatient area, seating arrangements, frequently utilised services departments such as labs, imaging and cash counters – should be appropriately located. NABH mandates clear signages.

The eighth P – feedback

Feedback from patients/families can be in different forms: Informal, formal filling in a questionnaire, on social media or feedback to their referring doctors. While questionnaires are a means for measuring patient satisfaction levels on discharge, patients may not express their true opinions in a questionnaire. Senior staff members should periodically meet with inpatients and outpatients to understand patient experiences from the attendants and patients themselves by devoting adequate time. This is termed management by walking around (MBWA). Unfortunately, most hospital managements content themselves by reviewing data in their offices as a substitute for the truth.

Hospitals cater to international patients by offering several facilities such as letters to obtain visas, stay for attenders, transport facilities, separate accommodation for long-staying rehabilitation patients and interpreters in foreign languages. Even though the number of international patients is small, it is essential to assess their satisfaction levels.

The marketing mix (Figure 8.7) of a corporate hospital is dependent on its strategy and the tactical use of various media. Print media is deployed for specific occasions, such as the inauguration of a new hospital, investment in

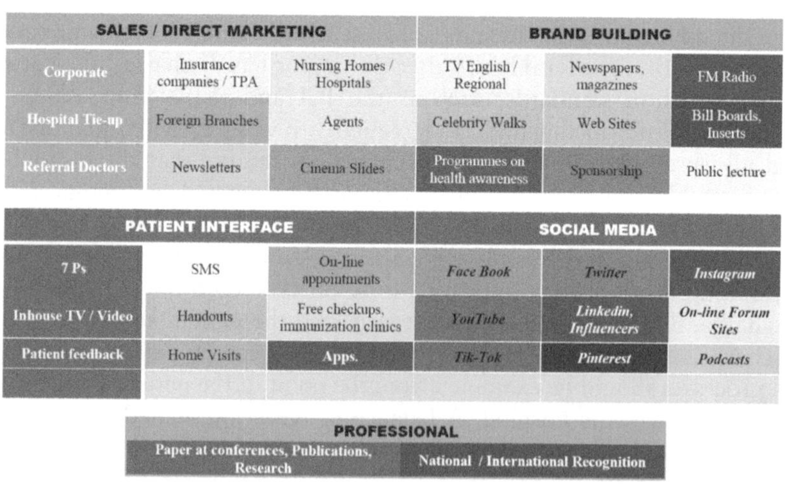

Figure 8.7 Marketing mix.

new medical equipment, senior doctors joining the hospital or acquisition of another hospital. Social media can be deployed on other occasions.

Patient groups can be categorised into different groups such as geriatric, women, youth, those with chronic illness and accident victims. It is essential that the media mix chosen be appropriate for the target segments. The management should also evaluate whether the campaigns are reaching the targeted segments.

Customer relationship management (CRM)

Customer relationship management (CRM) packages are widely used in various sectors such as consumer products, the service industry, pharmaceutical and healthcare (Figure 8.8). Modern hospitals have a wide range of databases, which generate data from master health checkups, inpatient and outpatient databases, prescriptions of retail pharmacy and data from clinics. The CRM software can draw upon these databases to trigger messages, emails and telephone calls.

Further segmentation into specific categories, such as geriatric patients, those with chronic diseases, paediatric patients, oncology patients and post-surgical cases, will help in sending reminders, improving immunisation and follow-up on rehabilitation programmes.

At a basic level, CRM captures key customer data, such as name, email id, phone numbers and health requirements. CRM can send birthday greetings, make enquiries with patients and follow up with rehabilitation patients,

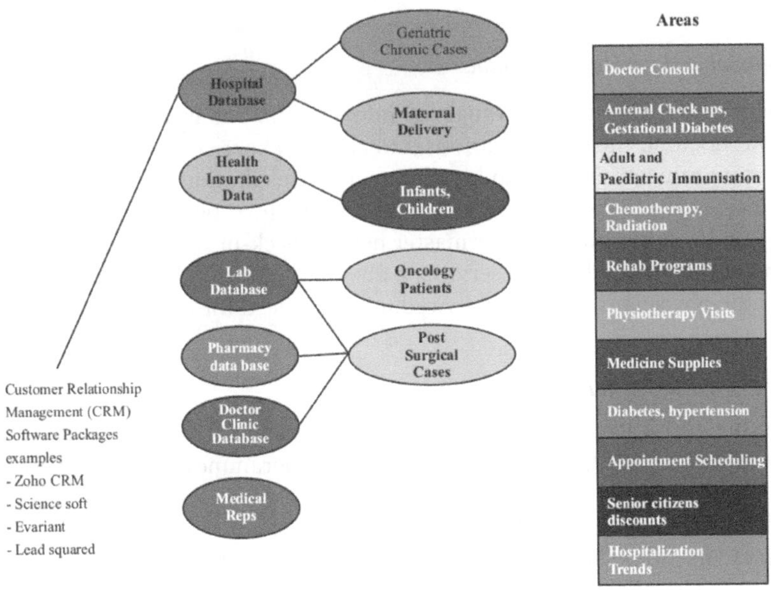

Figure 8.8 CRM in healthcare in India.

thereby building goodwill. Master health checkup patients may also need a follow-up, which the CRM can handle. CRM can be used imaginatively in a number of situations – with customers, suppliers and employees. This software enables keeping in touch in a world which is increasingly becoming insular.[24]

Home care

Some patients might prefer home care. In some cases, the hospitals recommend home care. Many hospitals arrange for nurses to care for the patient at their home. Oxygen concentrators could be rented, and doctor visits can also be arranged. Laboratories arrange for home blood collection and send the report results through email. The hospitals should constitute a team which can provide home care with lower costs without compromising on the quality of treatment. Some patients might require ICU facility or physiotherapy at home.

Websites as a marketing tool

Well-designed websites have become an important part of the marketing efforts of hospitals. Catering to different age groups, websites provide crucial information, offer several friendly features, provide navigation to various services offered by the hospital along with the profile of specialist doctors and payment gateways. Websites have shrunk distances and communication barriers, enabling hospitals to reach out to its target market easily.

Regional and pan-India hospitals

Websites provide a wide range of information, for example, information about doctors, their qualifications and clinical experience, enable patients to fix appointments and schedule online video consultations. Patients can order medicines from the pharmacy, fix laboratory investigations online, obtain lab results online and plan for master health check-ups. During the pandemic period, the value of online services gained appreciation by both the patients and the physicians, substantially reducing the need for hospital visits.

Health and wellness programmes

Websites offer a range of options, such as weight loss programmes, yoga and advanced yoga, five-kilometre running programmes and specialised programmes for patients with specific conditions such as asthma or sleep disorders. All these programmes cater to the needs of healthy citizens as well as patients. Some hospitals also offer Ayurvedic treatment as an alternative.

Access to health records

Patients registering with the hospital can access their personal health records, keep track of key parameters and allow consulting doctors to access relevant past data. This is a far cry from the days when the hospitals in India would not allow the patients to take their files home. Hospitals and most of the diagnostic laboratories send the test results online. Websites allow the patient to choose a particular technician to come for a home visit at a convenient time. Collection of samples, online payment and online test results eliminate the need for visiting the laboratories. In summary, websites are one of the ways to foster patient loyalty to hospitals.

Clinical outcomes

Many websites provide data on clinical outcomes for major treatments. This is a welcome step. Referring doctors and patients can decide whether they should choose a particular hospital on the basis of the data. Ashok Anantaram, the marketing expert, describes publishing data about clinical outcomes as the '*tangibilising the intangible*'.

Health video library

Websites feature a health video library offering expert advice on various diseases and typical symptoms. The purpose of this library is to inform and educate the patient and their families. Some examples are scientific information on the diagnosis and treatment of depression, gestational diabetes and the role of the family. The objective is to provide reliable scientific information for patient education.

Accreditations

Most corporate hospitals hold accreditations like JCI, NABH or National Accreditation Board for Testing and Calibration Laboratories (NABL). The accreditations assure patients of the hospital's commitment to maintaining the highest quality medical care standards. Websites offer detailed information about compliance.

Academics and research

Hospitals offer Diplomate of National Board (DNB) programmes in a number of specialties, have their nursing schools and provide courses in allied health sciences programmes, thus providing continuing medical education. Websites provide prospective students with information about the programmes offered, eligibility, duration, fees and application procedures.

Corporate information

Websites serve investors and the public by publishing annual reports on the site, addressing investor queries and presenting a host of operational data. Comparative analyses of various corporate hospitals can be valuable for the management student to appreciate the uniqueness of each hospital. The websites are constantly improving in their scope based on feedback from patients.

Logo, branding, co-branding and brand equity

Logo

Logos provide instant recognition of the hospital brand (Figure 8.9). The design of a logo would be based on inputs from the advertising agency, marketing and top management. Logo should utilise attractive colours, stylised wording and symbols to communicate messages about the company, the hospital and its philosophy. 'Logos should have great typography, simple colours, and a strong visual element'.[25]

All institutions spend large sums of money and effort to popularise their logo. Logos are prominently displayed on hoardings, newspaper advertisements, social media posts and in billboards with neon lighting.

Figure 8.9 Logos.

Branding

According to the American Marketing Association, 'A brand is a name, term, design, symbol, or any other feature that identifies one seller's goods or service as distinct from those of other sellers.' A brand name represents trust built over a period of time, based on patients' testimonials, media coverage, videos and social media.[26]

'Branding is endowing products and services with the power of a brand' (Kotler and Keller, 2015).[27] Brand equity helps in attracting patients to the hospital.[28] The brand name of a hospital serves as an identity for patients, employees, suppliers, the larger public, international patients, insurance companies, corporates and investors. Brand names, which signify the reputation of the institution indirectly, are also helpful in attracting doctors, nurses and other staff to join the hospital.

In the context of hospitals, reputed brand names, such as Apollo, Manipal, Fortis and Sankara Nethralaya, evoke emotions and perceptions built on 'word-of-mouth', personal experiences with the hospital and impressions formed over a period of time from several sources, including traditional and social media impressions.

Brand equity

Marketing expert Ashok Anantaram emphasises: 'Building and sustaining the brand equity is the core objective of every hospital, going beyond sales and marketing efforts. The entire organisation must be involved in sustaining a strong brand value'. Instant recognition of a brand offers a significant advantage, especially in cities where there are many corporate hospitals. Patients often have reasons to choose a particular hospital, and the trust associated provides a distinct advantage. Brand name helps in patient inflow, potential to charge higher rates for services and attract newer doctors to join the hospital.

Brand acquisition

When a hospital acquires another hospital, the decision to retain the original brand name depends on the brand equity of the acquired brand and the parent's brand equity. For instance, Manipal Hospitals acquired 100 per cent stake in Columbia Asia Hospitals, Bengaluru, and chose to change the brand name to the parent hospital in April 2021. Fortis retained both names of the Chennai-based hospitals Malar Hospitals as Fortis Malar. Since then, there has been another change. MGM Healthcare acquired Fortis Malar and changed the name to MGM Healthcare – Malar. Max Healthcare maintains the brand name everywhere, except in Mumbai, where it is called Nanavati Max Hospitals.

Apollo Hospitals uses nearly 20 sub-brands[29] to promote different specialties, such as Apollo Sugar (diabetes), Apollo Cradle (paediatrics), Apollo Clinics (outpatient), Apollo White (dental), Apollo Spectra (day-care surgery) and Apollo Pharmacy. The multi-brand strategy appears to be a long-term plan to compete with other well-known single-specialty hospitals. It could also potentially lead to forming a separate company for each brand.

Semiotics

Semiotics, in the context of branding, involves the study of how ideas or objects communicate through colours and symbols used in logos. 'Semiotics, put simply, is the study of how an idea or object communicates meaning – and what meaning it communicates. For example, 'coffee' is a brewed beverage, but it also evokes comfort, alertness, creativity'.[30]

Symbols consciously or subconsciously evoke meanings beyond the surface. Every aspect of the logo, including colours and stylised letters, conveys a set of meaning. The original designers of a logo may or may not have meant any great symbolism. Apple now represents innovative technological products, wonderful designs, a status symbol and an instant recognition for all the products such as phones, watches and iPads. Successful products create myths about the greatness of a logo. Companies like Apple, Nike, Coca-Cola, MRF and Apollo Hospitals are readily recognised by the public by their symbol. The symbol of red ribbon instantly reminds of AIDS awareness around the world. On the other hand, failed brands and symbols are quickly forgotten, highlighting the impermanence of the brands.

Adverting and promotional campaigns

Managements should ensure that the cost of marketing and the cost of acquiring patients are reasonable. Therefore, the selection of traditional or social media is done based on the effectiveness of each media in reaching out to the patient community.

Social media is also extensively utilised by all hospitals. Facebook, LinkedIn, Twitter and bookmarking sites, such as Pinterest, flip boards, blogs and YouTube, have become popular platforms. WhatsApp has become a powerful tool for forming friend, family and patient groups with physicians.

Rural India

Social media is also used extensively in rural India. In addition, promotion campaigns should be in the local language using local idioms. There are non-government organisations (NGOs) who use street plays, puppet shows and dance to create awareness about health and social practices. In a vast country like ours, there is immense scope for innovation in communicating with people. The public awareness about health and specific diseases is poor and, therefore, accurate presentation of facts is essential.

Print media

Print media in India, mainly newspapers and magazines, continue to be large, with over 380 million copies circulated every day.[31,32] Hindi newspapers dominate the newspaper market. While the young increasingly rely on other sources such as social media, print media still continues to be a significant player. So, hospitals utilise this medium for advertising the inauguration of a hospital, rare surgeries conducted at the hospital and other human-interest stories.

Traditional media continues to play a key part in reaching out to the communities. The launch of a new hospital is usually advertised in newspapers. A new medical team joining a hospital is splashed in regional and English newspapers. Articles and interviews in popular regional language magazines is another option.

Television

There are an estimated 210 million TV sets in India, providing options of up to 1,000 channels. Hindi channels are a crucial part of the TV spectrum.[33] Regarding TV viewing in India, a study shows that television viewing in the 15- to 30-year-old age groups has declined, while 31- to 50-year-old age group constitutes the largest TV viewing group.[33] Many channels have regular slots for interviews with senior doctors. During the pandemic, there was a surge in viewership of television programmes for interviews with medical experts. The Q&As with senior doctors on diabetes, pregnancy, childcare and stroke are also popular.

Hoardings

Hoardings continue to be popular for consumer products, consumer durables and airlines. Airport, bus stops, railway stations, highways, street corners and, indeed, any place that has reasonable traffic is a potential site for placing a hoarding. The cost of advertising depends on the location, size of the billboard and duration of exposure. Hospitals and laboratories extensively utilise hoardings for advertising.

FM radio[34]

FM radio has witnessed rapid growth. There are nearly 400 FM radio stations in 150 cities with an estimated 50 million listeners to radio programmes. Some hospitals use FM radio both for advertising their hospitals as well as for talks by medical experts. It is interesting to note that a large number of infertility clinics and laboratories seemed to favour this medium. Infertility clinics seem to be aggressive in the utilisation of social media as well, playing on the vulnerability of the couple. A senior doctor from a government hospital mentioned that even among the poor people, infertility treatments are popular.[35]

Digital media[36]

The patient group includes a large number of younger people and many tech-savvy senior citizens. Many digital platforms, such as websites, search engines, WhatsApp groups and other social media, have become an important source of information and communication. Every organisation uses digital media to their advantage, and private hospitals, labs and pharmacies are no exception. Some of the examples are discussed in this chapter.

Other media

It is common to see booklets or small handouts attached to morning newspapers at airports. Handbills are freely distributed by laboratories to households. Hospitals and laboratories utilise signposts to advertise their facilities. Each exposure serves as a reminder.

Social media and digital marketing

Digital marketing or online marketing is the promotion of brands using the Internet and other forms of digital communication, including email, social media, and web-based advertising, text and multimedia messages. Hospitals in the United States, such as The Mayo Clinic, Johns Hopkins and Cleveland Clinic, have created large audiences utilising social media.

> The Mayo clinic utilises Facebook and Twitter to inform the public about inspirational success stories. Cleveland Clinic has Facebook Q&A sessions on a wide range of subjects such as food borne illnesses, osteoporosis, and various interesting developments at the clinic. Johns Hopkins is very popular on YouTube. The programme on paediatric brain procedure for pancreatic cancers was considered outstanding.[37]

The National Health Service (NHS) in the UK uses social media extensively, particularly Twitter, Facebook, YouTube and LinkedIn.[38]

It is estimated that about 450–500 million users in India utilise some form of social media[39] for sending messages, sharing photos and forwards. Advertisers find these media attractive, which is evolving to reach out to specific groups such as youngsters and senior citizens.

Many hospitals and NGOs are present on social media. David Gonsalves, writing on healthcare marketing, opines that digital marketing helps improve sales and get more patients for the hospitals.[40] TAM Adex also reports a sharp increase in digital media advertising. Writing on the subject of social media effectiveness, Dam Eixred says, 'When you utilise the ad platforms available on networks like Facebook, Instagram, Twitter, you'll be able to target your exact customer by demographics'.

Social media effectiveness

Srinath Rajaram, an expert on social media, explained:

> Twitter (now called X) is a very powerful medium. When a patient complains about the poor quality of care or high hospital bills, his followers amplify and very soon there would be a large number of specific complaints on Twitter (now X). Hospitals have to be on Twitter (now X) if only as a defence mechanism.

Srinath further elaborated: 'When a patient responds to a wellness programme or a discounted master health check up on Facebook, hospitals marketing gets into the act'. He added, 'social media was closely involved in many public health programmes – pulse polio, COVID vaccination'.

Srinath goes on to say,

> You pay very little to advertise... you pay per click or per impression or per outcome. In the case of print media, the advertisers pay per insertion depending on the media depending on its circulation and readership, number of seconds of TV advertising on prime time. The outcomes cannot be easily measured. In the case of social media, it is based on effectiveness.

Parikh Hospital, based in Ahmedabad,[41] uses Twitter (now X) to advertise its laparoscopic surgery and general surgery services. Jawahar Eye Hospitals, Meerut, uses Twitter (now X) to advertise about its laser eye surgery. Several large hospital chains such as Apollo, Fortis and Max use various social media to boost their business.[42]

Apollo Hospitals have been utilising social media to run *Reel to heal* (information videos on COVID and vaccinations) and Twitter for conducting regular polls or surveys. The results of the surveys are posted on their blogs (a dedicated webpage for healthy lifestyle and medical information). It also uses hashtags, such as #38yearsofhealing and #runforahealthyheart, to make the public aware of its campaigns.[43] All these initiatives bring Apollo closer to the customer. Manipal Hospitals have a podcast named White Coat World, which is available on Google Podcasts, Apple Podcasts and Spotify. Similarly, they have a podcast called Up-close Medical, which says that it provides accurate medical information. Narayana Health utilises various social media platforms such as Facebook, YouTube and Instagram.

Narayana Health posts blogs on a range of medical information, for example, how to take care of asthma during monsoon, advanced cardiac care and other ailments.[44]

YouTube

Many well-known doctors in India, such as Dr V. Mohan on diabetes, Dr Devi Shetty on cardiac diseases and Dr Gagandeep Kang on viruses and, in particular, on COVID, have creatively utilised YouTube to educate the public. Some hospitals utilise YouTube for advertising their hospital in a short video programme. For example, Soundrapandian Bone and Joint Hospital, based in Chennai, is using YouTube to create awareness and also to promote its services.

QR codes

QR codes (quick response codes) have found increasing acceptance in a wide range of applications, including in the healthcare industry (Figure 8.10). QR codes can hold hundreds of information, more than conventional bar codes. In hospitals in the United States, QR codes are being used for patient identification, including links to patient case sheets. QR codes are being used in emails, newsletters, bills, flyers, hoardings and medical journals, which in turn provide links to hospitals' websites, success stories and cleanliness. Drug safety is another area. Important information about medical equipment and its linkage with operating manuals provides instant access.[45] A billion QR codes were used in India for issuing COVID vaccination certificates to citizens.[46]

Figure 8.10 QR codes.

Data analytics

Hospitals gather substantial patient data from diverse sources, including outpatients, inpatients, master health check-ups and pharmacy records. Artificial intelligence aids in identifying disease patterns and predictive analysis for a number of chronic diseases like diabetes. However, acceptance of data analytics and the privacy of data of individual patients are real concerns.[47]

Conclusion

For many decades, hospitals believed that 'word of mouth' and doctors' popularity are sufficient to attract patients. The twenty-first century has revealed that old management practices are no longer adequate. Hospitals have created an independent identity of their own. Competition, particularly among private hospitals, has necessitated the utilisation of marketing principles to get new patients and retain old patients, make profits, to grow and improve their valuation. Many marketing professionals have moved to the healthcare industry from various consumer and service industries. They have brought with them innovative strategies fully employing modern marketing concepts. The future promises to be even more interesting.

Notes

1 Apollo Hospitals, https://en.wikipedia.org/wiki/Apollo_Hospitals
2 Theory of demand, Tutor2u.net, https://www.tutor2u.net/economics/reference/theory-of-demand
3 List of million-plus urban agglomerations in India, https://en.wikipedia.org/wiki/List_of_million-plus_urban_agglomerations_in_India
4 Gupta Surojit, 'Nearly 1 in 3 Indians middle class, to double in 25 years: report', *Times of India*, 2 November 2022, https://timesofindia.indiatimes.com/business/india-business/middle-class-nearly-1/3rd-of-indias-population-to-be-2/3rds-by-2047-report/articleshow/95239621.cms
5 Prerna Gupta, 'Socio-economic classification in retail marketing', *PPMS*, https://www.ppms.in/blog/socio-economic-classification-in-retail-marketing/
6 Apollo Hospitals, Annual report, 2021–22, https://www.apollohospitals.com/apollo_pdf/AHEL-AR22-Full-Report-Final-(20220802).pdf
7 'Narayana Health's Dr Devi Shetty on the new health order at Microsoft Future Ready', *Economic Times*, 3 March 2022, https://economictimes.indiatimes.com/industry/healthcare/biotech/healthcare/narayana-healths-dr-devi-shetty-on-the-new-health-order-at-microsoft-future-ready/articleshow/89899615.cms?utm_source=contentofinterest&utm_medium=text&utm_campaign=cppst
8 'What is market segmentation?', *Qualtrics*, https://www.qualtrics.com/uk/experience-management/brand/market-segmentation/#:~:text=At%20its%20core%2C%20market%20segmentation,better%20understand%20the%20target%20audience
9 T. Ramamoorthy, S. Leburu, V. Kulothungan, and P. Mathur, 'Regional estimate of non-communicable diseases associated risk factors among adults in India: results from National Non-communicable Diseases Monitoring survey', *BMC Public Health*, 2022;22:article number: 1069, https://bmcpublichealth.biomedcentral.com/articles/10.1186/s12889-022-13466-5

10 J. Gangopadyaya and S. Sengupta, 'What does the future hold for India's ageing population?', *Life*, 27 July 2022, https://www.thecitizen.in/life/what-does-the-future-hold-for-indias-ageing-population-319293
11 Psychographic segmentation and its practical application in personalized patient engagement and activation, Upfront, White paper, https://upfronthealthcare.com/wp-content/uploads/2022/12/2022-Upfront-Psychographics-Whitepaper.pdf
12 Adele Revella, 'Psychographics and personas: how to get to the truth about why people buy', *Hotjar blog*, 23 February 2023. https://app.thejuicehq.com/content/rtLq8PmkxAdbuwooH7h7Cvav
13 Nicole Wintermeir, 'Who is the luxury consumer? A guide to the psychology of luxury', *Crobox*, 6 January 2021, https://blog.crobox.com/article/luxury-consumer-psychology
14 Alisa Meredith, 'Psychographics in your marketing – A beginners guide', *Hubspot Market Research Kit*, 17 August 2021, https://blog.hubspot.com/insiders/marketing-psychographics
15 '4 Hospitals leveraging social media to improve patient engagement', *HIT Consultant Media*, 27, February 2021, https://hitconsultant.net/2020/02/27/4-hospitals-leveraging-social-media-to-improve-patient-engagement/
16 Jared Cornell, 'Psychographic segmentation, variables, examples, and templates', *Proprofs*, 28 June 2023, https://www.proprofssurvey.com/blog/psychographic-segmentation/
17 Nir Eyal, *Hooked*, Penguin Random House UK, 2019.
18 'The best bipolar disorder apps of 2020', *Healthline*, https://www.healthline.com/health/bipolar-disorder/top-iphone-android-apps
19 'Labour survey shows rising trend in employment in organised sector', *NDTV Profit*, 28 April 2022, https://www.ndtv.com/business/labour-survey-shows-rising-employment-trend-in-organised-sector-minister-2927677
20 'Understanding the seven Ps of the marketing mix', *Oxford College of Marketing*, https://blog.oxfordcollegeofmarketing.com/2020/10/08/understanding-the-7ps-of-the-marketing-mix/
21 Julian Yudleson, 'Adapting Macarthy's four Ps in the 21st century', *Journal of Marketing Education*, 1999;21(1):60–67, https://journals.sagepub.com/doi/10.1177/0273475399211008
22 T. Srinivas, B. Srininivasa Rao, and U. Srinivasa Rao, 'An analysis of marketing mix in hospitals', *International Journal of Advanced Research in Management and Social Sciences*, 2013;2(4):187–207, https://www.researchgate.net/publication/369023123_AN_ANALYSIS_ON_MARKETING_MIX_IN_HOSPITALS
23 NABH Emergency Department Certification Program, August 2020, https://nabh.co/Images/PDF/Emergency_Brochure.pdf
24 'Role of CRM in healthcare industry', *SNAK Consultancy Services*, 20 May 2022, https://www.linkedin.com/pulse/role-crm-healthcare-industryrole-industry-snakconsultancyservices/
25 'What's the purpose of logos and why do they matter?' *Logo Geek*, https://logogeek.uk/logo-design/why-logos-matter/
26 'Branding insights from Philip Kotler', *Knowledge Capital*, https://www.kcapital-us.com/home/n/resources/philip-nirmalaya.pdf
27 'What is sub-branding? A guide to branding architecture', *Indeed*, 28 September 2022, https://www.indeed.com/career-advice/career-development/sub-branding
28 Adam Hayes, 'Brand equity: Definition, importance, effect on profit margin, and examples', *Investopedia*, April 2025, https://www.investopedia.com/terms/b/brandequity.asp
29 Apollo Group Brands, 14 August 2023, https://www.apollohospitals.com/corporate/company-overview/apollo-group-brands/

30 'Semiotics: The study of signs', *Encyclopaedia Brittanica*, 7 September 2023, https://www.britannica.com/science/semiotics
31 Tanushree Basuroy, 'Indian newspaper industry – Statistics and facts', *Statistica*, 25 January 2023, https://www.statista.com/topics/4726/newspaper-industry-in-india/
32 Tanushree Basuroy, 'Number of certified publications across India, by language', *Statista*, 9 March 2022, https://www.statista.com/statistics/945316/india-print-newspaper-circulation-by-language/
33 Television in India, Wikipedia, 17, September 2023, https://en.wikipedia.org/wiki/Television_in_India
34 'Radio industry listenership surges to 51 million', *Business Insider*, 9 April 2020, https://www.businessinsider.in/advertising/media/news/radio-industry-listenership-surges-to-51-million/articleshow/75063045.cms
35 FM Radio, Online Radio.in, https://www.adgully.com/digital-most-preferred-medium-for-hospitals-clinics-ads-in-jan-aug-21-tam-adex-109134.html
36 'Digital media most preferred medium for hospitals and clinics', *Adgully*, 21 September 2021, https://www.adgully.com/digital-most-preferred-medium-for-hospitals-clinics-ads-in-jan-aug-21-tam-adex-109134.html
37 'How hospitals can make the best use of social media', *AHA Trustee Services*, https://trustees.aha.org/articles/949-how-hospitals-can-make-the-best-use-of-social-media
38 NHS England – Examples Social media, https://www.england.nhs.uk/nhsidentity/identity-examples-categories/social-media/
39 Sam Wixted, 'Why marketing through social media is more effective?' *WebFx*, https://www.webfx.com/blog/general/why-marketing-through-social-media-is-effective/
40 Akanksha Rukhaiyar, 'Why digital marketing is so important to businesses', *Springboard*, 22 June 2022, https://www.springboard.com/blog/business-and-marketing/digital-marketing-importance/
41 Parikh Hospitals, X.com, 3 September 2022, https://x.com/ParikhHospitals/status/1566106984637640706
42 'Social media in India – Stats 2023 and platform trends', *OOGSA*, https://oosga.com/social-media/ind/#:~:text=How%20are%20users%20distributed%20in,33.4%20%25%20of%20the%20total%20population.
43 'How Apollo moved closer to the customer', March 2022. https://canit.in/marketing-insights/how-apollo-moved-closer-to-the-customer/
44 Narayana Health, X.com, https://x.com/NarayanaHealth?ref_src=twsrc%5Etfw
45 Apoorva Hegde, 'QR codes in health care- why it makes a difference', *Blog*, 14 September 2023, https://blog.beaconstac.com/2020/02/qr-codes-in-healthcare/
46 'India achieves major milestone: one billion vaccinations', Embassy of India, Poland, https://www.indianembassywarsaw.gov.in/news_letter_detail/?id=41
47 'Fortis Hospitals Mumbai launches social media campaign #AtFortisWePledge', *Bio Voice*, https://www.biovoicenews.com/fortis-hospitals-mumbai-launches-social-media-campaign-atfortiswepledge/

9 Human resource management

Tilak Shankar

Introduction

People working in organisations visibly perform the roles assigned to them, but they also invisibly bring their aspirations, need for recognition and likes and dislikes to their jobs. Therefore, managing large teams of professionals with diverse talent poses a challenge for leaders.

Douglas McGregor was one of the original thinkers in articulating the importance of management of human resources (HR) in organisations. He introduced the concepts of theory X and theory Y. According to theory X, employees are perceived as paid workers, while theory Y recognises them as human beings with emotions, feelings and aspirations. Frederick Taylor, in his groundbreaking work on industrial engineering, treated humans as inputs for production,[2] emphasising efficiency but neglecting their emotional dimensions. Abraham Maslow[3] (1908–1970), Ishwar Dayal, Kamala Chowdhry and many other original thinkers have added to our understanding of human behaviour in an organisational setting.[4] Some of these theories of human motivation and the need hierarchy of Maslow are valid today. In the last 60 years after McGregor's seminal work was published, HR practices have evolved significantly, but the underlying ideas of McGregor are still relevant. The industrial culture and HR practices that dominated the Indian industry in the late twentieth century and early twenty-first century, emphasising people management, have been replaced by HR practices assuming a strategic role in the services industry. HR practices in the manufacturing and service sectors have always been rooted in the Indian culture and ethos in a unique way. The service sector, which has emerged as a dominant sector of the Indian economy, employs millions of people.

People make a difference to an organisation

Several management thinkers have emphasised that, ultimately, people make organisations. It is not just medical equipment or buildings that make a great hospital, but it is the medical experts who work there to provide comfort and deliver high-quality care and nurses who help put the patient back to recovery and wellness. Hospital is a unique knowledge industry; it employs

DOI: 10.4324/9781003684947-11

highly qualified professionals, who make a difference through their ways of care and unique skills, and a large number of women in supporting functions. The hospital environment necessitates employees functioning under stress as hospitals function 24/7. The skill sets of professionals need constant upgradation.

New role for HR

The role of HR has evolved far beyond personnel record-keeping and routine administration. Industries such as software, telecom, banking, insurance, business process outsourcing (BPO), hospitality and healthcare are employing large numbers of skilled people. Organisations have challenges in recruiting, retaining and motivating predominantly young professionals, including a large number of women.

In the last few decades, there has been a paradigm shift in HR practices. The Indian manufacturing sector has a rigid hierarchy, strict gradations of jobs, inflexible payscales and slow promotion systems. The needs of the service sector are completely different. The services industry not only employs people with technical skills but also rewards good performers handsomely. Rapid career growth has become possible in today's services sector, along with attractive compensation. In organisations with diverse talent in terms of age and experience, achieving a balance between the seniors and juniors, between experience and fresh enthusiasm has become essential, particularly in the healthcare industry.

This chapter discusses three key areas in human resource management:

- Organisation development, structure, staffing and recruitment
- Compensation and benefits, including job evaluation and grading
- Skill development, education and technology absorption

Hospital as an institution of care

Hospitals are a knowledge institution employing highly qualified staff – medical, nursing and technical staff who require requisite skill, up-to-date knowledge and sound judgement while dealing with inpatients and outpatients. The physiology of each patient is different, and a mechanical approach to diagnosis and treatment would not be appropriate. While medical equipment provides substantial data, it is the doctor who uses his or her judgement in interpreting data for treatment. Beyond mere treatment, there is a unique human dimension attached to healthcare. The medical experts are required to save lives, alleviate pain and provide the patients with hope. The hospital environment is stressful for staff as the hospital works round the clock, especially the emergency department. Different points of care, such as operating theatres, children's wards, intensive care unit (ICU), post-operative wards and cancer wards, need alert medical staff who have to respond to patient needs promptly. The front-line staff are required to be alert, offering comfort to the patient even under difficult conditions.

The entire management should be appreciative of the stress levels of the staff. A senior hospital administrator pointed out, 'the doctor and nurse should be alert and compassionate even at 2 a.m. with a difficult patient'. HR practices and policies in a healthcare institution are therefore widely different from other service industry sectors.

Dual role of HR

HR is responsible for both transactional responsibilities and for overall organisational development. Both the above functions are equally important. Procedural responsibilities include salary administration, implementing timely increments, salary revisions, performance appraisals and initiating changes in HR policies. Organisational development (OD) includes the initiation of organisational changes, skill upgradation and new initiatives.

Organisational development

OD has been described as 'a critical and science-based process that helps organisations build their capacity to change and achieve greater effectiveness by developing, improving, and reinforcing strategies and structures'.[5]

Medical professionals need to be attuned to new scientific developments and hospital as an institution needs to encourage learning, new skills and be receptive to new ideas. In the last few decades, innovations in medical technology, drug development, global research findings and learnings from patient databases have revolutionised medical care. Indian hospitals have quickly adapted to global changes. Acquisitions and mergers in Indian healthcare require the integration of the two or more disparate organisations so that they start functioning as a single entity as quickly as possible. Organisations have to be nimble in not only accepting changes but also in providing a suitable atmosphere for growth. OD is a management tool for this purpose. OD requires a clear long-term vision with specific actions on organisational redesign, HR policies, development of key individuals and responding to external developments. The most important attribute is developing the capacity to change.

Organisational design (Figure 9.1)

Public health

The organisational structure in public health system is rigid and has largely remained immune to external changes. The system does not have the patient as its primary focus but pays more attention to systems and processes that

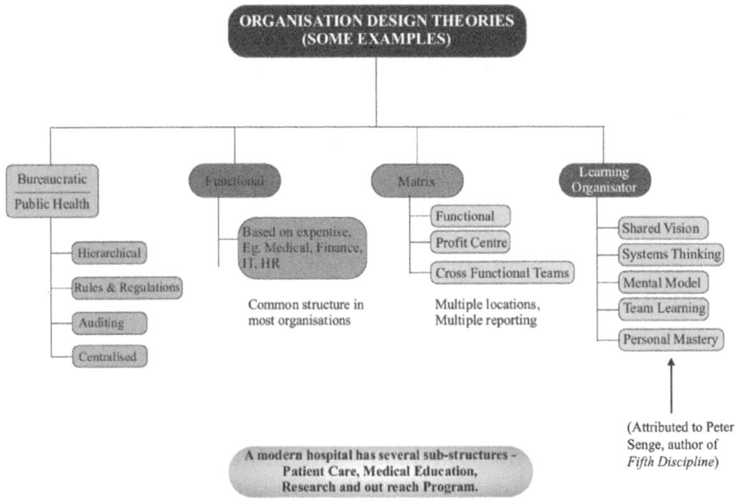

Figure 9.1 Organisational design.

may be outdated at times. HR systems are the same as for other government departments, and the unique needs of healthcare are not recognised.

Private sector

The private sector consists of small nursing homes, medium to large non-profit/charitable hospitals, medium to large for-profit hospitals and a chain of corporate hospitals. Private hospitals have grown in size, spread over several locations and their sales revenue has grown over the last three decades. Large corporate hospital chains have realised the importance of a flexible organisation structure, which responds to internal needs as well as external changes. Hospital chains in multiple locations require a matrix structure. A corporate structure with dual reporting of finance, marketing and HR functions has to facilitate management control while empowering the branches. Similarly, a profit centre concept has enabled growth, requiring a flexible organisational structure. Greater empowerment has been made possible with technology playing a role in creating centralised data. Contemporary medical technology combined with information technology has enabled nimble organisation structures.

Staffing characteristics

Hospitals experience high staff turnover of nurses and doctors. New recruits require adequate time to get familiar with the systems in the hospital. When a hospitals are acquired by other hospitals, organisational structures, job titles, salary scales in the two hospitals could be different, necessitating the integration of medical professionals and organisational culture. Successful integration is essential for the acquisitions to succeed.

Peter Senge, in his path-breaking work on learning organisation, has highlighted many aspects of a learning organisation.[6] A hospital requires constant upgradation of knowledge and flexibility in responding to changes. In addition to patient care, hospitals also engage in offering teaching programmes, bringing out publications and running research departments, each of which requires different approaches. Senge calls such organisations 'learning organisations'.

There have been many research studies on human motivation, organisational structures, compensation and conflict management. Every modern hospital has to constantly review its organisational structure, internal systems, staff compensation and composition of staff to remain cost-effective, balancing between short-term needs and long-term strategic directions. Patient care and cost implications have to remain the central focus. The hospital should also comply with quality accreditation standards.

Human resource planning

The National Accreditation Bureau for Hospitals (NABH) emphasises workforce planning, which includes strategic and operational aspects. This is the first of the 13 standards. In fact, after quality care, NABH accords the highest importance to HR management. It is essential that even if a hospital doesn't have formal accreditations, it should follow a systematic management process.[7]

Strategic HR planning involves five- or ten-year projections of human resources aligned with plans for growth, acquisitions, diversification and divestment. The National Health Service (NHS), UK, for example, prepares a 10-year plan in which prevention of heart attacks, strokes, dementia and many other plans for geriatric care are budgeted.[8]

Planning should not be a mere exercise of projecting the number of staff members over the next few years. Every assumption regarding future medical departments, skills required, new acquisitions and new activities has to be factored in.

Operational planning includes the projection of costs of human resources, staff productivity, skill development, automation, the number of staff in administrative departments, departments for outsourcing, job rotation and attrition analysis. Employee suggestion schemes help in improving efficiency. HR plays a crucial role in presenting recommendations to the board, ensuring alignment with organisational goals. NABH identifies HR as a priority function. There are a large number of activities in which HR should play a leadership role, bringing the human angle to focus.

Human resources in a hospital

In a modern hospital, different professionals play different roles in patient care: Medical doctors, medical council postgraduates or National Board students, nurses, technicians, physiotherapists, assistants, finance, administration, IT, HR and engineering services. In addition, there would be various outsourced staff.

Most hospitals have post-graduate students (DNB) who work round the clock in the hospital; their motivation is important. Nurses, who form the largest group of staff (exceeding 40 per cent of the total), are critical to the hospital. There are several sub-specialities in nursing: Intensive care unit, obstetrics and gynaecology, paediatrics, neonatology, oncology, psychiatry, major and minor operating theatres and wards.

Similarly, technicians working in laboratories, diagnostics, X-ray, CT, MRI, phlebotomists, physiotherapists and nutritionists are yet another key segment. There are several subspecialties in cardiology, pulmonology, orthopaedics and dietetics, which have highly qualified and experienced technical staff. There are over 100 subspecialties in allied sciences. So, specialisation is not only at the medical doctor level, but at all support staff levels as well, for adult patients and paediatric patients alike. Some institutions have separate research staff for clinical trials, and some highly qualified personnel undertake fundamental and translational research.

Organisational structure

The hospital's organisational structure should be dynamic. As the organisation expands to multiple locations in the country, a formal structure becomes imperative, facilitating smooth coordination and communication and ensuring the availability of medical and management expertise. Defined accountability for internal audit, fire safety and effluent disposal contribute to a well-structured organisation.

Top management

If the hospital organisation has a board of directors, it is led by a chairperson who may be designated as executive chairperson if the role is full-time, or non-executive chairperson if it is part-time. The managing director or the chief executive officer (CEO) manages the operations. The board of directors or trustees should focus on policymaking and overall direction for the organisation.

The chairperson can be a medical professional or a management professional. There have been discussions regarding the separation of roles between the CEO and chairperson of the board.[9] The objective is to ensure that there is a separation of roles between the operational role of the CEO and the independent role of the chairperson.

Some of the practical aspects, which are discussed in this chapter are the following:

- Formal and informal structure
- Corporate and regional organisations
- Hierarchy
- Optimal size of a hospital
- Clarity in roles and responsibilities
- Opportunities for career growth

Formal structure

Formal organisational structure is essential for all medium/large-sized hospitals. It should be patient-centric with a central role for medical care. Role definition becomes necessary, and the span of control (or direct reports) has to remain small. This enables the head of the institution to focus on developments in the external environment, its implications and broader aspects of long-term planning and strategy. There are many organisations where five to eight senior staff could report to the chairperson. Depending on the needs of the organisation, for instance, if the organisation is planning to raise funds from financial institutions or planning an acquisition, then finance may directly report to the chairperson.

All organisations should have a well-defined structure unless they are small organisations. As the organisation grows in size, complexity and operations in multiple locations, a formal structure is required. A formal organisation is required to detail various departments' main roles and responsibilities (see Figure 9.1), avoiding rigid structures and silos.

Many hospitals have functional structures – medical departments, nursing, laboratory, imaging, finance, IT and HR. The heads of each department would be functional experts. A profit centre structure, on the other hand, identifies distinct activities or businesses as profit centres. In a multi-locational group, each location could be a profit centre, and within that structure, there would be a functional structure.

In a hospital, the medical departments are usually grouped under a Medical Director or a Chief Medical Officer, who ensures coordination with all medical specialties. The Medical Director should balance their time between day-to-day functions and long-term planning and play a crucial role in guiding the board on long-term planning of medical resources and facilities. In addition, their attention needs to be focused on direct academic programmes, introducing quality improvements and initiating new research programmes. The Medical Director's job requires tact in dealing with other senior medical professionals and firmness in enforcing strict quality standards. There would be many sought-after specialists who will be heading speciality departments of centres of excellence and they have to be handled with respect and dignity and also with tact so as to achieve the organisational goals.

The nursing staff might be the largest workforce in a hospital, which would be headed by a Nursing Director or Nursing Superintendent, reporting to the Medical Director. Recognised as the backbone of a hospital, well-trained and adequately motivated nursing staff can be a differentiator in achieving patient satisfaction.

Management functions

In a modern hospital, management professionals – finance, HR, IT and marketing – could be drawn from other hospitals or industries. Given the high demand for IT professionals globally, some hospitals have outsourced their IT departments.

Management staff should be proactive in helping the medical departments with financial data, marketing concepts and use of IT. Basic appreciation programmes on IT, finance and HR for medical staff can be organised, for example, finance appreciation and IT appreciation. Qualified hospital administrators from reputed institutions may be appointed for management roles.

Finance organisation

In corporate hospitals, the Head of Finance would carry the title Chief Financial Officer (CFO) or Finance Director, a board position. All related functions, such as accounting, treasury, secretarial and management accounting, would be grouped together and function under this executive. The large inflow of funds through private equity, IPOs and other sources in recent times into big hospitals has highlighted the central role of the finance organisation. PE funds may appoint their own Finance Director.

Informal structure

All organisations usually have a combination of informal structures and formal hierarchy. Informal structures are those formed among staff due to reasons such as the influence of power groups. Several staff would desire proximity to existing or new power centres. There could be real or imaginary grievances against some individuals or the organisation. Such groups can act in constructive ways or disrupt harmony. Informal groups are a reality. CEOs may choose to ignore these groups or utilise them. When one informal structure integrates with the formal structure, new informal groups may emerge.

Dual reporting

Dual reporting becomes necessary when managers operate from multiple locations. Functions like procurement, sales and marketing, finance and accounts, IT, HR and medical departments may have a dual reporting structure. The functional heads report to the local head of operations in each location and to the corporate head overseeing centralised functions. Reporting to the local head would be described as administrative reporting, and reporting to the functional head would be termed as functional reporting.[10] A matrix structure could lead to tensions between the 'bosses'. Sharp differences could arise between the two bosses at the time of appraisals, transfers and promotions.

Span of control

In a hierarchical organisational structure, the span of control under each manager should be largely dependent on the seniority of staff reporting.[11] As the span of control widens, the head of functions would depend on information flows and feedback for effective management. Progression in the hierarchy demands broader management skills.

The number of reporting relationships in an organisation can give rise to conflicts, as there are essentially only in effect three levels – the implementing level, the decision-making level and the policymaking level. A flat organisational structure finds favour with some organisations. Theoretically, there should be only three levels in any organisation. However, there could be six, eight or more levels or designations to accommodate growth opportunities. Numerous levels of reporting will slow down decision-making and response times. There are conflicting goals when determining the number of levels in the organisation. The management has to choose between organisational effectiveness, employee aspirations, staff motivation and retention.

Staff to supervision ratio

A critical examination regarding the ratio of staff members to supervisors is essential. This exercise will help in examining the value addition at the level of each level of staff. Most hospitals have automated or computerised many services. NABH mandates nurse-to-bed ratio for ICU and wards. Ratios such as staff-to-bed ratio and average revenue per employee are utilised as broad indicators.

Cross-functional teams

Cross-functional teams bring about coordination between various departments, breaking down barriers and usually work on a common problem. For instance, a team comprising medical doctors, pharmacists and finance professionals could collaborate on cost reduction or on reducing energy costs. A third group could collaborate on improving patient satisfaction.

The right organisation size

Determining the right organisation size, in terms of the number of beds, the number of locations and the number of staff, is a subjective matter. In the past, it was believed that the optimum size for a tertiary hospital is around 500 beds and about 3,000 staff members. It was believed that a much larger hospital may lose the connect with the patient. This assumption has changed with advanced information technology. The concept of management bandwidth has undergone fundamental changes. Many tertiary care hospitals in India now have 2,000 beds or more in one location, spread over multiple buildings, employing 12,000 to 15,000 staff members. There is no longer a right or wrong size for any hospital.

Committees

All hospitals employ committees to facilitate coordination, for information sharing, and to review performance. Committees serve two broad purposes:

- To review performance considering patient census, bed occupancy, inpatient and outpatient incomes, quality metrics, staff attrition and progress on new projects.
- Committees help in disseminating information, identifying areas for improvement and building comradeship.

Empowerment

Decision-making is linked to capability at different levels and the extent of delegation. There are two broad kinds of delegation of power: Financial and non-financial. Financial powers include cheque-signing authority (though bank transfers have replaced cheques), issuing purchase orders, sanctioning of expenses, entering into annual maintenance contracts and sanctioning discounts on patient billing. Non-financial powers could involve activities such as sanctioning leave, initiating disciplinary action, issuing appointment letters and the like. Here again, technology has eliminated many activities. A simple ABC analysis would highlight the financial impact of different transactions requiring empowerment. ABC is a simple management concept, which categorises items depending on their importance. For example, inventory can be categorised based on their value and annual consumption and purchase decisions can be delegated. Integrated computerised systems require a completely different mindset. In a computerised system, the algorithm can make automatic decisions on the reordering of low-value items.

Recruitment and induction

Recruitment is a significant challenge in all human resource-intensive sectors (see Figure 9.2). In the case of hospitals, nurses form nearly 40 per cent of the total staff and their attrition is typically high after a two-year stint. Other technicians, doctors and staff from other industries are also in great demand. Fresh recruits are an important source. Many institutions build long-term relationships with major colleges, so that their brand equity is built up over a long period of time.

In addition, the determination of the quantum of salary revisions, the fitment of lateral entrants, identifying and taking corrective actions for attrition and constantly upgrading HR practices, such as performance management systems, require careful study.

HR departments have various recruitment options such as campus recruitment, job search sites, head-hunters, employee referrals, an effective system of selecting campuses for recruiting fresh talent, maintaining touch with the educational institutions and also building a favourable image by sending newsletters and sponsoring cultural programmes. Websites play a crucial role in attracting potential staff. Brand building is essential for the recruitment of fresh staff, especially through feedback from staff at educational campuses, that is, those already employed in the hospital, to the campuses. Many hospitals have their own nursing colleges and DNB programmes, and, in such cases, a balanced combination of internal and external recruitment is practiced.

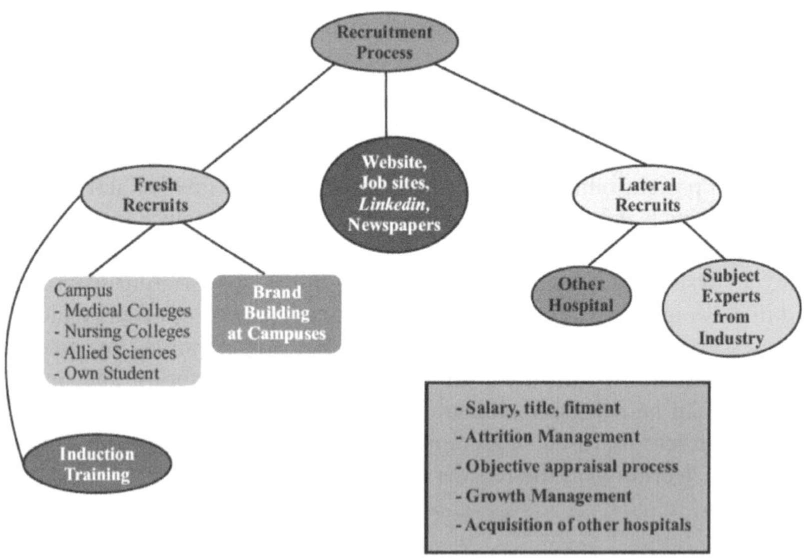

Figure 9.2 Recruitment and induction.

Induction

The first few days at work create a lasting impression, a key activity not always well understood. Employees entering their first job, at an impressionable age, will have a sense of anticipation and anxiety. Most organisations are not sensitive to the emotions of the young workforce. HR should ensure their first impressions are favourable by creating a welcoming atmosphere. Orientation programmes, elucidating organisational objectives, structure, key HR policies and a tour of the facilities, help the new employee. An HR representative is usually the contact point for the new entrants. Lunch and tea sessions where senior management executives interact with the new recruits give those freshers to the organisation an opportunity to understand the views of top executives. Young professionals are confident of their capabilities, unafraid of authority and expect comprehensive and honest responses to their queries.

During the induction training period, HR, in consultation with the heads of medical, nursing and laboratory departments, should ensure a structured training schedule. For example, one of the nurse trainees could work with housekeeping, pharmacies or the HR department on procurement, computerised systems or other topics. After three months, there should be a review, and the insights of new staff are extremely useful feedback to the hospital. This process is not only to inspire young entrants to the workforce but also to start building future leaders.

Lateral hires

Lateral recruitment has become necessary for senior managerial positions in finance, marketing, IT and health management. This might create ripples in salary levels, job titles and the age profile of the recruits. It is a common experience that whenever a recruit is hired from outside, it creates imbalances. Verification of credentials, that is, degree certificates, work experience and salary last drawn can sometimes yield unexpected results. There have been cases where the candidate's CV, even for a senior post, was found to be falsified. For medical doctors, an accreditation process should be made compulsory.

HR plays a key role in recruitment, striking a balance between requirements and broader organisational impact of the selected candidates as well as the cost implications. Organisations exercise caution in staffing decisions, including routinely replacing retiring staff.

Job grades

The relative importance of various jobs within a hospital can be established by a formal job evaluation system. These are different job evaluation methods to decide on the importance of each job in the organisation.

Job titles

The purpose of a job title is to define responsibilities to the individual working in an organisation and also to communicate their role to the external world. Job titles are typically organisation-specific. The titles could be based on government titles, named following the British or American designations and some are uniquely Indian. Senior positions may fall under four streams:

- Directors, deputy directors, joint directors, associate directors
- General manager, senior general manager, joint manager, manager, deputy manager, assistant manager
- Chief executive officer (CEO), chief financial officer (CFO), chief people officer or chief technology officer (CTO)
- President, Senior president, vice president and assistant vice president

Organisations adopt a combination of these designations, especially for marketing staff dealing with the external world, where high-sounding titles may be perceived as a necessity. In the Indian context, job titles play an important role in motivating the job holder and enhancing the person's self-image.

Job descriptions

NABH mandates formal job descriptions (JDs) at all levels, emphasising that JDs should not be created for mere compliance purposes but as tools reflecting the actual roles and responsibilities. There are varying views on the need for JDs. Some argue that role definition restricts the initiative of high-performing individuals, while others emphasise their utility in allotting job responsibilities, hiring staff, promoting staff and serving as a reference point in case of disputes. Periodic reviews of organisation structure, carried out internally or by external agencies, are crucial to identify areas of ambiguity, in assessing the adequacy of authority of different staff, as top management may not be aware of ground-level realities.

Organisation staffing and cost control

The design of the organisational structure and JDs should also focus on effective cost management. Salaries form the first or second most important cost item in all hospitals. There is a need for staff to provide effective patient care, moderated by cost considerations. Focus needs to be placed on staff productivity and additional staff have to be recruited only after clearly working out the need for additional resources. Human resources costs go up every year due to cost-of-living increases, increments and, where applicable, retirement benefits.

Departmental human resources costs

Department-wise salary costs can help identify major costs and their contribution to the hospital. Metrics should be established to measure and control costs across services, whether they are in-house or outsourced.

Personnel policies

Personnel policies have evolved significantly in the last few decades. Secrecy regarding policies is no longer possible. Management of a group of young professionals requires different HR skills. Young people have access to information about their own organisations as well as opportunities available to them elsewhere. Social media has been a great equaliser.

Productivity

Hospitals operating round the clock require additional staff. Human resources costs is a function of:

- Number of staff department-wise
- Staff to supervision ratio
- Cost increases due to cost-of-living adjustment, increments

Staff productivity

Staff productivity measures are common in many industries such as automotive, pharmaceutical and BPO industries. The hospital industry could develop such metrics based on NABH metrics.

Productivity can be enhanced by:

- Studying typical jobs performed in a day and identifying repetitive activities and their value addition
- Eliminating paperwork, examining work simplification methods
- Examining possibilities of using modern low-cost technology such as tablets for data capture, communication and reporting
- Automating repetitive work
- Combining two jobs into one
- Such studies are also required in government hospitals, which are paperwork-based

Narayana Health, a large tertiary care hospital with an all-India presence, has an effective system using mobile phones to transfer patient files and images and to link physicians, ICU staff and nurses. The mobile telephone-based system is not only employee-friendly but also integrates productivity with patient service.

A high degree of automation in the kitchen can help rationalise human resources. HR should work with all the departments and examine how human resources costs can be controlled by automation.

Compensation management

To attract new talent, salary scales should either match or surpass the 'market'. While low levels of compensation are often cited as a cause for high attrition, other factors also contribute to employee turnover. Effective compensation management is a crucial function within HR.

Benchmarking of salaries

Senior management may task HR with conducting a benchmarking exercise to compare salary levels with similar hospitals in the same region or pan-India hospital chains. The process may be carried out internally or outsourced, with participating hospitals sharing data based on a confidential agreement.

Methodological challenges include selecting comparable hospitals, accounting for their size, ownership differences, the number of specialties and differences in job titles across organisations. The salary and allowances mix may vary significantly. Non-profit hospitals also benchmark against the government of India and the state government payscales.

Pay commission

The Government of India implements a comprehensive job evaluation across all sectors that come under its jurisdiction. Once in 10 years, a central pay commission[12] is appointed, which studies and recommends to the government salary revisions required for job grades, payscales and allowances. The Seventh Pay Commission submitted its report to the Government of India in 2021 (Figure 9.3). There are about 40 levels that are equated across a variety of sectors based on education, experience and other factors. The government usually implements these recommendations, including in the public healthcare sector. Usually, state governments and some hospitals make revisions to their own salary scales accordingly. The healthcare sector is also covered by Pay Commission recommendations.

The Government of India and the state governments are the largest employers in India. The Government of India alone employs 33 lakh civilian employees and 14 lakh defence personnel. In addition, the government also pays pension to 53 lakh retired employees. It is relevant to point out that in the hospital sector, non-profit institutions benchmark their compensation to the Government of India scales.

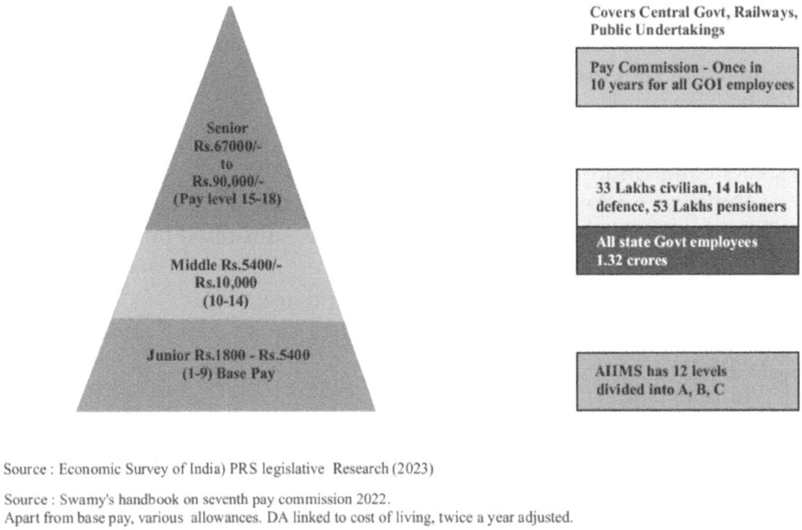

Figure 9.3 Seventh Pay Commission recommendations.

Sources: Economic Survey of India (2023), PRS legislative research (2023). Also Brinda and Sanjeev Muthuswamy, *Swamy's Compendium of Government Orders on Seventh Central Pay Commission Report* (2018), Swami Publishers.

Salary grades

Medical staff

Compensation practices for medical doctors vary. In non-profit institutions, medical staff are normally paid salaries. In some charitable hospitals, medical staff would be called consultants and compensated based on a 'fee-for-service' model, like for-profit hospitals. There would also be guidelines on the maximum fees that can be charged by consultants. There are also a small number of hospitals where the fee-for-service model is subject to a minimum guaranteed pay. In some hospitals, from the consultant's income, a small part would be set aside for attending conferences. DNB students would be paid a stipend as per the recommendations of the National Board.

Non-medical staff

In the case of all other staff, there would usually be eight to ten payscales, with the nursing staff comprising the largest number of grades. Generally, payscales would consist of the following elements.

- Basic salary
- Dearness allowance (DA) – either a fixed amount or a variable amount linked to the cost-of-living index. Some hospitals may not have a DA at all
- House rent assistance or housing in case of a remote location
- City compensatory allowance
- Conveyance allowance
- Night duty allowance, uniform allowance, subsidised lunch and dinner
- Creche benefits
- Medical benefits including hospitalisation insurance
- Retirement benefits – statutory provident fund, gratuity and sometimes pension
- Variable pay

The cost-to-company (CTC) approach is commonly used to manage compensation packages that encompass all outflows (pre-income tax) for employing the staff member, including allowances, DA and valuation of retirement benefits.

Increments

In private organisations, grade increments are provided annually, with high performers often receiving extra increments and promotions. Increments are predominantly performance-based rather than time-based. They may entail a fixed amount or a percentage of the basic salary. Consequently, employees with higher basic salaries in each grade receive larger salary raises.

Increments are determined by:

- Cost-of-living adjustments (COLA)
- Annual increments
- Performance-based increments
- Adjustments based on compensation studies

Performance-based increments

Performance-based increments are usually tied to formal performance appraisals. Some organisations follow a normal distribution curve, granting special or multiple increments to the top 10 per cent of the performers. However, certain managements may hesitate to reward individual excellence, as they feel that it could lead to poor teamwork. Good performers would be demotivated, resulting in attrition. Some organisations introduce 'variable pay' linked to performance for senior staff, accounting for a substantial portion of total compensation. Such systems could incentivise short-term results and foster unhealthy competition.

Performance appraisals

Adam Hayes defines performance appraisals as an annual process for assessing an employee's performance and contribution to the organisation.'[13] Performance appraisal systems have three broad objectives: (i) Integrate the organisation's goals into departmental and individual objectives; (ii) To assess the performance of each staff member and give feedback; and (iii) To link increments and promotions, identify training and development programmes and long-term potential for leadership. A sound system of performance appraisals will improve the hospital's brand image, attracting capable staff to its services.

Performance appraisal and goal setting

Individual appraisals should flow from the overall company goals and budgets. The main objectives of a private hospital are growth, quality, profitability and patient satisfaction. Charitable hospitals focus on financial self-sufficiency and patient satisfaction. The process of goal setting should be participatory, iterative and not merely an accounting exercise. Broadly, the goals of a hospital/company can be discussed under two headings: Revenues and costs.

Revenue is generated from medical departments, outpatient (OP) consultations, online consultations, operating theatres, laboratories, pharmacies and diagnostic tests. The revenues are further divided into departments, units within a department and individual practitioners. Goal setting will have two components: Quantitative and qualitative. Quantitative goals are based on departmental goals of revenue, profitability, growth and quality metrics. Qualitative goals should focus on the quality metrics for each specialty, human factor, teamwork, compassion for the patient, attitude to work and punctuality.

Medical staff evaluation

The primary objective of a hospital is patient care. Modern hospitals will have multiple yardsticks to measure the number of patients treated by each department, consultations, the number of major and minor surgeries and the quality of work through metrics. Evaluation of medical doctors is based on the quantity and quality of work, with numerous metrics employed for assessment. For instance, mortality and morbidity audits are conducted to ensure rigorous accountability for medical practitioners.

Senior surgeon Dr Arjun Rajagopalan, who served as Medical Director of a hospital, emphasised:

1. Mortality and morbidity (M&M) is easily the most venerable process. The vigour with which this is carried out depends on the institution's

character. Highly academic, teaching hospitals will carry out a no-holds-barred approach to discussions with the caveat that the proceedings are not to censure but to make sure mistakes don't get repeated. In most private hospitals, this is a perfunctory process where the exalted status of the doctor is not disturbed. When done well, the M&M is the most valuable component of physician competence and care assessment.
2. Random chart audits, where the case record is scrutinised under multiple, pre-established heads, are another good exercise. Some endpoints are length of stay, appropriateness of interventions to the condition and status at discharge, among others.
3. *Tissue committee*: Surgical procedures are assessed against the final pathological report to determine the appropriateness of the surgery.

A modern hospital should have a sound and rigorous M&M audit. The Medical Director plays a key role in this process.

Performance appraisal of cardiologists

Prof J. Sharada, a senior interventional cardiologist who is a professor at Meenakshi Medical College in Tamil Nadu, emphasises the importance of tailoring measures to account for the unique biology of each patient and admission conditions. Some examples of performance measures include cardiologists in an outpatient setting, heart failure patients[14] and interventional procedures.[15] Hospitals like the Apollo have developed their own Apollo Centre for Clinical Excellence (ACCE), and the measures are also published in their annual report.

In oncology, readmission rates and survival rates are valuable measures. In ophthalmology, assessing cataract patients' quality of life (QOL) is crucial. In other words, medical outcomes and long-term rehabilitation are important measures of the effectiveness of medical intervention.

Nurses

Nurses play diverse roles – in operating theatres, ICU, PICU and wards – and each of them requires different skills to manage work pressures. Accreditations such as JCI and NABH emphasise clear accountability in patient care, patient safety, infection control and case file updating. Night shifts (12-hour shifts) present challenges requiring alertness and quick corrective action. JCI and NABH have clear guidelines on nurses' performance assessment.

NABH has a special category of Nursing Excellence certification with 216 objective measures. At the beginning of the year, the Nursing Director should discuss with nurses regarding role expectations, specific tasks and the necessary training that they would require. Planning at the start of the year serves two purposes: Involving nurses in planning and communicating role expectations effectively. This approach fosters involvement, clarity, and effective relationships between the supervisor and team members. Similar considerations apply to all other medical support functions such as lab, diagnostic and imaging centres, pharmacy and physiotherapy.

Management staff appraisal

Management functions such as finance, IT, procurement, marketing, equipment maintenance, HR and diet kitchen should have clearly defined metrics.

For example, finance should be measured by the effectiveness of fund management, timely submission of tax returns, tax planning and managing surplus funds. Marketing should be measured by the number of patients, response rate to social media, effectiveness of sales calls and brand image of the hospital based on independent market research. Procurement should be measured by cost savings in procurement, elimination of stock-outs of critical drugs at any time, quick turnaround of stocks, developing good supply chains and obtaining favourable commercial terms with medical equipment suppliers. HR should be measured by attrition rates, human resources costs management, how quickly vacancies are filled and employee morale. IT should be measured by quick responses to bug fixing, appropriate development of customised software, customer-friendly technologies such as mobile technology and effective use of tools for data analytics. Equipment maintenance should be measured by uptime of critical equipment, stock levels, spare stocks turnover ratio and timely installation of new equipment. Evaluation of the diet kitchen should include cost per meal, feedback from patients and attendants, development of cost-effective alternative and nutritious food options and overall surplus from kitchen operations. Good management in each area determines the effectiveness of the management processes.

The system of goal setting for doctors is perceived to exert pressures, both in private hospitals, resulting in potential ethical compromises. Medical practitioners report pressures from management to examine more patients and order additional investigations and surgeries. Monthly reviews with senior doctors emphasise management concerns about the inadequate number of investigations prescribed by consultants. Corporate hospitals deny this accusation.

Self-appraisal

Self-appraisal is deemed effective when staff critically evaluate their own performance. Good performers tend to rate themselves low. However, average and below-average performers tend to exaggerate their achievements during self-assessment. The supervisor in discussions can help the staff member determine their actual performance. Self-appraisal is merely the first step in employee development.

Online appraisal

Most large organisations have transitioned to online appraisal systems, eliminating paperwork for a more efficient process. Both the appraiser and the appraised submit their assessments online with additional input from peers and other staff. Online appraisals have cut down the paperwork but have retained face-to-face meetings between the appraiser and the appraised. Without paperwork, the appraisal focuses on specific ways in which the appraised and the organisation can benefit.

360-degree appraisal

Some institutions have implemented a 360-degree staff appraisal, incorporating feedback from internal and external customers. All the staff who are involved in patient care participate in the process. Nurses regularly interact with doctors, housekeeping staff, dieticians and pharmacists. Their assessments will be communicated as generalised feedback. 360-degree assessments are not commonly practiced in many organisations. Such an exercise would require a certain degree of maturity, both by the appraised and their colleagues. There should be adequate training and broad consent *before* introducing such systems.

Feedback

Feedback is the most critical part of the entire appraisal process. Cultural differences may affect the impact of the feedback process, with direct feedback being more natural in some cultures. In others, the feedback would be nuanced. The tone of the meeting should focus on positive aspects, minimising defensive reactions. The meeting should be planned in advance, not fixed casually, in an informal setting. HR should highlight job rotation possibilities, training and development plans, constantly tapping the talents of the staff, to suit the needs of the organisation.[16]

Promotions

Every appraisal generates expectations, and inevitably, there will be disappointments or joy. There are several factors that merit discussion:

- Do promotions result in new roles?
- Criteria – is it essentially time-based (common in government organisations) or a combination of time- and merit-based?
- Extent of compensation revisions
- Handling disappointments among staff not promoted

The normal expectation typically involves a change in the job title along with higher compensation. However, in some cases, the title may change without significant changes in responsibilities or compensation. Dealing with disappointed staff requires HR intervention, explaining the reasons and implementing positive and tactful measures.

Succession planning

Senior management and the board have a key responsibility in succession planning. The board members should interact with senior staff and identify talent at different levels of the organisation. Different organisations follow different practices. Leadership roles require moving from a specialist role to broader organisational responsibilities. There should be a systematic process of identifying many leaders and grooming them for positions of higher responsibility.

Skill development

All healthcare institutions, particularly tertiary care hospitals, should institute a formal training and development system. The training programme should cover all categories of staff. Medical doctors are required to attend conferences and publish papers in peer-reviewed journals. Advancements in medical technology, use of robots, new drug development, findings of various clinical trials and use of artificial intelligence in diagnosis demand constant updating of knowledge, especially of medical professionals. Every professional – nurse, nutritionist, pharmacologist or physiotherapist – constantly deals with well-informed patients and so has to be prepared to answer their queries. Top management and HR should prepare a training calendar and ensure it is adhered to.

Dr R. Parivalavan, a senior surgeon, has suggested multiple areas for skill upgradation, such as data analytics skills, use of AI, genomics, personalised medicine, surgical skills in robotics and current trends in physiotherapy, among others. Nurses must work with online computerised systems and use techniques to access data from their desktops and mobile phones. Finance and marketing staff must understand medical jargon and use their understanding to serve their medical colleagues. Training can be classified into technical and management/soft skills training. Every large hospital should set aside a minimum period of training for all categories of staff. There should be a budget for such programmes. Some hospitals report in their annual report the average number of training hours per employee per year.

Factors influencing skill development and job performance

Employee morale[17]

Employee morale is important, and at the same time, a nebulous concept. There have been debates on whether high morale leads to job satisfaction and hence a lower staff turnover. There could be many reasons for low morale – poor financial performance of the hospital, job insecurity and rumours about a takeover and low salary. It is necessary for the management to be aware of these factors and the administration must initiate corrective action. Some hospitals have a formal system of measuring employee morale by an external agency. Such measurements are like 'dipstick' studies. One of the essential measures is regular and factual communication of various functional and HR issues impacting the company.

Employee attitude

Technical skills are essential for all jobs, but attitude impacts performance. Different types of attitudes – positive, negative and neutral – impact how individuals approach situations. A positive attitude is crucial for success in organisational and, in general, life situations. HR needs to identify the different personalities within the organisation and provide and create awareness of their strengths or drawbacks. HR acts as 'change agents' and also provides feedback to the department head. Attributes like caution, enthusiasm or resistance to change can be observed in various work situations. The proportion of staff with negative attitudes affects the quality of decision-making.

Managing staff turnover

Retirement age

Normally, full-time medical staff and other staff retire at the completion of 65 years and other staff at the completion of 58 years. In the case of most medical consultants, it may not be necessary to fix a retirement age. In not-for-profit hospitals, the medical staff could be full-time employees. The Medical Council of India has recommended 70 years as the retirement age for medical doctors. In exceptional cases, the retirement age could be extended by the institution. Rarely do organisations plan for retirement or succession of even important positions in the organisation. Extensions are given automatically.

Attrition

Attrition is a common problem in all hospitals. High attrition impacts the hospital in many ways, and it also influences the serving employees. The organisation incurs costs on hiring and training new employees. Patients are disturbed when senior doctors leave en masse. Trainee doctors, after completing their training and mandatory stay period, might leave the hospital for different reasons. In some hospitals, the annual turnover of nurses could be as high as 30–40 per cent. Attrition is also common among technicians, sales staff and administrative staff. In some hospitals, turnover of staff is computed on a monthly basis, which leads to wrong conclusions of the staff turnover problem. The correct method is to obtain the annual turnover of staff category-wise and divide the number of attritions by the number at the beginning of the financial year for each category.

Exit interviews

Exit interviews are generally held with the departmental head concerned and HR. It is essential that such meetings be held in an informal manner to understand the real reasons for resignation. There should be no hostility. HR should also introspect about the pattern of resignations at different levels and suggest solutions to the top management. It takes a skillful HR person to understand the real reasons through informal channels.

Some of the common causes, in our view, are:

- Dissatisfaction with salary and benefits
- Difficult working conditions
- Poor treatment by their immediate supervisor
- Lack of clarity about long-term prospects
- Long commute for those living away from the hospital
- Getting married
- Going back to one's hometown/state

Mergers and cultural integration

In recent years, there have been several cases of acquisitions and mergers. The success of the merger depends on cultural integration. Serious differences in value systems, quality systems, organisation structures, profitability levels, salary levels and titles could create problems in organisational mergers. Effective integration necessitates frequent meetings between senior teams to address personnel-related issues. Job security and redundancies should be handled sensitively, with HR playing a pivotal role in rationalising salaries, titles and redeployment strategies. Long-term perspectives and generous handling of personal issues are essential for successful mergers.

Internal communication, a key HR activity

Organisations employ various measures to ensure effective internal communication, disseminating information about the company's plans, changes in HR policies and organisational updates. Intranets are used in many routine matters, for example, leave status, provident fund (PF) status and expense statements submission. A senior manager mentioned, 'Nowadays, employees learn about their own company from LinkedIn', rather than their own Intranet. HR should keep track of LinkedIn posts to know what is being said about the company. In recent years, town hall meetings have become popular, in which the CEO and HR inform the staff about key developments in the organisation. Over time, such meetings are found to gain credibility, with the employees realising that they can ask questions and get honest answers. Internal newsletters are another way of encouraging staff members to contribute articles about their experiences.

HR as a partner

In the contemporary landscape, HR assumes a critical partnership role. Acting as a bridge between the management and staff, it has to represent the staff to the management. HR should communicate to the top management and the board about ground realities – staff morale, key issues and the need for change. HR should do its homework on the need for compensation change, organisational changes or the introduction of new policies to the top management.

Conclusion

Indian hospitals should adapt to contemporary information technology and adopt innovative policies. HR professionals should actively participate in major strategic developments, providing the human angle in the organisation's pursuit of growth and profitability. Staying attuned to the environment changes, HR should strategise how the organisation can effectively navigate and adapt to these shifts. Ultimately, the success of the organisation depends on its people.

Notes

1 Size, composition and distribution of health workforce in India: why, and where to invest? Human Resources for Health, https://human-resources-health.biomedcentral.com/articles/10.1186/s12960-021-00575-2
2 Fredrick Taylor, https://en.wikipedia.org/wiki/Frederick_Winslow_Taylor
3 Prof Abraham Maslow, https://www.simplypsychology.org/maslow.html
4 What is organizational behavior, and why is it important? Humanyze, https://humanyze.com/blog-what-is-organizational-behavior-and-why-is-it-important/
5 What is organizational development? A complete guide, Academy to Innovate HR, https://www.aihr.com/blog/organizational-development/#:~:text=is%20organizational%20development%3F-,A%20definition,strategies%2C%20structures%2C%20and%20processes.ocesses
6 Peter Senge, *The Fifth Discipline: The Art and Practice of the Learning Organization* (Kindle edition), Cornerstone Digital, 2010. See also https://infed.org/mobi/peter-senge-and-the-learning-organization/

7 NABH standards on HR. NABH standards lay emphasis on the HR function, second only to patient care. There are 13 standards which are detailed out. These standards spell out key concepts, procedures, and quality standards, etc., https://www.nabh.co/images/Standards/1.%205th%20Edition%20Hospital%20Std%20April%202020.pdf
8 NHS long term plan launched, Gov.UK, https://www.gov.uk/government/news/nhs-long-term-plan-launched
9 Separation of the chairperson and CEO roles in India: SEBI's missed opportunity, Faculty of Law blogs, University of Oxford, https://blogs.law.ox.ac.uk/business-law-blog/blog/2022/03/separation-chairperson-and-ceo-roles-india-sebis-missed-opportunity
10 Dual reporting: lines and working in a matrix structure, Office of HR, UN, https://hr.un.org/sites/hr.un.org/files/Dual%20Reporting%20and%20Working%20in%20a%20Matric%20Guidelines_July_29_0.pdf
11 A. Acharya, R. Lieber, L. Seem and T. Welc, 'How to identify the right "spans of control" for your organization', *McKinsey*, https://www.mckinsey.com/capabilities/people-and-organizational-performance/our-insights/how-to-identify-the-right-spans-of-control-for-your-organization
12 Seventh Pay Commission, https://getlegalindia.com/7th-pay-commission/
13 Performance appraisal systems in the hospital sector –a research based on hospitals in Kerala, https://www.scribd.com/document/207515348/PERFORMANCE-APPRAISAL-SYSTEMS-IN-THE-HOSPITAL-SECTOR-A-RESEARCH-BASED-ON-HOSPITALS-IN-KERALA
14 P.A. Heidenreich, G.C. Fonarow and K. Breathett, '2020 ACC/AHA clinical performance and quality measures for adults with heart failure: a report of the American College of Cardiology/American heart association task force on performance measures', *JACC* 2020:76(21):2527–2564, https://www.jacc.org/doi/10.1016/j.jacc.2020.07.023
15 PCI performance measures include patient selection, appropriateness, American College of Cardiology, https://www.acc.org/about-acc/press-releases/2013/12/19/14/12/12-19-13-pci-performance-measures
16 xxx
17 15 Employee morale survey questions you need to ask your employees, Question Pro, https://www.questionpro.com/blog/employee-morale-survey-questions/

10 Role of AI in India's healthcare sector

Mala Sarat Chandra

Healthcare challenges in India today

Rural versus urban healthcare disparities

Healthcare access in India is highly uneven across rural and urban areas. Nearly two-thirds of Indians live in rural regions, yet only about 27 per cent of the country's doctors and 33 per cent of health workers practice in rural areas. Urban centres enjoy most of the advanced hospitals and specialists, whereas rural communities have far fewer facilities. Rural India (≈65–70 per cent of the population) has only ~36 per cent of hospital beds, leading to long travel and delayed care for villagers.[1] The doctor-to-patient ratio in rural areas can be as poor as 1:10,000 or worse, far below the WHO guideline of 1:1,000. These disparities result in higher mortality rates – for instance, the rural infant mortality rate is 34 per 1000 live births versus 20 in urban areas.[2] Overall, rural Indians face significant hurdles in obtaining timely, quality healthcare due to geographic and resource inequities.

Infrastructure gaps and workforce shortages

India's healthcare infrastructure and workforce supply have not kept pace with needs. The nation has only about one doctor per 1,450 people (0.7 per 1,000), below the WHO-recommended one per 1,000.[3] This shortage is aggravated in government facilities; many primary health centres (PHCs) lack doctors, and community health centres (CHCs) have an acute deficit of specialists. According to the Rural Health Statistics report, there is an 83 per cent shortfall of specialist doctors at the CHC level (e.g. surgeons, paediatricians, obstetricians).[4] Infrastructure is also lacking – only 15 per cent of government primary care facilities meet Indian Public Health Standards, indicating deficits in equipment, medicines and basic amenities.[5] Many hospitals are overcrowded and under-resourced, leading to long wait times and compromised care. While programmes like the National Health Mission have added facilities, gaps remain in diagnostic labs, ambulance networks and intensive care unit (ICU) beds, especially in smaller towns. The workforce shortage extends to nurses and technicians as well. Such deficits in

DOI: 10.4324/9781003684947-12

infrastructure and human resources strain service delivery and undermine healthcare quality across India.

Affordability and low insurance penetration

Healthcare in India is largely paid out-of-pocket by patients, making affordability a major concern. Out-of-pocket spending accounts for about 50 per cent of total health expenditure in India, far above the global average of 17 per cent. This high cost burden pushes millions into poverty during medical emergencies. One reason is low health insurance coverage – at least 30 per cent of Indians (about 40 crore people) have *no* financial protection for health.[6] Even among those with some coverage, insurance limits are often low and many treatments are not fully reimbursed. Government-funded schemes like Ayushman Bharat (PM-JAY) have expanded coverage to the poorest 40 per cent of the population, issuing over 30 crore health insurance cards as of 2023, but the 'missing middle' of lower-middle-class families remains largely uninsured.[7] Private insurance penetration is also limited, covering only around 10–15 per cent of people. As a result, medical care can be financially ruinous – hospitalisations or chronic disease expenses frequently force families to deplete savings or take loans. While the out-of-pocket share has declined from 64 per cent a decade ago to about 48 per cent in 2022, it is still extremely high compared to other countries.[8] Improving insurance coverage and reducing out-of-pocket expenses are critical to make healthcare more affordable in India.

High disease burden: Communicable and non-communicable diseases

India faces a double burden of infectious diseases along with rapidly rising non-communicable diseases (NCDs). On the communicable front, India has the world's highest tuberculosis burden – accounting for about 26 per cent of global TB cases[9] – alongside malaria, dengue and other endemic infections. The COVID-19 pandemic further highlighted gaps in epidemic preparedness. Meanwhile, chronic conditions have become the leading killers. NCDs now cause roughly 61–62 per cent of all deaths in India, up from 38 per cent in 1990.[10] Cardiovascular diseases are a top cause (24 per cent of deaths), followed by respiratory diseases, diabetes and cancers. India is often called the diabetes capital, with an estimated 77 million people with diabetes and counting. Lifestyle changes and longer lifespans have led to surging rates of heart disease, stroke, obesity and hypertension, even as infectious diseases persist. This dual burden strains the health system, which must combat traditional public health challenges like TB and maternal mortality while also treating complex chronic illnesses. Limited healthcare resources and infrastructure struggle to manage this high caseload, resulting in suboptimal outcomes. For example, India's age-standardised death rates from NCDs are higher than many countries, and periodic outbreaks of infections

(TB, encephalitis, etc.) continue to occur. Managing both communicable and non-communicable disease burdens simultaneously is a core challenge for India's healthcare planners.

Systemic inefficiencies and regulatory challenges

India's healthcare sector also suffers from systemic inefficiencies and evolving regulatory frameworks. The system is highly fragmented – split between multiple public sector levels and a large unregulated private sector – leading to duplication and gaps in care. There are 50+ approvals and licences needed to establish or run medical facilities, making compliance complex.[11] However, enforcement of quality standards is inconsistent; for instance, after audits, only 15–18 per cent of government primary health facilities met required standards, reflecting deficits in staffing, equipment and services. Inefficient processes such as paper-based records, lack of data interoperability and siloed programmes lead to longer wait times and administrative bottlenecks. Essential drugs and supplies often face stock-outs due to supply chain issues. On the regulatory side, India is still developing clear guidelines for new healthcare innovations. The Clinical Establishments Act (2010) exists to regulate hospitals, but only a handful of states have implemented it fully. There is rising concern about quack providers in rural areas due to doctor shortages. Regulatory oversight of medical devices and AI-based health tools is nascent – the government has begun classifying certain software as medical devices, but detailed standards for AI in healthcare are still a work in progress. Data privacy and security regulations (like the new Personal Data Protection Act) will impact health data usage as well. Overall, the need is to streamline regulations to support innovation while protecting patients and to improve efficiency through better management and technology. Systemic reforms are gradually being introduced, but tangible improvements in governance and regulation remain a work in progress in Indian healthcare.

How AI is addressing these challenges

Artificial intelligence is emerging as a powerful ally to tackle India's healthcare challenges. From augmenting scarce medical expertise to streamlining workflows, AI technologies are being applied in diverse healthcare settings. In the following, we explore key areas where AI solutions are making an impact.

AI in diagnostics (imaging, pathology and predictive analytics)

AI is transforming diagnostics in India by providing faster, cheaper and more accurate analysis of medical data. In medical imaging, AI tools are helping radiologists interpret scans and X-rays – crucial in a country with an estimated 15,000 radiologists for 1.4 billion people.[12] For example,

Mumbai-based startup Qure.ai has developed AI models like *qXR* for chest X-rays to detect tuberculosis, pneumonia, lung cancer and *qER* for head CT scans to identify brain injuries. These tools can flag abnormalities within seconds. Deployed in over 130 health facilities, Qure.ai's system enabled screening of 120,000+ individuals for TB, and pilots in Mumbai saw 30–40 per cent increases in TB case detection by catching cases that were previously missed.[13] The World Health Organization has even endorsed such AI for TB screening in its guidelines.

In pathology, startups like SigTuple use AI-powered microscopes to automatically analyse blood smears and urine samples. SigTuple's platform can detect malarial parasites and abnormal cells or quantify blood counts with high accuracy, reducing the burden on pathologists. AI is also aiding predictive analytics – for example, algorithms that analyse electronic health records to predict which patients are at high risk of complications or readmission. At Apollo Hospitals, an AI-based Clinical Intelligence Engine parses patient symptoms and history to suggest possible diagnoses and necessary tests, ensuring doctors don't miss critical clues.[14] Overall, by assisting in image interpretation, lab diagnostics and risk prediction, AI is expanding the reach of quality diagnostics into underserved areas and enabling earlier detection of diseases.

AI in telemedicine and remote healthcare

To bridge the urban–rural gap, AI is boosting telemedicine and remote care initiatives across India. During the COVID-19 pandemic, telehealth platforms saw massive uptake, and many integrated AI to scale services. The Indian government's own telemedicine service eSanjeevani now conducts up to 150,000–200,000 remote consultations per day, assisted by an AI-powered Clinical Decision-Support System (CDSS) that helps doctors with diagnostic and treatment guidance.[15]

AI chatbots are also being used for preliminary symptom assessment and triage. For example, some hospitals deploy chatbot assistants on their websites or WhatsApp; patients describe symptoms and the AI suggests whether they should seek care, and even books appointments. Private telehealth startup Mfine offers an app where an AI triages cases to the right specialist and provides digital prescriptions; Mfine also supports AI-based vitals monitoring during video consults (Mfine raised $48 million in Series C funding in 2021 to grow its AI telemedicine platform[16]).

AI-powered remote monitoring devices are helping bring specialist care to far-flung areas. In cardiac care, for instance, Tricog Health installs internet-connected ECG machines in rural clinics – these use algorithms to instantly analyse ECG readings and alert cardiologists if a heart attack is detected. Tricog's network has performed over 2.37 million ECG analyses and identified 30,000+ heart attacks, delivering reports in under ten minutes to enable timely treatment.[17] Such solutions effectively extend expert diagnostics to villages that lack cardiologists. Tele-ophthalmology programmes have also adopted AI – Google and Aravind Eye Hospital partnered to deploy an AI model that scans retinal photos for diabetic retinopathy, referring high-risk patients for treatment.[18] By embedding AI into telehealth, India is managing to serve remote populations with specialist advice, reducing the need for travel and enabling 'virtual' access to quality care.

AI in hospital and patient management (automation and workflow optimisation)

Within hospitals, AI and automation are helping streamline operations and enhance patient management. Many Indian hospitals now use AI-enabled systems for tasks like appointment scheduling, billing and record management – reducing manual effort and errors. AI-driven chatbots at hospital helpdesks can answer common patient queries and guide them to the right department, easing the load on staff. In clinical workflows, AI is assisting doctors by organising information and suggesting actions. For example, Apollo Hospitals' AI engine mines medical literature and patient data to provide decision support during consultations, saving doctors from having to manually research every detail.[19] This helps doctors keep up with the latest treatments and not overlook important symptoms or drug interactions. The electronic medical record (EMR) platforms like HealthPlix incorporate AI to auto-fill forms and provide prompts – HealthPlix's AI-powered EMR is used by over 10,000 doctors, offering suggestions at the point of care to reduce cognitive load.

AI-based optimisation is also improving resource allocation in busy public hospitals. Machine learning models predict patient footfalls in emergency rooms, so staffing and triage can be adjusted dynamically. In some smart hospitals, AI tracks real-time bed availability, ICU occupancy and even predicts which patients might deteriorate and need intensive care. This allows early interventions. Predictive analytics for hospital operations is becoming common – for instance, AI can forecast the stock levels for medicines and oxygen based on usage patterns, helping administrators prevent shortages. Robotic process automation (RPA) bots handle repetitive clerical tasks like insurance claims processing. Overall, by automating routine processes and providing data-driven insights, AI is enabling hospitals to serve more patients efficiently with the limited workforce available, thereby partially offsetting staff shortages and improving patient experience.

AI in drug discovery and personalised medicine

In the pharmaceutical and biotech domain, AI is accelerating research and enabling more personalised therapies. Drug discovery typically takes years, but AI models can analyse enormous chemical and genomic datasets to identify promising drug candidates much faster. Global pharma companies as well as Indian firms are using AI for computational drug design – sifting through libraries of molecules to predict which might bind to a target protein of a disease. This was demonstrated during COVID-19 when AI systems helped suggest molecules for antiviral drugs. In India, startups like AarogyaAI are leveraging genomics and AI to combat diseases like tuberculosis – AarogyaAI's tool analyses genetic sequences of tuberculosis (TB) bacteria to quickly detect drug resistance, enabling personalised TB treatments (traditionally, such tests take weeks). Another area is precision oncology: OncoStem Diagnostics, an Indian startup, uses machine learning on tumour profile data to predict cancer recurrence risk, which helps in tailoring follow-up treatment plans for breast cancer patients.

There are also collaborations between research institutes and tech companies – for example, the Tata Memorial Centre and IIT inaugurated a national cancer imaging biobank (Comprehensive Archive of Imaging), which provides anonymised scans to train AI models.[20] By mining this data, AI can discover imaging biomarkers that predict tumour behaviour, aiding personalised cancer care. Tech giant Microsoft, in partnership with Apollo Hospitals, developed an AI risk score for cardiac disease by analysing 400,000 Indian health records, which can identify at-risk individuals even without obvious symptoms. This allows personalised preventive care for those individuals. Furthermore, AI helps pharma manufacturing by optimising clinical trial design – selecting optimal patient cohorts and predicting outcomes to make trials more efficient. While still an emerging field in India, AI-driven drug discovery and personalised medicine hold immense potential, especially given India's rich genetic diversity and disease burden – AI can help develop treatments tailored to Indian populations and fast-track solutions for endemic diseases.

AI in surgical robotics and emergency response

Robotics augmented by AI are beginning to play a role in surgical care and emergency response in India. Surgical robots can assist doctors in performing precise, minimally invasive procedures. While most surgical robots (like the Da Vinci system) are imported, India recently developed its first indigenous surgical robot, the SSI Mantra, created by SS Innovations. This robot, equipped with AI-driven controls, has successfully performed over 1,000 complex surgeries including urological and cardiac procedures.[21]

Remarkably, in 2024 surgeons used SSI Mantra to conduct India's first telerobotic surgery across a 286 km distance, with the robot operating on a patient in one city under surgeon control from another city.[22] This feat, made possible by AI and high-speed networks, hints at a future where top surgeons could operate remotely on patients in rural hospitals. Beyond the operating room, AI is aiding emergency medical response systems. For instance, the startup ZENZO launched a nationwide ambulance network leveraging AI for dispatch optimisation. ZENZO connects 25,000+ ambulances across

450 cities via a central platform, using an AI backend to deploy the nearest ambulance and chart the fastest route (accounting for traffic) to achieve sub-15-minute response times.[23] This is crucial in improving outcomes for trauma or cardiac arrest cases. In some metros, experimental AI systems use live traffic and emergency call data to pre-position ambulances in anticipation of demand peaks. AI is also being used in emergency rooms for triage support – tools like Early Warning Score systems analyse patient vitals and history to alert doctors of high-risk patients (e.g. sepsis or shock) so that immediate care is given. During natural disasters or mass incidents, AI-based decision systems can help allocate limited emergency resources to where they are needed most. While still early, these AI and robotic applications in surgery and emergency care are extending the reach and speed of lifesaving interventions in India's vast and often logistically challenging environment.

AI for disease surveillance and epidemic prediction

Given India's susceptibility to disease outbreaks – from seasonal dengue to pandemics – AI is being deployed to strengthen public health surveillance. The National Centre for Disease Control (NCDC) has partnered with the Wadhwani Institute of AI to augment the government's Integrated Disease Surveillance Programme. Wadhwani AI developed an AI-powered outbreak monitoring system that automates scanning of huge volumes of data (news reports, social media, local bulletins) in multiple languages to detect early signals of disease outbreaks.[24] This system, operational since 2022, filters and analyses over 100,000 media sources, generating alerts for public health officials if unusual disease clusters or symptoms are reported. By catching early warning signs (for example, a spike in 'mystery fever' news in a district), the AI can prompt quicker investigation and containment measures, potentially preventing wider epidemics.

During the COVID-19 wave, Indian states also used AI models to forecast case surges and plan hospital capacity. AI-based predictive models estimated the spread of infection based on mobility and testing data, helping authorities impose targeted restrictions. Beyond humans, AI is aiding surveillance of disease vectors: programmes analyse satellite and weather data to predict dengue or malaria outbreaks by identifying high-risk areas (e.g. with standing water post-monsoon). In community health, simple AI tools are being used for syndromic surveillance – a chatbot might collect symptom information from thousands of primary clinics to flag any unusual patterns (like clusters of diarrhoea that could mean a water contamination issue). On the policy side, the health ministry is creating digital health records under the Ayushman Bharat Digital Mission, and linking AI for analytics – for instance, detecting trends in chronic disease prevalence in certain regions to guide interventions.[25]

Overall, AI's ability to parse big data in real time is improving India's disease surveillance, allowing a shift from reactive to more predictive public health. This is vital for a country aiming to eliminate diseases like TB by 2025 and better manage any future pandemics.

Investment in AI-driven healthcare

Public sector investment and government initiatives

The Government of India has recognised AI as a national priority and is investing in enabling its healthcare potential. In 2018, NITI Aayog (the government think tank) released a national AI strategy identifying healthcare as a key sector for AI-driven transformation.[26] Since then, the government has launched various initiatives to support AI in health. The Ministry of Health designated the All India Institute of Medical Sciences (AIIMS) New Delhi, Post-Graduate Institute of Medical Education and Research (PGIMER) Chandigarh and AIIMS Rishikesh as Centres of Excellence for AI in healthcare, tasked with developing and adopting AI solutions in clinical care.[27] The government's flagship Ayushman Bharat Digital Mission (ABDM) is building the digital infrastructure (such as unique Health IDs and data exchange standards) needed to leverage AI at scale. ABDM will integrate cutting-edge technologies like AI, IoT and blockchain with health systems to enable interoperable electronic health records for every citizen – a foundation that significantly expands data available for AI analytics while maintaining privacy.

Specific government-supported AI projects are also underway. For example, NITI Aayog, Department of Biotechnology, and IITs set up an Imaging Biobank for Cancer to compile over 20,000 annotated radiology and pathology images of Indian cancer patients, providing a rich dataset to train AI for cancer detection. NITI Aayog has piloted an AI algorithm for early diabetic retinopathy screening in collaboration with Google, which is being validated against eye specialists' diagnoses.[28]

The Indian Council of Medical Research (ICMR) has also launched AI research schemes (e.g. in pathology and outbreak analytics). Importantly, policymakers are formulating guidelines – 'Responsible AI in Healthcare' approach documents were published in 2021 to ensure ethical and safe AI deployment.[29] These recommend frameworks for data privacy, algorithmic transparency and bias monitoring. Overall, public sector investment is focused on creating an ecosystem (data, standards, institutions) for AI to flourish. While government health spending in India remains around 1.5 per cent of GDP, within that, the allocations for digital health and AI have grown in recent budgets. Going forward, continued government support – through funded research, public–private partnerships and progressive regulation – will be pivotal in scaling AI across India's vast public health apparatus.

Private sector investments and venture capital trends

The promise of AI in Indian healthcare has attracted substantial private sector and venture capital (VC) investment, especially in the last five to six years. Numerous health-tech startups with AI-centric models have emerged and raised funds from both domestic and global investors. Health-tech was among the top-funded startup sectors in India during the pandemic years, peaking in 2021 when health-tech companies raised about \$3.2 billion in funding.[30] This marked a sharp increase as digital health solutions (telemedicine, remote monitoring, online pharmacies, etc.) saw mass adoption. In 2022, there was a dip in funding to \$1.4 billion amid a broader startup funding slowdown, but it was still the second-highest year on record. Early-stage investments remained robust with a 26 per cent year-on-year rise, indicating investor confidence in new health AI ventures.[31]

The major global tech companies have also entered the fray – Google, Microsoft, Intel and IBM have all launched healthcare AI initiatives in India (for instance, Microsoft's AI Network for Healthcare with Apollo Hospitals on heart risk, and Google's tie-up with Aravind Eye for eye disease AI). Pharmaceutical companies are partnering with AI startups for drug research. In terms of venture capital, Sequoia Capital, Accel and Chiratae Ventures have been identified as top investors in Indian health-tech, actively backing AI-driven startups. Other prominent investors include Nexus Venture Partners, India-focused funds like Pi Ventures (which specialises in AI), international funds like General Atlantic and SIG, and strategic investors such as Alphabet's investment arm and medical device companies. Corporate hospital chains (Apollo and Narayana Health, among others) are also investing in AI startups or developing solutions in-house. The funding landscape shows a healthy mix – from big-ticket late-stage rounds (e.g. Tata Digital's \$125 millioni in 1mg e-pharmacy in 2022, Temasek's \$135 million in HealthKart nutrition platform) to seed funding for niche AI health apps. With over 1,000 Indian health-tech startups funded to date,[32] the ecosystem is vibrant. While a global funding winter cooled some late-stage deals in 2022, the overall trend remains positive. Investors are particularly keen on startups addressing massive gaps – like scalable diagnostics, chronic disease management and healthcare access for the masses. Going forward, as successful case studies emerge and AI proves its value in reducing costs and improving outcomes, one can expect renewed private investment. Both the public sector and private investors are recognising that AI in healthcare is a high-impact growth area, and funding is being channelled accordingly to drive innovation.

AI funding in Indian startups: recent trends and major investors

Recent funding trends underscore a shift toward AI-powered healthcare solutions. During the COVID era, venture funding poured into telehealth, diagnostics and wellness apps, many with AI at their core. For example, Pristyn Care (which uses AI for surgical workflow optimisation) and PharmEasy (which employs AI in its supply chain) became unicorns. By 2022, as the market normalised, investors became more selective, favouring startups with clear monetisation and proven tech. Health-tech funding in 2022 was 70 per cent concentrated in the first half of the year,[33] after which rising interest rates led to caution. Late-stage funding (>$100M rounds) slowed, while early-stage flourished. Notably, Sequoia and Accel – who were early backers of companies like Cure.fit, SigTuple and Qure.ai – remain bullish and have continued to invest, cementing their spot as top investors in the segment. Chiratae Ventures (formerly IDG Ventures) has built a health-tech portfolio including AI-based mental health platform Wysa. Other active investors include Lightrock India, Qualcomm Ventures, HealthQuad, Eight Roads and Bharat Innovation Fund, which have funded AI-driven ventures ranging from deep-tech diagnostics to biotech.

We are also seeing convergence of healthcare and tech investors; traditional life-sciences VCs are now looking at AI startups, while tech investors are hiring medical experts for due diligence. In addition, large Indian business groups like Reliance and Tata have made strategic acquisitions in digital health (e.g. Tata acquired 1mg, Reliance invested in Netmeds and Strand Life Sciences), injecting more capital and helping the companies scale. International agencies and impact funds are another source of investment for socially impactful AI health solutions – for instance, the India Health Fund (backed by Tata Trusts and Global Fund) supported Qure.ai's TB screening deployment.[34] The overall trend indicates that while pure funding numbers may fluctuate year to year, the interest in AI for healthcare is secular and strong. India's massive healthcare market (expected to reach $650 billion by 2025) and the proven ability of AI to address structural issues make it a 'sunrise' sector. As a result, we can expect diverse stakeholders – government, venture capitalists, corporate venture arms and global Big Tech – to continue channelling capital into India's AI-powered healthcare innovations.

Innovative AI healthcare startups in India

India is home to a growing crop of innovative startups that are applying AI across the healthcare spectrum. Below are some leading AI-driven healthcare startups, their focus areas, and contributions[35]:

- Qure.ai – A Mumbai-based AI radiology startup (founded 2016) that provides automated medical imaging diagnostics. Qure.ai's algorithms (*qXR*) can read chest X-rays to detect TB, COVID-19, lung nodules and more within seconds, and *qER* analyses head CT scans for stroke and trauma. Deployed in 50+ countries, Qure.ai's tools have significantly improved TB detection rates in public health programmes.[36] The company raised $40 million in 2022 led by Novo Holdings and HealthQuad to expand its global footprint.
- Niramai – Bengaluru-based startup (founded 2016) focusing on early breast cancer detection using AI. Niramai (which stands for 'Non-Invasive Risk Assessment with Machine Intelligence') developed *Thermalytix* – a solution that uses a high-resolution thermal camera and AI algorithms to

identify breast tumours. It's radiation-free, low-cost and portable, ideal for screening camps in rural areas that lack mammography. Niramai's technology has been used in thousands of screenings and helped catch early-stage cancers in asymptomatic women. The startup has garnered funding (including $0.6 million in a 2023 round from Pi Ventures and Axilor Ventures) to further develop the product and expand screenings.

- SigTuple – A Bengaluru-based startup (founded 2015) applying AI to microscopic analysis for lab diagnostics. SigTuple's platform Manthana can analyse blood smears, urine and semen samples by automatically identifying cells, pathogens and anomalies in digital microscope images. This enables faster and more consistent pathology results, addressing the shortage of skilled lab technicians. SigTuple has partnered with diagnostic chains to deploy AI-powered digital pathology in labs and even peripheral clinics through cloud-based analysis. It raised $4.3 million in Series C funding in 2023 (led by Endiya Partners and Accel) to scale its solutions to more healthcare facilities.
- Tricog Health – A Bangalore-based cardiac care startup (founded 2014) that combines cloud-connected devices and AI to provide rapid ECG diagnostics. Tricog's flagship InstaECG service equips clinics with IoT-enabled ECG machines; the ECG traces are sent to the cloud where an AI algorithm (validated by cardiologists) interprets them and returns a report within five to ten minutes. This has been lifesaving for heart attack patients – Tricog has analysed over 2.3 million ECGs and identified 75,000+ critical cases (30,000+ heart attacks), often in small towns where cardiologists are not present. By 2023, Tricog announced it had touched ten million lives globally with its AI-driven remote cardiac solutions. The company has backing from investors like UTEC-Japan and the University of Tokyo Edge Capital.
- Mfine – A health-tech startup from Bangalore (founded 2017) offering an AI-powered digital healthcare platform. Mfine allows users to consult with doctors via chat or video, book lab tests and manage health records through an app. AI is used for preliminary symptom checking, routing the patient to the appropriate specialist and assisting doctors by suggesting possible diagnoses based on the chat triage. During the pandemic, Mfine's usage spiked for COVID consultations, and it introduced AI-based tools to monitor patients' oxygen levels and temperature remotely. Mfine has raised significant funding ($48 million Series C in 2021 led by Moore Strategic Ventures and Beenext) to grow its network of partner hospitals and strengthen its AI capabilities.
- HealthifyMe – A Bengaluru-based wellness startup (founded 2012) that uses AI to provide personalised diet and fitness coaching. HealthifyMe's mobile app employs an AI nutritionist named 'Ria', which can automatically track users' meals (using image recognition to log food) and give tailored diet advice and workout plans. The AI analyses a user's food intake, activity and goals to offer suggestions in multiple languages,

making healthy living guidance more accessible. With over 25 million downloads, HealthifyMe has become a popular digital nutritionist in India and Southeast Asia. It raised about $75 million in 2021 (from LeapFrog, Khosla Ventures and others) to enhance its AI coach and expand internationally. The startup's success reflects rising demand for preventive health and weight management solutions powered by AI personalisation.

- Wysa – An AI-driven mental health app (originating from Bangalore, founded 2016) that provides an 'AI friend' for users to talk to and improve their mental wellbeing. Wysa's chatbot uses therapeutic techniques (cognitive behavioural therapy (CBT), meditation, mood tracking) in a conversational manner, helping people cope with anxiety, stress or depression. Importantly, it breaks barriers of stigma and access by being available 24 × 7 anonymously. Wysa has over four million users globally and has proven especially useful during the pandemic's mental health toll. It also offers an enterprise version for employers. Wysa raised $20 million in Series B funding in 2022 led by HealthQuad and others, and has been approved by the NHS in the UK – showcasing an Indian AI health innovation making a global impact.
- AarogyaAI – A Delhi-based biotech startup (founded 2019) leveraging AI for infectious disease diagnostics. AarogyaAI has developed a proprietary machine learning algorithm that can rapidly analyse the genome of tuberculosis bacteria from a patient sample and predict drug resistance. This enables clinicians to know within hours which TB drugs will be effective for a patient, as opposed to conventional culture tests that take six to eight weeks. Fast genotypic diagnostics powered by AI are crucial for India's goal to eliminate TB by 2025. AarogyaAI was a winner of the IBM Watson AI XPRIZE and has received grants and seed funding to bring its solution from lab to field.

The above list is illustrative, not exhaustive. Other notable AI-driven health startups include Forus Health – affordable retinal screening devices with AI for eye care; OncoStem – AI-based cancer recurrence prediction; PharmEasy – e-pharmacy optimising logistics with AI; Predible Health – organ-specific imaging AI (e.g. liver disease); and Reliance's Jio HealthHub platform integrating AI health analytics. Together, these startups showcase the breadth of innovation – from preventive care to diagnostics to chronic disease management – being pioneered in India's health AI ecosystem.

Future outlook for AI in Indian healthcare

Predicted AI adoption trends in healthcare

The adoption of AI in Indian healthcare is poised to accelerate in the coming years. Industry analysis projects that AI in Indian healthcare will grow at ~40 per cent CAGR, reaching a market size of around $1.6 billion by 2025.[37] This rapid growth is fuelled by the pressing need to overcome system challenges and the increasing availability of enabling data and technology. Surveys show that many Indian healthcare organisations have begun their AI journey – for instance, 82 per cent of pharma and life sciences companies have adopted AI at least at a pilot scale, and AI adoption among healthcare providers is about 68 per cent (though 92 per cent of those are still proof-of-concept projects).[38] This indicates strong interest that has not yet been fully translated to scaled deployments. Over the next five years, we can expect these pilots to convert into production systems as confidence builds.

Key areas likely to see high AI uptake include diagnostics (radiology AI could become standard in many hospitals), decision support in clinical workflows, hospital operations optimisation and consumer health management via apps and wearables. The COVID experience demonstrated the value of digital health solutions, so hospitals and insurers are now more willing to invest in AI for telehealth, remote monitoring and predictive analytics for resource planning.

The government's push for digital health records will also catalyse AI adoption – as data becomes more centralised and interoperable, it will unlock myriad AI applications (from personalised medicine to population health analytics). Market forecasts suggest that by 2030, AI could potentially add $25–30 billion to India's healthcare industry through improved productivity and new services. That said, the adoption will likely be uneven in the near term – large corporate hospitals and pharma companies (and health-tech startups) will lead the way, while smaller clinics and rural facilities take longer to integrate AI due to cost and skill barriers. Yet, as scalable AI solutions (like cloud-based diagnostics) mature, even smaller providers may simply 'plug into' these AI services. Overall, the trajectory indicates that AI will move from experimental to essential in Indian healthcare over the next decade, fundamentally altering how care is delivered and experienced.

Policy and regulatory landscape for AI in healthcare

Policymakers in India are increasingly cognisant of creating a conducive yet safe regulatory environment for AI in healthcare. A balance must be struck between encouraging innovation and safeguarding patient safety and privacy. Currently, India is working on multiple fronts to achieve this.

Data regulation: The recently enacted Digital Personal Data Protection Act (2023) classifies health data as sensitive personal data, with strict requirements for consent and protection. This law will influence how patient data can be used to train AI models. The government is expected to formulate specific guidelines for health data anonymisation to allow research while preserving privacy.

AI-specific guidelines: NITI Aayog's 'Responsible AI' principles emphasise transparency, explainability, accountability and fairness.[39]

In healthcare, this means AI systems should ideally be interpretable by clinicians and auditable for biases or errors. We may see sectoral guidelines – for example, the health ministry could require validation studies for critical AI diagnostic tools before clinical use, similar to drug trials. Notably, the Central Drugs Standard Control Organisation (CDSCO) has started to categorise certain AI-based software as medical devices which require certification. Though still nascent, this regulatory pathway is being defined: for example, an AI software that provides radiology diagnosis can fall under Medical Device Rules – needing registration and evidence of safety/effectiveness. Telemedicine practice guidelines (2020) already recognise artificial intelligence/machine learning (AI/ML)-based solutions as decision-support tools that the doctor can use, but the ultimate responsibility lies with the human practitioner. This principle of *human-in-the-loop* is likely to remain a cornerstone of regulation – AI will be seen as assisting, not replacing, medical professionals. The government is also investing in building capacity for AI governance. Initiatives like AIIMS and the Indian Institute of Technology (IIT) joint research units and the centres of excellence are partly to develop homegrown expertise that can inform policy. We can anticipate that in a few years, India will have a more formal approval process for AI algorithms (much like the US Food and Drug Administration's (FDA) process for AI/ML medical devices). Additionally, standards for interoperability (through ABDM) will ensure different systems and AI solutions can work together, which is more of a policy issue than technology. On the ethical front, the emphasis will be on AI not exacerbating inequalities – for example, ensuring that AI works for different demographics and doesn't inherit biases (like under-diagnosing diseases in women or certain castes due to skewed training data). In summary, India's regulatory landscape is evolving to keep pace with AI – with a clear intent to promote innovation while instituting checks for safety, efficacy and ethics. Continued dialogue between regulators, medical community and AI developers will shape guidelines that allow AI to flourish responsibly in healthcare.

Challenges and opportunities for scaling AI solutions

As India pushes forward with AI in healthcare, it faces several challenges that must be addressed, as well as immense opportunities that can be realised:

- *Challenges*: One major challenge is the lack of quality data for AI training – much of India's health data is unstructured or not digitised, and data silos persist between institutions. Efforts like ABDM aim to fix this, but it will take time to gather large, clean datasets representative of India's diverse population. Another hurdle is the shortage of skilled professionals who can develop and deploy AI in healthcare; there is a need for more data scientists with biomedical knowledge and clinicians trained in data-driven methods. There is also resistance to change among some healthcare workers – doctors may be sceptical of AI outputs or fear that automation could diminish their role. Building trust through explainable AI and training will be key to adoption. Cost and infrastructure pose issues, especially for smaller centres – AI solutions often require reliable electricity, internet and hardware like GPUs, which may not be readily available in rural hospitals. Furthermore, regulatory uncertainty can slow down innovation – startups may be unclear on approval requirements for AI tools, and too much red tape could stifle agile development. Lastly, concerns about algorithmic bias and errors loom large: if an AI misdiagnoses a patient, it's unclear who is liable, and if AI is trained predominantly on urban hospital data, it may underperform for rural patients. All these factors mean scaling up AI to all corners of Indian healthcare will not be trivial.

- *Opportunities*: On the flip side, the opportunities are extraordinary. AI offers a chance for India to leapfrog traditional healthcare constraints – by augmenting its limited doctors and nurses with intelligent tools, it can drastically expand access. For example, AI-powered screening can allow one radiologist to oversee what would have required ten radiologists' workload, bringing diagnostics to underserved areas. Preventive and personalised care can get a boost – AI can help identify at-risk individuals for diseases like diabetes or cancer far earlier, enabling interventions that save lives and costs. There is also a huge opportunity for India to become a global innovation hub for frugal healthcare AI – solutions developed for India's low-resource settings (like Niramai's portable cancer screening or Tricog's remote cardiac care) have demand in other emerging markets across Asia, Africa and Latin America. This could drive economic growth and exports of Indian health-tech. Additionally, AI can assist the government in achieving public health goals: models to optimise vaccine supply chains, predict disease outbreaks or monitor health programme performance can greatly improve efficiency. The demographic trends (a relatively young tech-savvy population but with rising chronic diseases) mean a big market for AI-driven wellness and chronic disease management tools. From a patient perspective, AI integration can empower individuals – via smartphone apps for self-monitoring and AI chatbots for counselling, healthcare can become more continuous and home-based rather than episodic and hospital-based. If challenges are met with the right strategies – investing in infrastructure and skills, strong public–private collaboration and adaptive regulation – India has the opportunity to set a model for AI-assisted healthcare at scale, improving outcomes for its 1.4 billion citizens. In the long run, effective use of AI could be a key factor in India achieving universal health coverage by making quality care more accessible and affordable for all.[40]

Conclusion

The role of AI in India's healthcare sector is rapidly expanding from experimental pilots to impactful real-world applications. AI is helping doctors make better decisions, extending healthcare to remote areas, optimising hospitals and empowering patients. India's unique healthcare needs have fostered innovative homegrown AI solutions that are now gaining global recognition. While challenges of implementation exist, the convergence of enabling government policy, enthusiastic private investment and entrepreneurial energy is accelerating AI adoption. With a supportive ecosystem, AI has the potential to transform Indian healthcare – bridging gaps in access and quality, augmenting the healthcare workforce and ultimately improving health outcomes for millions. The coming years will be critical in scaling up successful pilots, regulating wisely and ensuring that the benefits of healthcare AI are distributed equitably across urban and rural India. The strides made so far provide an encouraging glimpse of a future where AI is an integral part of a smarter, stronger Indian healthcare system.

Notes

1 Kalyani Sharma, 'Bridging the urban–rural divide', *Express Healthcare*, https://www.expresshealthcare.in/news/bridging-the-urban-rural-divide/445455/#:~:text=Abrarali%20Dalal%2C%20Director%20and%20CEO%2C,in%20healthcare%20infrastructure%20between%20urban
2 'Rural health system in India | Importance, problems, statistics', *Rural Duniya*, https://ruralduniya.com/rural-health/#:~:text=,Open%20defecation%20rates%20remain%20high
3 'State of healthcare in rural India 2024', *Dristi IAS*, https://www.drishtiias.com/daily-updates/daily-news-analysis/state-of-healthcare-in-rural-india-2024#:~:text=country%20is%205%25.%20%2A%20Doctor,to%20a%20shortage%20of%20doctors
4 'Rural health system in India | Importance, problems, statistics', *Rural Duniya*, https://ruralduniya.com/rural-health/#:~:text=,Open%20defecation%20rates%20remain%20high
5 'Reasons for systemic healthcare regulation failures in India', *Forum IAS*, https://forumias.com/blog/reasons-for-systemic-healthcare-regulation-failures-in-india/#:~:text=Unrealistic%20Standards%3A%20The%20Clinical%20Establishments,facilities%20meet%20their%20own%20standards
6 Samrat Sharma, 'The uninsured: 40 crore Indians are a medical emergency away from financial ruin', *India Today*, 17 July 2024, https://www.indiatoday.in/diu/story/40-crore-indians-are-a-medical-emergency-away-from-financial-ruin-2568229-2024-07-17
7 'Health insurance for India's missing middle', *Dristi IAS*, https://www.drishtiias.com/daily-news-analysis/health-insurance-for-india-s-missing-middle#:~:text=,any%20financial%20protection%20for%20health
8 Mahua Venkatesh, 'India's health insurance coverage is among the lowest, something the centre needs to worry about', *The Secretariat*, https://thesecretariat.in/article/india-s-health-insurance-coverage-is-among-the-lowest-something-the-centre-needs-to-worry-about

9 'India accounts for 26% of global TB burden, the highest: WHO', *The Siasat Daily*, https://www.siasat.com/india-accounts-for-26-of-global-tb-burden-the-highest-who-3122576/#:~:text=of%20the%20global%20target%2C%20a,highest%20%E2%80%94%20global%20TB%20burden

10 Press Information Bureau, 'Status of non-communicable diseases (NCDs) in India', *Ministry of Health and Family Welfare*, https://www.pib.gov.in/PressReleaseIframePage.aspx?PRID=1796435#:~:text=According%20to%20the%20study%20report,in%202016

11 'Reasons for systemic healthcare regulation failures in India', *Forum IAS*, https://forumias.com/blog/reasons-for-systemic-healthcare-regulation-failures-in-india/#:~:text=Excessive%20Regulations%3A%20India%20has%20numerous,making%20compliance%20complex%20and%20cumbersome

12 Arunima Rajan, 'AI in radiology: Amit Gandhi on teleradiology's role and the future of personalised healthcare', *Healthcare Executive*, https://www.healthcareexecutive.in/blog/ai-in-radiology#:~:text=,tailored%20treatment%20strategies%2C%20that

13 'Qure.ai's AI tool boosts TB detection rates in India', *Radiology AI*, https://radiology-ai.org/2024/04/26/qure-ais-ai-tool-boosts-tb-detection-rates-in-india/#:~:text=The%20tangible%20outcomes%20of%20this,crucial%20for%20effective%20TB%20management

14 'From disease surveillance to aiding diagnoses how AI tools are revolutionising Indian healthcare', *Deloitte*, https://www.deloitte.com/in/en/pages/life-sciences-and-healthcare/articles/From-disease-surveillance-to-aiding-diagnoses-how-AI-tools-are-revolutionising-Indian-healthcare.html

15 'From disease surveillance to aiding diagnoses how AI tools are revolutionising Indian healthcare', *Deloitte*, https://www.deloitte.com/in/en/pages/life-sciences-and-healthcare/articles/From-disease-surveillance-to-aiding-diagnoses-how-AI-tools-are-revolutionising-Indian-healthcare.html

16 Jayanti Dubey, 'Top 5 AI-powered startups transforming India's healthcare landscape', *Digital Health News*, https://www.digitalhealthnews.com/top-5-ai-powered-startups-transforming-india-s-healthcare-landscape#:~:text=In%202021%2C%20Mfine%20raised%20%2448,funding%2C%20led%20by%20Moore%20Strategic

17 'InstaECG by Tricog delivers more accuracy', *Biospectrum* (Tricog analysed 23.7 lakh ECGs, detected 75k+ critical cases, 30k+ heart attacks, 6–10 min results), biospectrumindia.com

18 Rajroshan Sawhney, 'How AI is making eyesight-saving care more accessible in resource-constrained settings', *Google in Asia blog*, https://blog.google/around-the-globe/google-asia/arda-diabetic-retinopathy-india-thailand/#:~:text=,to%20investigate%20whether%20AI

19 'From disease surveillance to aiding diagnoses how AI tools are revolutionising Indian healthcare', *Deloitte*, https://www.deloitte.com/in/en/pages/life-sciences-and-healthcare/articles/From-disease-surveillance-to-aiding-diagnoses-how-AI-tools-are-revolutionising-Indian-healthcare.html

20 'AI in healthcare: India's trillion-dollar opportunity', *World Economic Forum*, https://www.weforum.org/stories/2022/10/ai-in-healthcare-india-trillion-dollar/#:~:text=Similar%20applications%20are%20possible%20in,improve%20outcomes%20for%20cancer%20research

21 'India's very own indigenousy developed surgical robotic system – SSI mantra – achieves 1000 surgeries milestone', *Medgate Today*, https://medgatetoday.com/indias-very-own-indigenousy-developed-surgical-robotic-system-ssi-mantra-achieves-1000-surgeries-milestone/#:~:text=,surgeries%20using%20SSi%20Mantra

22 'SSI Mantra: India's first surgical robotic system', *GS Times*, https://www.gstimes.in/current-affairs/ssi-mantra-indias-first-robotic-system/#:~:text=India%E2%80%99s%20indigenous%20surgical%20robotic%20system%2C,proctoring
23 'India's largest AI-driven ambulance network launched by ZENZO', *Express Healthcare*, https://www.expresshealthcare.in/news/indias-largest-ai-driven-ambulance-network-launched-by-zenzo/447462/#:~:text=Key%20features%20include%20GPS%20tracking%2C,operations%20through%20a%20dedicated%20app
24 'From disease surveillance to aiding diagnoses how AI tools are revolutionising Indian healthcare', *Deloitte*, https://www.deloitte.com/in/en/pages/life-sciences-and-healthcare/articles/From-disease-surveillance-to-aiding-diagnoses-how-AI-tools-are-revolutionising-Indian-healthcare.html
25 Press Information Bureau, 'Ayushman Bharat Digital Mission creates longitudinal Electronic Health Record (EHR) facilitating interoperability of health data', https://www.pib.gov.in/PressReleaseIframePage.aspx?PRID=1908041#:~:text=and%20longitudinal%20electronic%20health%20record,performance%20of%20the%20health%20services
26 Nirupam Bajpai and Manisha Wadhwa, 'Artificial Intelligence and Healthcare in India', CSD Working Paper Series: Towards a new Indian model of information and communications', csd.columbia.edu
27 Press Information Bureau, 'AIIMS Delhi, PGIMER Chandigarh and AIIMS Rishikesh as centre of excellence for artificial intelligence', https://www.pib.gov.in/PressReleaseIframePage.aspx?PRID=1908041#:~:text=AIIMS%20Delhi%2C%20PGIMER%20Chandigarh%20and,of%20Excellence%20for%20Artificial%20Intelligence
28 'Health Ministry to use Artificial Intelligence in safe way in public health', *Economic Times*, 12 July 2019, https://economictimes.indiatimes.com/industry/healthcare/biotech/healthcare/health-ministry-to-use-artificial-intelligence-in-safe-way-in-public-health/articleshow/70189259.cms
29 Press Information Bureau, 'AIIMS Delhi, PGIMER Chandigarh and AIIMS Rishikesh as centre of excellence for artificial intelligence', https://www.pib.gov.in/PressReleaseIframePage.aspx?PRID=1908041#:~:text=NITI%20Ayog%20has%20published%20two,Responsible%20AI%E2%80%9D%20in%20August%202021
30 Aryaman Gupta, 'Funding for healthtech companies falls 55% to $1.4 bn in 2022: Tracxn', *Business Standard*, 29 March 2023, https://www.business-standard.com/companies/start-ups/funding-for-healthtech-companies-falls-55-to-1-4-bn-in-2022-tracxn-123032900863_1.html
31 'Healthtech funding fell 55% in 2022; Sequoia, Accel top investors: Tracxn', *YourStory*, 29 March 2023, https://yourstory.com/2023/03/total-funding-healthtech-sector-2022-late-stage-deals-tracxn-report
32 Paromita Gupta, 'Tracxn's Healthtech India Report 2023: Funding into the segment plummets 55% in 2022', *Entrepreneur*, https://www.entrepreneur.com/en-in/news-and-trends/tracxns-healthtech-india-report-2023-funding-into-the/448594#:~:text=Tracxn%27s%20Healthtech%20India%20Report%202023%3A,taken%20into%20consideration%20while
33 'Healthtech funding fell 55% in 2022; Sequoia, Accel top investors: Tracxn', *YourStory*, https://yourstory.com/2023/03/total-funding-healthtech-sector-2022-late-stage-deals-tracxn-report
34 'Artificial intelligence game changer in tracking cases of tuberculosis', *Qure.ai*, https://www.qure.ai/news_press_coverages/artificial-intelligence-game-changer-in-tracking-cases-of-tuberculosis
35 'Top 5 AI-powered startups transforming India's healthcare landscape', *Digital Health News*, https://www.digitalhealthnews.com/top-5-ai-powered-startups-transforming

-india-s-healthcare-landscape#:~:text=match%20at%20L147%20In%202022%2C,regions%20with%20a%20shortage%20of
36 'Qure.ai's AI tool boosts TB detection rates in India', *Radiology AI*, 'https://radiology-ai.org/2024/04/26/qure-ais-ai-tool-boosts-tb-detection-rates-in-india/#:~:text=The%20tangible%20outcomes%20of%20this,crucial%20for%20effective%20TB%20management'
37 'AI in Indian healthcare market projected to reach $1.6 billion by 2025', *Silicon Review*, https://thesiliconreview.com/2024/08/indian-healthcare-market-projected-billion#:~:text=AI%27s%20integration%20into%20healthcare%20is,growth%2C%20promising%20enhancements%20in%20diagnostics;
38 'Advancing healthcare in India: Navigating the transformative impact of AI', *NASSCOM*, https://nasscom.in/knowledge-center/publications/advancing-healthcare-india-navigating-transformative-impact-ai#:~:text=,AI%20use%20cases%20to%20production
39 Press Information Bureau, 'Update on Artificial Intelligence (AI) in health sector', https://www.pib.gov.in/PressReleaseIframePage.aspx?PRID=1908041#:~:text=NITI%20Ayog%20has%20published%20two,Responsible%20AI%E2%80%9D%20in%20August%202021
40 'Advancing healthcare in India: Navigating the transformative impact of AI', *NASSCOM*, https://nasscom.in/knowledge-center/publications/advancing-healthcare-india-navigating-transformative-impact-ai#:~:text=In%20the%20short%20term%2C%20AI,in%20achieving%20universal%20healthcare%20coverage

11 Quality as a management tool

Tilak Shankar

Introduction

The National Accreditation Board for Hospitals and Healthcare Providers (NABH), a constituent board of the Quality Control of India (QCI), was set up in 2005 to 'establish and operate accreditation programmes for hospitals, healthcare providers and sets benchmarks for the progress of the health industry'.[1] The standards of NABH are subject to triennial reviews, and the latest revision was made in 2020. Smaller hospitals, which constitute the majority of private hospitals (with less than 50 beds), have specific requirements for accreditation.[2] But only a limited number of small hospitals opt for this accreditation since it is perceived that extensive infrastructure changes and accountability on a number of parameters are needed. Hospitals that opt for NABH accreditation go through external assessments. NABH accreditation, though created by the Quality Council of India – Government of India wing, is not mandatory for hospitals. Very few government hospitals have been accredited so far. The total number of accredited hospitals is very few – about 500.[3]

NABH-accredited hospitals include corporate hospitals, for-profit private hospitals, non-profits. The organisation structures, objectives, size and speciality are different. These are generic guidelines and not specific to any one speciality. NABH is basically an operational quality standard with detailed quality metrics for all departments of a hospital. A lesser-known section is the standards for the Board of Directors/Trustees. In this chapter, the entire discussion is on management aspects alone. The NABH standards (January 2025) can be referred to for a detailed guideline covering all standards. An effective implementation of the accreditation standards will greatly strengthen the functioning of the top management.

Quality is also a management tool since the standards highlight that quality flows from the top. If the leadership is enthusiastic about adherence to clearly defined standards, then automatically, it percolates to the entire hospital. When the top is lukewarm, then there would be only procedural compliance. Top management should govern by establishing high ethical values, instituting clear roles for each board member and ensuring highest standards of professionalism.[4]

DOI: 10.4324/9781003684947-13

NABH and National Accreditation Board for Testing and Calibration Laboratories (NABL) standards require hospitals to keep track of a large number of parameters such as patient service levels, emergency care, patient safety, employee safety, operating theatre and infection control. It is surprising as to why the Government of India and state governments have not insisted that all hospitals, including government hospitals, should be accredited. NABH is not merely a quality control certificate to be showcased as a marketing tool. It is intended to improve the way their hospitals are being managed. One of the key benefits of NABH accreditation is that it provides a formal method of improving management processes.

NABH as a management tool

Every well-run institution should have systems of budgetary control and management reporting through dashboards for reviewing the data to be gathered as per NABH requirements. NABH defines five management standards consisting of 36 discrete areas of responsibility.[5] Implementation of these standards acts as a guide for effective management.

The five standards mentioned in NABH clearly state that the Governing Board and each board member should be closely involved in the hospital's functioning and spelling out specific policies and procedures (Figure 11.1).

Five standards

Let us examine these five standards:

- Responsibility of the governing body and its role.
- Ethical leadership.

QUALITY AS A MANAGEMENT TOOL

NABH STANDARDS FOR MANAGEMENT	NABH + OUR INTERPRETATION
Governing body roles	Specific roles for each board member in sub-committees, based as their professional background and interest. Ex-Offico & Independent Members.
Ethical leadership	Strict formal ethical guidelines on purchase of capital equipment, drug & consumable, tests, morbidity audit, kickbacks. Report in Annual report
Leadership in day-to-day management	Appoint professionally qualified for all non-medical functions, compliance reports.
Professionalism	Senior management focus on long term planning strategy, external developments using management tools, succession planning.
Patient safety, overall risk management	Implement patient safety and employee safety. Risk management - fire safety, legal developments.

Figure 11.1 Five standards defined by NABH.

- Leadership in day-to-day management and its responsibilities.
- Professionalism in functioning.
- Patient safety and overall risk management.

A reading of these standards reads like chapters from a management textbook. These are not idealistic goals but directions in which all hospitals should move towards. Accredited hospitals are mandated to follow these standards, along with the other standards. However, in accredited hospitals, the sad truth is that management standards are not followed, but it need not be overemphasised that adherence to them will enhance the performance of the hospital.

Responsibility of the governing board

Normally, there would be about 10 to 15 Board members in a private company or a non-profit, including members from the management group, independent or non-executive members. The Chairperson of the Board could be an executive or non-executive member.

Even though there could be as many as 15 members, in actual practice, only a few are usually actively involved in the governance of the institution. Some of the members will play only a nominal role and merely attend Board meetings. If the board members are not from the healthcare sector, unless they are actively involved their contribution to governance in any case will be limited. An active member however can bring objectivity, professional expertise and external perspective and can contribute to the long-term interest of the institution.

The Chairperson plays a central role in all institutions. The roles of the different non-healthcare Board members in a hospital should normally be linked to their professional backgrounds – banker, accountant, lawyer, administrator, social worker, industrialist and management expert. Generally, the Chairperson of a Trust does not allocate specific roles to any individual trustee, even though formal roles for Board members will increase their involvement. In many cases, the Chairperson may not want to share their authority with the other Board members.

Members who have an executive role in the hospital management, as ex officio members, represent their viewpoint at the meetings. In addition, it is necessary that there should be an independent oversight of the functioning of the hospital. This can be facilitated only if there is a large representation by independent members on the Board. There should be a clear distinction between the operational role of the management members and a distinct role for the governing body.

It is necessary to quantify the 'performance' of the institution. Performance can be defined in financial terms, quality parameters, education, research and community initiatives. It is necessary for each Board member to monitor actual performance in consultation with the operating members and initiate necessary corrective action. Unfortunately, most members either do not have the time or adequate understanding to contribute to improvements in different areas.

Corporate hospital boards

Typically, corporate hospitals will have 12–15 members on the Board, with approximately half of the members being 'independent' members. There have been attempts by the government to separate the positions of Chairperson from that of the Chief Executive or Managing Director. The main objective of this move was to ensure an independent review authority in the form of the Chairperson. Recently, the separation of the two roles has been made voluntary. A study of the annual reports of various corporate hospitals reveals a considerable amount of data presented regularly, facilitating Board members to examine the reports and suggest corrective action.

In listed companies, it is mandatory to have sub-committees of the Board members, in areas such as investor relations, investments, audit, remuneration and corporate social responsibility. Each of these committees plays a different role in the overall governance of the Board. An ethics committee with a clear mandate would be a crucial addition. The Board of Trustees or Directors with their professional expertise and skills of handling varied situations, professional backgrounds in industry, accounting, banking, administration, business, management, law and social work can add significant value to the hospital. However, it is also important to appreciate that managing hospitals is completely different from an industrial organisation or a bank or a law firm. The important differentiator is that the hospital is an institution involved in patient care guided by medical professionals who form the core strength of the hospital. The Board members should engage in conversations with various levels of staff members, including nurses and HR, and visit the hospital premises. NABH standards clearly define specific contributions that are expected from the Board members. The Board members themselves should offer to play specific roles in the overall governance of the institution.

Ethical leadership

A crucial part of the NABH management standards emphasises 'transparency in various dealings, the practice of denying medical treatment to poor patients for monetary reasons, conflict of interest, disclosure of ownership interest, affiliations or accreditations to a specific department or to the whole hospital'. It is necessary to evolve suitable systems to collect feedback from the patients and devise ways to gain insights into the perceptions of the community. This data should be systematically examined by an independent Board member.

A process has to be put in place to scrutinise whether medical professionals are prescribing expensive tests and prescribing expensive branded drugs when cheaper generic drugs may be available. This process can be undertaken by internal committees and reported to the Board. There is a perception from newspaper reports that consumable items are being charged at very high rates by the hospitals and overstay is encouraged in the ICU or in the wards. The Board should approach the findings in an objective manner. The focus should not be to second-guess medical management. However, in a profit-oriented corporate hospital, there have been doubts whether medical decisions are also being made for commercial reasons. Critics point out that there is a difference between 'profits' and 'profiteering'. There is always an ongoing debate on whether a hospital should have only the shareholder interest in mind or work in the larger interest of society as well.

During the COVID-19 pandemic in 2020 and 2021, there was a widely held belief that many hospitals were overcharging their patients at a time of acute medical crisis. The government and insurance companies intervened to warn the erring hospitals. The responsibility ultimately vests with the Board. The Chairperson should issue guidelines on ethical practices in capital purchases, medicine and consumable purchases, overcharging of patients and 'referral charges'. The Medical Director should issue guidelines on various ethical medical practices, which should be followed by the entire medical team. A formal code of ethical conduct should be drafted and made publicly available. There should be a mechanism to ensure that all these directives are followed in letter and spirit. The Board of Directors, in their annual report, should inform the shareholders on the ethical aspects of management. In the case of other institutions, it should be published on their website.

The National Medical Commission and National Board should also publish a list of hospitals that follow good ethical practices. It is ultimately in the long-term interests of all corporations themselves to follow ethical practices, instead of waiting for the government to rein them in through legislative measures.

Leadership in management

The author has witnessed many healthcare leaders who have displayed vision, concern for the patient and affection for the staff. Some examples have been provided in the chapter on leadership (Chapter 6). Dr S.S. Badrinath, former Chairman of Sankara Nethralaya, very often would visit the outpatient department at 7 a.m., talk to patients, speak to the staff and if he observed any areas which needed to be cleaned, he would attend to it personally. Dr Rangarajan, Founder of Sundaram Medical Foundation, would make personal enquiries about family members of the staff in his morning rounds. Dr V. Shanta, former Chairperson of Cancer Institute, would insist on the best food for every child in the children's free ward. Leadership flows from the personality, beliefs, concern for the poor and converting standards into actions. They should set examples for others to follow.

NABH emphasises the importance of strong and empowering leadership in healthcare organisations, viewing it as crucial for building a culture of quality and patient safety. NABH-accredited hospitals are expected to have leaders who empower their staff, promote continuous learning and foster a positive work environment.

- *Empowering leadership:* NABH values leaders who empower their staff by connecting employee objectives with organisational goals, believing in their subordinates' abilities and promoting participation in decision-making.
- *Continuous learning and development*: NABH accreditation encourages a culture of continuous learning and professional development for all staff, including medical and paramedical personnel.
- *Positive work environment:* NABH standards aim to create a positive and supportive work environment where staff are satisfied and motivated.
- *Patient safety and quality*: NABH standards emphasise the importance of leadership in ensuring patient safety and delivering high-quality care.
- *Organisational culture*: NABH accreditation helps organisations develop a strong culture of quality and patient safety at all levels, including leadership.

The top management of a hospital typically consists of a team comprising Medical Director, Nursing Director, Head of Finance and Administration and Head of Human Resources. NABH recommends that heads of HR and finance should be 'a person qualified in hospital administration'. In the last two decades, many teaching institutions have been offering a master's degree in hospital administration (MHA). Hospitals should collaborate with the teaching institutions. The undergraduates in this MHA programme are drawn from a variety of backgrounds, including medicine, dentistry, economics, engineering and physiotherapy. Some management institutes also have medical graduates who enrol as students. NABH standards also require that the key leaders be familiar with various statutory requirements and implement them. A compliance report should be obtained from the management. NABH standards lay emphasis on spelling out key result areas (KRAs), classified into medical, financial, operational and other administrative areas, with a central focus on the patient. In a multi-specialty hospital, various clinical and direct support departments will have clear measures, also defined in the NABH. For every speciality department such as cardiology, orthopaedics, oncology, intensive care unit (ICU) and direct support departments such as laboratories, imaging and blood bank, there are several operational parameters as well. Similarly, in the case of the nursing department which employs the largest number of staff, there are clearly defined performance measures. Some hospitals also have an additional 'nursing excellence'[6] certification, which has additional quality measures. Nurses should be empowered so that their full potential is utilised. There are very few boards – charitable or corporate boards – which have a nurse on them. Many hospitals do not have formal appraisal systems based on quantitative KRAs.

Professionalism

Professionalism is required at all levels in a hospital. Professional standards are defined by the respective professional associations, for example, professional standards for a medical doctor, nurse or a chartered accountant. These standards should be no different in a hospital setting also. It is possible that in some cases, professional standards might conflict with financial goals of the organisation and may be compromised. For example, when an accident victim is admitted to a hospital, the attending doctor should treat the victim without worrying about the ability of the patient to pay the hospital bill. Hospital management may provide only temporary treatment. A chartered accountant may be required to implement policies that may conflict with professional standards. But in reality, many of these actions do take place. It is difficult to maintain the highest professional standards.

NABH standards may not revolutionise professional standards overnight. But there should be a progressive change over a period of time. The burden of change is with the Board and top management of each hospital.

NABH standards document lays emphasis on professionalism, particularly by the leadership team. NABH emphasises that leadership should focus on long-term planning, strategy, external environment and policymaking, along with managing operations on a day-to-day basis. Most of the time, a marked deviation from professionalism is observed. In Board meetings, the agenda is largely focused on routine transactions. NABH standards, on the other hand, emphasise the use of management tools to interpret external and internal environments. Charitable institutions mostly are inward-looking, with little attention paid to examining the changing environment and the emerging challenges. Patients could choose a well-run government hospital as compared to a poorly run charitable hospital.

Professional standards should be complied with not merely to meet NABH requirements but because they are in the interest of the institution itself. It will be unfortunate if governments bring in punitive legislation to force hospitals.

Internal scanning

NABH standards prescribe a focus on internal scanning. Unfortunately, most of the senior management do not focus on internal developments impacting their hospitals. We will take two examples to illustrate this point – employee morale and patient satisfaction. Employee morale is critical to every organisation, namely, the morale of doctors, nurses, technicians and other staff. Medical doctors 'are the engines in any hospital pulling all other carriages', says a senior hospital administrator. Patients develop loyalty to individual doctors. So, low morale of doctors, especially key doctors leaving the hospital, could have an adverse impact on the hospital. In the case of patients with chronic illnesses, they could gravitate towards the doctors. We have come across instances in which senior doctors have been peremptorily dismissed by the management. Boards should be sensitive to these internal developments.

Many hospitals also have in-hospital training programmes, for example, Diplomate of the National Board (DNB) and a post-graduate course where the students train for three years. They are at the forefront of providing care and work round the clock for a government-prescribed stipend. The dean of academic studies of the hospital is expected to coordinate their training needs and their morale. The dean largely restricts their interest to academic matters. The needs of the students – working conditions, food, transport if they are staying outside the premises – could be issues affecting their morale. Very few students, after completing their training, continue with the parent hospitals. The HR department should have the pulse of their morale. In many hospitals, similarly, it is not uncommon for even senior doctors to have many concerns or complaints. Nurses who constitute the largest group of staff members are often the most neglected. Hospitals are immune to a high attrition rate. The nurse's attrition levels are rationalised by arguing that it is common. Some have a system of employee morale survey by an external agency in which interviews are conducted with employees and specific areas for improvement are reported to the Board.

Patient satisfaction

Patient satisfaction depends primarily on medical outcomes; however, many other factors also contribute. In some hospitals, the Chairperson would go on around every morning, listening to patients, examining the kitchen and restrooms. Unfortunately, this is not a common practice. Some Chairpersons rarely visit the hospital, instead prefer to have virtual meetings. In fact, many senior staff members also do not 'manage by walking around'. Patient complaint system does not capture the 'real' complaints of the patient or their attenders. Patients tend to be deferential to their doctors and are hesitant to articulate their 'real' views. The senior management and the Board go largely by summary of the hospital complaint system. However, in the long run, each one of these changes could affect the hospital. NABH standards, thus, can help the institution to improve by both external and internal scanning systems.

Strategic planning

The NABH lays emphasis on strategic planning for all accredited institutions. This is defined as 'a general plan to achieve one or more short term and long-term goals under conditions of uncertainty.'[7]

The strategies could include marketing, financial, product/service and human resources. Every institution should have an understanding of likely future developments and their implications. NABH standards suggest that the institution should formally state its vision, mission and values. Some institutions, particularly charitable institutions, believe such an exercise is unnecessary. NABH standards mention political, economic, social, technology (PEST), PESTLE (PEST plus legal and environment) to track environmental changes in the socio-economic environments. There are frequent legislative changes which have an impact on hospitals. Concepts such as environment scanning and strengths, weakness, opportunities and threats (SWOT) and technology forecasting are scoffed at by the leadership of many such institutions. There is a misperception that only corporate hospitals need these 'new-fangled' ideas. There have been several significant environmental advancements in the medical field impacting large hospitals and nursing homes in the last few decades.

Strategic planning requires that the senior management studies various environmental developments impacting their hospital. Nursing homes and small hospitals in future may be required to obtain quality accreditation, computerise their case sheets and strengthen their internal systems. Middle-class patients are becoming aware of their health needs, thanks to the internet and social media. Mobile phones are used for patient–doctor communication. The rapid increase in non-communicable diseases, growth of fitness centres and webinars have contributed to greater awareness about wellness. A large number of YouTube videos in local languages have enhanced awareness even among illiterate citizens. FM radio's popularity and its extensive usage by infertility hospitals is a case in point. There have been major medical technological changes in the last few decades. Many home diagnostic kits, such as blood pressure apparatus, pulse oximeters, peak flow meters and oxygen concentrators, are becoming common in middle-class homes. Some middle-class homes even convert their houses into mini-hospitals. There are a large number of wearables which are in use. Some hospitals have started utilising artificial intelligence (AI) to help in better diagnosis, as well as to serve underserved geographical areas.

The provision of insurance by governments has made access to private and corporate hospitals easier. Government and private insurance schemes have resulted in greater patronage of private hospitals, posing a challenge to non-profits. Some of the external changes may be subtle, while others may be evident even in the short term. Individual hospitals cannot simply ignore external developments. It is important that the top management and the Boards should periodically meet and review the impact of environmental changes.

Corporate hospitals

We will briefly discuss the strategic requirements for long- and short-term planning. In recent years, there have been initial public offers (IPOs) from some hospitals, diagnostic laboratories, pharmacies and health insurance companies, resulting in acquisitions, friendly or hostile.

Foreign funds have been acquiring hospitals in India. Motherhood chain of maternity hospitals acquired by a Singapore fund is one of the several instances of this trend. Pharmacy chains have become attractive investments for acquisition. All these hospitals are required to be aggressive in their marketing strategies, offering substantial discounts in the case of laboratories. Many hospitals have started 'hub and spoke' model, a chain of diagnostic centres requiring the acquisition of more patients.

The NABH standards recommend that the senior management and the Board should constantly evaluate strategic options available, such as expansion, discontinuing some departments or diversify, targeting foreign patients, by establishing foreign branches, partnership with other institutions and establishing a nursing school.

Effectiveness of committees

NABH standards recommend a regular review of the functioning of the committees, where meetings tend to be ritualistic and members are not enthused about the meetings. Critical review membership of the committees, replacement of those who do not contribute. The objectives of each committee should be examined in the contemporary context, and the Chairperson should be rotated regularly. A summary of the proceedings, agenda for meetings should be made available to the next higher level of committees.

Change management

NABH standards emphasise the importance of change of management, an inescapable part of an organisation's life. For example, hospital-wide computerisation has made patient information available on desktops and mobile phones rather than on case sheets. Communication to patients and blood test reports are sent through email from hospitals and laboratories. Robotic surgery is fast becoming common. The change process involves training the doctors, nurses, technicians and other staff, explaining the need for change and identification of 'change agents'. Disruptions and resistance to change are also equally common. Resistance is directly proportional to the magnitude of change – greater the change, greater is the resistance. For many years, resistance to computerisation and introduction of NABH itself arose due to the lack of familiarity with its benefits. Every organisation has staff members who are pro-change, and many favour the status quo. Leadership plays a critical role in change management. Enthusiastic leadership can set the tone and the speed of change by involving outside experts. A good model to emulate is the Japanese style of extensive internal consultations for ensuring success. This investment in time and effort by the leaders is essential to ensure that all major changes are successful.

Succession planning

NABH standards place considerable emphasis on succession planning urging the Board and the senior management to ensure smooth succession at the helm and department level. Successive leaders should build on the founder's vision and develop it further. In some cases, the change of guard can take place during the lifetime of the leader or after a turbulent change – over the founder's departure.

In the case of corporations, there are company law guidelines on the retirement age of directors. In the case of non-profit organisations, there are no formal guidelines. For the medical staff, normally superannuation is at 70 years of age. For other staff, it would be 58 or 60 years of age. Strangely, many organisations do not plan for the retirement of their senior staff. Extensions are given to the incumbents for several years. A sense of 'indispensability' is created by continuing the incumbents. Timely retirement is necessary for all organisations. There should be a good mix of experience and youthful exuberance in every organisation. Succession is essential to keep pace with the changes in the environment. A static organisation and staffing are not in the best interest of any organisation.

Change in leadership

NABH standards highlight the need for change in leadership, particularly for founders actively involved in the organisation. Convincing present leadership of the necessity, when they believe they know 'what is best' for the organisation. The Board should play a crucial role in ensuring orderly change in leadership.

Patient safety and risk management

Patient's safety

NABH discusses various patient safety aspects, such as waiting time in emergency, safety precautions during surgery and errors in medication or blood tests. The top management and the Board should periodically examine this critical aspect as part of their monthly or quarterly review.

Risk management

The Board should have a contingency plan for fire accidents, floods and other emergencies, prioritising patient safety and evacuation. Financial crisis as seen during the epidemic also necessitates contingency plans. Boards should actively participate in drawing up plans for overcoming such challenges as discussed in the chapter on management science.

Conclusion

NABH standards should be treated as a prescription for growth. A well-balanced, active Board will strengthen the institution towards greater excellence. The Board will help explore the hidden potential of the hospital, thereby benefiting patients and staff alike. Ethical practices will benefit the hospital in the long run, even if it means compromises on the profit levels. A hospital is not like any other profit-making enterprise, routinely churning positive cash flows. It is a professional institution meant to adhere to the highest professional standards. Patient safety and staff safety should be an integral part of the functions of the hospital. Faithful adherence to NABH standards will strengthen the institution.

Notes

1 NABH Standards, *National Accreditation Board for Hospitals and Health Care Providers*, 4th edition, December 2015, https://kgmu.org/download/NABH-Book.pdf
2 Small Healthcare Organisations, *NABH Standards for Small Healthcare Organisations*, August 2020, https://nabh.co/Images/PDF/gib.pdf
3 'NABH Accreditation Statistics', *The Healthcare Manager*, https://expresshealthcaremanagement.blogspot.com/2019/06/nabh-accreditation-statistics.html#google_vignette
4 NABH Accreditation Standards for Hospitals, 6th edition, 1 January 2025, https://portal.nabh.co/images/Standards/NABH%20Hospital%20Accreditation%20Standard%206th%20Edition%20January%202025.pdf
5 NABH Standards – Responsibility of Management, Quality Council of India, NABH international, undated, https://international.nabh.co/standard.aspx
6 Nursing Excellence Certification, Mathew Verghese, Nursing Officer, AIIMS New Delhi, Introduction to NABH and Nursing Excellence, 24 September 2020, https://www.slideshare.net/mathewvallanamatathil/introduction-to-nabh-nursing-excellence
7 Strategic Planning, Wikipedia, https://en.wikipedia.org/wiki/Strategic_planning

12 Management of support services

Tilak Shankar

Introduction

Senior management or Board members typically don't accord sufficient importance to support services in a hospital such as the diet kitchen, laundry, engineering services, including biomedical engineering, housekeeping, water supply, medical gas, waste disposal, transport and security services (Figure 12.1). These activities are given prominence only when there is a crisis. Medical oxygen is a good example. During the COVID-19 pandemic, acute shortage of medical oxygen resulted in hospitals scrambling for required quantities. Poor service in any of these departments is immediately noticed, resulting in patient dissatisfaction. The total cost of all these services could range from 15 to 20 per cent of the total expenditure of a hospital. Therefore, purely from a cost perspective, effective management of these services is essential.

Hospitals are mandated to comply with various regulatory requirements, and National Accreditation Board for Hospitals and Healthcare Providers (NABH) accredited institutions have specific quality monitoring standards. It is desirable that even if a hospital is not accredited, it should adhere to these processes. The individual departments must be professionally managed to improve patient satisfaction and achieve cost savings. Given the widespread use of computerised systems in many hospitals, monitoring activities can be facilitated, even at a granular level.

Some of the services may be outsourced and some of them could be managed in-house, but the ultimate responsibility should vest with the management. Diet kitchen, for example, should ensure timely service, supply high-quality and appropriate diet as prescribed and supply warm food by courteous staff. This service is required 365 days a year. Biomedical services ensure that all medical equipment is in working order. Biomedical waste disposal is a statutory requirement and full compliance and within budgets at high levels of quality.

DOI: 10.4324/9781003684947-14

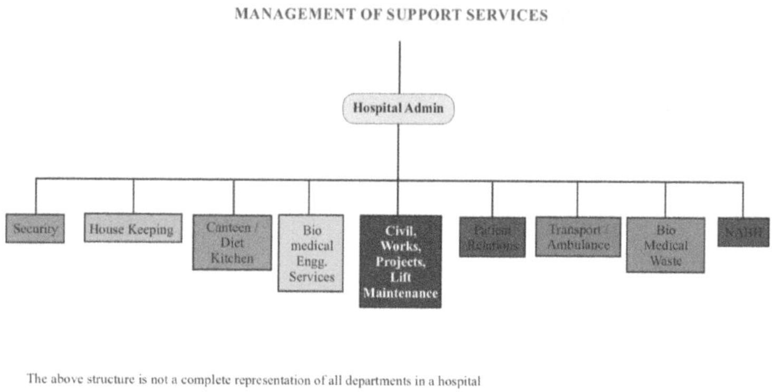

Figure 12.1 Management of support services.

Organisation structure

The head of administrative or support departments should be an experienced administrator. Hospitals should employ those who have obtained a Masters in Hospital Administration (MHA) degree to be responsible for these activities. Key staff, for example, nutritionist, should be in charge of diet kitchen, and biomedical engineer should manage medical equipment maintenance. Unfortunately, some of these functions do not get the attention of the top management in many hospitals.

Parameters for management control

These broadly encompass:

- Compliance with all the existing rules and regulations.
- Ensuring patient satisfaction.
- Adherence to financial budgets.
- Adherence to measurable outputs.

Compliance

All hospitals must comply with many government rules and regulations. Compliances for operational aspects such as fire safety, lift maintenance, disposal of medical waste, effluent treatment and food waste apply with equal force to all hospitals, including government hospitals. A compliance report should be submitted on a quarterly basis to the Board of Directors or Trustees.

Budgeting

Financial and operational budgets should cover all aspects, including human resources, materials and consumables, annual maintenance contracts (AMC) and other overheads. If some services are outsourced, then the budgeting should reflect such expenses. Food budgets should be linked to the number and types of meals served, laundry by kilos of clothes washed and engineering services by value of spare parts utilised. Regardless of whether the activity is managed in-house or outsourced, the ultimate accountability vests with the management.

Measure of performance

The overall performance is measured by a number of financial indices such as income and quantitative metrics like the number of patients handled. It is crucial that these overall measures are sub-divided into various departments and sections. NABH defines numerous quality-related areas emphasising correlation between performance, patient satisfaction and financial and quantitative parameters. For example, housekeeping quality indicators are defined in NABH standards – frequency and type of cleaning of high-risk areas such as isolation rooms, intensive care units (ICU) and infectious diseases wards. There are also guidelines for the disposal of biomedical waste and a list of disinfectants and chemicals that can be used. Employee needle-stick injuries and employee safety should be closely monitored.[1] Similar metrics are also defined for other services, in great detail.

Scope for cost savings

Efficiency improvement and cost savings are achievable in every aspect of the hospital's operations. 'We are operating a tight ship' is the frequently heard defensive response from many administrators. The truth is it is not always well managed. Cost savings are required in many industries to compete in their business accomplished through innovative (small and big) use of new material, use of new technologies, improvement in work practices and employee suggestion scheme. Healthcare should be no exception. There should be a constant endeavour to search for cost savings by eliminating wastages. For example, solar energy and recycling of wastewater are areas where cost savings can be accomplished. It is essential that each section identifies small and big ideas for efficiency improvement, and cost savings as part of their annual plan with staff being encouraged to make improvements.

Patient satisfaction

There are a range of services which collectively determine patient satisfaction. A brief discussion on the management processes in each of the support services follows. Any malfunctioning or deficiency in these services lead to a high level of patient dissatisfaction.

Diet kitchen and cafeteria

In a typical 500-bed hospital, food department supplies between 1,500 and 2,000 meals a day along with snacks and coffee/tea from the cafeteria. The food department should generate cash surplus after meeting all the direct and indirect expenditure including provision of subsidised food/free food for some patients and food at subsidised rates for the staff. Cafeteria caters to visitors and outpatients. Cafeteria services may be outsourced. The in-house food supply should be in line with the diet prescribed by the physician and the nutritionist. The decision to run the food services in-house or outsource is commonly referred to in management parlance as 'make or buy'. One of the main reasons is that outsourcing is believed to be less expensive. However, a detailed cost–benefit exercise is rarely undertaken. Many charitable institutions coordinate with non-government organisations (NGOs) to supply food to poor patients, sometimes under an Annadhana scheme as it is relatively easy to raise funds for providing free food.

Costing of food services

The in-house costs should include salary of the staff in the kitchen, material used, cost of cooking gas, notional cost of space, cleaning costs, amortisation of various equipment and other fixed costs. The total costs should be amortised over the number of major and minor meals served over a month. Food may be charged separately or as a part of room charges.

Investments in cold storage, modern kitchen equipment and vessels, and trolleys for food transport are essential. Predicting the number of meals should take into account past data – day of the week, bed occupancy, number of patients in the ICU, bed category-wise and non-vegetarians – to minimise wastage. Analysis of fixed costs of the kitchen and variable costs of each meal aids in amortisation. Automated kitchens, whether outsourced or in-house, contribute to efficiency. Compliance with NABH standards, irrespective of whether they are NABH-accredited or not, requires measures such as medical screening of all kitchen workers and pest control.

The layout of the kitchen should be carefully planned. Ventilation, light, easy flow of material and storage will help in greater efficiency. Wastage and pilferage should be closely monitored. Disposal of paper plates and cups should be done scientifically. A neglected area is screening of kitchen workers for possible infections, such as hepatitis. There should be a well-defined protocol in every hospital and periodic reports sent to the Head of Administration about the tests carried out on staff. Food distribution to patients needs to be done in temperature-controlled service trolleys (hot food kept hot, and cold food kept cold).

The cost of food, whether it is passed on to the patient or absorbed by the hospital, should be reasonable. Hand-held tablets can be utilised by nutritionists and communication with the kitchen should be automated. Barcodes/QR codes may also be considered. The nutritionist should be innovative. In the children's wards or in a children's hospitals, food can be nutritious without being boring. Hospitals should provide low-cost, yet nutrition-dense food. Kitchen can be profitable even in non-profit hospitals.

Housekeeping

Housekeeping is vital for hygiene, but it often receives insufficient attention in public areas and private rooms compared to boardroom toilets. The selection of contractors' annual activity should be based on the credentials of the agency, references from other similar hospitals, number of staff proposed to be deployed, frequency of cleaning toilets and common areas and nature of chemicals to be used. Hospitals should employ their own staff to supervise by carrying out surprise checks. In addition, patient complaints should also be taken into account.

A senior hospital administrator of large charitable hospital pointed out:

> Although wards, critical areas and OT are monitored, public areas including toilets and corridors are neglected, OP or IP – patient to toilet ratio, particularly in free patients' wards, is neglected. Poor maintenance of fixtures, furniture, furnishings, blinds, area priority matrix is not determined for fixing the frequency of cleaning, based on footfalls, type of activity performed, high risk vs low risk. A checklist is rarely used.

NABH has documented detailed procedures. The COVID-19 epidemic has highlighted the criticality of this function.

Quality indicators

The following are some of the quality indicators:

- Patient satisfaction rate on housekeeping.
- Compliance rate to safety practices while doing housekeeping functions.
- Compliance rate to biomedical waste (BMW) regulations.
- Compliance with frequency of cleaning as determined.
- Needle-stick injury (when the skin is accidentally punctured by needles used for patients) rate among housekeeping.

(*Source*: 'Checklist of housekeeping services for NABH accreditation', Healthcare Manager, https://expresshealthcaremanagement.blogspot.com

/2018/03/checklist-of-hospital-housekeeping-services-quality-accreditation.html).

Hospitals should take these guidelines seriously and assign responsibilities to hospital staff.

Engineering services

The engineering services should handle a wide range of specialised departments such as civil, mechanical, electrical and electronic sections. Proprietary items will be maintained under AMCs. It is essential that there should be an electronic record of all equipment, their uptime, frequency of servicing, downtime, causes for downtime and cost of repairs. Regular electrical safety audits are necessary to eliminate electrical risks. A planned preventive maintenance scheme is essential not only for electrical but also for other utility equipment, items such as wheelchairs, stretchers, furniture items, cleaning of AC ducts/filters, air handling units and cleaning/replacement.

Fire safety

Fire safety is another area which requires serious attention and the highest levels of compliance. Newspapers periodically report fire accidents in hospitals, including in government hospitals in intensive care units (ICUs), children's wards and other areas, which result in loss of lives. Very often, small fire mishaps are not even reported. The management of the hospital and the Board are legally responsible for such accidents. Prof. Kanchan Choudhary of the Indian Institute of Technology, Kharagpur, highlights three critical ingredients for hospital fires[2] – fuel, including a wide range of gases, oxidants and ignition. It is common knowledge that storage of gases is not given much importance. Fire is *never* an accident and must be prevented. The management should, with the help of experts and fire departments, take corrective action on time. There must be regular fire drills, so that staff are trained to handle evacuation most efficiently. There have been instances where the Board of Directors and the Chairperson have been arrested for major fire accidents.

Water supply

There are many cities in India where an adequate quantity of water is a problem, particularly during summer. This results in the hospital buying water from tankers at a high cost. Hospitals also buy drinking water in bottles. A small number of hospitals have installed systems for providing drinking water from the atmosphere.[3] While it is a good alternative, these systems require investment in equipment, sufficient humidity in the atmosphere and operating costs are high.

Laundry services

Laundry services could be handled in-house or outsourced. Many hospitals have large industrial-scale laundry machines, with dryers, often on the premises. Very few government hospitals have automatic washing machines. Some hospitals use disposable sheets. It should be ensured that all hospitals adhere to the quality indicators.

General facilities

Patient-safety devices like grab bars, bed rails, safety belts on stretchers and wheelchairs, fire alarms, smoke detectors, call bells and fire safety devices are simple areas which should not be ignored. Periodic preventive maintenance of items which have a high 'wear and tear' is important.

Facility inspection rounds to ensure safety should be conducted at least once a quarter. There should be suitable documentation and closure of gaps. A checklist, prominently displayed, will act as a reminder. As alternate sources for electricity, diesel generator sets, solar energy, uninterrupted power supply, gas and water must be provided as a backup for any failure/shortage and their functioning should be tested.

During night shifts, most hospitals lack an emergency response team. This lacuna should be corrected. Minor incidents are not reported, with the result the management is unaware of such problems.

Electricity

Electricity is the lifeline of a hospital. All medical equipment, ICU wards, computers and lighting require uninterrupted power 24/7, 365 days a year. Hospitals depend on supply from electricity boards, supplemented by diesel generator sets and solar power. Electricity is an expensive and scarce resource, and its optimal use and close monitoring are critical. Electricity is also a major item of cost.

Other items

Facilities for the differently abled – special toilet, wheelchair accessible entrance – are critical aspects that are sadly neglected. Disposal of non-functioning items, unwanted material and scrap material should be carried out periodically. All hospitals must have a contingency plan, ensuring that critical systems and services do not fail, or that failures are recovered within minimum time frames. Ambulance is another vital service. Some states, for example, Tamil Nadu, have a good system of networking of all ambulance services which are connected through apps, so that the arrival time of the ambulance, where it is required, is minimal.

Medical gas

During 2020–2022, in the two long years of COVID-19, the importance of medical gas came to limelight in unfortunate circumstances. Medical gas availability is taken for granted most of the time but proved to be a critical need.

Crèche

Crèche is a legal requirement, depending on the number of women employees – the children of nurses, technicians and doctors should be provided this facility, either free of charge or at concessional rates. If the hospitals are in a position to have an in-house crèche, they should provide this facility either in-house or at some other proximate facility. Hospital management should view this as an essential measure, which is legally mandated.

Transport

Many hospitals own or hire buses for transportation, owned by the hospitals, operated by contractors or are completely outsourced. Buses and cars could be used for the transportation of staff, trainees from their hostels, patients from one location to another and patients from camps. Efficient management includes route planning, operational costs and adherence to time schedules.

Central sterile supply department (CSSD)

This section is responsible for maintaining a healthy and safe environment, minimising infections and providing a timely supply of sterilised items. Hospital-acquired infections are a major cause for nosocomial or hospital-acquired infections. Operating theatre requires all surgical instruments, trays, linen and dressing material to be sterilised. CSSD is responsible for this vital function.[4] A professionally managed CSSD is critical for all hospitals.

Mortuary

It is necessary to provide a mortuary within the hospital for safe custody of bodies, before and after postmortem. It should be located in a separate building on the ground floor, easily accessible from the wards, emergency department and operation theatres, preferably away from the general public traffic.

Green hospital

In recent years, there has been a heightened awareness of environment, urging organisations to go beyond legislative requirements and actively save our fragile environment. Hospitals should aggressively identify areas for savings on electricity, water consumption and recycling of wastewater. Many developments such as light-emitting diode (LED) lights, sensor lights, energy-efficient fans and energy-efficient air conditioners are now popular in homes and institutions for cost savings and concern for the environment. There are many areas for cost savings and for energy conservation in all hospitals.

D. Suresh, an expert on alternative energy, has implemented several energy savings projects in offices, hospitals and educational institutions. He suggests:

1. *Rooftop solar*: In recent years, solar including rooftop solar has become common. With high-quality and inexpensive solar cells, power can be tapped from solar energy and used directly or stored in batteries. One kilowatt costs between INR 40,000 and INR 50,000 including solar panels, necessary stands, mounting structure, with a life of about 25 years. The cost per kilowatt is constantly going down. Depending on the total roof area available, the size of the panels and the kilowatt of energy can be determined. In some cities, net metering is permitted, in which excess electricity can be banked.
2. *Cooking gas*: Utilising kitchen waste is another way to save the environment. Every large organisation – hospital, hotel, educational institution, factory, office – generates a large quantity of cooking waste every day. Employees, patients, students and visitors make use of the cafeteria every day. This waste generated from the kitchen can be converted into cooking gas through a simple process. The byproduct from this process can be used as organic manure. Any kitchen waste – cooked, uncooked, excess, spoilt, daily vegetable peeling – can be used. In a large college hostel, about 1,000 kg of waste is generated every day, which can be converted into cooking gas.

Suresh continues:

> *Kitchen garden and hydroponics:* Wherever there is land area, a kitchen garden can be easily developed. Government hospitals have plenty of land area where kitchen gardens can be grown. Depending on the soil conditions and water availability, fruits and vegetables can be grown. In fact, the modern trend is hydroponics where kitchen gardens can be developed without land at all. The capital cost is low, virtually no maintenance and highly profitable. In some places, exotic vegetables and fruits are grown 365 days a year.

Air to water: Equipment for the generation of water from the atmosphere is now produced in India and is commercially available. It is used in hospitals with a large capacity (1,000 litres per day). This equipment uses electricity to generate water and requires atmospheric humidity (https://www.airowater.com/).

All hospitals should get advice from experts and draw up a plan for moving towards a 'green' organisation over a three- to five-year period. Capital investment required is minimal and the benefits are substantial.

Departmental reviews

Senior managements in hospitals should review the functioning of all support services once a quarter to ensure compliances, service levels to patients, costs and safety of patients and staff. It is essential to obtain patients' feedback, review effectiveness of outsourced agencies and get surprise checks.

The departmental review should encompass various aspects including:

- Expenditure in rupee terms, as well as in terms of cost of service per patient.
- Workflow and how it can be optimised and wastages should be minimised.
- Physical layout of the work spot, for example, location of kitchen, laundry and stores department.
- Number of staff deployed in each area – shift-wise where applicable.
- Extent of automation and how further automation can improve efficiency.

Conclusion

Support services are an unglamorous but important service area playing a crucial role in patient satisfaction. Support services employees work behind the scenes. Without ancillary services, primary physicians will not be able to function effectively. The staff should be professionally qualified at supervisory levels. Where possible, there should be job rotation to maintain the freshness of approach.

Notes

1 'Checklist of housekeeping services for NABH accreditation', *The Healthcare Manager*, https://expresshealthcaremanagement.blogspot.com/2018/03/checklist-of-hospital-housekeeping-services-quality-accreditation.html
2 K. Chowdhury, 'Fires in Indian hospitals: Root cause analysis and recommendations for their prevention', *Journal of Clinical Aesthesia* 2014;26(5):414–424, https://pubmed.ncbi.nlm.nih.gov/25113423/
3 'Water from air machine', *Maithri*, https://www.maithriaqua.com/post/water-from-air-machine
4 'Importance of CSSD (Central Sterile Supply Department) @ JSS hospital, Mysuru', JSS Hospital, https://jsshospital.in/importance-of-cssd-central-sterile-supply-department-jss-hospital-mysuru/

Part III

Financing healthcare in India

13 Financial management in corporate hospitals

Tilak Shankar

Introduction

The finance manager has a dual role – operating as a member of a team in a hospital and fulfilling responsibilities of the corporate entity. Finance is not another small department in a hospital, as it carries a significant voice in Board meetings and plays a key role in all decision-making involving expenditure. All investors require a well-qualified and competent person to head this function. In this chapter, key contributions of the finance manager in a hospital is being explored.

Good financial health is fundamental for all healthcare organisations. Financial goals vary depending on the objectives of each institution (non-profit or for-profit), but financial self-sufficiency or profitability depends on the competent management of financial resources. In a complex healthcare environment, the role of finance cannot be overemphasised. The focus of this chapter is on (for-profit) private hospitals. Management processes would apply to non-profits as well. Good processes are not the prerogatives of any one sector.

In the last four decades, since the advent of large private hospitals and corporatisation, finance has come to play a transformative role in the functioning of the hospital. Finance's role is no longer restricted to maintaining books and accounts, regulatory compliance or rationing of available resources. In recent years, the emphasis has been on utilising a wide range of funding options, availing of equipment manufacturer financing, strategies to improve the value of the enterprise and financial engineering.

> Financial engineering is an interdisciplinary branch of the investment industry that makes use of applied mathematics, statistics, computer science, financial theory, and economics to conduct quantitative analysis.[1]

Hospitals are generating large sums of funds from private equity firms, venture capitalists or stock markets in addition to utilising own funds and investing surplus funds. The focus is slowly shifting to utilising resources profitably, rather than rationing funds. The availability of investments bringing in substantial funds has resulted in acquisitions, diversification and rapid growth

DOI: 10.4324/9781003684947-16

of large hospitals, laboratory chains, insurance companies and start-ups. In corporate hospitals and large private hospitals, finance department performs a pivotal role like in other profit-oriented organisations. There are, however, differences in the role of the finance function. The medical team is the most valued human resource and the *prima donna*s of a hospital. Finance function is also critical as it plays a significant role in shaping the organisation's financial health. Other departments such as marketing or HR also carry out their respective functions on a day-to-day basis towards achieving organisational goals. The main objective of finance is value maximisation in the long term for the company. The challenge for private/corporate hospitals lies in achieving continuous growth and profitability. It should be pointed out that high profits of hospitals invite disapproval from fellow medical professionals, scrutiny from government authorities and criticism from the larger community. It is expected that private hospitals will perform the role of a noble service-oriented profession. The main role of finance is to critically examine all major expenditures, which may not be popular.

Corporate and large private hospitals have to strike a delicate equilibrium between profit maximisation and providing affordable medical care. Even though their excessive focus on profits has drawn criticism from some quarters, private/corporate hospitals have grown exponentially in the last four decades, becoming a dominant part of India's tertiary care. Quality tertiary care is now available in nearly all major cities of the country.

Financial management in large hospitals

The focus of this chapter is on (for-profit) private hospitals, which are one of the main drivers of the healthcare industry. The growth of other segments, that is, pharmaceutical industry, retail pharmacy, diagnostics, medical devices, medical software and health insurance, has also been equally impressive, but the focus in this chapter is not on these sectors.

Corporate hospitals have been growing rapidly in the last two decades. The first corporate hospital in India, Apollo Hospitals, was established in 1983. The hospital quickly filled part of the vacuum that existed in tertiary care in India. There was a latent demand for good-quality medical care, which was not being met by the existing hospitals at that time. There was a need for entrepreneurs with vision and courage who could establish high-quality healthcare institutions. Growth required steady flow of funding, preferably at a low cost. In the early 1980s, the capital market was not well developed. and obtaining bank loans also was difficult. The environment has dramatically changed since the 1990s in many ways, and funding avenues have rapidly become available for the well-managed, profitable large hospitals. Funding agencies prefer to fund medium/large hospitals, that is, based on the number of beds.

At present, corporate hospitals have to compete with other healthcare companies, but also with all other highly profitable sectors such as retail and software, for raising funds. It should also be pointed out that hospitals have been experiencing a good growth rate with high operating margins. During 2020–2024, hospitals have been growing at the rate of 18% p.a., thereby attracting investments. Earnings before interest, taxes, depreciation and amortization (EBITDA) margins also have been attractive.[2]

The attractive profits, along with impressive growth and branding, have helped hospitals to raise large funds from the market.

Role of finance

The basic role of finance in all organisations is maintaining books of accounts as per statutes and submission of financial statements. Broadly, a finance department carries the following functions:

- Implementing financial policies, developing robust procedures and internal controls.
- Controlling of operations through detailed budgeting, monitoring actuals, tariff determination, service mix and deploying surplus funds.
- Raising cost-effective funds.
- Reviewing service mix for revenue and profit optimisation.
- Expenditure control.
- Evaluation of capital expenditure proposals and new projects.
- Working capital management.

In addition, finance plays a key role in evolving strategies in an environment where fundraising has become increasingly sophisticated.

Adherence to accounting standards and regulations

All registered companies must adhere to the standards of the Institute of Chartered Accountants of India.[3] Some examples of standards are accrual-based accounting, matching of revenue and expenses, materiality in accounting and conservatism.

The companies also have to comply with various Company Law regulations and taxation rules. The primary function is to ensure the integrity of all financial transactions, compliance with governmental requirements and presenting statements as per professional standards. Investors and general public depend on the published accounting information and hence data integrity is a basic requirement. There should be a strong internal audit function to ensure data reliability, in addition to compliance with various statutory laws and regulations.

Financial statements, including profit and loss statement, balance sheet, cash flow, medical quality performance and directors' report, are submitted annually to the shareholders. Some of the non-profit institutions have different accounting systems from corporates, following a cash-based accounting and not an accrual system. Market valuation of a hospital company is largely based on its profits, earnings per share, dividend record and shareholder wealth maximisation. The annual reports depict the financial health of the company succinctly.

The statements are generally in electronic format and available on the website of the hospital and are prepared adhering to accounting standards[4] and complying with Companies Act[5] on disclosure.

Finance is closely involved in the operations of the hospital whenever financial transactions occur. IT-based integrated accounting systems are the basis for tracking of transactions and audit trails. Control functions such as budgeting, evaluation of capital expenditure proposals, tariff determination, monitoring of performance and approval of major revenue expenditures require close coordination with medical and other departments. The finance function is concerned with the impact of the above-mentioned expenses on company's financial performance, particularly on major capital expenditure, new projects and revenue expenditure.

The primary focus of a hospital is patient care, while the company's objective is to maximise its revenues and profits. There are often conflicts between these goals. The financial health, as required by the investors, is the continued profitability of the hospital. Thus, controlling the operations with a view to increasing profits becomes one of the key roles of finance.

Budgeting and costing

Budgets and costing systems incorporate fundamental principles of measurement, development of metrics, tracking mechanisms and accountability. The budgeting process helps in a critical examination of the functioning of various departments and processes within each department. Finance plays a central role in this process, with budgets broadly classified into revenue and capital budgets. Revenue budgets are prepared by compiling income from various departments and other incomes such as interest income. Expenses are categorised into salaries, medicines, electricity charges and repairs department-wise. Budgets estimate expenditure at the department/corporate level, while controlling costs at individual transaction level. All operational activities of the hospital are regularly tracked by financial parameters ensuring that all expenditures are monitored and accountability for results is identified. Hospitals incur fixed costs in the form of salaries and factor in the depreciation of buildings and equipment. Amortisation of fixed costs is accomplished by utilisation of facilities. Multiple metrics can be employed to monitor efficiency of operations such as average length of stay, bed occupancy and staff to bed ratio. Further analysis would be done department-wise and case mix-wise.

Capital expenditure evaluation

Hospitals incur large amounts of capital expenditure every year towards replacements, new medical equipment purchase and new buildings. It is essential that each investment either serves a strategic purpose and/or is financially viable. In addition, there could be cost-saving capital expenditures, for example, solar installations and automated laboratory equipment.

Finance uses a variety of tools. The return on investment (ROI) evaluation ensures that the cost of capital and capital itself are recovered from inflows. The capital expenditure proposals are ranked according to their ROI. If the proposal earns more than the cost of funds and has acceptable cash flows, such proposals are accepted. Some strategic capital expenditures may not necessarily meet ROI standards. Leasing is an option due to the high obsolescence of medical equipment as long as net cash flows are positive. Laboratory equipment is available on a use basis. A judicious mix of capital expenditure and leasing is a happy combination.

Revenues

The hospital's revenues broadly come from doctor charges (less payment to consultants), operating theatre charges, charges for investigations including imaging, physiotherapy, use of various equipment, bed charges, lab investigations, pharmacy sales and charges for food offered to patients.

Operational costs

The operational costs comprise salary, depreciation, annual maintenance costs (AMCs) and fixed costs. These costs are not dependent on bed occupancy rates. Incomes from medicine are variable with the level of activity and are controllable even at a granular level. The purchase cost of medicines and salaries (excluding consultant's compensation) account for 40–45 per cent of the total operating costs in hospitals. It is essential that finance closely monitors these two items.

Medicines include doctor-prescribed medicines, other medicines, consumables and implants. These are usually charged based on the maximum retail price (MRP). For other items, patients are charged based on guidelines provided by the finance department. The pharmaceutical companies offer discounts for large purchases. Regarding salaries (excluding consultant's fee-for-service payments), finance closely monitors staff levels, performance ratings, administrative staff costs, salary revisions, productivity, scope for automation and outsourcing of non-core activities. Outsourcing is common for security, housekeeping and canteen services, as they are non-core functions. In other words, finance keeps a close watch on sources of income and control of expenses to ensure overall profits of the hospital.

Tariff determination and review

Hospitals provide different medical services, including tests and investigations, minor and major surgeries, and dispense thousands of prescriptions at varying levels of profit. Finance plays a key role in tariff decisions, considering service costs and competitors' pricing. Surpluses (sales minus costs) are generated from pharmacy, laboratory and other investigations. Similarly, periodic price revisions are undertaken to ensure prompt cost recovery whenever costs go up. Facility utilisation directly impacts their actual costs, with higher utilisation lowering the cost. For instance, the operating theatre (OT) costs are allocated on an hourly rate to recover fixed and variable costs, aiming for optimal utilisation. When the OT is optimally utilised, costs are recovered and surpluses are generated from OT. Higher the utilisation, surpluses will be higher. The same concept is relevant for all expensive medical equipment.

A detailed costing system is essential not only for pricing decisions but also for expenditure control. Quality accreditation standards require measurements for a large number of key indicators, which may be integrated with the costing system.

Costing as a management tool

Financial data, that is, profit and loss statement, balance sheet and funds flow, indicate the overall health of the company. Cost data reveal the 'actual' cost of providing a service and profit-generating areas, which can then be used to guide action on whether to continue certain activities or to increase the prices of select services. Costs serve as a basis for determining the pricing, but unique services may be priced well above cost. Skimming the cream is a strategy applied when a new product or service is introduced by the organisation. The product or service would be charged at a high price point till the service matures and competition enters. At a later stage, price normally will start coming down. In some situations, the initial pricing could be low to popularise the service. Regardless of the pricing strategy, understanding the cost of major services is crucial. Breakeven is accomplished when fixed costs are recovered.

Management decisions like equipment purchase or infrastructure expansions hinge on cost data. Cost data should be disseminated to the concerned department for effective control. Fixed costs, variable costs, incremental costs, along with budgeting and operational metrics, are basic tools for management control. Fixed costs like employee salaries persist irrespective of the percentage of bed occupancy or depreciation and will be incurred irrespective of the extent of utilisation of equipment. Variable costs like electricity or consumables should be fully recovered. For example, most corporate hospitals have an average bed occupancy of 60–70 per cent. So, room tariff should be fixed based on the projected average occupancy. Costing along with budgeting forms the foundation for expenditure control across all departments. Operational metrics like the utilisation of operating theatres, utilisation of various testing equipment and number of tests carried out in the laboratories are vital. Higher the utilisation, lower are the costs, since the fixed costs of investment in equipment and staff costs get spread out over a longer time frame. Quality accreditation metrics, for example, bed-to-nursing ratio, should be integrated with the costing system. Budgeting and costing are not mere financial numbers. Annual budgets are built on a set of assumptions regarding number of inpatients, outpatients, day-care patients, case mix of various departments, tariff revisions during the years, salary revision costs and a large number of other factors. Costs, amortisation periods and obsolescence of medical equipment similarly vary depending on utilisation of various equipment. It is possible that there could be substantial variations during the course of the year. Hence, the advantages of budgets and their limitations should be borne in mind.

Make or buy decisions

The hospital frequently has to take decisions with regard to performing some activities in-house (make) or outsourcing them (buy). Some hospitals opt to lease laboratory equipment rather than purchasing it. In some cases, medical equipment manufacturers may provide the equipment free of charge and charge a higher rate on consumables.

Finance evaluates the advantages and disadvantages and provides recommendations on operational areas such as catering, laundry services or housekeeping. Many non-core services may be carried out in-house or outsourced. These decisions are reviewed annually, considering the long-term costs to the hospital, accountability for quality and track record of the agency selected. An essential criterion is whether it would release management time for the core activities of the hospital, that is, patient care.

Finance, in essence, needs to serve as the conscience keeper of the company's finances and the protector of the minority shareholders. The head of finance advises the board of directors on the financial viability of all the investments.

Compliances and investor relations

Operating within the rigid framework of various acts and laws, hospitals must ensure that compliances under various regulatory mandates and obtain renewal of licences (lift, fire safety, blood bank, pharmacy, pollution control) as applicable. It would be a good idea to appoint a special officer for compliance. Finance has to report to the Board that all laws are being complied with.

Companies with a large number of shareholders – varying from small holdings to large holdings – necessitate prompt and effective communication from the finance department. Secretarial department, which functions under finance, should effectively interact with all the shareholders.

Monitoring capital-intensive operations

Corporate and private hospitals operate in a capital-intensive industry, marked by rapid technological changes requiring frequent modernisation and replacement of medical equipment. Funds are required at different stages – when a new hospital is being set up, to fund cash losses in the initial stages and for major expansions, acquisitions and diversification.

In every hospital, there are demands from all medical departments to acquire the latest medical equipment. The demand for new equipment from specialty departments usually far exceeds internal fund availability. Finance has to balance these demands, keep its cost of funding low, satisfy key departments and 'star' doctors, monitor the utilisation of existing facilities, improve service mix and control costs. A combination of financial acumen and tact is required.

As discussed earlier, capital expenditure decisions are based on projections about the number of patients, revenues and profits. Actuals may not align with these assumptions. Taking these factors into account, finance has to follow prudent financial policies at all times. It has to ensure that rigorous analysis is carried out prior to investment and monitor actual performance. Monitoring of revenues generated by all major investments is essential for financial stability.

Structure of the finance organisation

The finance function typically holds a prominent position at the Board of Directors level. The Director – Finance, whose equivalent positions are Vice-President or Chief Financial Officer, assumes multi-faceted roles as a bookkeeper, controller, compliance officer and adviser to the Board on major financial matters. Within the finance function, various sections such as accounting, treasury, management accounting, internal audit and secretarial would be headed by appropriately qualified professionals. The finance organisation should be lean. Many of the finance professionals are often recruited from diverse private sector companies infusing hospital operations with a robust commercial orientation. See Figure 13.1 for finance structure organisation.

Corporate and regional organisation: Dual structure

In cases where companies have multiple hospitals in the same city, in a region or across India, there could be a corporate finance organisation at the headquarters with staff at various other locations. Some entities function as subsidiary companies with their staff reporting to the corporate office

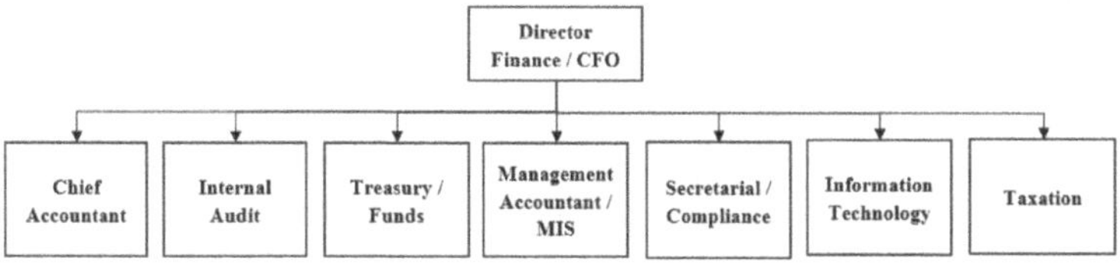

Figure 13.1 Finance organisation in a hospital.

functionally and administratively to the local hospital head. This dual structure is applicable not only to finance but also to other functions like marketing, IT, HR and quality. Consolidation of accounts takes place at the headquarters, while secretarial matters and treasury are managed centrally from the corporate office.

Profit centre[6]

In multi-locational groups like Apollo, Fortis, Manipal Hospitals and Max Hospitals, each location can be termed as a profit centre. These locations generate income, invest in facilities and generate profit or loss. Profitability in relation to investments is a key metric for evaluating these centres, while cost centres are measured by other metrics. It is believed that profit centre concept contributes to profit maximisation.

One of the primary goals of a corporate hospital is shareholder *value maximisation*, or in simple terms, maximising the company's value to its shareholders.[7] At two levels – strategic and operational – finance plays a pivotal role in accomplishing both these goals. Financial policies are designed to achieve growth and profitability.

Strategic roles of finance

The strategic role of finance could encompass both short term and long term. Finance would provide a dispassionate financial analysis of each major proposal. A large number of operational decisions of purchasing new equipment and adding new hospitals and chain of clinics ultimately require corporate approvals. Similarly, strategic moves to acquire or merge with other hospitals, overseas branches, diversification and initial public offer (IPO) and private equity (PE) funding will be based on financial implications for the Board to decide.

New hospital or expansion

Finance function takes a crucial role in determining the optimal source of funding for a new hospital. Collaborating with the medical team, finance assesses the total cost of the hospital and examines the optimal way of funding. The iterative process involves the estimation of cost of land, construction, number of rooms, beds, medical departments and non-medical equipment, projected number of patients, operating costs and the overall financial viability. A detailed project report would be prepared by finance as the basis for raising money from investors and lenders.

Management of funds

Funds can be broadly divided into short term (up to one year) and long term (five to ten years). The source of funds could be internal funds or borrowings, with the cost of capital being a critical factor in determining the source. There are a number of factors which determine the source of funds. Finance has to ensure that the overall dependence on borrowing (measured by debt–equity ratio) does not affect the health of the company adversely. In the case of borrowings, repayment of interest and principal amount and cash outflows determine the soundness of the expenditure. Working capital management is crucial because hospitals deal with daily fund generation from corporate billing and billing on insurance companies. The payments from insurance may be delayed at times. Expenditures towards the purchase of medicines, salaries, capital equipment purchases and advance payments have to be managed using collections and bank funds. Finance should ensure that they get the best terms for all fund-based and non-fund-based needs (such as bank guarantees and letters of credit).

The responsibility for fundraising vests with the finance department. Apart from bank funds, internal sources are retained earnings and other internal funds of the company. Fund management would be handled by treasury, which manages all the cash flows, deals with the banks and financial institutions and obtains favourable terms from them and invests excess funds.

Internal controls and audit

Checks and balances are essential for ensuring financial integrity of all transactions in small and large organisations. Finance establishes clear policy guidelines for operational decisions such as equipment purchase, procurement of medicines and consumables, disposal of old equipment, staff hiring, compliance with billing schedule and giving discounts/concessions to patients. In a computerised environment, any deviation from financial policies is immediately identified.

Audit

Audits of the books of the accounts are broadly two types: statutory and internal. Statutory auditors who are appointed by the shareholders as required by the Companies Act report to the shareholders about the financial health of the company. Auditors technically report to the shareholders. Statutory auditors depend on a robust system of internal audit in the company. There could be other types of auditors – internal auditors and forensic auditors to investigate frauds.

Development of financial goals

The strength of a company lies in its short-term focus. Investors in the listed companies require quarterly reports and detailed annual accounts. Finance, in consultation with all departments, identifies revenue generation goals for the short term, considering the main medical and all the supporting departments. An optimal mix of services is considered examining both revenue (top line) and profits (bottom line). Some departments such as sugar clinics, cardiology and oncology generate revenue for many support services. Surgical departments utilise operation theatres, order consumables and help in improved bed occupancy. Some hospitals charge a premium charge for its brand. Pressures on pricing from the community, government and insurance companies have led to fixed-price surgeries or packages.

Multi-specialty hospitals face competition not only from similar hospitals but also from well-established single-specialty hospitals. Each hospital benchmarks itself against competition by evaluating the competitor facilities and charges. In addition, subtle attempts are made to attract doctors and their teams. The competition could be in select departments such as cardiology, orthopaedics or oncology. It is not uncommon that senior doctors and their team en masse migrate to a competing hospital.

Long-term goals

Long-term goals involve strategic considerations such as growth, acquisitions, mergers, private equity funds and initial public offering (IPOs) and de-risking. This is discussed in Chapter 14.

Revenue optimisation

A key goal of all private hospitals is revenue optimisation (Figure 13.2). The revenue models differ depending on the hospital. Some depend largely on hospital services, while some have de-risked their revenue model by diversifying into retail pharmacies, diagnostic laboratories, health insurance and various specialty clinics such as dialysis and dentistry to realise income. De-risking is to ensure that the fortunes of the organisation are not dependent on one or a few activities.

There are many levers which the hospital can employ for revenue increase such as improved ALOS, better bed occupancy, tariff modification and average revenue per occupied room (ARPOB). ARPOB is an important indicator, which ranges from INR 40,000 to INR 50,000 per day, and has been increasing year after year to meet the revenue goals.

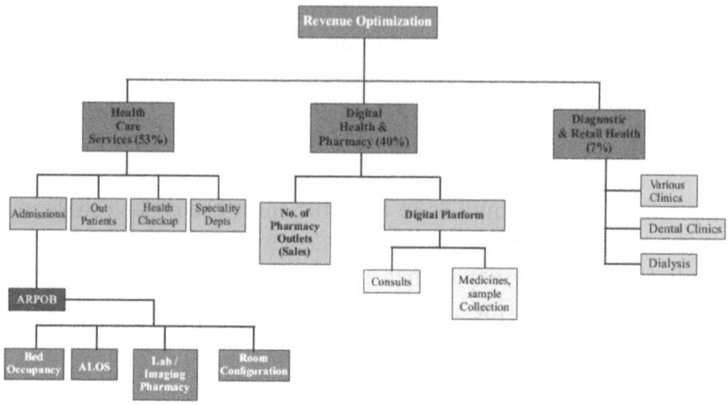

(Source: - Annual report, Apollo Hospitals 2022-23)
ARPOB - Average Revenue per occupied bed
ALOS - Average length of stay

This hospital has de-risked its business, all levers can be changed for revenue optimization. Other hospitals have other business models

Figure 13.2 Revenue optimisation.

De-risking

In recent years, corporate hospitals have been experiencing a steady decline in ALOS in tertiary departments. ALOS ranges between three and five days per patient (in hospitals like Apollo and Fortis). The bed occupancy has been around 65–70 per cent. Investment in beds is a fixed cost and hence high bed occupancy is essential. There has been a trend towards day-care surgeries, home-based treatment and home care. Hence, there is a pressure to attract more inpatients. Sales efforts are constantly employed to attract more inpatients. It is advisable for hospitals to diversify revenue sources from related businesses such as chain of pharmacies, well-equipped clinics, diagnostic laboratories, dental clinics and dialysis centres. Apollo Hospitals offers a great example of de-risking by diversification (Figure 13.3). Each hospital has chosen its own model.

Long-term strategies

Long-term strategies will be based on selection from various opportunities, internal organisational strengths, quantum of fund availability, borrowings and cost of funds. One of the important sources is the internal generation of funds. Dividends to shareholders is no longer a major factor. Companies normally declare dividends on the par value of the share. The rest of the post-tax profits would be retained in the company. Retained earnings is an important source for expansion and diversification. The Board of Directors based on a five-year plan would decide on future strategies including funding options. The Board might consider raising funds by way of rights issue, debentures. It might also consider approaching PE funds or respond to overtures from PE

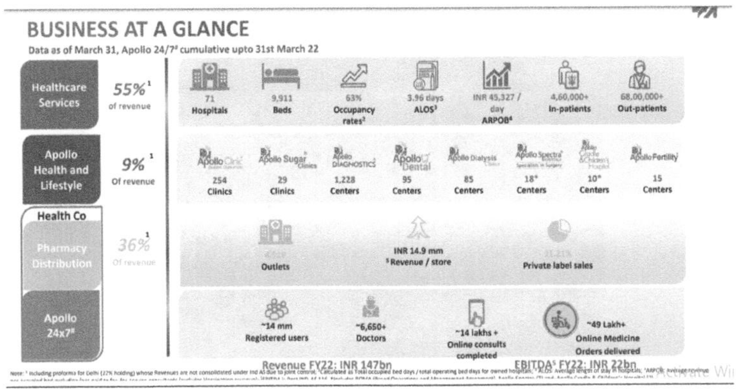

Figure 13.3 De-risking strategy of Apollo Hospitals.

funds. In all cases, factors such as dilution of owners' equity, earnings per share would be taken into account.

Capital structure: The main consideration in selecting the source of finance would be the cost, commitments associated with the source and whether the returns are after tax or before tax. The Chief Financial Officer or the Finance Director of a hospital should consider the risk appetite of the management and offer advice on the downside of any major proposal to the Board.

Revenues and profitability are dependent on efficient use of resources and cost control of expenses. The cost structure of the largest corporate hospital, Apollo Hospitals (2022–23), is illustrated in Figure 13.4. This is only a pointer, and the cost structure of other hospitals could be different.

Materials covering a wide range of items form one of the largest items of expenditure, and also an important cost and profit-generating area. In each of these items, the purchase cost depends on various commercial aspects such as price, payment terms, frequency of purchase, inventory levels and usage control. Each of these should be managed by professionally qualified staff.

The second major item is salaries – both of medical doctors and other staff. Normally, most of the medical staff are consultants, and their incomes are linked to the number of patients treated. In the case of the full-time staff, their productivity should be monitored for operational efficiency as well as for cost control. Investors could decide to cut down the staff numbers if the profit targets are not being met.

Apollo Hospitals generated a healthy 18 per cent on income (financial year 2022–23), which is comparable to companies in other industries (Figure 13.4). This percentage of profits is also substantially higher than their profits of 2021–22.

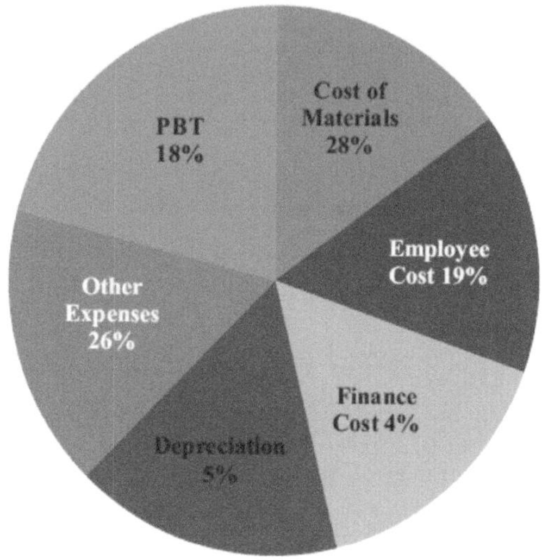

(Source Apollo Hospitals 2022-23 Annual Report)
Charitable Hospital Cost Structure will be different

Figure 13.4 Cost structure of a hospital.

Operating metrics and financial ratios

Profits and surplus are built by a large number of departments and number of patients for which there is a need for building operational metrics. Hence, hospitals rely on a wide variety of metrics for performance evaluation, divided into departments and specific activities within each department. Operational metrics such as the number of consultations per doctor, number of chemotherapy cycles, number of bone marrow transplants, ALOS, average bed occupancy for each category of room, number of major and minor surgeries per operating theatre, number of admissions and discharges per day, number and value of pharmacy prescriptions per doctor and each department, number of CT scans.

Financial ratios: Financial ratios such as average revenue per occupied bed, net margin on sales, earnings before interest depreciation and amortisation (EBITDA), debt–equity ratio and earnings per share are tracked by the finance department. Such ratios are common across industries.

Working capital management

Working capital is a key aspect of all industries. Working capital is funded by internal or bank funds, and each source has an interest cost attached to it. Hence, the quantum should be efficiently managed. In the case of hospitals, the importance would vary depending on the nature of the hospital. Inventory, receivables and advances constitute the major items. If the hospital handles a large number of patients under government insurance schemes, then receivables would require close attention. It is learnt that it could take up to a year for the government to settle bills, and the delay could cause cash flow problems.

Inventory would include a large number of medicines, spare parts, implants and consumables, which should be monitored to avoid expired drugs, obsolete spares and non-moving items.

Rapid changes

Some hospitals have diversified into related businesses tapping into the large and growing unorganised private healthcare sector. Hence, many hospitals have diversified into a chain of diagnostic laboratories, pharmacies and wellness centres. If the company decides to set up a chain of retail pharmacy business, it offers significant advantages like bulk purchases, storage and distribution and helps in brand promotion, which in turn helps the corporate image. There are other business strategies such as developing sub-brands so that at a later date, if required, these sub-brands can be spun off as separate companies. Corporate finance has triggered radical changes in corporate strategies in Indian hospitals. IPOs and private equity investments have been changing the hospital landscape.

Acquisitions should be carefully considered to ensure that there is a strategic fit with the parent organisation, whether based on new departments or specific locations or the expertise of renowned doctors. The focus on patient service often guides acquisition, and the timing may coincide with or follow an IPO. Or an allopathic hospital may acquire an established Ayurvedic hospital.[8] Acquisitions are guided by addition to top line and combating competition. Chapter 14 deals with the PE and IPO investments into the Indian healthcare sector.

Management information system or dashboard (MIS)

It is believed that 'data is the new raw material for making critical decisions, making forecasts, simulation opening up opportunities for the finance function'. All hospitals generate millions of data – operational and financial, which can provide insights for future.[9]

All hospitals would have some form of MIS in which financial data would form a central part. Hence, finance function will be responsible for collating and analysing MIS data. Combining operational data with financial data, including budgets, provides a holistic picture. Information technology and data analytics help with in-depth analysis. Every hospital, depending on its major focus areas, could utilise information for its future planning. Similarly, revenue generation department-wise and growth trends will help in future investments.

Timely operational and financial information is fundamental for effective management. Management information system (MIS) in many hospitals tends to be a routine ritual, with monthly MIS reports being mere presentation of statistics. Financial data and statistical data are presented as isolated sets of data. Only a critical analysis of data can help in sharper focus on performance and effective intervention in the governance of the hospital.

Importance of financial data in hospitals

Medical team would be concerned with various aspects of patient care – admissions, treatment, discharges, quality of care and skill development. The administrative team, on the other hand, would focus on all non-medical aspects. Finance explores scope for revenue enhancement and cost control through vast volumes of data generated every day. Finance has an overview of the entire hospital, which can be utilised for analysing trends and exploring strategic options.

IT, artificial intelligence and data analytics

IT, AI and data analytics enable the hospital to meet all these objectives while improving profitability.

There have been three major changes in IT in the last two decades:

- Real-time, cloud-based systems linking all departments and all locations and connecting patients through mobile phones.
- Data analytic tools facilitating improvement in patient services, enhanced use of resources and generating revenues.
- Artificial intelligence creating new frontiers.

The motto of the hospital IT strategy is defined as 'IT is not merely an enabler but a strategic differentiator'. The medical team, starting from the Chairperson, is actively involved in defining its requirements to the IT team. The headquarters of the hospital has a large team of IT professionals. This has resulted in imaginative use of IT in medicine and management.

Importance of management controls

MIS is a compilation of statistics from medical and commercial departments, facilitating analysis both for operational and strategic objectives. MIS has been redefined in the context of modern IT systems. A large volume of data is created every minute in a hospital collating both operational and commercial information thanks to integrated computerised systems. Information is available on the cloud, desktops and mobile phones at all times. The focus of all

MIS is analysing data on a monthly and annual basis to ensure that the key objectives of patient care remain within acceptable standards, in line with budgets and in case of corporate hospitals as per investor expectations. At senior levels, normally the data would be a summary or reporting by exception. Some CEOs, however, prefer detailed information on a daily basis, while others are content with summaries.

The concept of MIS has undergone a fundamental change – from a paper-based static system to a dynamic real-time, hospital-wide computerised systems with data analytics, mobile telephony and artificial intelligence and data analytics tools.

Private hospitals represent a wide spectrum of hospitals – ranging from small nursing homes (two-thirds of the private hospitals in India), charitable hospitals and large for-profit hospitals. In the case of nursing homes, which mainly handle primary and secondary care, the 'owner' focuses on daily performance and cash balances at the end of the day.

In the case of large hospitals, the focus shifts to multiple aspects, including patient care, financial performance and quality adherence. Modern corporate hospitals are multi-locational (pan-India or regional) multi-specialty and multi-divisional. Influx of large funds has facilitated the growth of hospitals and has enabled related diversification. Naturally, it has created investor pressures for performance. Therefore, MIS has to be fine-tuned for efficient management of the company.

MIS: A paradigm shift

In the last four decades, corporate hospitals have established themselves as important providers of tertiary care medical services. They have also obtained international and national quality accreditations. They are listed on stock exchanges requiring excellent management control and reporting on both operational as well as on financial areas. Investors demand regular reporting on all key areas. It is natural that IT has become a key tool in ensuring that the hospitals function efficiently to meet the needs of the patients and meet the expectations of the patients and investors.

Main focus areas of MIS

Patient satisfaction is achieved in many ways such as provision of quality care, minimal waiting time, offering affordable care and facilitating necessary communication systems with doctors. Each of these actions requires close coordination among various departments and real-time communication.

Efficiency of operations

A modern hospital functions under the strict protocols of various accreditations such as Joint Commission International (JCI), National Accreditation

Board for Hospitals and Healthcare Providers (NABH), National Accreditation Board for Testing and Calibration Laboratories (NABL) and College of American Pathologists (CAP), where quality is constantly measured. Similarly, investors expect regular reporting of results. The expectations of revenue growth and profitability can be achieved only by efficient operations. IT, data analytics and other management tools help in close monitoring of every single activity in the hospital.

Revenue growth and profitability

There are several metrics for monitoring revenue and profitability. ARPOB, ALOS, volume of inpatients and outpatients, revenue from allied activities, cost structure and increases, number of ICU patients, EBITDA margins and case mix are reported in annual reports of corporate hospitals. Internal analysis should be benchmarked against competing hospital's performance, changing epidemiological trends, optimal use of new medical technologies and new medicines. Profit improvement arises from utilisation of all resources such as operating theatres, expensive imaging equipment and pharmacy prescriptions.

IT is a strategic enabler

IT is used in many hospitals primarily as a data processing device. This is sub-optimal use of the power of the technology. The full potential of IT, data analytics and AI needs to be fully leveraged both for the patient communities as well for the hospital's profitability. At higher levels of management and at the Board of Directors levels, there is a need to study the broad trends of patients, disease pattern, medical technology, emerging opportunities for diversification, fund availability and its implications for the hospital.

Data analytic tools

Data analytic tools are a rapidly evolving technologies to improve hospital functioning. A modern hospital is required to constantly improve patient care and cut costs. These can be accomplished by employing appropriate tools of AI and data analytics. By forecasting operating theatre utilisation, minimising readmissions, minimising medical errors, improving inventory management and many other operational improvements, operations become efficient. Each improvement enhances patient satisfaction and helps in profitability.[10]

A wide range of analytic tools is available to interpret a vast amount of data that are generated on a daily basis. Some of the following examples clearly highlight the acceptance of data analytics in Indian hospitals.[11,12]

Narayana Health using AI: A case study

The author spent two days at Narayana Health to understand the management processes at the hospital in Bengaluru. Narayana Health, a pan-India multi-specialty hospital, has a large IT department and has been developing data analytic tools for its chain of hospitals. One of the reasons for its effectiveness is the active role played in the software development by their Chairman, Dr Devi Shetty. In this section, we would be discussing specifically how MIS powered by AI and data analytics can facilitate efficient management.[13]

A quick analysis of financial data reveals the following:

Financial year	*2019–20*	*2023–24*
Revenue from operations (INR million)	31,278	50,182
Profit after tax (INR million)	1224	7896
PAT as % revenue	3.9%	15.7%

Source: Annual reports.

Growth in revenue in revenue and profits are not merely due to data management. Data are effectively utilised by management to improve performance, facilitated by multiple factors including close monitoring of all key factors.

NH has nearly 40 facilities (including 18 hospitals) with nearly 6,000 beds. During 2023–24, it handled nearly 2.5 million outpatients and 240,000 inpatients. The hospital chain has nearly 100 plus specialty and sub-specialties, employing 20,000 employees (2,400 doctors). The hospital chain operates in a competitive environment in all the cities where it is operating. It has recently diversified into health insurance.

A sizeable part of the total revenue (47 per cent) comes from insurance patients, that is, corporate insurance, Central Government Health Scheme (CGHS), state government insurance schemes and corporate patients' insurance schemes. The government schemes and CGHS generate lower revenue per patient. Management of receivables assumes importance since the settlement period for bills government schemes are much longer.

Hospital insurance claims

Health insurance coverage in private hospitals is increasingly becoming common – both government insurance schemes as well as private insurance schemes. Hence it is necessary that IT systems comply with the requirements of various schemes, which have different limits and sub-limits on the sum insured, allowable and disallowances. This is an important patient-oriented service. It is essential that hospital systems facilitate maximum permissible amounts are obtained by the hospital as well as by the patients. Medha

Analytics ensures that all the requirements of the insurance companies are taken into account. Vivek Rajagopal of Medha Analytics explains:

> Insurance companies have certain formats, standards, inclusions and exclusions in the way the claims need to be recorded and presented. Based on the claim, the insurance company many raise queries on certain items, disallow or deny certain items. This presents a revenue loss for the hospital or the patient. The hospitals typically put in place a mechanism to analyse why the denials or disallowances happened and the process controls they can put in place to minimise these.

IT, AI and data analytics in NH

Narayana Health's IT is built on two systems – Athma ERP and Medha Analytics – both developed in-house by their IT team. The architecture is shown in Figures 13.5 and 13.6.

Athma ERP and apps

Athma is a new-age healthcare platform which accesses healthcare technology for doctors, clinics, laboratories, hospitals, diagnostic centres and pharmacies. All the solutions, desktop and app, have been developed based on user requirements.

Some of the apps are discussed below:

Aadi (doctor's app)

'Aadi acts as a digital assistant, enabling real-time communication among care team members and providing live updates on patient data through integrations with lab and radiology systems.'

Aadi allows doctors to conduct virtual rounds seamlessly while being stuck in a traffic or in an important meeting. Aadi has been able to save 40 per cent of doctor's time during ward rounds and has helped reduce medical errors by 65 per cent.

Namah (nursing app)

Nurses at NH facilities were overwhelmed with paperwork, having to fill out over 20 forms for a single patient in addition to providing timely care. Manual handovers to the next shift were also hectic and time-consuming. A special app for nurses, Namah, aims to reduce paperwork by streamlining digital documentation and facilitating digital shift handovers, allowing nurses to spend more quality time with patients. As a result, NH has been saving nearly three days per nurse each month through the digital documentation.

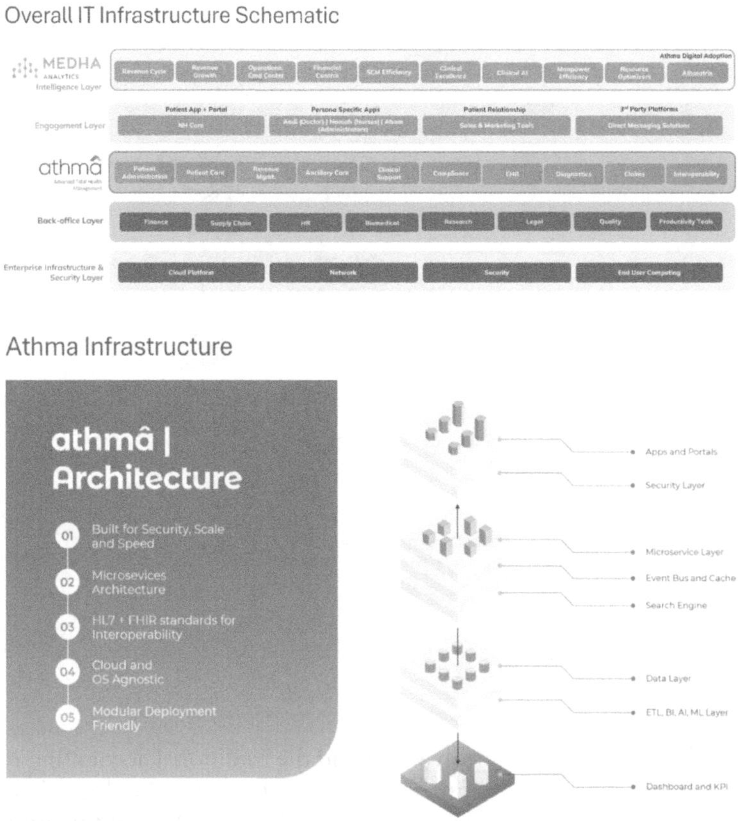

Figure 13.5 (top) Overall architecture; (bottom) Athma infrastructure.

NH Care app (patient's app)

NH Care is an app designed to provide utmost convenience and a seamless experience for patients visiting NH facilities. Currently, NH Care is one of the highest-rated hospital apps in India, boasting a 4.8 rating and over 1.6 million downloads. 'The app allows patients to book appointments, order medicines, and access their reports anytime, anywhere, effectively eliminating lengthy queues at hospitals and significantly improving the overall patient experience', says Vivek Rajagopal.

Narayana Health employs AI Bot (AI assistant), machine learning and real-time AI analysis for high-quality affordable healthcare.[14] AI is used for early diagnosis, remote area consultation, drug discovery and personalised medicine.[15]

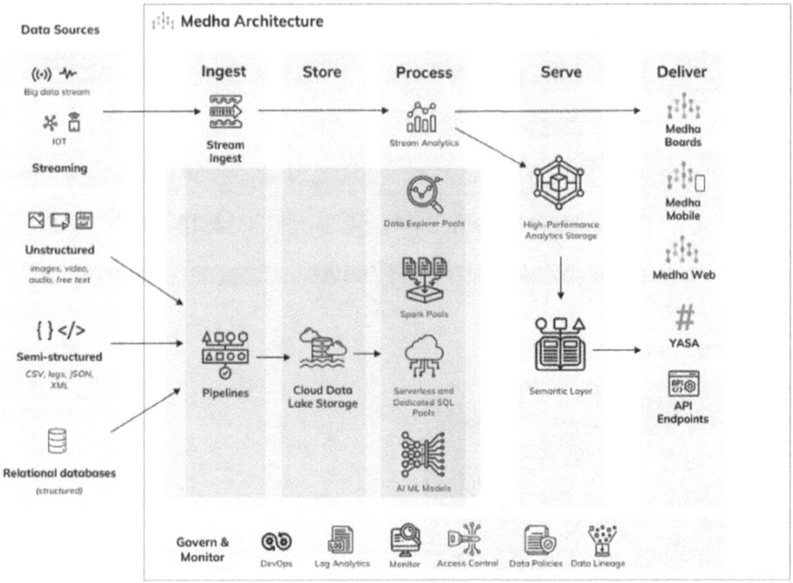

Figure 13.6 Medha Analytics.

Conclusion

Finance function's role has evolved beyond the traditional accounting role. A modern hospital operates in an environment of rapid technological change, competition and various governmental regulations. Data automation and knowledge explosion necessitate fresh approaches to financial management. A finance manager should play the role of a strategist, a data manager and a fund manager all at the same time. In the near future, the role and the complexity of these professionals are likely to grow even further.

Notes

1 'What is financial engineering'? Certificate in Quantitative Finance blog, https://www.cqf.com/blog/what-financial-engineering
2 'Private hospitals to add ~10,000 beds over this fiscal and next', Crisil Ratings, 28 February 2025, https://www.crisilratings.com/en/home/newsroom/press-releases/2025/02/private-hospitals-to-add-10000-beds-over-this-fiscal-and-next.html
3 https://www.pw.live/ca/exams/indian-accounting-standards
4 Accounting standards, 'https://www.pw.live/blogs-ca/list-of-indian-accounting-standards-issued-by-icai-2023
5 Companies Act, https://www.mca.gov.in/content/mca/global/en/acts-rules/companies-act.html; https://www.indiacode.nic.in/handle/123456789/2114?sam_handle=123456789/1362(2)
6 Profit centre concept, https://www.investopedia.com/terms/p/profitcentre.asp

7 Value maximisation, concept steps, implications, strategies, advantages and disadvantages, https://theintactone.com/2023/05/08/value-maximization-concept-steps-implications-strategies-advantages-and-disadvantages/
8 Acquisition of Ayurvedic hospital by Apollo Hospitals, www.thehindubusinessline.com/companies/apollo-hospitals-to-acquire-60-per-cent-stake-in-ayurveda-hospital-chain/article65974967.ece
9 Data management, PwC, https://www.pwc.de/en/finance-transformation/data-management.html
10 'Eight ways to use data analytics in healthcare', Infosys BPM, https://www.infosys-bpm.com/blogs/healthcare/ways-to-use-data-analytics-in-healthcare.html
11 https://www.softwaresuggest.com/healthcare-analytics-software
12 Vikram Thaploo, 'India will move from a "Data-Driven" approach to a "Data-First" approach in 2023', *Financial Express*, 24 April 2023, https://www.financial-express.com/business/healthcare-india-will-move-from-a-data-driven-approach-to-a-data-first-approach-in-2023-3058460/
13 We are grateful to Narayana Health (NH) headquartered in Bangalore, a multi-specialty, multi-locational tertiary care corporate hospital for sharing information readily. A special thanks to Chairman Dr Devi Shetty, Ms Sandhya, CFO, Mr Vivek Rajagopal and Mr Jagdeesh of Medha Analytics/IT.
14 'Narayana Health uses data analytics and AI to provide affordable, high-quality healthcare', *Microsoft*, https://news.microsoft.com/en-in/features/narayana-health-uses-data-analytics-and-ai-to-provide-affordable-high-quality-healthcare/
15 Naitik Ganguly, 'The growing influence of AI in Indian healthcare: what does the future hold?', https://www.linkedin.com/pulse/growing-influence-ai-indian-healthcare-what-does-future-ganguly

14 Private equity (PE) investments and initial public offer (IPO) in the healthcare sector in India

Tilak Shankar

Introduction

The human endeavour from time immemorial has been to live long. All human beings want to prolong their life, preferably healthily. Medical technology, vaccines and newer medicines have been constantly evolving to meet this need along with increasing awareness of nutrition and lifestyle changes. There are an estimated half a million people who are hundred years old or more in different parts of the world. More and more people also want to live long.[1]

Modern allopathic medicine, supported by traditional medicine, has helped people all over the world to increase their life expectancy. Technology has been playing a pivotal role in bringing about a revolutionary change, enhancing the accuracy and precision of interventions and treatments. Rapid progress in tertiary care has made advanced treatment possible for various ailments. Modern tertiary hospitals require substantial investments and constant upgradation. The medical fraternity involved in patient care also has to keep pace with medical developments. New bacteria, viruses, lifestyle changes and poor environment, however, pose a constant challenge to life in general. The COVID-19 pandemic highlighted the frailty of humans to new infections, consuming hundreds of thousands of lives in 2020 and 2021, exposing large gaps in global and Indian healthcare. Thus, the process can never be said to have been completed.

India's healthcare needs have grown dramatically in the last few decades – quantitatively and qualitatively – due to rising income levels, urbanisation, growing pollution in many cities and changes in lifestyles and food habits. According to various estimates, Indian healthcare is expected to reach $638 billion by 2025.[2] Small nursing homes, which are part of the unorganised health care system in India, have been the backbone of the healthcare network and still continue to play an important role in villages, towns and cities. But many larger private hospitals (single specialty and multi-specialty), which were set up or have grown in the last few decades, have made a difference to tertiary care in the country. Advancements in medical care in India have been on par with international standards.

DOI: 10.4324/9781003684947-17

Against this background, the focus of this chapter is to evaluate the effect of private equity (PE) and retail investors (through initial public offers (IPOs)) on the healthcare industry. PE funds offer attractive valuation for the company and, in turn, the hospitals are required to comply with multiple financial requirements. The PE funds are focussed on short-term financial performance and would drive the investing entity to generate more revenue and profits. To meet this goal, the hospital starts focusing on case mix, length of stay of the patient, tariff, cost reduction and compliance with financial metrics.

The private healthcare sector had been hamstrung by shortage of funds, especially in the 1980s and 1990s. Expensive funds (for example, borrowing at higher interest rates) result in an increased cost of medical care. In the last two or three decades, a new source of funds has emerged for the Indian private healthcare system. In parallel, medical advancements have provided technologies for cancer treatment, transplants of various organs, robotic surgeries, infertility treatment and gene research – all to create life, identify diseases early, improve the quality of life post-treatment and most importantly, prolong life.

PE funds and listing on the stock exchange through IPO have provided Indian private hospitals, especially those concerned with tertiary care, with what appears to be an unending source of funds to create new capacities and push the frontiers of medical knowledge and medical practice.

Growth of tertiary care

In the last few decades, tertiary care has grown manifold, especially after the infusion of investments:

- State-of-the-art tertiary care with highly skilled medical personnel and formal quality accreditations has been created in multiple cities in India. More than 80,000 tertiary care beds are now available and treatment is on par with international standards with very little waiting time. Clinical outcomes are benchmarked with international standards. Patients from other countries now throng Indian hospitals for quality of care and at a fraction of cost compared to the advanced nations. In countries having a nationalised healthcare system, long waiting times are very common. It can be expected that in the next few years, there could be a larger inflow of patients from other countries visiting Indian hospitals, a phenomenon termed 'medical tourism'.
- Large inflow of funds has benefitted the hospitals, owners and the patient community. High-quality tertiary beds have been created with these investments and with company's own funds. The availability of funds has enabled the installation of expensive equipment, for example, proton therapy, robotic surgical theatres, expensive computed tomography (CT) facilities, magnetic resonance imaging (MRI) equipment, laboratory

equipment and many other critical facilities for providing quality care to patients.

- A medical ecosystem has emerged to support hospitals – diagnostic laboratories, imaging centres, retail pharmacies, fitness centres, senior citizen homes, home care services, medical software, medical devices and medical, nursing and allied health sciences education. This ecosystem is, however, available only in large cities and towns.

All major hospitals have multiple educational programmes (DNB), thereby creating large number of specialist doctors, nurses and other staff. These specialists have largely been absorbed by various private hospitals. Cardiac surgeries, multi-modal treatment for cancer and complex orthopaedic surgeries are routinely carried out in many private hospitals. For example, about 150,000 cardiac bypass surgeries were annually carried out in India as of 2019, with 60 per cent on a beating heart mode.[3]

Transplants of heart, liver, kidney, lung and hand are being carried out in India by private hospitals specialise in these procedures. Many leading hospitals have carved a niche for themselves by undertaking robotic transplants of kidney (for example, in Apollo Hospitals, Yashoda Hospital, Citizens Specialty Hospital and Medanta) and liver (for example, in Max Healthcare, Amrita Hospital and Rela Hospital). The Asian Institute of Gastroenterology, Hyderabad, has become a referral centre in Asia for advanced gastrointestinal procedures. There are 11 proton therapy centres in different parts of India, each centre established with large investments. There are an estimated 5,000 MRI equipment in India in various hospitals and stand-alone imaging centres, each costing INR 4 to 12 crore. Many stand-alone laboratories and imaging centres have upgraded their facilities, particularly in cities since equipment and their test results are accepted by hospitals. It is also reflective of the profitability of such investments for both hospitals and stand-alone centres. It also highlights the availability of funds and the attractiveness of return on such investments.[4]

What are PE funds?

Private equity funds are 'pooled funds from various individuals by a fund which then invests in various companies with the objective of generating attractive returns'.[5]

The PE funds can be Indian funds or foreign funds who invest in various industries. Indian healthcare has become an attractive option for the PE funds because of its size, growth potential and profitability.

PE funds have invested in single specialty and multi-specialty hospitals, laboratories, start-ups, imaging centres and health insurance companies. The access to PE/IPO funds, in addition to investor funds, is providing hospitals and other companies with the capacity to invest in cutting-edge technology and treatment, enhancing the quality and level of care provided and also creating opportunities for higher income and profits.

In this chapter, the focus is on the following:

- Private hospitals who have accessed PE funds and stock markets (IPO).
- Changes in recipient hospitals/companies, as a result.
- Short-term and long-term implications of these investments to the patient community.

PE investment in Indian healthcare has been extensively covered in the media over the years.[6–14] It is believed that in addition to funds, PE bring in strategic management expertise and a global perspective. There have also been concerns about the excessive focus on profits undermining patient care. There have been concerns about PE taking over the management of the hospitals.

Private equity and IPO in the healthcare sector

Bain & Company, a global management consulting firm, provides a snapshot of PE investment in healthcare in India[15]:

> Investors are increasingly looking at India's healthcare sector ... with an increased interest in health providers, pharmaceuticals, diagnostics, and single-specialty providers since 2020. India's healthcare sector saw deal values reach $4.3 billion in 2022, at approximately 8% of total investments ... KKR's exit from Max Healthcare grabbed headlines with an exit value of $1.6 billion in 4 years driven by a significant EBITDA expansion, followed by other large exits such as Everstone's exit from Sahyadri Hospitals and Carlyle's and British International Investment's IPOs of Medanta Medicity (Global Health) and Rainbow Hospitals ... which have resulted in high average revenue per occupied bed (ARPOB), improved utilisation, and increased margins ... listed health providers have generated two to three times the returns of the Nifty index in recent years.

In five years between 2016 and 2021, Max Healthcare, Manipal Hospitals and Care Hospitals, for example, have received large private equity investments to enable their growth and acquisitions.[16,17] PE funds are also started investing in primary healthcare. Tata group, for example, acquired 1mg, an online pharmacy store, to enter the retail pharmacy field.[18]

Recently, the PE fund Temasek acquired a majority stake in the second-largest chain of hospitals in India – Manipal Hospitals.[19] This is an instance of an investor taking over the operations of the hospital by acquiring a majority stake. PE funds prefer to invest in unlisted companies, so that they can exit at the time of the company going public and when the company monetises its value. Sambhav Kumar, writing in *Businessworld*, states,

PE firms focus on companies with significant growth potential or those needing operational improvements. Once they acquire a stake, they inject capital, restructure operations, and aim to enhance the company's value. After typically four to six years, PE firms exit the investment, usually by selling the company or taking it public.

Further, he cautions that

the increased involvement of PE firms in India's healthcare sector may bring short-term growth but could come at the cost of quality, affordability, and access to care. As private equity continues to make inroads into healthcare, patients and policymakers must remain vigilant to ensure that the primary focus of the healthcare system – patient well-being – remains intact.[20]

Tables 14.1–14.3 provide a summary of investments in the healthcare sector through private equity and IPOs. Estimates suggest that approximately INR 3,20,000 crore have been invested in the healthcare sector through private equity and IPOs between 2018 and 2024.

PE fund investments have been from both foreign and Indian funds. In case of foreign funds, their investment has been converted to INR, year-wise. The conversion into INR had ranged from INR 67 to a USD in 2016 to INR 83 to a dollar in 2024.

Sources:

PE investments

1. https://www.niti.gov.in/sites/default/files/2023-02/InvestmentOpportunities_HealthcareSector.pdf
2. https://www.pwc.in/assets/pdfs/industries/private-equity/reflections-indian-private-equity-in-2017.pdf
3. https://bwhealthcareworld.com/article/why-private-equity-firms-are-betting-big-on-indian-healthcare-501365
4. https://www.hfsresearch.com/research/private-equity-growth-must-not-undermine-patient-care-in-indian-healthcare/#:~:text=Private%20equity%20(PE)%20money%20has,levels%20of%20%243%2D4%20billion.

IPO

1. https://www.chittorgarh.com/report/sector-wise-ipo-list-in-india/96/209/
2. https://www.business-standard.com/markets/ipo/india-s-healthcare-pharma-sectors-achieve-record-ipo-issuance-since-2019-124122200062_1.html

Table 14.1 PE and IPO funds invested in Indian healthcare

Year	*PE investment (in INR crore)*	*IPO investment (in INR crore)*
2016	8,457	3,112
2017	9,712	2,302
2018	12,984	1,070
2019	27,729	1,249
2020	21,780	6,493
2021	44,674	8,730
2022	44,551	4,044
2023	51,757	9,370
2024	44,171	14,811
Total	**2,65,814**	**53,722**

Table 14.2 Inpatient numbers of select hospitals

Hospital	*IP Volume*
Apollo Hospitals Enterprise Limited (AHEL)	5,69,988
Fortis Healthcare Ltd (FHL)	2,50,000
Global Health Ltd. (Medanta) (GHL)	1,55,915
Kauvery Hospitals	14,194
Krishna Institute of Medical Sciences Limited (KIMS)	1,91,000
Max Healthcare Institute Ltd (MHIL)	2,15,000
Narayana Hrudayalaya Limited (NHL)	76,000
Rainbow Children's Medicare Ltd	87,736
Shalby Ltd	85,363
Yatharth Hospital and Trauma Care Services Limited (YHTC)	17,054

Source: Annual reports of companies, FY 2023–24.

Table 14.3 Healthcare companies listed in the stock exchanges

Particulars	*No. of companies*
Hospital and healthcare services	32
Medical equipment/supplies/accessories	9
Pharmaceuticals and drugs	185
Laboratories and diagnostic centres	9
Biotechnology	1
Total	**236**

Source: https://groww.in/stocks/filter?closePriceHigh=100000&closePriceLow=0&industryIds=59,70,80&marketCapHigh=3000000&marketCapLow=0&page=3&size=15&sortType=ASC.

Based on discussions with some PE funds, it is relevant to highlight certain features:

1. In the last nine years (2016–2024), PE investments have been much larger than funds raised from IPOs.
2. The amount of funds invested by PE in a company is negotiated depending on their needs. PE funds decide on the valuation of the hospital/company based on revenue multiples or EBITDA multiples or a combination of both. National hospitals seem to get better valuation than regional hospitals.
3. PE investments have been in multi-specialty, single-specialty hospitals, for example, ophthalmology, infertility, nephrology and children.
4. Unlisted companies are preferred since it will enable the companies to go public.
5. Valuation of the company is a key step in the negotiation between PE funds and the company.
6. PE funds take substantial stake in the investing entity, through either equity or compulsorily convertible preference shares. The valuation automatically provides a premium to the investors.
7. IPO also provides substantial premium to the investing company. The above process automatically increases the value of the company substantially.

Valuation

Based on the author's discussions with a large PE fund (who prefers to remain anonymous), the following key points may be noted:

- Valuation depends on whether it is a single specialty or a multi-specialty, single location, regional or has a national spread.
- The valuation would be a combination of revenue and EBIDTA multiples.
- Different PE funds might invest in the same hospital at different points of time.
- Valuation could be different multiples, for example
    - Single location: two times revenue and 11 times EBIDTA.
    - Regional chain: three times revenue, 18 times EBITDA.
    - National chain: four times revenue and 25 times EBIDTA.

The percentage of stake acquired by a PE fund could range from 20 to 100 per cent in the entity, depending on the deal value.

Inpatient numbers of select hospitals

Tertiary care hospitals have been able to attract large numbers of inpatients and outpatients. The numbers have been growing rapidly year after year. It is also relevant to point out that each inpatient generates a substantial income and profit to each hospital (see Table 14.2).

Number of healthcare companies listed in the Indian stock exchanges

There are 236 healthcare companies listed on stock exchanges as of January 2025 (Table 14.3).

The list in Table 14.3 includes pharmaceutical companies including many foreign companies that have been operating in India for many decades. Hospital companies have entered the stock exchanges in the last three decades. In addition, a small number of labs and health insurance companies have also gone for an IPO.

A large number of unlisted private companies operate large tertiary care hospitals. Private hospitals (both listed and unlisted) have grown rapidly in the last four decades, largely driven by owner funds and PE funds. Several hundred companies prefer to stay private, even though their market capitalisation would improve on going public.

Investment by PE and retail investors (through IPO) has multiple implications, some positive and some developments that are worrisome, which are discussed later in this chapter. It may be useful to examine the management process by which decisions on inviting PE funds or going public are taken by the Board of Directors.

Strategy and the funding process

The process of inviting PE funds or going public requires very careful consideration by the Board of Directors. It is a strategic move of choosing a completely different path. The final decision would depend on the risk appetite of the main investors and an evaluation of the pros and cons of the decision. The advantages of PE/IPO funds are many – increasing shareholder value, greater visibility and a seat on the high table of opinion makers in the industry. On the other hand, there would be irreversible changes in management control, new directions for the hospital or the holding company, greater accountability to the investors and the public and the glare of constant publicity.

Preparing for investment

Some of the steps that the company should undertake *prior to PE funds* investment are as follows:

- A five-year business plan should be prepared internally and vetted by an external expert.
- Marketing department has to identify specific locations or hospitals for expansion of the business.

- Internal and external valuation needs to be arrived at based on the proposed business plan.
- Discussions should be held with potential PE funds.
- In case of an IPO, compliances with various regulatory agencies, approaching qualified institutional investors for underwriting, determination of premium and other formalities need to be completed (see Annexure 12.1).

The main promoter of the company who may also be the Chairman plays a critical role. As the main shareholder, he or she might have a risk appetite and decide to launch an IPO or to invite PE funds to invest in their company. The Board will also decide whether fresh capital should be issued. The main promoter also would consider the possibility of dilution in its shareholding. Shares issued at a premium automatically increase the wealth of the promoter who is a dominant shareholder in the company. It is also possible that the management bandwidth in the company might not be adequate to take on a larger challenge. Finance has a key role in advising on the pros and cons of such strategic decisions.[21]

Shareholder's agreement

Shareholder's agreements are a normal feature in all investments by PE funds. The main features of the agreement where the *prior consent* of the fund would be required are:

- Changes to the capital structure of the company.
- Approval of the business plan.
- Appointment or removal of key employees.
- Entering a new line of business or terminating any existing line of business.
- Capital expenditure in excess of INR ___ crore (defined by the PE).

In effect, the PE funds take management control of the company. They expect high returns (for example, 25 per cent) on their investment on an annual basis. They will drive the company to obtain their financial goals.

Venture capital funds

Venture capital funds typically invest smaller amounts than PE funds in a business, with an investment window of five to seven years, usually investing in risky ventures. Angel investors invest at the take-off stage, invest what is called seed capital and may expect the company to attract PE or venture capital funds at an appropriate stage so that they can exit.

Investments by PE funds have been in the form of compulsorily convertible preference shares with the option to convert at the choice of the fund, normally at a pre-defined period. This option implies that technically, ownership remains with the original promoters, but PE funds de facto have a key operational role.[22]

In return for such investments, hospitals have to make commitments on future income growth and operational profits, financial metrics in a pre-defined time period. If the hospital is unable to meet the targets, then the fund retains the right to convert preference shares into equity shares and obtain control of the company.[23]

Strategic options

The PE fund, along with the promoters of the company, would examine multiple strategic options of either staying with healthcare or diversifying into related or unrelated areas. It is believed that a company should stick to what it is good at, rather than venture into unknown territories. Tom Peters refers to this as 'sticking to the knitting'.[24] If the management believes that their core competence is healthcare, they might focus on this line of business.

It is possible that the Board of Directors of the company might diversify into related areas like pharmacy, diagnostic laboratories, medical software and health insurance. One of the key factors is the composition of the Board of Directors who can provide an external, objective assessment of opportunities. The Chairman of the Board plays a pivotal role in strategic decisions, considering factors like raising large funds from IPO or inviting private equity funds, with a view to provide *value maximisation* for the shareholder.

Alignment of strategic goals with financial goals

Corporate strategies can be broadly classified into organic and inorganic growth. Both forms of growth could include geographical expansion, establishing a chain of clinics and day-care centres, exploring overseas markets, diversifying into related businesses like health insurance, developing medical software or a chain of diagnostic centres. The expansion strategy may target 'low-hanging fruits', businesses with low entry barriers, for example, infertility centres, dental clinics, dialysis centres, retail pharmacy chains and laboratories. The objective is to attract more patients, improve sales and enhance brand equity. Growth and expansion into new territories are contingent on various factors including availability of medical and nursing human resources, suitable locations for a new hospital and, importantly, financial viability.

In every hospital, decisions on new hospitals or major expansions are undertaken based on multiple considerations including financial viability. Every decision need not be based solely on financial assessment; however, ignoring financial viability totally weakens the entire company. Acquisitions aid in expanding the national or regional footprint or entering new geographies or new areas of business. There could be clash of cultures. The parent companies' interest should be the only priority in any acquisition. Acquisitions should strengthen the parent company's brand equity, attract new patients and improve earnings per share (EPS) in the medium term.

Company boards and PE funds prefer the acquisition route in preference to greenfield projects as greenfield projects have a longer gestation period and may incur cash losses in the initial years. Acquisitions result in immediate revenues, which satisfy IPO and private equity funding.

Long-term strategies

Obtaining funds at a premium, from the PE fund or IPO, is similar to riding a tiger. The hospital is required to start utilising the funds with very little waiting time. The focus will shift to improving revenues, profits and earnings per share and hence share prices. The focus has to shift from hospital operations to overall strategy. Three large hospital chains – Apollo Hospitals, Max Healthcare and Narayana Health – had raised more than Rs 8,500 crores as of 2022–23 by way of share premium. This is at once an opportunity and a challenge. The companies can acquire other hospitals, start greenfield projects or diversify into allied healthcare areas. The challenge is to ensure that share prices rise quarter after quarter, based on performance. This pressure percolates to the entire hospital.

Financial strategies require an assessment by the Board whether they should opt for equity funds, go public and select other financial instruments.

Corporate and financial strategies are closely interlinked (Figure 14.1). Organic growth is opted for when there are opportunities for expansion and

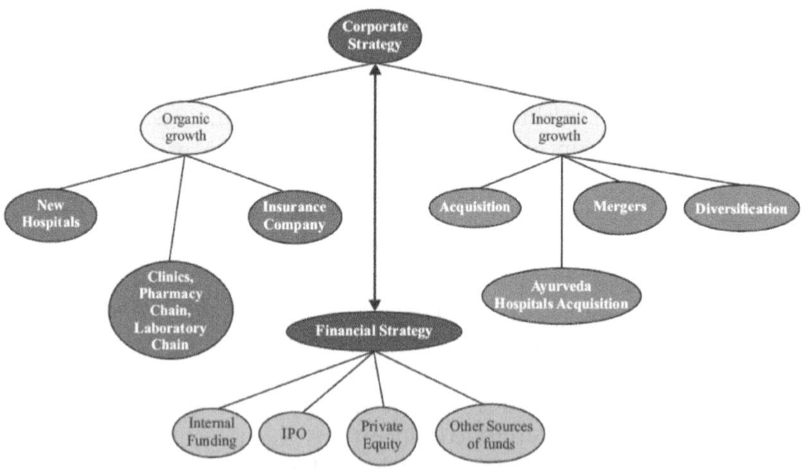

Corporate strategy directs financial strategy and in turn finance spurs new corporate strategy.

Figure 14.1 Interlinking of corporate and financial strategies.

growth. On the other hand, inorganic growth helps achieve rapid growth, which requires companies to be ready with projects or targets for acquisition, ensuring that funds are deployed judiciously and expeditiously. Financial strategy propels the growth cycle just as corporate strategy directs finance to initiate private equity investments or IPOs. Acquisitions should be carefully considered to ensure that there is a strategic fit with the parent organisation, whether based on new departments or specific locations or the expertise of renowned doctors. The focus on patient service often guides acquisition, and the timing may coincide with or follow an IPO. Or an allopathic hospital may acquire an established Ayurvedic hospital.[25] Acquisitions are guided by addition to top line and combating competition.

With new funds, there would be added emphasis on branding, rationalisation of resources and organisational changes. Cost-cutting would become important. Large inflow of funds also has other implications:

1. PE funds and other funds are likely to substantially increase their investments in future in healthcare, as they have experienced very good returns.
2. Partly as result, corporate hospitals would have further consolidated their presence in tertiary care. There has been consolidation in laboratories and retail pharmacy sectors as well, which should be beneficial since the quality of care and reliability of test results from laboratories should improve.
3. Large fund inflows have put pressure on the other non-funded healthcare companies to increase their own incomes and profits. The healthcare companies in general are required to treat more patients, increase revenue per bed and revise tariffs. Marketing efforts would be intensified. Hospitalisation charges would increase rapidly.

Value maximisation

The market value of a hospital/company or its share price is based on various factors such as growth record, profitability, image, number of beds in prime locations and quality accreditations. While profit maximisation is generally considered the central goal of a company, PE funds require higher rate of growth in a shorter time frame. Corporate hospitals strive to enhance shareholder wealth through strategies like share price maximisation, acquisitions and mergers. Corporate hospitals focus on quarterly results, annual profit reporting and increasing shareholder wealth by share price maximisation.

Impact on hospitals

It is interesting to study the importance of share premiums in the finances of the company (Figure 14.2).

A comparison of three corporate hospitals reveals that equity capital contributes a relatively small proportion, that is, 6–12 per cent of their funds.

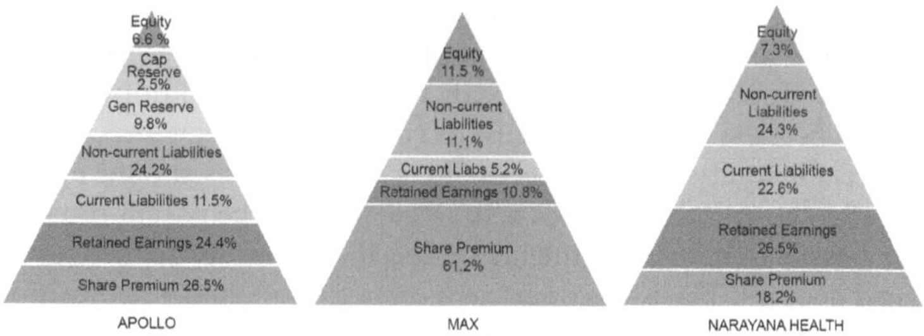

Figure 14.2 Capital structure of select hospitals.

Source: Annual reports of the respective hospitals FY 2022–23.

The maximum funding comes from retained earnings and share premium. Share premium could be from a PE fund or IPO, or both. Retained earnings is a clear sign of the Board's conservative policy of rewarding the shareholders through share price appreciation rather than through dividends on the par value of the share.

Management perspective of PE/IPO funds

The large inflow of funds has benefited the hospitals, owners and ultimately has offered tertiary care for the affluent patient community and middle-income groups as well. It has enabled the installation of expensive equipment, for example, proton therapy, robotic surgical theatres, expensive CT scans, MRI equipment, laboratory equipment and many other facilities.

It should be pointed out that even before the inflow of PE funds, many private and corporate hospitals had initiated multiple improvements in their infrastructure and offerings, responding to the needs of the patients. Hospitals have been hiring highly qualified medical specialists, nurses and other allied medical sciences staff. Hospitals have opted for rigorous quality accreditations, obtaining accreditations such as the Joint Commission International (JCI), National Accreditation Board for Hospitals and Healthcare Providers (NABH) and National Accreditation Board for Testing and Calibration Laboratories (NABL). A high degree of digitisation has improved patient data retrieval and improved the research and teaching quality. As discussed in the other chapters, these companies have realised the importance of applying various management concepts. With the influx of PE/IPO funds, the emphasis is slowly shifting to 'super profits'. Now Indian hospitals have started competing not only with other hospitals but also with all other industries for fundraising, financial performance and market capitalisation.

The large inflow of funds into Indian healthcare, from a management perspective, is a welcome development. All institutions have started focusing on various metrics to improve operational efficiency and profits. Management techniques, however, do not necessarily focus only on profits as the sole goal of an enterprise. Affordable care should also be one of the objectives of any private company.

PE and IPO funds have made financial results a primary goal of the invested companies. In addition, PE funds also require strategic interventions from the management. PE funds, for example, 'persuade' the management to look for regional expansion, setting up overseas hospitals, consider acquisitions, plan mergers and examine diversification opportunities. Similarly, there would be regular monitoring of average revenue per occupied bed (ARPOB), average length of stay (ALOS), case mix, tariff revision, acquisition of new equipment and its utilisation with a view to improving profit margins and obtaining competitive advantage. Earnings before interest depreciation taxes and amortisation (EBIDTA) has become the primary focus of the hospital administration.

Impact of the investments

The primary (and perhaps the only) interest of PE and IPO investors is financial, that is, short-term revenue and profit growth. The focus of the hospital management, however, should necessarily lie on patient care and translational research, and these two goals have to be carefully balanced. With increased competition, each hospital chain has to differentiate itself from others in terms of its offerings. Hence, the focus has started shifting towards case mix, branding, marketing, patient retention and higher levels of profits.

Acquisitions, mergers and market capitalisation

The availability of large funds has accelerated the pace of acquisitions. Over 150 acquisitions and mergers in healthcare took place in the first half of 2022 alone.[26] Several acquisitions and mergers have led to the creation of oligopolies. The top three hospital chains – Apollo Hospitals, Manipal Hospital and Aster-DM (after the recent merger of both hospitals) – have nearly 30,000 beds together (see Table 14.4). It would appear that 10,000 tertiary beds for each chain is a new benchmark for obtaining a leadership position in healthcare in a particular region. Each hospital chain has focused on a specific geographical area in the country. Oligopolies in all businesses start dominating

Table 14.4 Total beds and revenues of sample hospitals

Particulars	*No. of hospital chains*	*No. of beds*	*Revenue (in INR crore)*
Listed	23	53,197	58,101
Private	29	33,595	14,068
Total	**52**	**86,792**	**72,169**

Note: Data for the financial year 2023–24.

the mind-space of the consumer community, dictate prices and attract even more investments. The leading hospitals have built up a strong brand image over many years with a national or regional footprint. All these hospitals have created ten to 12 centres of excellence focusing on niche areas, which has become a point of differentiation. Their pricing for various services has become a benchmark for other hospitals either nationally or in their main region.

Sample study

The author's team selected 52 hospitals that have a bed strength of more than 250 beds across the country for analysis. The list includes large and medium-sized hospitals and both listed and unlisted private hospitals. The purpose was to study bed strength and sales income of hospitals, which represent secondary care, and in the case of large hospitals mainly tertiary care. The idea is to understand how large hospitals dispense medical care. All the data pertains to the year 2023–24. The total bed strength of these hospitals was 86,000, of which the large six hospitals had about 40,000 beds (approximately 40 per cent of the total). The top six hospitals accounted for about 66 per cent of the revenue of the sample hospitals. It came be seen from Table 14.5 that the large hospitals are beginning to play a dominant role in tertiary care attracting patients by their size and reputation.

Tertiary care beds

In the last few decades, there has been substantial increases in tertiary beds (Table 14.4).

The list of 52 hospitals is provided in Annexure 12.2.

Table 14.5 For-profit hospitals: Dominance, beds and revenue

Hospital	*Geographical spread*	*No. of beds*	*Revenue (INR crore)*
Apollo Hospitals	All India	10,134	19,059
Manipal Hospitals	Kerala and Karnataka	9,500+	5,510
Aster-DM Healthcare and Care Hospitals	South and West India	8,000	5,303
Narayana Hrudayalaya	Karnataka and East India	6,074	5,018
Max Healthcare	National Capital Region (Delhi) and northern states	4,300+	5,406
Fortis Healthcare	North India and metros	4,500+	6,893
Total		39,938	47,189
Grand total (sample of 52 hospitals)		**86,926**	**71,714**
Percentage		46%	66%

It can be seen that a small number of hospitals have created nearly 90,000 tertiary/quaternary care beds with all supporting departments in about two to three decades. These hospitals have created capabilities for handling complex medical cases, including transplants and robotic surgeries. This is keeping with the trend in many developed countries. Transplants require live or cadaver organs. A system for harvesting cadaver donations has also been established.

From a company point, complex medical cases generate large revenues – at various stages – pre-treatment, during surgery and follow-up procedures. Such cases also enhance the reputation of the hospital and its medical team.

It is relevant to point out that growth, acquisitions and effective management have benefited the larger hospitals. Hence a small number of large hospitals have begun to dominate the tertiary medical care sector in India through regional and national footprint and image building (see Table 14.5).

There has also been a gradual concentration of tertiary hospital beds in select cities. Over a period of time, it can be expected that a few regional/national leaders would emerge for tertiary care. It is common to find patients travelling long distances to visit a specific hospital in major cities of their choice. Dominance by a few hospitals would put patients at a disadvantage.

Healthy profit margins and market capitalisation

Corporate hospitals' operating profits showed a healthy operating margin of 22–23 per cent and a revenue growth of 8–10 per cent per annum, with a substantial addition of beds (FY2023–24).[27] Healthy revenue growth and profits of corporate hospitals have resulted in very large increases in market capitalisation in a short period of three to five years (see the section 'Market capitalisation').

Increase in hospitalisation costs

The rapid growth in medicare facilities has come at a cost to the patients, with hospitalisation costs going up on a yearly basis. Tertiary care requires investment in expensive equipment that requires a higher return on investment (ROI). For making investments to scale up growth, PE or IPO funds are needed. It means that the patients have to pay higher charges. It is often alleged that hospitals resort to unbundled services and 'surge' pricing (increasing prices based on higher demand). It is also alleged that even a routine master health check-up is provided at exorbitant prices in an exclusive ambience.[28]

Impact of medical inflation

Many middle-class patients also get treated for many serious illnesses at large private hospitals. They depend on their meagrely savings and borrowings. It is reported that 23 per cent of medical costs are funded from borrowings, and about 62 per cent are out-of-pocket expenses are funded from the patient/ families.[29]

Some sections of the patient communities are even more seriously affected. Senior citizens, those with multiple chronic illnesses such as diabetes, hypertension and lung diseases requiring frequent testing and hospitalisation, are most affected by the steadily rising medical costs. Insurance schemes exclude pre-existing illnesses. Indebtedness due to medical expenses is a well-known phenomenon. High medical costs can result in delayed access to physicians or hospitals, which can further exacerbate medical costs. Dr. K. Srinath Reddy defines this phenomenon as 'foregone care', as even when patients know that they should get their illness treated, they do not do so because they cannot afford the treatment costs.[30] Anecdotally, it is common knowledge that patients discontinue their oral tablets or doctor visits for treatment of diabetes because of costs. It is also a well-known fact that borrowing from money lenders even for short periods is very expensive.[31]

Health insurance

To meet the increasing cost of care, health insurance is one of the options. This can be seen in the massive growth of the medical insurance sector in the last two decades. Health insurance is now a mature industry with an annual premium income of INR 1,00,000 crore and is in a strong position to influence the hospitals.[32] It is also reported that the health insurance costs rose by 450 per cent between 2021 and 2024 as the healthcare inflation rose by 14 per cent in FY 2024.[33] While this figure of 450 per cent increase is an exaggeration, nevertheless there has been a sharp annual increase in health insurance premiums,[34] ultimately impacting the patient communities. Other patients (who do not have adequate health insurance or are uninsured) are required to settle larger hospital bills by themselves. It is also believed that high insurance premiums are resulting in discontinuance of health insurance.

ARPOB

Financial management of modern hospitals has evolved multiple techniques to enhance revenues. One common metric is the Average Revenue Per Occupied Bed (ARPOB). This figure is reported in the annual reports of all corporate hospital companies. This figure is arrived at based on the case mix, type of room, tariff for different services, optimal use of operating theatre (OT), effective use of medicines and consumables. Of the above variables, case mix perhaps is the most important factor. The goal for every large hospital is to benchmark with other hospitals and constantly improve its own ARPOB number. A comparative picture of this metric across the sample hospitals is provided in Table 14.6. ARPOB has been increasing every year, reflecting increases in operating costs as well as due to higher profit margins.

Table 14.6 ARPOB of major hospitals

Hospital	*ARPOB (INR)*
Max Healthcare Institute Ltd (MHIL)	78,000
Global Health Ltd/Medanta (GHL)	61,890
Fortis Healthcare Ltd (FHL)	60,887
Apollo Hospitals Enterprise Ltd (AHEL)	57,488
Rainbow Children's Medicare Ltd	55,853
Jupiter Lifeline Hospitals Ltd	54,871
HealthCare Global Enterprises Ltd (HGEL)	41,802
Aster DM Healthcare Ltd	40,100
Shalby Ltd	37,517
Krishna Institute of Medical Sciences Ltd (KIMS)	31,916
Yatharth Hospital and Trauma Care Services Ltd (YHTC)	28,571

Source: Annual reports of companies, 2023–24.

A single occupied bed thus can generate a revenue of between INR 1.27 crore and INR 2.00 crore per annum in the high ARPOB hospitals. A 500-bed hospital can generate revenues up to INR 1,000 crore per annum at 100 per cent occupancy. There is pressure on the hospitals to constantly change the bed configuration, make revisions to tariffs, introduce a large number of high-revenue cases, cut costs and increase profits year after year. Most hospitals do not admit government insurance patients since the revenues from such patients are low.

ARPOB is improved by a number of measures including reducing the length of stay of the patient, improving case mix and implementing various operational improvements. There have been instances of hospitals discharging patients after a major surgery to free up the bed for the next patient. The author can vouch for such practices from the experience of a family member. It should be pointed out that reducing hospital stays minimises the probability of getting hospital-acquired infections.

Tertiary care hospitals focus on the ALOS helps to serve a larger number of patients as well as to improve their revenues and profits (Table 14.7).

Table 14.7 Average length of stay (ALOS)

Name of the hospital	*ALOS*
Apollo Hospitals Enterprise Ltd (AHEL)	3.30
Fortis Healthcare Ltd (FHL)	4.28
Global Health Ltd/Medanta (GHL)	3.20
Krishna Institute of Medical Sciences Ltd (KIMS)	4.11
Max Healthcare Institute Ltd (MHIL)	4.10
Narayana Hrudayalaya Ltd (NHL)	3.50
Rainbow Children's Medicare Ltd	2.65
Shalby Ltd	3.83
Yatharth Hospital and Trauma Care Services Ltd (YHTC)	4.80

Source: Annual reports of companies, FY 2023–24

Though improving profitability through efficiency of operations is necessary, excessive focus on revenues is not desirable for a healthcare institution.[35]

Inpatients

Inpatients are the most important indicator for any hospital. A visit to any large private hospital or one of its clinics will highlight the demand for tertiary services (Table 14.2).

Trends in case mix and focus on quaternary care: Two hospitals

In this chapter, Max Healthcare and Fortis Hospitals have been taken as examples of case mix for revenue maximisation and profitability. Nearly half the number of inpatients at Max Healthcare undergo complex, high-revenue-generating surgeries or procedures. Max Healthcare operates 22 hospitals across ten cities in India. The demand for such complex surgeries is partly because of the need for such services and patients' ability to pay high charges. In addition, the hospital's focus on higher revenue-earning case mix can be seen in Figure 14.3. The hospital carries out robotic surgeries, transplants and cardiac surgeries, in addition to neurological, orthopaedic and oncology surgeries. In addition, it carries out CAR-T cell therapy, a modern scientific innovation, for certain types of blood cancers.

Fortis operates 28 hospitals with 4,500 beds (Figure 14.4).

Quaternary care is considered an extension of tertiary care. All large hospitals offer quaternary care. All major hospitals offer quaternary care. Some hospitals may only provide quaternary care for particular medical conditions or systems of the body.[36]

Market capitalisation

Market capitalisation (market cap) represents the value of the company; share prices multiplied by the number of outstanding shares.[37] A steady increase in market cap represents good financial performance by the company, and a sharp increase reflects a resounding approval by the stock market. The

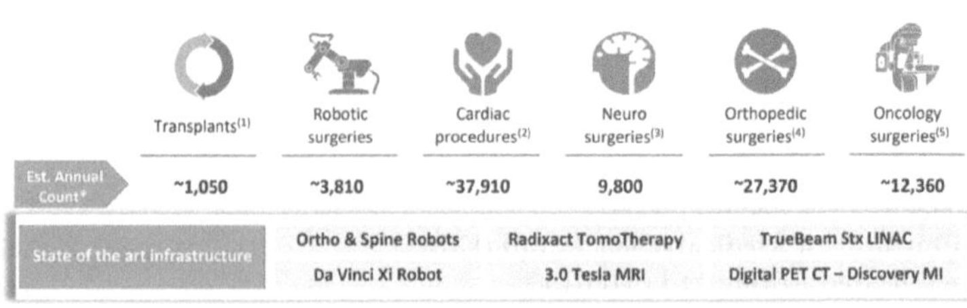

Figure 14.3 Max Healthcare: Procedures performed.

Source: Annual report 2023–24.

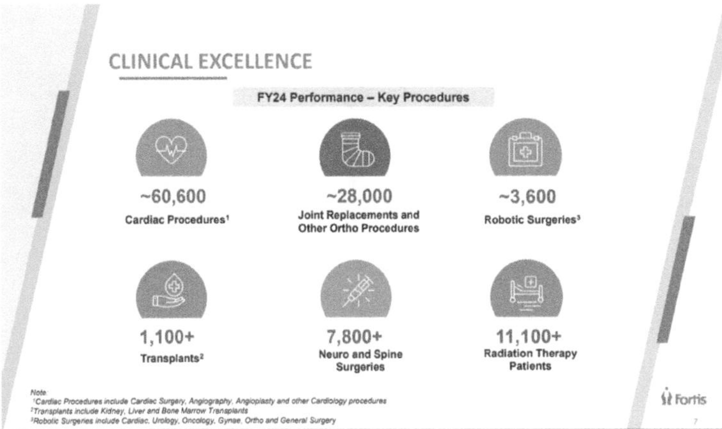

Figure 14.4 Fortis Hospitals: Procedures performed.

Source: Annual report 2023–24.

increase enriches the shareholders including the promoters, PE investors and retail investors. A sample of five corporate hospitals in our study (Table 14.8) shows that all of them have increased their market cap by six times in five years, an incredible record. One of them – Max Healthcare – improved its market cap by nearly six times in three years. The share prices of Max Healthcare, for example, had increased more than fourfold from INR 330 per share to INR 1,200 per share in three years (FY 2022–23 to 2024–25). Max Healthcare incidentally has the highest ARPOB among the sample hospitals.

It is relevant to point out that the fast-moving consumer goods (FMCG) industry, which includes international giants like Unilever, P&G, Brittania and others like ITC and Godrej have shown a market cap increase of only 1.5 times in six years (2019–25) (see the following table and all figures are in INR crore).

Table 14.8 Market capitalisation of select hospital companies

Name of the hospital	*Market capitalisation (in INR crore)*		
	FY 2024	*FY 2021*	*FY 2019*
Apollo Hospitals Enterprise Ltd	1,02,115	41,739	16,986
Max Healthcare	1,16,845	19,946	NA
Fortis Healthcare	53,609	15,023	10,252
Narayana Hrudayalaya Ltd (NHL)	27,200	8,299	4,368.21
Krishna Institute of Medical Sciences (KIMS)	26,401	7,346	NA**

Source: Annual reports.

	2025	*2024*	*2021*	*2019*
Hindustan Unilever	5,32,112	5,70,875 (2,34,95,91,262*2,429.68)	5,35,464 (2,34,95,67,819*2,278.99)	3,79,403 (2,16,47,04,405*1,752.68)
ITC	5,12,078	5,40,588 (12,48,47,21,471*433.00)	2,63,163 (12,30,88,44,231*213.8)	3,49,077 (12,25,86,31,601*284.76)
Brittania Industries	1,16,698	1,20,841 (24,08,68,296*5,016.9)	84,414 (24,08,68,296*3,504.6)	74,552 (24,03,18,294*3,102.2)
P&G	45,379	54,021 (3,24,60,736*16,642.10)	39,904 (3,24,60,736*12,292.9)	32,964 (3,24,60,736*10,155.18)
Godrej Consumer Products	1,13,697	1,23,200 (1,02,28,20,329*1204.5)	74,486 (1,02,24,86,273*728.5)	73,963 (1,02,21,66,096*723.6)

*Based on last three months' average market prices (Jan till Mar 2024).
Sources:

In other words, the PE/IPO funds have inspired the hospitals to improve every aspect of their operations with a sharp focus on market share prices. It would appear that over a period of time, such PE/IPO-funded hospitals might become islands of exclusivity for a small number of the privileged population who require high-end care and who can afford hospital rates.

Impact on the patient community

This rapid growth due to PE funds and IPOs has also led to sharp increases in hospitalisation costs for all major ailments, both in rural and urban areas. This has meant that those who cannot afford it are either denied or some patients, out of desperation, have been forced to sell their assets to settle the hospital bills. These increased charges need not be attributed to private equity investments or IPOs alone, since inflation in healthcare costs is an ongoing phenomenon due to a greater focus on profits.[38]

Ethics of corporate and private hospitals

Concerns about the excessive focus on profits and growth leading to unethical practices in corporate hospitals have been expressed. In their seminal book titled *Healers or Predators*, Samiran Nundy, Keshav Desiraju and Sanjay Nagral[39] bemoan the various unethical practices of the corporate hospitals. In this book, several practising doctors and administrators have highlighted the rapidly falling ethical standards in several private hospitals. The Competition Commission of India has also brought to light exorbitant charges levied by the largest hospital chains in India.[40] The government has expressed its concern about the high charges in corporate hospitals in various fora. These practices have led to a general perception that corporate hospitals are only for the rich and famous, yet corporate hospitals are overcrowded, since tertiary care is needed by many, including the middle class.

The Board of Directors of all healthcare companies should not wait for the government to pass punitive legislation for the regulation of private hospitals. All these companies, particularly independent directors on hospital Boards, should play a proactive role and represent public opinion.

Key issues for Indian private healthcare

The fundamental question is whether profit-making should be the primary purpose of a hospital. A related question is whether higher levels of profits and market cap are compatible with patient care for a country like India. Is it necessary for private hospitals to make more profits than other companies? Is it desirable to create islands of care in a poor country like India? Strangely, even smaller islands or islets of exclusivity are being created within these islands for the rich and famous. The relationship between PE and the hospital company should be reviewed. Hospitals are now a strong entity, and they don't have to play a subordinate role to PE funds. If excessive focus on profits is affecting medical practice, then hospitals should not compromise on their core goal of caring for patients. It is clear that many PE funds are wooing healthcare clients since the healthcare sector has consistently delivered results. It is necessary to strike a balance between PE goals and the larger good of the patient community.

There are similar questions for the health insurance industry as well. A steep increase in premium is discouraging a large number of middle-class Indians from renewing their medical insurance. At present, premium is automatically revised upwards based on the claims ratio. The insurance company also makes profits from its investment, which is actually premiums paid by millions of insured persons.

The main goal of the insurance industry should be to enlarge the insurance market rather than restrict it to a few. Insurance companies and third-party administrators should publicise on their website the rates for various procedures negotiated with each hospital. There is a tendency to deny the insured the full value of the amount insured with the insurance company. The insurance industry should 'persuade' large hospitals to accept government insurance schemes.

India should retain the benefits of new fund sources, but there should be a balance in favour of patients. Large hospitals need to find ways to provide high-end medical care without excess profiteering. It is time for policymakers and thinking Board members to intervene and bring about the urgently needed reforms in the healthcare sector.

Conclusion

The large fund flow has benefited tertiary care in India. Modern medical technology along with necessary digitisation technology, highly skilled medical personnel and patient-oriented quality care are available in various cities. However, the balance is shifting towards expensive tertiary care for the affluent, and a weak public health system is unable to cope with the private sector. There is an urgent need for a major course correction in our healthcare system to make it inclusive, affordable and accessible to everyone who needs care.

Annexure 14.1

IPOs in healthcare

IPOs require various approvals by various government authorities and underwriting by qualified institutions. The share premium is arrived at step by step.[41]

IPO underwriting requirements[42]

These IPOs in the hospital and diagnostic sectors had ranged from INR 500 crore to INR 2,000–2,500 crores per issue, from existing capital and/or new issue of shares. The infusion of a large quantum of funds has encouraged each hospital to expand, acquire other hospitals and diversify. The objectives of IPO are required to be mentioned in the *red herring* prospectus.[43] (A red herring prospectus is a preliminary document informing the potential investors and Securities and Exchange Board of India (SEBI) about the company's operations and future plans.)

It is interesting that diagnostic laboratories which do not require large investments also have raised large amounts from an IPO. Some examples are Vijaya Diagnostics (INR 1,895 crore), Krishna (INR 1,213 crore) and Metropolis (INR 1,200 crore). All these IPOs have been issued at substantial share premiums. The inflows have helped them to open a large number of centres and modernise the facilities centres that are acquired by them.[44] There are other companies in the analytics and technology sector which also have raised funds through IPOs, for example, Syngene (INR 550 crore) and Take Solutions (INR 150 crore)[45]. Star Health Insurance company raised INR 2,000 crore by way of a fresh issue, monetising its potential.[46]

Annexure 14.1 List of 52 hospitals chosen for the author's study

Name of the hospital[a]	*Whether listed?*	*Beds*[b]	*Consolidated revenue (INR crore)*
Apollo Hospitals Enterprise Ltd (AHEL)	Yes	10,134	19,059
Artemis Medicare Services Ltd	Yes	750	879
Aster DM Healthcare Ltd	Yes	5000	3,699
Billroth Hospitals	No	650	
Blue Sapphire Healthcare Pvt Ltd (BSH)	No		412
Care Hospitals (Quality Care India Ltd)	No	3,000	1,604
Dr. Agarwal's Eye Hospital	Yes		319
Ganga Medical Centre and Hospitals Pvt Ltd	No	650	100–500
Fortis Healthcare Ltd (FHL)	Yes	4,500	6,893
Global Health Ltd/Medanta (GHL)	Yes	2,823	3,275
GPT Healthcare Ltd (ILS Hospitals)	Yes	560	361
HealthCare Global Enterprises Ltd (HGEL)	Yes	~2000	1,908
Hinduja Healthcare Ltd	No	640	
Jaypee Healthcare Ltd (JHL)	No	504	421
Jupiter Lifeline Hospitals Ltd	Yes	1,194	1,060
Kailash Healthcare Ltd (KHL)	No	2,200	
MGM Healthcare Pvt Ltd	No	500	352
Kauvery Hospitals	Yes	450	181
Kovai Medical Center and Hospital Ltd	Yes	1975	1,020
Krishna Institute of Medical Sciences Ltd (KIMS)	Yes	4000	2,498

Name of the hospital[a]	*Whether listed?*	*Beds*[b]	*Consolidated revenue (INR crore)*
Lotus Eye Hospital and Institute Ltd	Yes	300	48
Maitreya Medicare Ltd	Yes	555	48
Manipal Hospitals	No	9,500	5,510
Max Healthcare Institute Ltd (MHIL)	Yes	4,300	5,406
Medica Hospitals	No	564	611
Metro Institutes of Medical Sciences Pvt Ltd (MIMS)	No	1,762	1,375
Moolchand Healthcare Pvt Ltd (MHPL)	No	500	
Narayana Hrudalaya Ltd (NHL)	Yes	6,074	5,018
Nephro Care India Ltd	Yes		27
Paras Healthcare	No	2135	1,129
Rainbow Children's Medicare Ltd	Yes	1,935	1,297
Sahyadri Hospitals Pvt Ltd	No	1000	718
Seven Hills	No	300	
Shalby Ltd	Yes	2000	934
Wockhardt Hospitals Ltd	No	1,600	1,154
Yashoda Hospital & Research Center Ltd (YHRC)	No	4,000	432
Yatharth Hospital and Trauma Care Services Ltd (YHTC)	Yes	1,650	671
Devadoss Hospital	No	200	
Dr. Mohan's Diabetes Specialities Centre	No		153
Vasan Healthcare	No		189
Unihealth Hospitals	Yes	1200	49
Asarfi Hospital Ltd	Yes	250	84
Vijaya Diagnostic Centre Ltd	Yes		548
Lakeshore Global Lifecare	No	470	419
Royal Care Hospital	No	401	333
Marengo Asia Healthcare Pvt Ltd	No	1,280	345
Gleneagles Healthcare Pvt Ltd	No	1,500	659
MIOT Hospitals Pvt Ltd	No	1,000	
Image Healthcare Ltd	No		9
Ford Hospitals	No	200	33
Guwahati Neurological Research Centre	No	720	326

[a]The above hospitals considered are based on publicly available information and is not a comprehensive list of all hospitals having more than 250 beds.
[b]The bed strength of some hospitals is based on the position in March 2024.

Notes

1 'There are now more than half a million people aged 100 or older around the world', *World Economic Forum*, 17 February 2021, https://www.weforum.org/stories/2021/02/living-to-one-hundred-life-expectancy/

2 'Indian healthcare market projected to reach $638 billion by 2025, report reveals', *FE Healthcare*, 27 November 2024, https://www.financialexpress.com/business/healthcare-indian-healthcare-market-projected-to-reach-638-billion-by-2025-report-reveals-3678354/#:~:text=The%20Indian%20healthcare%20sector%20is,CAGR%20growth%20during%20this%20period

3 Srinivasa Rao Apparasu, 'Bypass surgery with beating heart safe bet in India, says latest study', 1 November 2019, https://www.hindustantimes.com/india-news/bypass-surgery-with-beating-heart-safe-bet-in-india-says-latest-study/story-X6JAQ1mQITRFQqpGvfFszO.html
4 'Magnetic resonance imaging market in India: size and share analysis – Growth trends and forecasts (2025–2030)', *Mordor Intelligence*, https://www.mordorintelligence.com/industry-reports/india-magnetic-resonance-imaging-mri-market#:~:text=India%20Magnetic%20Resonance%20Imaging%20Market%20Research%20FAQs,USD%20439.67%20million%20by%202030
5 Private Equity Funds, Investor.gov, U.S. Securities and Exchange Commission, https://www.investor.gov/introduction-investing/investing-basics/investment-products/private-investment-funds/private-equity
6 'Why are private equity firms interested in India's healthcare sector?' *BW Businessworld*, 26 September 2024, https://www.businessworld.in/article/why-are-private-equity-firms-interested-in-india%E2%80%99s-healthcare-sector-534248
7 'Private equity must not undermine patient care in Indian healthcare', *HFS*, https://www.hfsresearch.com/research/private-equity-growth-must-not-undermine-patient-care-in-indian-healthcare/#:~:text=Private%20equity%20(PE)%20money%20has,levels%20of%20%243%2D4%20billion.
8 'Private equity targets India's healthcare sector with record investments', https://www.ft.com/content/335558f1-bdb3-4f38-ab31-2c447a9500c7
9 'PE-VC investments in India's healthcare sector fall in 2024, shows data', *Business Standard*, 1 December 2024, https://www.business-standard.com/industry/news/pe-vc-investments-in-india-s-healthcare-sector-fall-in-2024-shows-data-124112900930_1.html
10 P.B. Jayakumar, 'PE's health takeover', *Fortune India*, 5 July 2024, https://www.fortuneindia.com/long-reads/pes-healthcare-takeover/117415
11 Shivam Tyagi, 'Why private equity firms are betting big on indian healthcare?' *BW Healthcare*, 7 December 2023, https://bwhealthcareworld.com/article/why-private-equity-firms-are-betting-big-on-indian-healthcare-501365
12 'Indian healthcare industry receives USD 1B investment in just five months', *Medical Buyer*, 3 June 2024, https://medicalbuyer.co.in/indian-healthcare-industry-receives-usd-1b-investment-in-just-five-months/
13 'Reflections: Indian Private Equity in 2017', *Pricewaterhouse Coopers*, https://www.pwc.in/assets/pdfs/industries/private-equity/reflections-indian-private-equity-in-2017.pdf
14 'Investment opportunities in India's healthcare sector', *NITI Aayog*, https://www.niti.gov.in/sites/default/files/2023-02/InvestmentOpportunities_HealthcareSector.pdf
15 'India private equity report 2023', *Bain & Company*, https://www.bain.com/insights/india-private-equity-report-2023/#:~:text=India%27s%20healthcare%20sector%20saw%20deal,approximately%208%25%20of%20total%20investments
16 Kaustabh Kulkarni and Indulal PM, 'Private equity pours money into India primary healthcare', 5 January 2013, https://www.reuters.com/article/us-india-heathcare/private-equity-pours-money-into-india-primary-healthcare-idUKBRE9030UB20130104 Indium Healthcare Valuation update – June 2023, Indium Capital Advisors, 28 June 2023, https://www.linkedin.com/pulse/indium-healthcare-valuation-update-june-2023-indium-capital/?utm_source=share&utm_medium=member_ios&utm_campaign=share_via
17 Shraddha Nair, 'Private equity firms prefer convertibles to direct equity', *LiveMint*, June 7, 2010, https://www.livemint.com/Money/rkcStm18Wex1Z8yPvnAFuO/Private-equity-firms-prefer-convertibles-to-direct-equity.html

18 Digbijay Mishra, 'After Big Basket, Tata Digital acquires online pharmacy 1mg', 11 June 2021, https://economictimes.indiatimes.com/tech/startups/tata-digital-to-acquire-majority-stake-in-1mg/articleshow/83393293.cms?from=mdr Aman Rawat, 'Tata Digital-owned 1mg raises $40 million in fresh round at unicorn valuation', 6 September 2022, https://www.vccircle.com/tatadigital-owned-1mg-raises-40-million-in-fresh-round-at-unicorn-valuation#:~:text=Tata%20Digital%20had%20acquired%201mg,Tata%20Digital%20in%20April%202021
19 'Singapore's Temasek acquires majority stake in Manipal Hospitals for $2 billion', 8 April 2023, https://bwhealthcareworld.com/article/singapores-temasek-acquires-majority-stake-in-manipal-hospitals-for-2-billion-472147#:~:text=Singapore's%20Temasek%20Acquires%20Majority%20Stake%20In%20Manipal%20Hospitals%20For%20%242%20Billion,-BW%20Online%20Bureau&text=In%20a%20recent%20announcement%2C%20India's,per%20of%20the%20hospital%20chain
20 Sambhav Kumar, 'Why are private equity firms interested in India's healthcare sector?' *BW Businessworld*, 26 September 2024, https://www.businessworld.in/article/why-are-private-equity-firms-interested-in-india%E2%80%99s-healthcare-sector-534248
21 Micheal Jensen, 'Value maximization and stakeholder theory', *Harvard Business Review*, 24 July 2000, https://hbswk.hbs.edu/item/value-maximization-and-stakeholder-theory
22 Compulsory convertible preference shares, https://www.dmshah.in/wp-content/uploads/2017/03/Writeup_CCPS.pdf
23 Shraddha Nair, 'Private equity firms prefer convertibles to direct equity', 7 June 2010, https://www.livemint.com/Money/rkcStm18Wex1Z8yPvnAFuO/Private-equity-firms-prefer-convertibles-to-direct-equity.html
24 Rick Segal, 'How Tom Peters taught me to knit', *Forbes*, 6 March 2013, https://www.forbes.com/sites/gyro/2013/03/06/how-tom_peters-taught-me-to-knit/
25 'Apollo Hospitals to acquire 60 per cent stake in Ayurvedic hospital chain', 6 October 2022, www.thehindubusinessline.com/companies/apollo-hospitals-to-acquire-60-per-cent-stake-in-ayurveda-hospital-chain/article65974967.ece
26 Nagesh Joshi, 'Healthcare mergers and acquisitions (M&As): disruption-led growth', 21 December 2022, https://www.healthcareradius.in/features/healthcare-mergers-and-acquisitions-mas-disruption-led-growth
27 'Corporate hospitals to see 8-10 pc revenue growth in FY24: Report', 17 August 2023, https://m.economictimes.com/industry/healthcare/biotech/healthcare/corporate-hospitals-to-see-8-10-pc-revenue-growth-in-fy24-report/articleshow/102811643.cms
28 'Unbundled charges by private hospitals to push healthcare costs', 17 October 2024, https://medicalbuyer.co.in/unbundled-charges-by-private-hospitals-to-push-healthcare-costs/
29 'Medical inflation in India: Current rate, causes and impacts', *Onsurity Editorial*, 29 November 2024, https://www.onsurity.com/blog/medical-inflation-in-india/#:~:text=The%20index%20further%20revealed%20that,from%20getting%20quality%20medical%20care
30 K. Srinath Reddy, 'Forgone care: The blindspot of our health system', *Indian Express*, 15 March 2025.
31 Aman Gupta, 'The rising cost of healthcare expenses in India: Implications for the future', LinkedIn, 2 July 2023, https://www.linkedin.com/pulse/rising-cost-health-care-expenses-india-implications-future-aman-gupta
32 'Value of health insurance gross direct premiums written in India from financial year 2013 to 2024', Statistica, https://www.statista.com/statistics/1452834/india-health-insurance-gross-direct-premiums/#:~:text=In%20the%20financial%20year%202024,nearly%20906%20billion%20Indian%20rupees

33 Bindu Shajan Pedarappan, 'Healthcare cost inflation soaring, raising health cover premiums', *The Hindu*, 26 December 2024, https://www.thehindu.com/business/healthcare-cost-inflation-soaring-raising-health-cover-premiums/article69023505.ece

34 Neelanjit Das, 'Health insurance premium shot up over 25% last year for 52% policyholders, finds survey; here's how the impact can be reduced', *The Economic Times*, 10 May 2024, https://m.economictimes.com/wealth/insure/health-insurance/health-insurance-premium-shot-up-over-25-last-year-for-52-policyholders-finds-survey-heres-what-you-can-do-to-reduce-the-impact/articleshow/109923308.cms

35 'Beyond the balance sheet: The Indian hospital CEO's guide to boosting EBITA margins', Navig Health, 14 May 2024. https://www.linkedin.com/pulse/beyond-balance-sheet-indian-hospital-ceos-guide-boosting-o2oof

36 Levels of healthcare, Physiopedia, https://www.physio-pedia.com/Levels_of_Healthcare#:~:text=Quaternary%20care%20has%20been%20defined,of%20national%20or%20international%20centres

37 'Market capitalization', Corporate Finance Institute, https://corporatefinanceinstitute.com/resources/valuation/what-is-market-capitalization/

38 A. Minhas, 'Average medical inflation in India from 2018 to 2022, with forecast for 2023', Statistica, 3 February 2025, https://www.statista.com/statistics/1466124/india-average-medical-inflation/

39 Samiran Nundy, Keshav Desiraju, and Sanjay Nagral, *Healers or Predators – Healthcare Corruption in India*, New Delhi: Oxford University Press, 2018.

40 'Hospital chains abused their dominance to charge exorbitant prices: Report', *Business Standard*, 23 September 2022, https://www.business-standard.com/article/current-affairs/hospital-chains-abused-their-dominance-to-charge-exorbitant-prices-report-122092300441_1.html

41 Jatin Pareek, 'What are the IPO requirements in India?', 2 March 2023, https://www.wintwealth.com/blog/what-are-the-ipo-requirements-in-india/

42 Mahak Agarwal, 'The basics of bringing an IPO', 6 September 2023, https://vinodkothari.com/2023/09/the-basics-of-bringing-an-ipo/

43 'What is the red herring prospectus', HDFC Bank, 2 January 2025, https://www.hdfcbank.com/personal/resources/learning-centre/invest/what-is-a-red-herring-prospectus

44 Healthcare service provider IPOs in India, Chittorgarh, https://www.chittorgarh.com/report/sector-wise-ipo-list-in-india/96/222/

45 Healthcare Research: Analytics and technology IPOs in India, Chittorgarh, https://www.chittorgarh.com/report/sector-wise-ipo-list-in-india/96/233/

46 'Star Health and Allied Insurance Company Ltd IPO', Chittorgarh, https://www.chittorgarh.com/ipo/star-health-ipo/1184/

Part IV

Looking to the future

15 Public health reforms

Tilak Shankar

Introduction

An estimated 450 million people rely on public health system to fulfil their healthcare needs in India. It need not be overemphasised that India needs a strong public health system to address the twin challenges of basic health needs and medical treatment to millions of underprivileged citizens and the middle class. The public health system, although robust in a few states, is lagging behind in providing optimal care across most of India. Fundamental reforms are needed to revamp the public health system so that it delivers on its promise of healthcare to millions of people. Poor management of even available resources is the biggest reason for the unsatisfactory health outcomes.

Reforms are needed at three levels across different time frames: immediate, short term and long term:

- *Immediate measures* (within the next seven to ten years): The first step is to ensure that all public hospitals and health centres function on par with any modern private healthcare facility. Filling medical vacancies at the community health centre (CHC) level is perhaps the most urgent and probably the biggest challenge. The upgradation of facilities, setting suitable standards of care with accountability and infusing the requisite number of healthcare professionals at all levels needs to be fulfilled over a time period of seven to ten years, which may appear quite challenging, but in the author's opinion, a realistic time estimate. Experience of well-performing states should be replicated in all states.
- *Short term* (next 10–15 years): The Kerala model of empowering all public health centres (PHCs) and community health centres (CHCs) with supervision from district health officers should be implemented across the country. At present, PHC data are collated and processed electronically at a central location. At the health centre or hospital level, manual records of case sheets are used. Manual records should be abolished at the PHC/CHC level. Expense approval should be automated. A health district should be viewed as an integrated entity including accredited social health activist (ASHA) workers, Integrated Child Development Scheme (ICDS) centres and other departments. Basic data analytic tools

DOI: 10.4324/9781003684947-19

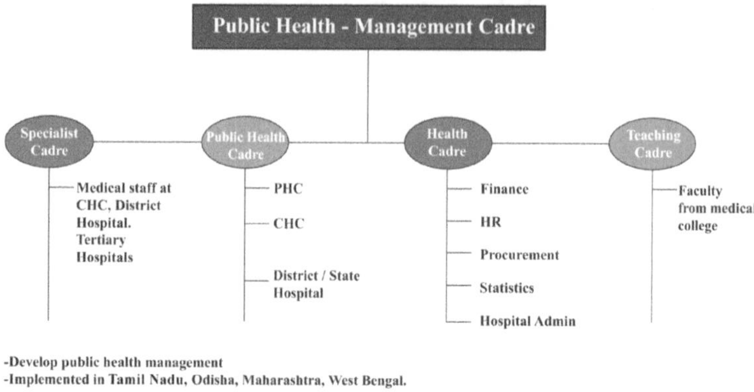

Figure 15.1 Public health management cadre.

should be employed to link expenditure and staff vacancies with health outcomes. Public health has a goldmine of raw data, and when digitised, it can be used to improve health outcomes dramatically.

Public health management cadre (Figure 15.1) has been recommended by the Government of India with an integrated approach to addressing public health challenges in rural areas and towns.[1] The cadre consists of multiple disciplines of health, management, statistics and others.[2] Public health cadre has been implemented in some states in 2022 and even earlier. There should be an assessment of the health outcomes as a result of this intervention.

- *Long term* (next 20 years): Major changes including seamless digitisation, substantial investment in nutrition supplementation programmes, development of medical leadership for hospitals and research institutions and human resource development. Public health should grow and work along with non-profit, private and corporate sectors.

The present scenario

Healthcare comprises two components: treatment at hospitals and clinics and promotion of the population's wellness by addressing the basic causes of poor health. The underprivileged sections of society in India (an estimated 350–450 million) rely solely on the public health system for all their medical needs. The health challenges faced by children and adults are diverse including malnutrition, iron-deficiency anaemia, tuberculosis (TB), stunting and wasting, under-five mortality, morbidity and non-communicable diseases (NCDs) such as cardiovascular diseases, diabetes and respiratory illness. India has a twin problem of both communicable and non-communicable diseases causing morbidity and mortality. If the public health does not keep pace with the changing healthcare environment, there is a risk of this system becoming obsolete.

India's public health system should be evaluated in the context of the twenty-first century. There have been rapid advancements in medical technology, information technology, medicines, quality standards and translational research studies in India. We have an enviable network of sub-centres, primary health centres and community health centres throughout the country. We also have the advantage of last-mile connectivity through ASHA workers and ICDS centres. Yet India's health outcomes are poor. One of the main reasons is poor management of resources. Requirements such as frequently prescribed medicines, shortage of consumables, non-availability of continuous power supply and breakdown of medical equipment require prompt attention. The present systems are not equipped to handle even simple requirements. Unfortunately, even purely administrative decisions on fire safety, supply of water and electricity, tackling staff shortages, housekeeping and effluent treatment are not competently handled by the administration at present. Medical personnel cannot be held responsible for administrative incompetence.

Majority of the patients visiting government hospitals are from the underprivileged sections and low- or middle-income groups. Some of them, especially in remote areas, reach the nearest health centre or hospital with great difficulty. They could be visiting the hospital or the health centre for a snake bite, diarrhoea, high fever, diabetic complications, tuberculosis, cataract or other illnesses, which require prompt and compassionate attention. The patients may not have easy access to public transport or government ambulances from their residence. There would be a long wait to see the doctor (if he/she is available), have an X-ray taken or get a blood test done, if the equipment is in working condition. The hospital pharmacy may or may not have the drugs prescribed by the doctor. The patient may have to buy them from a nearby pharmacy. All these are simple managerial problems, for which there are easy solutions.

They would have spent most of the day at the hospital. If they are daily wage labourers, they would have lost their daily income. Minimal facilities such as clean bed sheets (not disposable sheets), running water, electricity and clean surroundings are a luxury in government hospitals. In addition, patients are forced to use unclean toilets and, in some places, confront stray dogs and pigs. These experiences make the hospital stay a nightmare for the poor in India. Patient focus unfortunately is absent in public health. Unfortunately, most Indians have become inured to the sorry state of affairs.

Anecdotally, we understand that in some states, patients are forced to travel for several hours to a reasonable private healthcare facility. It is necessary to consider alternative health models, which can produce good health outcomes. Most of the government hospitals operate from their own properties. The upkeep of these facilities is characterised by neglect. The author has witnessed crumbling walls and dump yards in the middle of the hospital. ‘Budgetary constraints’ is the common refrain for the state of affairs.

The vast public health system in India is not uniformly dismal. Some states are performing exceptionally well. Tamil Nadu has remained one of the top states in public healthcare delivery. During 2023, nearly two million patients (including 25 per cent pregnant women) were provided free ambulance services in Tamil Nadu with the help of global positioning system (GPS) system, which tracks the response time.[3] Taking this as an inspiration, it would be beneficial if every state, even if the ambulances are outsourced, could provide this facility 24/7 to fulfil the urgent medical care requirement of emergency patients.

Bright spots

The history of allopathic public healthcare spans about four centuries. The Government General Hospital in Chennai[4] is the oldest hospital in India, founded in 1664 by the East India Company. Currently, it has over 2,700 beds and has been running a network of medical, nursing and several allied health sciences teaching programmes for many years. Recognised as one of the most respected institutions for teaching, research and patient care in Tamil Nadu, this hospital alone handles about 12,000 outpatients, and about 2,300 inpatients in a day. As a referral hospital, it draws substantial crowds from other government hospitals as well, but it also reflects the characteristics of large teaching hospitals, with referral from other hospitals. There are many shining examples of well-run hospitals in spite of the poorly functioning healthcare system overall. Many government hospitals in Kerala are well run, providing primary, secondary and tertiary care. There is a high degree of delegation to PHCs with the active involvement of the local panchayat.[5]

In spite of poor service levels, the poor have very little option but to approach a government hospital. Continued dependence on public health is a strong reason for a larger role for this sector.

Inadequacy of medical staff at public healthcare facilities

In the last few decades, many private medical colleges have been sanctioned by the Medical Council of India. There is an acute shortage of medical staff and specialist doctors in the country,[6] as mentioned in Chapter 1. The number of graduate and postgraduate (PG) doctors, graduating every year, is grossly inadequate in relation to the patient needs. There is a very high percentage of vacancies (up to 80 per cent of sanctioned posts for specialists) at community health centres (CHCs), and 96 per cent of the 6,000 CHCs in the country are in rural areas. Each CHC has 30 sanctioned beds, and thus nearly 200,000 hospital beds are merely beds. There is reluctance for specialists to work in rural areas for a variety of reasons.

The number of students graduating out of government and private medical colleges is roughly the same. Many of the private medical colleges charge a substantial quantum of 'capitation fees', pushing up the spend on college education substantially. This discourages private medical graduates from joining government hospitals or non-profit institutions as they want to earn higher salaries in private medical care institutions. This further depletes the number of doctors/specialists joining government service.

There is a small number of Diplomate of the National Board (DNB) graduates who specialise at the postgraduate level from for-profit private hospitals, but they also prefer to work with private hospitals. Even though they are considered equivalent to Medical Council of India (MCI) graduates, very few DNB graduates join the government service, further adding to the imbalance and weakening our public health.

Even though there are more than 60,000 seats in postgraduate (PG) courses, they are spread over a large number of disciplines, making those qualifying with post-graduate degrees grossly inadequate to meet the demand for specialists. Hence, there are acute shortages for gynaecologists, paediatricians, neonatologists and general surgeons. This shortage has a direct impact on health outcomes.

There are about one million allopaths and an equal number of Ayurveda specialists. The Government of India had wanted Ayurveda specialists to undertake surgeries, which was not acceptable to the Indian Medical Association as they felt it would interfere with their medical standards. There has since been an impasse.[7] The net result, particularly in rural India, is the presence of a large number of quacks (unqualified practitioner) numbering about one million who treat patients and conduct surgeries.

Public health expenditure and controls

Expenditure on public health ranges between 1.3 and 2.0 per cent of our GDP, shared by the central government (one-third) and the state governments (two-thirds). The Government of India spent about INR 74,000 crore in 2021–22, and in addition, typically each state spends between INR 10,000 crore and INR 35,000 crore per annum, depending on the size of the population and its overall budget.[8] The Government of India's expenditure includes operational expenditure of the All India Institute of Medical Sciences (AIIMS), funding of various national missions and support for national research institutions. Public health expenditure has remained low for several decades.

The low expenditure on public health emphasises the need for a substantial increase, but that alone may not achieve the desired results. A higher level of capital expenditure is likely to lead to more wastage, implementation delays, cost overruns and corruption. Efficient healthcare delivery requires proper medical staffing and good management. The central and state governments employ thousands of staff, with substantial public funds being spent. It is therefore felt that strict centralisation, governmental accounting and control are needed. It is automatically assumed that strict controls and audit minimise corruption, which has not been the case. In addition, outdated procedures and extensive paperwork are incompatible with providing good medical care.

In the twenty-first century, information technology (IT) offers real-time data of expenditure, outcomes and grassroots level data, rendering rigid manual paperwork-based mindset unnecessary. The prevailing audit orientation often sidelines the primary goal of delivering quality, with expenditure seldom being correlated with medical outcomes.

Traditionally, health expenditure is measured in relation to the nation's GDP. In our view, per capita expenditure state- wise and indeed district- wise are better indicators to assess the adequacy of expenditure. Figure 15.2 highlights both public and private health expenditure systems wise.

- There are huge disparities among states in total per capita expenditures.
- Public health expenditures are very low and as a result 40–75 per cent of the per capita expenditure in all the states is spent by the poor citizens who are forced to avail private care. State governments are unable to fund even the minimum required health expenditures, due to their low Gross State Domestic Product (GSDP).

State budgets are not related to the health needs of the population. For example, many large states in India have a high infant mortality rate and still spend inadequate amounts on healthcare (Table 15.1).

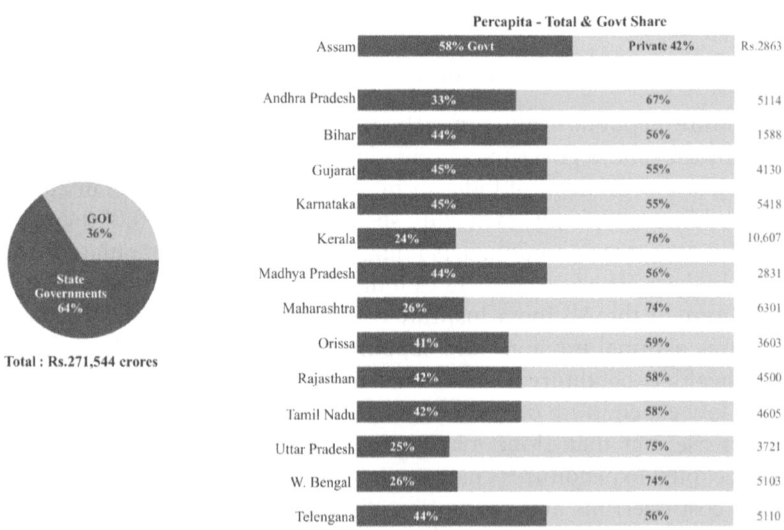

Figure 15.2 Per capita public health expenditure.

Source: National Health Accounts, 2019–20 (published 2023).

Table 15.1 Comparison of public health expenditure of some states

State	*Public health expenditure (INR per capita)*	*% of GSDP*	*Infant mortality rate*	*Population (million)*[a]
Assam	1,657	1.7	36	35
Madhya Pradesh	1,247	1.1	43	69
Orissa	1,494	1.3	36	45
Rajasthan	1,662	1.3	32	78
Uttar Pradesh	951	1.3	38	228

Source: National Health accounts 2022–23.
GSDP: gross state domestic product; IMR: infant mortality rate; population: 2020 figures.
[a]List of Indian states by population, https://statisticstimes.com/demographics/india/indian-states-population.php

Structure of public health in India

Public health services serve as the primary lifeline for large sections of our population both in urban and rural areas. The central and state governments have also undertaken many initiatives in addressing the long-term health needs of the vulnerable population. Creation of wellness centres, food fortification programmes, nutritional supplementation, noon meal schemes and breakfast programmes for school children are necessary steps to tackle malnutrition, stunting and wasting and mortality of children under the age of five.

India has a strong grassroots-level structure of ASHA workers and anganwadi centres as envisaged in the ICDS programme. However, these initiatives come under different ministries, and grassroots-level coordination becomes laborious. The diffusion of accountability and bureaucratic delays often hampers the effective implementation of these programmes. The public health system is governed by a bureaucratic framework.

Max Weber (1864–1920), credited with the term bureaucracy, defined bureaucratic systems as follows:

> Bureaucracy is an organizational structure characterized by many rules, standardized processes, procedures and requirements, designated number of desks, meticulous division of labour and responsibility, clear hierarchies and professional, almost impersonal interactions between employees.

This definition remains relevant in contemporary India. As expenditures increase, the size of bureaucracy grows, and it gets even more rule-bound. According to the Weberian bureaucracy, such a structure is deemed suitable for all big organisations – government or private. In Max Weber's bureaucratic model, qualifications and competence are the sole criteria for hiring and promotion of workers.[9] The evolution of the bureaucratic system spans over a hundred years, extending its scope across various types of organisations in industry, government and social sectors, in different parts of the world. India had implemented the bureaucracy in full force, adding its own flavour. Bureaucrats have often applied similar principles across different sectors without considering the specific requirements of each sector.

We will focus on three conceptual issues regarding public health administration in India. They are:

- Is a bureaucratic system suitable for healthcare?
- Does the size of the state, with its population and geographical spread, determine the quality of healthcare? Is a smaller decentralised structure more suitable for a large populous state? Are they more suited for providing at least minimal care to rural and underprivileged sections of our population?
- Assuming that government systems are the only option available, are there advantages in a highly decentralised, empowered and simpler bureaucratic structure utilising information technology to deliver superior care? What are the metrics for determining the superiority of a decentralised structure? How can we demonstrate the superiority of a decentralised structure?

The public health system is funded by the Government of India and the states from their overall revenues. In recent years, the Government of India has established one or more national-level institutions in each state totalling 22, titled All India Institute of Medical Sciences (AIIMS). Additionally, the Government of India also funds all national programmes such as the Rural Health Mission and Digital Health Mission covering both capital and revenue items.[10[]

Organisational structure of public healthcare system

At the Government of India level, the Health Secretary, who belongs to the Indian Administrative (IAS), heads the health department. Similarly, in each state as well, the Health Secretary is an IAS officer, in charge of the health department. Both central and state governments have a well-structured hierarchy of officers – medical and administrative personnel responsible for various sub-departments. Staffing norms are defined at all levels with recruitment strictly adhering to 'sanctioned' posts.

State health departments are organised as directorates comprising various medical, nursing and administrative departments, operating within government pay scales, audit requirements, staffing norms and expenditure control. The presence of an IAS officer at the helm is a clear indication that the focus of the healthcare department is on administration and expense control. A hospital should be headed by a medical professional, who understands the field of healthcare supported by administrative staff.

A bureaucratic organisational structure is not suitable for healthcare for the following reasons:

- Healthcare is a unique service sector, where hospitals are dedicated to serving the patients 24/7, with the primary focus of saving lives and alleviating the suffering of the patient. Each hospital or a health centre's administration needs to prioritise on a day-to-day basis micro-level aspects including availability of appropriate medicines, maintenance of medical equipment, a steady supply of consumables and round-the-clock staffing. In the absence of these essentials, specific staff should be accountable. Dealing with poor, illiterate and sick patients requires compassion, a quality not facilitated by bureaucratic systems, further worsened by large numbers of patients and their attendants who throng hospitals.
- Effective healthcare leadership demands a comprehensive understanding of medicine and hospital management and requires continuity of leadership. A superficial approach, based only on authority, is grossly inappropriate to manage a modern healthcare system. In fact, such a system may be detrimental to patient care.
- Many hospitals and research institutions engage in sophisticated scientific research work employing hundreds of highly qualified staff. Hospital management requires an appreciation of the work pressures faced by the medical and nursing professionals.
- Modern hospitals require constant upgradation of equipment. Strategic decisions on the purchase of medical equipment requires good understanding of medical technology and decisions regarding purchase of specific equipment require a deep understanding of prioritisation and clinician needs. Such decisions cannot be taken based by an administrator who little understands the medical field.
- Health policies should be based on an understanding of scientific findings of various research studies, appreciation of specific health or nutritional inadequacies of the population and require specific medical solutions to many public health challenges. Unfortunately, health policies are based on administrative convenience and fund availability.
- States which have large populations, with a centralised power structure, struggle to deliver even a reasonable level of healthcare as evidenced from all health statistics. While the administration cannot bear the full blame, it plays a significant role in the observed shortcomings.
- Human resources have to be managed with tact and finesse. Medical and technical staff in every public hospital are highly qualified, and there are a large number of sub-specialties and super-specialties in every field of medicine. The doctors heading these departments are experts in their fields and deserve respect. We have encountered many situations where

the IAS officers treat medical staff poorly, because of their rank. Often even junior-level administrators deal with senior medical staff with power and authority, rather than knowledge. Administrative decisions are frequently driven by financial and administrative considerations rather than medical needs.

Choice of government or private employment

Every government doctor, nurse and technician has the option of working in private hospitals. Recruitments, compensation, motivation and performance management should be unique to medical, teaching and research institutions. However, the bureaucratic structure demands uniformity and follows precedence.

Empowerment

There are a large number of operational decisions, for which the field staff should be empowered. If a low-value consumable or a medicine is urgently needed at a hospital, the medical staff should be empowered to buy these items. If a patient with diabetes requires insulin, the doctor should be empowered to provide them from the hospital pharmacy. There are simple methods of linking patient profile with medication in every single case to prevent misuse. There is corruption in spite of controls at present.

The motivation levels of all staff are critical for delivering high-quality care, in servicing patients – whether it is a paying patient (a small number) or free patients. There are well-defined quality accreditation standards (National Accreditation Board for Hospitals and Healthcare Providers (NABH), National Accreditation Board for Testing and Calibration Laboratories (NABL)) for all aspects of care. Government hospitals do not have the requirement of obtaining quality accreditations.

Given all these issues, a bureaucratic structure is clearly unsuitable for the healthcare sector.

Assessment of health outcomes

Healthcare systems should primarily be assessed based on the outcomes. In our view, the health of the mothers and children stands out as the most crucial indicator of any healthcare system worldwide. Unfortunately, our health system falls significantly short on this factor, with unsatisfactory statistics on infant mortality rate (IMR), maternal mortality rate (MMR), under-five morbidity and mortality and incidence of severe iron-deficiency anaemia among expectant mothers. Society should move away from being fatalistic and superstitious. They should believe that quality healthcare that is timely and affordable is our fundamental right as enshrined in Article 21 of the Constitution of India.

Let us briefly examine the current status of healthcare in the country.

Health index of states

In 2019–20, the National Institution for Transforming India (NITI Aayog) had ranked all states on various health indicators. The summary index derived from 24 different criteria, including health outcomes, key processes and inputs, governance and information, revealed no surprises. Each one of the above criteria collectively determines the health index ranking.

Kerala secured the top spot, with a score of 82.2 out of 100, with Tamil Nadu scoring 74.4 and UP a far distant 30.[11] The ranking reflects the net result of variables such as per capita expenditure on health, health outcomes, number of vacancies of medical staff and size of the states. Lack of a good organisation structure is a key factor contributing to the poor health outcomes in certain states. Unfortunately, many of the above indicators for a number of poorly performing states exhibit the same characteristics year after year, and indices are merely viewed as a set of numbers for publication and not as a road map for addressing performance gaps. A detailed study by local authorities could highlight specific actions needed even at each district level. The objective of ranking is for the state to identify specific factors that contribute to continued poor performance. For example, if the large number of vacancies is one of the causes, then corrective action should be initiated at the district level.

States with a large population

There are several states which have a large population and several administrative districts: Uttar Pradesh – 200 million, 75 districts; Bihar – 104 million, 38 districts; Madhya Pradesh – 78 million, 55 districts; Maharashtra – 112 million, 36 districts.[12] with populations per district ranging from 10 lakh to 40 lakh.[13] The functioning of healthcare in these districts is affected adversely because of the geographical size and large population under their jurisdiction. As the population, number of districts and geographical distance increase, overall administration, including healthcare, becomes difficult.

Per capita expenditure

Health expenditure is based on Gross State Domestic Product (GSDP) of the state. Economically less developed states like Uttar Pradesh allocate limited funds for healthcare, spending a total amount of INR 1,650 per capita (private and public) on health compared to Kerala, which spends six times this amount (public and private). A combination of low expenditure, large population and high medical staff shortage contributes to poor medical and health outcomes.

A detailed comparison of district-wise infant mortality, maternal mortality, under-five mortality, vaccination of children and correlation with availability of obstetricians and gynaecologists and paediatricians will highlight the simple fact that mere buildings cannot deliver good maternal care. Health policy should be based on the correlation and in-depth analysis between various factors contributing to poor medical outcomes. It cannot be based on administrative convenience.

Optimum size of a state

There have been debates about the appropriate size for a state, particularly in relation to the population it serves. This is also true of healthcare systems. There are several states which have relatively small populations and geographical areas. The extent of urbanisation also varies significantly from one state to another. Hence, healthcare should be decentralised to the district level with each district being treated as a separate healthcare entity.

Staffing norms

Bureaucratic organisation structures bound by rules and rigid staffing norms need to be reviewed. The norms have evolved over a period of time to minimise nepotism and corruption. For example, as per the norms prescribed, all the PHCs and CHCs have sanctioned positions for washing clothes, providing security and housekeeping. It is necessary to review the need for employing staff for non-core functions. All these jobs may be outsourced to another government agency with defined accountability. This will help the medical team to focus on their core job. In recent years, many systems have been computerised. The staffing needs should be reviewed, for example, the government should consider recruiting bio-medical engineers to maintain medical and other electronic equipment at district headquarters, hiring software engineers to maintain computer systems and digital data capture and employing nutritionists to advise the patients on nutrition. Studies should be carried out to introduce greater automation, procuring washing machines, modernising and automating the kitchen, ensuring running water and maintaining toilets and washroom facilities. Alternative means of supplying food from a centralised kitchen to many PHC/CHCs should be explored. These are simple measures. Staffing norms should be reviewed periodically, in consultation with local management to ensure that staffing norms are contemporary and meet the needs of the patients.

There are governmental norms for sub-centres, PHCs and CHCs, including in tribal and hilly areas. However, there are shortfalls in the number of centres compared to the norms. Even in a functioning CHC, vacancies up to 80 per cent of sanctioned posts for specialist positions severely compromise health delivery. Unless the PHC/CHC is fully staffed and medical equipment is in working order, it cannot provide even minimum patient care. Anecdotal evidence suggests that the percentage of functioning medical equipment is a mere 20–30 per cent in many government hospitals.

A smaller state is an advantage

Kerala with a relatively small population – 33 million, in 14 districts – and a small geographical area (38, 863 sq. km) spends INR 10,300 crore on health (for 2021–22), nearly 12 per cent of its state budget.[14] Kerala has a highly decentralised organisation up to district and PHC levels, a model discussed later in the chapter.

Tamil Nadu, which has a population of 72 million and an area of 130,363 sq. km, has an impressive health record and spends INR 18,632 crore on health. Of its Budget Estimate (BE) for 2021–22, about 8 per cent was allocated towards healthcare. The Government of Tamil Nadu employs more than 120,000 staff in the health department, administered by 15 directorates.[15] There are an estimated 100,000 beds in Tamil Nadu serving a population of 77 million. The hospital beds in all the government allopathic hospitals – primary, secondary, and tertiary care hospitals – serve a large number of inpatients. The state has more than 350 paediatric intensive care units (PICU) in all the districts to tackle the infant and under-five mortality. Thus, Tamil Nadu has taken specific action to address infant and maternal mortality in a systematic manner.

The GSDP of Uttar Pradesh (geographical area of 250,968 sq. km) was INR 21,23,000 crore for the financial year 2022–23, and INR 33,309 crore was budgeted for health and family expenditure, which works out to 15.5 per cent of its state budget.[16] Despite a higher allocation to healthcare in its budget, the per capita expenditure on health is low because its population is more than 240 million (2023 estimates).

In Madhya Pradesh (area of 340,258 sq. km), IMR, for example, is six times that of Kerala per 1,000 live births. The above examples highlight the interplay of low per capita expenditure, large geographical area and large vacancies of doctors resulting in poor medical outcomes. Each of these factors has to be addressed individually.

Such figures are disheartening and should not be acceptable to policymakers. Per capita expenditures on health per year, private and public sources together are shown in Table 15.2.

Table 15.2 Per capita health expenditures for select states

State	*Per capita health expenditure (INR)*
Kerala	9,183
Tamil Nadu	2,077
Uttar Pradesh	1,650

Kerala's decentralised model

Kerala provides an alternate model of public healthcare spending as well as decentralised administration. Kerala has been home to the Ayurveda system for several centuries, as well as a robust allopathic system. Patients have the flexibility to use either system or both systems. According to Raman Kutty,[17] Kerala had implemented decentralised healthcare for several years and has been continuously making improvements and extending the model to the entire state:

> Kerala has demonstrated that it can provide effective healthcare, maintain low infant and maternal mortality rates and address the needs of the vulnerable population. The state has several initiatives such as a Weekly Iron and Folic acid Supplementation (WIFS) Programme and Adolescent Friendly Health Clinics (AFHCs) for adolescent health. Kerala has also planned ahead the health needs of its senior citizens. The proportion of adults over the age of 60 is expected to double by 2050, and the state is already developing geriatric care wards and geriatric-friendly facilities. The state is also a leader in palliative care with its own Pain and Palliative Care Policy (2008), which focuses on community-based home care initiatives. Kerala's palliative care network contains over 60 units and serves more than 12 million individuals. In addition, the state is investing in health information systems to compile household level data designed to help with population health management and surveillance of communicable diseases.

There are several striking features of the Kerala model. Some examples:

- About 35–40 per cent of the state health budget expenditure is passed on to local governments for their management.
- A three-tier system of village panchayat, block and district level supports the PHCs and CHCs.
- The PHCs and sub-centres were brought under the villages so that there could be better coordination and control.[18]
- Improvements have been found in terms of availability of facilities and service delivery. Most of the institutions are equipped with medicines as per their needs. The overall capacity of public health management professionals and local management staff has improved. Dual control of the healthcare institutions by elected officials and medical personnel has been sorted out.[19,20]

Kerala's healthcare model may not be perfect, but there are several key lessons for the rest of the country.

Experts concur that preventative and curative services are best done at the PHC and CHC level. One of the key features in the Kerala model is the grassroots-level care. At the PHCs and CHCs, for example, all the basic secondary care is provided. High priority is given to quality standards.

An exemplary CHC in Kayyur in Kasargod district has obtained a 99 per cent rating by the National Quality Accreditation Standards. The rating is based on compliance with standards set by the national body, on outpatient facility, lab facilities, patient-friendly systems and infection control.[21] The strength of the healthcare system is how well the patients are treated at the first point of contact with the public health network. All these patients are treated free of charge.

Tamil Nadu also has 40 out of the 424 CHCs that have received similar accreditations. Tamil Nadu has also set up infertility clinics, for which there is a huge demand, many of which at present are managed by the private sector, resulting in expensive treatment protocols. The state has also established a computerised centralised procurement system to lower drug prices.

Healthcare can only be built bottom-up by systematically decentralising and building quality systems at CHC/PHC level in coordination with local authorities. Such a model brings healthcare closer to the people it serves. They respond better to local needs.

Specific model for each state

While the Kerala model need not be the only solution for all the shortcomings of a bureaucratic structure, each state in India should develop suitable ways to decentralise authority to PHCs and to the district level. There needs to be a detailed discussion with the districts on their specific health issues that require urgent attention, for example low levels of immunisation among children, prevalence of high levels of iron-deficiency anaemia among adolescent girls and expectant mothers, infant and maternal mortality, stunting and wasting, and diabetes.

Funding and staff allocation should be aligned with each specific health need, and fund allocation should be based accordingly. The million-strong ASHA workers and an equal number of anganwadi workers should be utilised for follow-up work. They should be equipped with modern hand-held electronic devices, smartphones and other simple medical equipment and provided training on the usage of equipment and data transfer.

Ensuring proper utilisation of all facilities

It is not uncommon to find crates of equipment left unopened for long periods of time. Similarly, many expensive and smaller items are reported to be out of order. Broken dental chairs are not uncommon. Fire accidents due to poor wiring result in loss of lives. Absence of signage is a common problem. All these simple administrative matters should be handled effectively.

Remedial measures for a highly functioning public healthcare system

- A complete revamp of the present system of centralised, bureaucracy-controlled management of healthcare has to be made by replacing it with management by medical professionals and a patient-centric system with specific accountability for results. The immediate first step is to ensure that all positions are filled either by recruitment or by co-opting from the private sector. Minimal improvements by undertaking building repairs, provision of water and electricity round the clock will help the patients and their families.
- Assessment of capital and revenue expenditures for each state should be based on the citizens' health needs. There are huge variations in health outcomes across states and within each state. Innovative fundraising, including public donations and obtaining loans through health bonds, should be considered. Project management has to be monitored with the help of modern management tools.
- Accountability should be defined for each category of staff. Authority should be decentralised along with simplification of all procedures and should be carried out prior to digitisation.

Bureaucracy should be replaced by a health management organisation both at the state as well as at the central government. The concept of public health cadre should be extended to strengthen all sections of the healthcare organisation. The leadership of healthcare should be in the hands of medical professionals with patient care as their main focus. Bureaucracy should play a supporting role and not a leadership role. A separate public health cadre, which is already functioning in seven states, should be implemented in all the states by employing medical doctors with suitable training in administration. Quality accreditation should be obtained for all hospitals and clinics. Quality is a fundamental right of poor patients, not a luxury.

Application of management principles

There is a perception that management theories and practices are only for profit-oriented corporate hospitals. Nothing could be farther from the truth. It is the right of every citizen to expect good service, irrespective of whether the patient is being treated in a government or in a private hospital.

In the other chapters, we have discussed the role of management techniques and concepts that can significantly improve healthcare services. Application of simple techniques such as queuing theory can minimise patients' waiting time. This book details the importance of financial management, social marketing, quality and supplementary services in Part II.

Innovation at workplace

Highly qualified medical and technical staff have to be managed with sensitivity and encouragement. The present system lacks focus on identifying leadership qualities as the staff realise that top positions are reserved for IAS officers. The Confidential Report (CR) system does not focus on the identification of leadership qualities of the staff members. Systematic efforts should be made to develop medical leaders and identify and encourage self-motivated staff. The author has come across outstanding medical professionals and professors in government service, whose skills should be more effectively utilised by encouraging them to innovate in their work.

In recent years, there has been extensive computerisation in government, right down to the PHC level. Authorisation of high-value expenditure within the budgets can be made online by the higher authority as is being done in the private sector. Expenditure can easily be linked with medical outcomes. When the budgets for public health are projected to increase substantially, it is likely that the bureaucracy will grow even bigger. This should be prevented before it becomes a fact.

Future budgets

What would constitute a realistic public health budget for India? Traditionally, health expenditures are measured as a percentage of GDP of the country. While this is a useful statistic, it is a macro figure and should not be the basis of determining the health budget. Budgets should reflect the health needs of the population, size of the population in each state and other requirements for efficient functioning. One potential parameter could be per capita public and private expenditure across states. There is a large amount of data on state-wise per-capita health expenditure (both private and public health) available in the National Health Accounts, highlighting the vast inter-state data and mix of private and public expenditure.

Currently, state health budgeting is based on the state's budget and on the state's GDP. Health expenditure at present is based on the number of functioning health centres and hospitals, staffing, prevailing salary scales, cost of medicines and other operational expenses. Thus, budgets are not linked to the health and major medical needs. It is imperative to align health expenditure with specific health objectives. On this basis, it can be seen that the state of Kerala spends close to INR 10,000 per capita (inclusive of private and public health expenditure). Even if we conservatively take only half of the total Kerala's health expenditure on a national scale, the fund requirement can be arrived at. Thus, a careful study should be undertaken on funding required for revenue and capital expenditure.

Outcome-based budgets

Health budget should result in measurable and vastly improved medical and health outcomes. In other words, major illnesses should be addressed by health expenditure and the root cause must be eradicated or reduced over a defined period. At present, budgets are prepared based on heads of expenditures such as salaries, medicines and capital purchases. The focus should shift to budgeting for minimal acceptable health outcomes.

Budgets should focus on reducing mortality and morbidity to acceptable levels in a defined time frame with defined accountability. For example, the medical needs of mothers and children. The incidence of IMR, MMR and under-five mortality is at unacceptable levels in many parts of India. State governments focus only on the reduction of ratios but should also take into account the number of infants who die at childbirth. Loss of every life – rich or poor – is a tragedy. Based on recent years' data (2020), about 700,000 infants die at the time of birth, and another 25,000 mothers die during childbirth. Pregnancy and childbirth are the major causes of death for girls in the age group of 15–19 years in India.[22]

IMR and MMR are caused by both short-term factors as well as long-term causes. It is essential that expert groups discuss specific actions and budgets required to address each major health problem. Both communicable diseases and NCDs such as diabetes, cancers and respiratory illnesses should be budgeted based on specific district needs, as the long-term complications necessitate prompt diagnosis. There should be specific expertise for initial diagnosis, treatment, follow-up and rehabilitation.

Budgets based on operational and quality metrics

Future budgeting needs close involvement of both medical and administrative wings. There are a large number of medical and financial metrics that are available in various public and private hospitals and in the public domain. These metrics should be used for building a budget. National health standards prescribe extensive metrics even at the department level in a hospital.

About two-thirds of the expenditure is incurred by the states. Many states would not be able to allocate a larger health budget from their own revenues. The Government of India has to subsidise the shortfall based on an assessment of the effectiveness of the additional allocation. States which are performing well on the health front should be rewarded. Wherever required, international funding and floating of health bonds may be sought. There should be independent measurement of health outcomes for future funding assistance.

Reinvigorating the public healthcare system

Any sudden increase in public health expenditure on health and medical education is not advisable. The present system is not capable of handling any sudden or large increase in capital or revenue expenditure. The focus should not be on creating more hospitals but on strengthening and improving the functioning of the existing hospitals. Existing medical colleges themselves are not able to fill many faculty vacancies, so creating new medical colleges would not help. The shortages of specialists as well as graduate doctors should be addressed by relaxing the present norms for creating more seats and collaborating with private hospitals. The Medical Council of India and the National Board should work together. The Government of India has also suggested a collaboration between Ayurvedic and allopathic systems.

If all the existing government beds (about 70,000 beds)[23] at various levels are well staffed and adequately funded, then we may not need any immediate increases in beds, except in specific districts.

The pedagogical advancements in teaching and the use of technology should be fully leveraged. Retirement age for all medical/faculty positions may be increased. We understand that the Medical Council of India itself is considering increasing the age limit for doctors.

Doctors working in other private hospitals should be allowed to teach and practice at government medical colleges as visiting doctors and visiting faculty. It is relevant to point out that the High-Level Expert Group (HLEG) had recommended a short-term programme of three years for medical practitioners. A cadre of Nurse Practitioners should be introduced with greater empowerment and professional responsibilities, which is a common practice in many developed countries. This will help in mitigating the acute shortage of doctors.

There should be a systematic planning of health infrastructure in consultation with key stakeholders, spread over a 10- to 15-year time frame, year by year. Responsibility for timely completion should be determined.

Grassroots reforms (Figure 15.3)

Reforms should commence from 'bottom-up' – from PHC upwards. Simple repetitive activities, for example, washing clothes, housekeeping and kitchen, should be outsourced to other government agencies. The focus of the staff should thus be on patient medical care.

All existing systems should be reviewed by organisation and methods (O&M) studies, followed by eliminating outdated procedures. At present, all PHC data are already computerised for data gathering purposes. However, patient-oriented systems at the PHC are manual. Manual systems

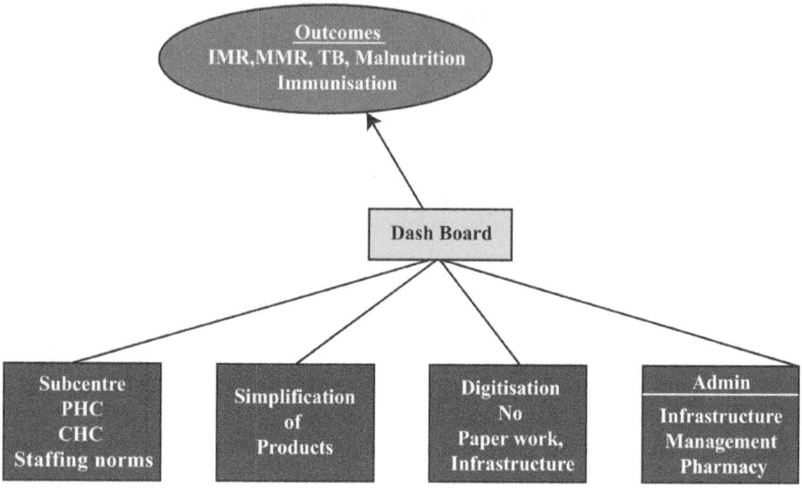

Figure 15.3 Public health grassroots reforms.

are inefficient and do not provide for referral in complex cases, for example high-risk pregnancy. All manual systems should be replaced by online systems with adequate training for all staff. Operating theatre scheduling, case sheets, pharmacy, staff attendance, asset registers and routine accounting should be computerised. There should be clear accountability for results for all staff – medical and administrative. All human resource systems should be revamped. Performance of each centre would be based on health outcomes, which will be posted on the government website every month.

Decentralisation

India has already overtaken China to become the most populous nation in the world. Uttar Pradesh alone has a population of more than 240 million. Many states like Bihar and Maharashtra also have large populations, particularly in rural areas. It is difficult to manage a large population and large territories centrally.

India has 766 districts. Among the larger states, the number of districts ranges from 10 districts per state going up to 75 districts in Uttar Pradesh. Health care is delivered to millions of citizens on a daily basis from thousands of hospitals and health centres. As discussed earlier, in a service-oriented sector, there is a need for prompt local response to local emergencies. Hence, there is a need for a decentralised approach to health delivery. Kerala, a small state, has shown the right example by approaching health delivery through panchayats and local health centres.

Public–private partnerships (PPP)

The health challenges of a state cannot be met by governments alone. They need to take assistance from public service-minded non-governmental organisations (NGOs), non-profit hospitals, citizens, volunteers, corporates and trusts. These collaborative efforts should be planned and coordinated at the district level. The author has come across many charitable hospitals, which take help from volunteers and retired employees who wish to help. Single-specialty hospitals such as Sankara Nethralaya and Arvind Eye Hospitals extensively make use of NGOs and volunteers. Some NGOs, for example, Ekam, help government hospitals in crowd management, training of nurses and in medical equipment maintenance. Seven Hills Hospitals in Mumbai works with the local government through a PPP arrangement by providing some free care. Hospitals in the North-East work with charities and NGOs. Ramakrishna Mission works with governments as well as on its own. Some citizen groups work with schools for the visually handicapped and differently abled individuals. These efforts should be multiplied by involving a large number of citizens and should be coordinated so that there's no overlap in the efforts of those who wish to assist.

The concept of PPP has been in vogue for many years. However, it has had a limited currency in healthcare so far. The challenges of providing healthcare to 1.4 billion Indians have to be shared by all the health systems and citizens in different ways. There is a wide chasm between what is needed by the community and the present collaborative efforts. Public hospitals are vigorously guarding their turf and the private sector is not sufficiently motivated to participate more fully in this process. This logjam needs to be broken.

There are areas where both public and private sectors can work together (Figure 15.4). Some examples are the following. Qualified doctors from private hospitals as well as retired medical professionals can be utilised as visiting faculty in government medical colleges. Medical equipment can be

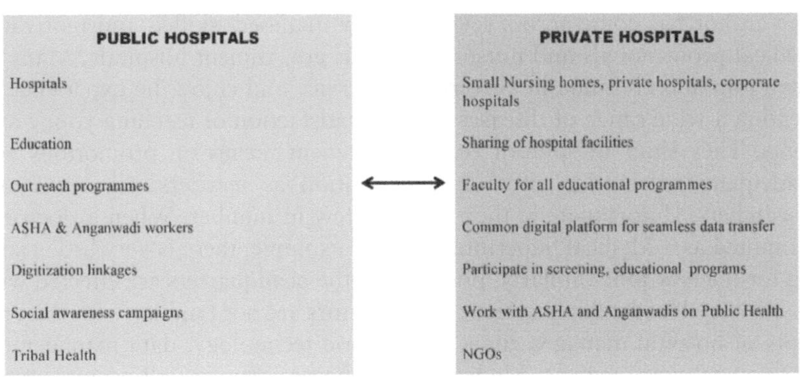

Figure 15.4 Public health–private health collaboration.

shared. Private sector may participate in screening programmes, in public education, as well as work with ASHA workers and anganwadi workers. The proposed digitisation of public hospitals should include small nursing homes and corporate hospitals so that patient data can move seamlessly between government and private hospitals, particularly during emergencies.

Effective utilisation of government insurance schemes

The Government of India and many state governments offer free medical insurance. The Comptroller and Audit General of India (CAG) has pointed out several shortfalls[24] in the implementation of the Ayushman Bharat scheme. The main goal of the scheme is to provide an option to the citizens to avail of medical care at a private hospital of their choice. This is a commendable idea. However, it has been observed that various insurance schemes benefit mainly the private hospitals[25] because of the preference of the patients. Poor service quality at the government hospitals and health centres is the main reason. In principle, poor citizens should not be denied treatment at well-known private hospitals and hence insurance cover is a welcome initiative. It should also be noted that many large corporate hospitals do not offer such governmental insurance schemes in their hospitals because the reimbursement from such schemes is not attractive. Besides, claims are not settled in time by the government.

The Government and the corporate sector should work together to address such issues and arrive at an acceptable solution. The medium-sized private hospitals and some large hospitals benefit from government insurance schemes. The scheme implementation should be improved based on various studies. We would suggest that the funds earmarked for such insurance schemes may at least partially be used to strengthen the public health systems.

Leadership development

The author has come across several highly qualified, skilled and motivated medical professionals and nurses in various government hospitals. Many of them join and continue in Government service and enjoy the experience of treating a wide range of diseases and the satisfaction of teaching young students. They shine in spite of rigid government norms on promotions and inadequate recognition of their contribution as teachers, clinicians and researchers. Unfortunately, they are very few in number. When a doctor is promoted as a Medical Superintendent for example, there is very little training for the new job. Similarly, positions in the headquarters are effected with no advanced leadership training. Most doctors are not familiar with the concepts of hospital management – information technology, data management or financial management. Medical staff who are trained will perform more effectively. Promotions in government are based largely on seniority, and such time-based promotions don't seem to affect motivated professionals.

The appraisal systems are based on Confidential Reports (CR), which are a relic of the old colonial system. Promotions to higher positions require a broader span of responsibilities involving completely different skill sets. It is seen that the senior medical officers are required to be responsible for administrative duties with no training in management. Very few officers are trained before they are promoted to higher jobs. It is also important to select the 'right' leaders, rather than only based on seniority.

Universal healthcare (UHC)

UHC is practised in some form in 72 countries in the world (see Figure 15.5). UHC has been recommended by many experts as the appropriate solution for India. UHC is the provision of free healthcare for all citizens in government and private hospitals. The Government of India and the states will be required to fund the total expenditure from their tax revenues. Normally, UHC refers to medical care at hospitals. Other expenditures on long-term health would continue to be funded by the state and the central governments.

It would be useful to evaluate whether a full-fledged UHC is preferable to the present arrangement of public health plus state-funded insurance schemes. In countries where UHC is operational, public health systems are reasonably strong, well funded by the state and have effective systems of quality accreditations, long-term planning and modern information technology support. The Indian healthcare situation is different.

At present, public health facilities offer free healthcare and in addition, government-funded insurance schemes provide the choice of treatment in government or private hospitals. Many developed countries such as Japan, UK, Canada and many parts of Europe have successfully implemented UHC for many decades. These countries spend 8–10 per cent of their GDP on

Recommended for India by HLEG*	UK - National Health Service (NHS)
• Comprehensive preventive, curative, promotive & rehabilitative health care for all citizens free for charge • Increase health exp. to 3% of GDP, option to choose private or Govt. hospital • Increase taxation. • Integrate insurance scheme with UHC. • Essential drugs free of cost • Govt. rejected the idea as too radical. • No progress on UHC.	• UHC in vogue for 75 years • Strong public health supplemented by private hospitals through private insurance • All citizens covered. First resort. • Funded by Govt 10% of GDP. • Taxation rather than insurance • 180 quality standards for hospitals with monitoring authority & disciplinary action. • Detailed metrics for outcome. • Public Health - Main recourse to all citizens.
* High level Expert Group of Planning Commission (2010)	UHC in some form in 72 countries in the world.

Figure 15.5 Universal healthcare (UHC).

healthcare, funded from general taxes. The UHC is built of a strong foundation of a well-run public health system.

Dr Srinath Reddy points out in his book *Make Health in India*[26] that UHC was extensively discussed by a High-Level Expert Group (HLEG), appointed by the Planning Commission of India, in October 2010. The HLEG had recommended that a universal healthcare system should be introduced in India.[27] The HLEG made many recommendations including the increase of public health expenditure to 3 per cent of GDP by the year 2022, a mandatory deduction (something like health surcharge) from salaried employees, increase in primary health expenditure to at least 70 per cent of total expenditure and doubling the number of ASHA workers. There are many good recommendations that are worthy of implementation. The main proposal of UHC was not accepted by the Ministry of Health, which viewed it as too radical. Possibly, the recommendations of the UHC may be brought up again in the future.

It can be argued that UHC is not a viable idea at the present juncture for different reasons. In economically developed countries, for example, UK, many European countries and Canada, there has been a tradition of a strong public health system providing comprehensive care, supported by adequate funding. Private hospitals are very few in number in these countries. For example, UK citizens are required to have private insurance if they are to use the private hospitals. India's neighbour Sri Lanka (population of 23 million) has an excellent network of government hospitals and very low infant and maternal mortality among other achievements.[28]

The public health system in India is weak; hence, the introduction of UHC at the present moment is not suitable. Under the proposed UHC, private sector will benefit further and, over a period of time, and the public health system may disappear altogether. There is also a proposal for restricting public health's role to regulation rather than operating hospitals. This will ensure that the healthcare system will be dominated by the private sector in the future.

The health insurance schemes of the Government of India and various state governments already offer the option of private hospitals. We believe that instead of further expanding health insurance schemes, governments should spend some part of such funds for strengthening the public health system. According to a study by the *Indian Express*,[29] in many states up to two-thirds of the expenditure is at private hospitals. The main reason for choosing private hospitals is the poor functioning of many public hospitals. It would therefore appear that the first step should be to strengthen public system, ensure it is performing on a level-playing field and then evaluate the options of UHC.

Conclusions

An efficient public health system is central to overall healthcare, particularly for the underprivileged and middle-income families. The public health system with its responsibility for promoting good health through various interventional programmes involves significant financial outlays. There is a need for strengthening this effort, ensuring that the outcomes justify the expenditure.

While government hospitals and health centres have reasonable facilities, they are poorly maintained and bureaucracy hinders effective utilisation of even existing facilities. There is a constant need to modernise medical equipment for treatment and for teaching purposes. The present centralised public health system needs fundamental reforms. There should be decentralisation, and the grassroots level centres should be empowered.

The healthcare departments at the central and state government levels should be headed by a medical professional with strong administrative capabilities. Bureaucrats should be in charge of administration only. Before they are posted to the health department, these administrators should have spent at least ten years in health departments and preferably have health management qualifications.

Accountability for results should be the future paradigm. A public health cadre setup is functional in some states. This should be extended to all states in India as well as at the government of India level.

Notes

1 T. Sundararaman and Daksha Parmar, 'Professionalising public health management', https://www.india-seminar.com/2019/714/714_t_sundararaman_daksha.htm
2 *Booklet for Public Health Management Cadre: Guidance for Implementation 2022*, Ministry of Health and Family Welfare, Government of India, https://nhsrcindia.org/sites/default/files/2022-04/Public%20Health%20Management%20Cadre%20Booklet.pdf
3 'Chennai had highest number of users of 108 ambulance network in 2023', *The Hindu*, 10 January 2024, https://www.thehindu.com/news/cities/chennai/chennai-had-highest-number-of-users-of-108-ambulance-network-last-year/article67724029.ece
4 Rajiv Gandhi Government General Hospital, Chennai, https://en.wikipedia.org/wiki/Rajiv_Gandhi_Government_General_Hospital
5 Shweta Kulshreshtha, '12 government hospitals in Kerala', Clinicspots, https://www.clinicspots.com/blog/government-hospitals-in-kerala
6 '80% shortfall of specialist doctors in CHCs: Health Ministry report', *The Hindu*, 13 January 2023, https://www.thehindu.com/news/national/80-shortfall-of-specialist-doctors-in-chcs-health-ministry-report/article66370205.ece
7 'India's doctors protest against allowing ayurvedic surgeons to perform 58 procedures', *BMJ* 2020;371:m4840, doi: 10.1136/bmj.m4840.
8 National Health Estimates, published in 2018, Ministry of Health and Family Welfare, Government of India, https://www.mohfw.gov.in/sites/default/files/NHA%202021-22_up.pdf

9 'Max Weber theory of bureaucratic management', Harappa Blogs, 23 December 2021, https://harappa.education/harappa-diaries/max-weber-theory-of-bureaucracy-2/
10 AIIMS hospitals in various states and proposed projects, https://www.mapsofindia.com/my-india/government/list-of-all-india-institutes-of-medical-sciences
11 'Health care: Kerala retains top spot, UP at the bottom among large states', *Financial Express*, 28 December 2021, https://www.financialexpress.com/lifestyle/health/health-care-kerala-retains-top-spotup-at-bottom-among-large-states/2391474/
12 List of districts in India, 16 September 2023, https://en.wikipedia.org/wiki/List_of_districts_in_India
13 District wise population, https://en.wikipedia.org/wiki/List_of_districts_in_India
14 PRS legislative research, Kerala budget analysis 2021–22, 7 June 2021, https://prsindia.org/budgets/states/kerala-budget-analysis-2021-22-113
15 PRS Legislative Research, Tamil Nadu budget analysis 2021–2022, 21 August 2022, https://prsindia.org/budgets/states/tamil-nadu-budget-analysis-2021-22
16 PRS legislative Research Uttar Pradesh budget 2021–22, 26 February 2021. https://prsindia.org/budgets/states/uttar-pradesh-budget-analysis-2021-22
17 V. Raman Kutty, 'Rethinking the Kerala "model" in health', https://www.india-seminar.com/2012/637/637_v_raman_kutty.htm
18 D. Lakshmi Narayana and K.K. Hari Kurup, 'Decentralisation of healthcare in Kerala: Some issues', February 2000 (IDEAS/RePEc search), https://www.researchgate.net/publication/5127034_Decentralisation_of_the_Health_Care_Sector_in_Kerala_Some_Issues
19 Jos Chathukulam, 'Reflection on decentralised healthcare systems in Kerala', *Mainstream Weekly*, 30 January 2016, http://www.mainstreamweekly.net/article6189.html
20 V. Raman Kutty, Rekha Raveendran, and Biju Soman, 'Health systems transformation plan, decentralisation and local decision making in health – The Kerala experience, health action by people', 26 February 2023, https://twitter.com/HSTPIndia/status/1630138167016783874
21 'Kayyur PHC selected as the best in the country by national health mission', *News Experts*, 20 June 2019, https://www.newsexperts.in/kayyur-phc-selected-best-country-national-health-mission/
22 'Maternal health: UNICEF's concerted action to increase access to quality maternal health services', https://www.unicef.org/india/what-we-do/maternal-health#:~:text=This%20translates%20to%208%2C580%20additional,and%2019%20years%20of%20age
23 K. Srinath Reddy, *Make Health in India: Reaching a Billion Plus*, Orient Blackswan, 2019.
24 Audit Reports – Comptroller and Auditor-General, 2023, https://cag.gov.in/en/audit-report/details/119060
25 'Ayushman Bharat scheme favours private hospitals', *Editorial, drishtiias.com*, https://www.drishtiias.com/daily-news-editorials/ayushman-bharat-and-the-role%20-of-private-hospitals
26 K. Srinath Reddy, *Make Health in India: Reaching a Billion Plus*, Orient Blackswan, 2019.
27 High Level Group Expert Group – UHC, https://nhm.gov.in/images/pdf/publication/Planning_Commission/rep_uhc0812.pdf
28 Ramya Kumar, 'Public–private partnerships for universal health coverage? The future of "free health" in Sri Lanka', Globalization and Health, 28 November 2019, https://globalisationandhealth.biomedcentral.com/articles/10.1186/s12992-019-0522-6

29 M. Kaunain Sheriff, 'Over half of Ayushman Bharat beneficiaries used scheme to access private care; 53% patients in five southern states', *Indian Express*, 10 March 2024, https://indianexpress.com/article/express-exclusive/over-half-of-ayushman-beneficiaries-used-scheme-to-access-private-care-53-patients-in-five-southern-states-9203944/lite/

16 Future trends in Indian healthcare

Tilak Shankar

Introduction

India is already the most populous nation (1.4 billion people) in the world, overtaking China, and the population is projected to grow further to 1.66 billion by the year 2050.[1] Moreover, the socioeconomic status of people remains in various strata, defined by a large gap between the rich and the poor. A critical assessment of the healthcare systems is needed so that the healthcare needs of all the segments of the population are met. Providing accessible healthcare to the needy sections of the society is the government's responsibility as healthcare is a fundamental right according to the Constitution. Roughly, two-thirds of the population is dependent on the government for their healthcare needs. Only one-third of the population can afford private healthcare. The concerning situation is that the public health system is threatened by the stupendous growth of the private healthcare sector. Its long-term consequences are dire, and there is an urgent need to keep the public healthcare system vibrant.

The role of the government at present consists of delivering preventive healthcare programmes, addressing the long-term basic health needs of the underprivileged, and providing them with medical care. Continuing this system is essential to ensuring accessible healthcare for almost two-thirds of the population.

Seven major trends in Indian healthcare

In the next few decades, while there are likely to be multiple healthcare developments – demographic, epidemiological, medical and technological that would have an impact on healthcare – the focus of this chapter is on the following seven trends in Indian healthcare:

1. Private (for-profit) medical care hospitals would grow and continue to dominate tertiary care and may enter secondary care as well.
2. Medical technology, information technology, medical research, new medicines and nutrition would play an important role in healthcare as well.

DOI: 10.4324/9781003684947-20

3. Health insurance companies will grow and exercise greater control over private hospitals. Insurance premiums will go up sharply.
4. Some unethical practices in the private sector, motivated by reasons other than patient care, are already a cause of concern and seem likely to become prevalent in the future, and the healthcare practices, driven by higher profits, might result in increased costs to the patients.
5. Inequities in healthcare, widely prevalent at present, are likely to rise further.
6. Public healthcare system is likely to decline further.
7. The healthcare ecosystem is poised to become larger, encompassing stand-alone laboratories, imaging centres, medical software and retail pharmacies, and start-ups are likely to play even a larger role in the delivery of healthcare services.

A brief discussion on each of these trends and its implications for individual hospitals as well as for the healthcare system as a whole is taken up first.

1. *Private medical care*

Private (for-profit) healthcare sector in India is marching towards a (near) total dominance of medical care. Corporate hospitals and other private hospitals have become exclusive providers of tertiary care to higher-income groups and the middle class that can afford the cost of care. These hospitals are located in large cities, and it has become common for a large number of people from other parts of the country to travel to large cities for medical care. Only certain sections of the society (i.e., people who can afford the high cost of care) have benefitted from high-quality medical treatment provided by highly qualified and experienced specialists with very little waiting time. Waiting times for the commencement of treatment is an important consideration. For example, in UK, which has a National Health System (NHS), the diagnosis of cancer, for example, could take up to 28 days and commencement of treatment for cancer could take up to 62 days after diagnosis.[2]

In Indian hospitals, particularly in private hospitals, waiting time is very low. It is also easy to get appointments with senior doctors. Cardiology is one of the most important centres of excellence in all private hospitals. Many hospitals create multiple units in cardiology to cater to patients. For example, Apollo Hospitals, located at Greams Road in Chennai, has 18–20 senior cardiologists, 46 ICU beds and 15 operating rooms.[3] This enables patients to get quick appointments. Many hospitals have international and national quality accreditations and publish their treatment outcomes. Private hospitals offering high-quality medical care have been established in multiple cities in the last few years, taking it within the reach of a large middle-class population.

At a macro level, large investments in tertiary and quaternary care have had a cascading effect of reduced investments in the much-needed public healthcare, especially in primary and secondary care hospitals, predominantly run by the government. Laboratories, imaging centres and retail pharmacies are enlarging their footprint. Using the latest available technology, retail pharmacies attract patients by offering physician consultations online, providing substantial discounts and also offering home delivery of medicines. Tests can be ordered from home and the results delivered by email or phone (through WhatsApp). These ancillary healthcare institutions have also played a significant role in creating awareness about preventive healthcare.

Corporatisation of hospitals is likely to increase substantially in the coming decades. There are fears that under the public–private partnership (PPP), the private sector might effectively take over secondary care from the government. It is believed that governments might restrict their role to just regulating the healthcare sector rather than directly providing medical care at hospitals and health centres. A former health secretary to the Government of India, Dr. K. Sujatha Rao, has warned against the government's declining role in public healthcare, as it would deny the poor access to affordable healthcare.[4,5] Though she articulated this fear in the context of Andhra Pradesh, it holds good for the entire country.

Profitability of private hospitals

Just to stress the direction in which private healthcare is headed, a sample study of 12 large hospitals – multi-specialty and single-specialty hospitals for the financial year 2023–24 – highlights the fact that private hospitals are highly profitable. Private hospitals in India generate an operating profit margin or earnings before interest depreciation and amortisation (EBIDTA) of 20 per cent on revenues and some up to 33 per cent on revenues (Table 16.1). As discussed in the earlier chapters, the value of companies (market cap) of some companies went up five times in as many years and one hospital by five times in just three years. Such financial performance is highly unusual.[6] It is relevant to point out that in the fast-moving consumer goods (FMCG) companies, one of the profitable sectors of the Indian economy, the market capitalisation went up 1.5 times in a similar period.

The high operating margin in hospitals is a result of various measures:

- High degree of operational efficiency, service mix and quick turnover of patients (early discharges).
- High profits partly due to large margins from sale of medicines and consumables and other measures.
- Huge demand from many sections for quality tertiary services in spite of patients being aware of expensive treatment costs. Hospitals periodically raise the costs despite them being high already.

Hence, tertiary care offered by private hospitals is restricted only to affluent people and those with health insurance (available at a high annual premium).

Table 16.1 EBITDA of 12 large hospitals

Name of the hospital	*Amount (INR crore)*		*EBITDA as a % of revenue*
	Revenue	*EBITDA*	
Apollo Hospitals Enterprise Ltd (AHEL)	19,059	2,497	13
Max Healthcare Institute Ltd (MHIL)	5,406	1,670	31
Fortis Healthcare Ltd (FHL)	6,893	1,306	19
Narayana Hrudayalaya Ltd (NHL)	5,018	1,228	24
Global Health Ltd (Medanta (GHL))	3,275	874	27
Krishna Institute of Medical Sciences Ltd (KIMS)	2,498	653	26
Aster-DM Healthcare Ltd	3,699	591	16
Rainbow Children's Medicare Ltd	1,297	429	33
Kovai Medical Centre and Hospital Ltd	1,020	363	36
HealthCare Global Enterprises Ltd (HGEL)	1,908	347	18
Jupiter Lifeline Hospitals Ltd	1,060	264	25
Artemis Medicare Services Ltd	879	140	16
Average EBITDA% (Total EBITDA/Total revenue)	**52,011**	**10,361**	20

Hospitals are also making large profits on drugs, consumables and diagnostics according to a study.[7] It is also well known that hospitals purchase large quantities of various medicines at a substantial discount. These discounts are not passed on to the patient. The present situation is such that affordable charges to patients and high profits by hospitals cannot coexist. The boards of hospitals can determine a 'more reasonable' profit margin and should discontinue the present questionable practices. The boards should also establish an ethics committee to identify every undesirable practice that should be discontinued, monitor ethical practices continuously and make it a part of their annual report.[8]

2. *Technological advancements*

Rapid technological advancements are sweeping the healthcare sector, and both public and private hospitals will also be influenced by these changes. Apart from offering tertiary healthcare, large private hospitals are offering preventive healthcare, enabled by technology (e.g., AI) as well as a favourable ecosystem made up of imaging centres and testing laboratories. The public primary and secondary healthcare system falls woefully behind in acquiring the latest equipment for testing and diagnosis. In the future, not-for-profit and many private hospitals' survival, growth and indeed relevance would depend on the ability to differentiate themselves from the more affluent private hospitals. The Government of India has announced a national digital mission for all government hospitals (2020).[9] The main objective of this mission is to eliminate paperwork (including case sheets) and facilitate data transfer across locations for effective medical intervention (e.g. in pregnancy). Teaching and research activities are also expected to be benefitted from digitisation of all data.

Medical equipment hardware, robotics, AI and advanced software, cloud data storage, mobile telephony and drones have already revolutionised healthcare. Modernisation of medical technology on a regular basis would be essential for all the hospitals. Information technology (IT) has made online data for medical care, teaching and research easily accessible to experts. Data analytics has made it possible to make sense of a humongous amount of data, thereby enabling effective management. 'Medical treatment is moving from disease treatment to disease prevention, diagnosis more precise, portable and more intelligent'.[10]

Each hospital should invest in biomedical technologists and IT experts to guide the management. Eric Topol in his book, *The Patient Will See You Now: The Future of Medicine Is in Your Hands* (Basic Books, 2015), has visualised that the patient will become more powerful. In the Indian context, there are signs that the patient is more aware of their rights, well-informed and will choose the hospital and doctor of their choice.[11]

There are many other developments. Considerable research on micronutrition (iron, folic acid and zinc) for the underprivileged sections who are deficient in micronutrients is being undertaken. Fortification of a wide range of foods, rice and wheat, low-cost food alternatives, common salt, use of millets, tea, pickles and nutraceuticals are also being given attention.[12]

3. *Health insurance and its influence over private hospitals*

Health insurance was relatively unknown till 2000, restricted largely to the public sector. Health insurance started in India with the employee's state insurance scheme (ESIS) in 1948. Government employees were covered by the Central Government Health Scheme from the 1950s. General Insurance Corporation of India (GIC), a state insurance firm, was the first to offer a standardised health insurance policy, called Medi-Claim policy, in 1986. The Insurance Regulatory and Development Authority of India (IRDAI) was formed by the Government of India in 1999, and in 2000, the insurance sector was opened to private companies, allowing for 26 per cent foreign direct investment (FDI). Star Health became the first exclusive healthcare insurance company to be formed in 2006. Today, there are seven exclusive health insurers in the country[13] and more than 30 companies in total offering health insurance. The increased cost of care led to a huge uptake of insurance by people, primarily to manage the hospitalisation costs in private hospitals. The health insurance premium crossed INR 1,00,000 crore in early 2025, growing at a rate of 10 per cent from the previous year.[14] Thus, health insurance companies have begun to play an active role in funding medical treatment in private hospitals. Government and private insurance companies have expanded their coverage over the years. The health insurance market in India is projected to reach INR 2 trillion by 2028.[15] Now insurance companies or third-party administrators (TPAs) are scrutinising hospital costs and negotiating package charges with hospitals. The insurance industry is exercising greater influence over private hospitals since they are armed with vast data (granular) based on insurance claims. Some hospitals have also ventured into the health insurance business. It is possible that insurance companies might acquire or start new hospitals. Government insurance schemes may also further encourage some sections of private sector hospitals to grow faster. Health insurance is becoming costlier driven by medical inflation, as health insurance companies have been promptly increasing premiums to adjust for higher claims. As FDI is allowed, many health insurance companies operate as a joint venture between an Indian company and a foreign partner, which is in most cases an insurance company operating in foreign countries. The health insurance companies have also raised funds from stock markets. As a result, health insurance companies, like private hospitals, are increasingly becoming profit-driven. With both hospitals and insurance companies focusing on profits, it is only going to drive the cost of medical care in India further north.

4. *Ethics of care: Focus on profitability and questionable practices*

While increases in hospital costs have been keeping millions of patients out of the tertiary system and putting a strain on the middle class, there are widespread concerns about the questionable practices of many private sector hospitals. The infusion of PE funds pressures hospitals to aim for super profits or profits beyond reasonable levels. Even though there have been instances of PE funds acquiring a majority stake in hospitals, taking the hospital administration firmly under their control. PE funds also drive mergers and acquisitions, creating large hospital chains. For listed hospitals, there is a need to continuously deliver shareholder value and increase in share prices. Hence, there is immense pressure on hospital management to ensure high levels of profits.

Dividends on par value of shares are no longer attractive. Hence share price increase has become the focus of investors. It is alleged that these pressures lead to many undesirable practices being followed. Profits are partly linked to questionable practices.

Even individual practitioners resort to certain highly deplorable practices such as earning incomes from 'referrals and commissions'. It's alleged that hospitals pay individual doctors for referring patients for further treatment at specified hospitals. Doctors are paid varying commissions depending on the revenues generated by each referral to the hospital.[16] It is also reported that individual practitioners are being paid 'referral' charges for prescribing tests at a specified laboratory and ordering tests from imaging centres.[17] It is alleged that in the case of kidney transplants for example, there is a system of commissions to the referring doctors.[18] The Indian Medical Association (IMA) clearly prohibits kickbacks and referral charges, as the IMA code of conduct items 14 and 15 specifically denounce gifts, gratification and pecuniary benefits from pharma companies, equipment suppliers and diagnostic centres.[19] To discourage such untoward practices, necessary controls and effective and prompt punitive action are required. In 2017, the Government of Maharashtra finalised a draft Prevention of Cut Practice in Healthcare Services Act to deter kickbacks in the medical ecosystem as a whole.[20] But it was quietly buried as there were apprehensions about its implementation and protests by the medical community as the Act proposed harsh punishments.

There are other reports about hospitals levying high charges for hospital consumables, retaining substantial discounts offered by pharmaceutical companies for volume purchases, resorting to 'surge pricing' (prices increasing on demand) and additional charges for certain procedures and use of operating rooms.[21] Many undesirable practices are also well documented. The Competition Commission of India (CCI) had carried out an enquiry into corporate hospital practices. The final report of the Commission is awaited.

5. *Inequities in healthcare*

Inequities and imbalances have grown over the years in India's healthcare system. There is a palpable rural versus urban divide. Tertiary care offered through private hospitals has grown multifold, whereas primary and secondary healthcare offered by the government has not kept pace.[22] South India scores over North India in healthcare delivery. On a large number of health parameters – infant mortality, maternal mortality, under-five mortality, percentage of institutional delivery, per capita health expenditure – there are sharp differences between South Indian and North Indian states, with the South performing better.[23]

The long-term preventive health needs of the underprivileged have not been receiving enough attention, resulting in stunting and wasting, malnutrition, iron-deficiency anaemia in adolescents and expectant mothers and low child and adult immunisation. Millions of people are being treated at government hospitals and health centres every day. There is poor attention to the quality of patient care at government hospitals and health centres. A weakened public health system will further aggravate the suffering of the poor. There is a strong need for interventions on multiple fronts from both the central and state governments towards targeted nutrition supplementation. There is a growing threat of non-communicable diseases (NCDs), which requires screening early intervention. Morbidity and mortality from NCDs pose a growing threat.[24]

6. *Decline in public healthcare*

The decline in public healthcare in most states of India is obvious. In this respect, some of the southern states have performed relatively better, evident in health outcomes in these states, as Nilakantan reveals in his book, *South vs North: India's Great Divide*. There is greater decentralisation and many operational improvements are being regularly implemented in states like Tamil Nadu and Kerala, which rank high in health indicators. In the rest of the country, shortages of doctors and specialists, poor maintenance of medical equipment, inadequate infrastructure and lack of sensitivity towards patient care have been silently accepted by millions. Low funding, delays in the execution of new projects and too much centralisation have impeded medical care in nearly 200,000 health centres.[25]

There seems to be an alternate view that governments should only regulate and not manage hospitals. If it happens, it will further weaken the role of the government in ensuring healthcare access to the deprived sections of society. The fact that some of the states are performing relatively well reaffirms the belief that public health system can deliver stellar medical outcomes.

Universal healthcare (UHC)

WHO defines universal healthcare as 'access to full range of quality health services'.[26] More than 70 countries in the world have some form of universal healthcare, built on a strong public health system. For example, the National Health System (NHS), the public health service of the government of UK, is highly respected and one of the most successful public health systems in the world. This system provides primary, secondary and tertiary care to the entire British population. A strong public health system is common in most developed and developing countries. The idea of UHC for India has been frequently evaluated by various committees and independent experts. Though UHC was recommended by one of the expert committees, it was considered unsuitable for India by the Ministry of Health and Family Welfare.

7. *Expanding health ecosystem: PE funds and IPO in labs and retail pharmacies*

Laboratories, imaging centres, retail pharmacies, fitness centres and AYUSH centres are also engaged in providing medical services. These are likely to grow. The start-ups in healthcare are large in number – covering areas such as medical software, wearable devices, low-cost diagnostic equipment, mobility devices, early disease detection, home-based care and many others. This represents the robustness of small institutions and innovative enthusiasm of the young techies. It bodes well for the future of Indian healthcare.[27]

The entire ecosystem made up of laboratories, retail pharmacy chains, imaging centres and single-speciality hospitals also has raised large amounts of funds from PE funds and through IPOs. This has enabled all recipients to modernise, grow and diversify. Tata 1mg, a company which is part of one of the largest business conglomerates in the Indian industry, went for an IPO in 2023, acquired multiple retail pharmacies and effectively leverages technology for supplying medicines, providing medical consultations and other services.

In other words, the entire health ecosystem is now dominated by the infusion of funds from private equity and companies that raised funds from the stock market. It is but natural that the primary focus of well-funded hospitals and other institutions is on profits. This has resulted in sharp increases in hospitalisation costs, higher laboratory/imaging charges and increased health insurance premiums. In the case of hospitals, there has been a deliberate shift towards a more profitable case mix generating higher revenues (detailed in the chapter on private equity, Chapter 12). At a macro level, a profit-oriented, efficient organisation is a great advantage both to the investors and the larger society. However, a single-minded focus on profits in healthcare would be unsuitable for the vast majority of the Indian population.

Implications for the future

The present market-driven health system in India has many serious implications. A robust tertiary care, well-funded and competently managed private hospitals, with a focus on patient care, is most certainly required. India will be benefitted immensely from a larger number of quality-accredited hospitals, laboratories and retail pharmacy chains in the organised sector. These developments can help in raising the reliability levels of medical care offered through well-qualified staff by leveraging technology. The huge demand for quality tertiary care has been a long-felt need. This is reflected in the large and growing crowds in many hospitals and the growth of stand-alone labs and retail pharmacy outlets.

If the government decides to move out of managing hospitals, millions of the underprivileged and large sections of the middle class would be severely affected. It is estimated that about 230 million people come under the underprivileged category.[28] There are varying estimates of the middle-class population; one estimate puts the figure at 430 million.[29] There can be further stratification within this overall figure. The upper segments of the middle class can access private hospitals, while the lower segments would depend on charitable hospitals.

Government-funded health insurance schemes

The government believes that state-funded health insurance may be a possible alternative solution for meeting treatment costs. The insurance cover offered by the government, however, meets only a part of the hospital bill. The rest of the hospital bill has to be settled by the patient, which a large number of patients cannot afford to. Many private hospitals do not admit patients under the government's insurance schemes. A further weakened public health system could put several million patients at hardship, and they would be forced to seek private care, pay for doctor consultation and for tests and treatment costs.

Under this scenario, the medical needs of the middle class and the underprivileged progressively would be left to the market forces. Large sections of India's population will be forced to look at other options for their medical needs, or their debt burden will increase. Higher hospitalisation costs could lead to a shift to alternative medicine, and the public could seek the services of quacks in larger numbers. These changes would impact a significant section of the population. It should be pointed out that even the affluent sections would at some stage find the high hospitalisation cost unreasonable.

Building a resilient healthcare system for India

Dominant private system is unsuitable

A dominant private medical care system for secondary and tertiary care would be clearly unsuitable for a large section of the Indian population. A country with a large rural population and a population on subsistence, lacking knowledge about health, needs government's support in the form of a robust public health system. For this reason, the budgetary allocation for public healthcare has to be increased from the current abysmal levels (1.9 per cent of the GDP in 2023–24). Private healthcare system is absolutely necessary for tertiary and quaternary care, and India has already emerged as a popular destination for quality medical care. A combination of a robust private medical card and a slack public health system does not bode well because if the health problems of the population go unattended, then tackling the endemics would pose a huge challenge to the government. Preventive healthcare should be widely practised to prevent non-communicable diseases (NCDs) at the individual level. The government has to play a proactive role in preventive healthcare of the millions that are dependent on the public health system. This apart, the Government of India and the states have to evolve a comprehensive strategy to address respective health challenges faced by the population in each state. Technology at a low cost can be a saviour in most instances. The potential of young entrepreneurs who are eager to start up in the healthcare sector should be recognised and encouraged so that they can be productively employed by the entire healthcare system.

Alternate models

To build a resilient healthcare system, a few models of healthcare may be considered. These models are currently in practice either in India or in some parts of the world.

- Value-based healthcare model.
- Public health model that delivers to the healthcare needs of the population: A stronger, well-funded and well-managed public healthcare system that delivers quality services and outcomes matching the health needs of the population it serves. This model could take inspiration from quite successful ones in Western European countries. Although there is a public health system operating in India at present, urgent reforms are needed to make it robust and efficient.
- Revitalising the non-profit/charitable hospitals through a community participation model: India has a vibrant network of not-for-profit/charitable health institutions that are providing a high quality of care using a different model of revenue generation and services to all sections of the society. This network has to be nurtured and funded through corporate social responsibility mandates and, if needed, suitable legislative action taken for corporates to contribute to non-profitable health institutions.
- Public–private partnership model: In this model, the services of the private sector hospitals are mandated to cater to the healthcare needs of all the citizens, not just a privileged few, and the private hospitals need to work in partnership with the public healthcare institutions in a symbiotic way. Some areas of cooperation could be private hospitals working with government institutions to deliver chilled and adult vaccination programmes and in the screening for diabetes, kidney diseases, tuberculosis, cancer, cataract and other eye ailments. Senior private doctors should participate as faculty in the government-run medical and nursing colleges. There are many other examples which are discussed in other chapters.

Value-based healthcare model

In a value-based healthcare model, payments are made to the provider based on the quality of services rendered. It was introduced as part of the Affordable Care Act in the United States.[30] The performance measurement domains in the US hospital value-based purchasing programme consist of the following four areas: clinical outcomes (25 per cent), safety (25 per cent), person and community engagement (25 per cent) and efficient and cost reduction (25%). The National Health Authority of India has also proposed a comprehensive system of value-based healthcare in which payments are linked to health outcomes and incentives are paid based on the outcomes. It has been suggested that the Government of India's insurance scheme – Pradhan Mantri

Jan Arogya Yogana (PMJAY) – one of the world's largest health insurance schemes, costing about INR 9,500 crore, may bring hospitals under the value-based model.[31]

Value-based healthcare model will be extremely difficult to implement in India. The model calls for patient orientation by the physicians and hospitals and measurement of outcomes, which in turn will offer incentives. India's public health system and 'fee-for-service' models are strongly antagonistic to the proposed model. A lot of preparation is required involving medical experts, medical associations and management experts. It may be desirable to commence with non-profit hospitals in the Indian context.[32]

If the value-based model is implemented in the private sector, the quality of services will become the top priority of the healthcare institutions. Only top-notch private institutions are delivering quality care at present and a culture of quality will percolate to all levels of the healthcare system.

Public healthcare model that delivers to the needs of the population

India's public health system can be strengthened only by undertaking fundamental, bottom-up reforms. A robust public health is a sine qua non for a country like India. Policymakers should imagine alternative solutions to strengthen public health. For example, diabetes is emerging as a major NCD in India. In the UK, the NHS provides insulin pumps for type-1 diabetic patients or continuous glucose monitors (CGM) for other diabetic patients. There is no such provision for poor patients in India. Similarly, with increasing lung problems, government hospitals should provide oxygen concentrators to needy patients.

Funds for public health can be mopped up using sources such as healthcare bonds and international soft loans. Public donations will have to be explored for specific requirements such as equipment, buildings and free food. To generate some income and more importantly to bring about a greater patient orientation, about 10 per cent of the beds may be converted into 'pay wards' to bring about some additional revenue and more importantly improved service levels in medical care. Some states already have started this facility. There should be decentralisation to the primary health centre (PHC) levels and medical and administrative staff should be held accountable for their performance. Most government hospitals have costly imaging equipment for MRI and CT scans. Private hospitals can leverage these facilities by asking patients to go to government facilities for imaging or other services available. Many smaller nursing homes may not have expensive diagnostic medical equipment. The revenues from pay wards, other services and treatment under government insurance schemes may be utilised for repayment of loans. This will bring greater focus on efficiency and accountability at operational levels. There should be a revamp of the staffing structure with the induction of bio-medical engineers and software experts at the district headquarters.

Community participation model

There are hospitals in the United States, such as Mayo Clinic, a highly reputed chain of hospitals, and MassGen, which provide care under the Medicare program. Mayo Clinic is extensively involved in many community initiatives also.

In India too, the community healthcare model is well established by ophthalmic care organisations such as Sankara Nethralaya and Arvind Eye Care, as well as the Cancer Institute. These are provided by not-for-profit institutions that raise funds through donations as well by charging patients (cross-subsidisation) who can afford the cost of care. The services are provided free of cost to poor patients as the income from affluent patients and donations is used to provide healthcare for the community as a whole. The role of non-profit institutions is discussed in the chapter on non-profit hospitals (Chapter 5). Governmental support in the form of CSR mandates to not-for-profit hospitals will go a long way in bolstering community healthcare. The definition of CSR projects should be reviewed in the context of present-day medical needs.

Public–private partnership model: Private hospitals need to work with government hospitals

This public–private partnership model need not be on the lines practised in other areas of the economy such as infrastructure. Private for-profit hospitals should be actively involved in public health. They are part of the Indian society. They should share resources with government hospitals, offer specialists, participate in public screening camps, vaccination programmes, provide faculty support and enlist in the government insurance schemes. Many charitable institutions are already undertaking all these activities. If required, the government may bring necessary legislation to require private hospitals to participate in national healthcare programmes.

Other measures to tone up the healthcare system

These models apart, other measures are needed to revitalise the healthcare system and make it dynamic in response to the problems currently faced.

Regulations

Private healthcare has to be regulated to ensure quality, and suitable regulations have to be in place to also rein in their charges at a certain level. If the private hospitals come together and agree on a range of rates for different services, it will help the patient community to plan their treatment well. As impracticable as it may sound, the government can help regulate the fees charged by hospitals by bringing together private healthcare institutions and persuading them to be transparent in their fee structures.

The state governments and the Centre should implement strong measures to control quacks. A large number of laboratories do not have quality accreditations, which may be corrected through regulation. Spurious and adulterated drugs are freely available.[33] Such drugs are harmful and should be banned, and manufacturers, distributors and retailers should be prosecuted. The focus should be on the effective implementation of the existing laws. If necessary, strong legislation has to be passed that has 'teeth' for eliminating quacks and spurious drugs.

Low-cost funding

Private equity funds can join hands with the Government of India to introduce low-cost long-term funds to government hospitals and charitable hospitals. A large fund base will partly help the modernisation of hospitals. Such a system of external funding will also bring about greater accountability on the part of the management of each hospital. The international funding organisations should also be enlisted for supporting the public healthcare system.

Role of health insurance industry

Health insurance companies cannot be mere observers of the rising hospitalisation costs and cannot sustain through their regular increases in insurance premiums. One of the roles of the insurance industry as a service industry is to increase the number of insured, make insurance more affordable to all sections of the population and influence hospitals by effective control of their charges and publish the rates agreed with various hospitals.

India needs different and multiple solutions

The healthcare needs of multiple Indias (signifying the diversity of the population and its healthcare needs) require different solutions. Our collective healthcare needs are very large, requiring coordinated efforts of both government and the private sector. Collectively, at present India's healthcare system is not delivering quality, timely or affordable care to the millions of underprivileged Indians. While our medical technology has improved, management capabilities have been grossly inadequate. There is considerable management talent in society, which can be tapped by the government and charitable hospitals. Government should create public health boards consisting of lawyers, engineers, bankers and social activists to advise on the efficient management of resources. The availability of doctors, better utilisation of equipment and focus on the patients will bring greater confidence in public health. Even small operational improvements in governmental medical care can challenge private medical care significantly. This is easily doable.

The government should take concrete measures to strengthen the non-profit or charitable healthcare sector. Many specific steps have been recommended by NITI-Ayog[34] such as providing attractive tax benefits to donors, making available low-cost funds and providing grants for capital expenditure. A separate fund should be created for this purpose.

Management challenges

There are different challenges for hospitals depending on whether they are government, charitable (not-for-profit) or for-profit. In the last few decades, rapid changes in the environment have necessitated all institutions to adopt modern approaches to managing the hospitals. It is evident that management techniques are a vital ingredient in delivering affordable, patient-oriented quality care. Some of the private sector companies have demonstrated how modern management can help in achieving their goals.

Information technology would play a key role in communication, data transfer across departments and locations and data analytics for analysing the humongous amount of data and teaching and research.

Forecasting

Government hospitals, large private hospitals and charitable hospitals should study the trends in technological developments that will impact them. Each hospital has to decide on what type of technology is required for its patients and make it affordable. Senior management can no longer be content with handling day-to-day patient care alone. Technology forecasting is essential to study disease patterns, developments in medical technologies, new drugs and information technology. Clinical forecasting is being carried out in different parts of the world to examine trends in diseases such as infectious diseases, cancer, liver and circulatory systems of the human body. Artificial Intelligence is being employed for forecasting disease patterns.[35]

India has a huge database – from hospitals' own databases as well as from various sample studies on the incidence of diseases, research papers and conference presentations. Similarly, developments in medical equipment, medical devices, wearables, drugs and medicines, robotics, internet of medical things (IoMT), AI and nano-medicine are already playing significant roles, and they should be integrated with regular medical practice. IoMT for example is 'providing patients and providers with enhanced access to a patient's healthcare information, IoMT reduces the need for unnecessary doctor's office and hospital visits. IoMT also lowers costs for both patients and providers'.[36,37]

These changes are likely to impact all the hospitals. Modernisation of medical equipment requires appropriate skill development at each hospital. Similarly, changes in teaching methods would be required. Technological changes would demand a higher quantum of capital expenditure. There should be planning for cost-effective funding to meet rapid technological developments. This is particularly true for charitable institutions.

Health informatics trends

Health informatics is emerging as a major differentiator between hospitals.[38] Institutions which are aware of the power of IT can improve patient care and obtain a competitive advantage. IT can be utilised for efficiency improvement as well as for predicting likely trends based on data.[39] There are several developments which can impact health delivery. For example, India has an incredible database and data analytics tools can be employed to make sense of them.

Social marketing

This book has a chapter on marketing of corporate hospitals (Chapter 8). One of the biggest challenges is to create health awareness or social marketing among the one billion-plus citizens. Non-communicative diseases (NCDs) pose a major health challenge. Some of the NCDs are chronic diseases. Early detection of NCDs can minimise or eliminate complications, reduce admissions in hospitals, drastically reduce treatment costs and eliminate the suffering of the patient. NCDs affect the rich and poor alike. Strategies need to be devised for educating the population and providing adequate facilities for testing, provisioning for adult and child vaccination and follow-up. Social marketing by public health is equally, if not more, important. There are a large number of health problems caused by the use of tobacco, poor compliance with child immunisation, diabetes (100 million diagnosed and undiagnosed),[40] cancer (one in nine in their lifetime),[41] preventable blindness, strokes and many other diseases. These conditions require public awareness and periodic preventive check-ups. Simple YouTube videos can help in patient education. FM radio can be effectively leveraged to spread the message. Some charitable hospitals undertake screening camps. Private hospitals should participate in such camps. Corporates should fund such programmes as part of their responsibility. NGOs should be encouraged to be actively involved in all the districts.

Mobile phones, TV and stage plays and posters in local languages can be useful media to reach out to the public.[42] Social media such as Facebook, X (formerly Twitter), Instagram and WhatsApp are also popular, some even in rural areas. A large proportion of the population has smartphones. It is necessary for public health officials to imaginatively employ various media to educate the public. In other words, the focus should be on prevention in addition to treatment.

Financial management

The third major area is financial management. In the case of private hospitals, treatment costs have been rising steadily and there is a need to control costs through operational efficiencies. The chapter on financial management has dealt with major developments impacting large private hospitals. Similarly, there is a need to revamp the entire public health system. Budgeting, effective utilisation of funds and introducing 'pay wards' are required to mop up resources for the public health system.

Conclusion

Indian healthcare system is desperately in need of a change. A balanced system serving different sections of the entire Indian population is essential for ensuring that all citizens have access to quality healthcare at all times. Simple operational improvements and decentralisation of public healthcare system can bring immense relief to millions of people who are dependent on it for their healthcare needs. A robust non-profit system should support medical, educational and community services more actively to meet the multiple needs of the society. Ethically managed private healthcare institutions, which provide high quality of care, not only inspire trust but also ensure that critical health issues are addressed to global standards.

Notes

1 'India's population expected to rise till 2050 and then decline: UN', NDTV, 19 April 2023, https://www.ndtv.com/india-news/indias-population-expected-to-rise-till-2050-and-then-decline-un-3961880#:~:text=The%20UN%20analysis%20stated%20that,would%20dip%20to%20131.7%20crore
2 'Cancer waiting times', Cancer Research, https://www.cancerresearchuk.org/about-cancer/worried-about-cancer/cancer-waiting-times
3 Apollo Hospitals, Greams Road, Chennai, https://www.bdhci.com/hospitals/apollo-hospital-greams-road-chennai
4 'Ex-Health Secretary warns against healthcare privatisation', *Deccan Chronicle*, 23 February 2025, https://www.deccanchronicle.com/news/ex-health-secretary-warns-against-healthcare-privatisation-1862999
5 'Commercialisation of health services can be a recipe for disaster, says Sujatha Rao', *The Hindu*, 21 September 2024, https://www.thehindu.com/sci-tech/science/commercialising-health-services-can-be-a-recipe-for-disaster/article68664340.ece
6 'Indian hospitals operating profit margin to remain healthy, over 22% in FY24: ICRA', *BW Healthcare*, 16 August 2023,' https://bwhealthcareworld.com/article/indian-hospitals-operating-profit-margin-to-remain-healthy-over-22-in-fy24-icra-487824
7 Dr. Mahboob Khan, 'Indian private hospitals making profits up to 1,737% on drugs, consumables and diagnostics: Study', LinkedIn, 27 November 2023, https://www.linkedin.com/pulse/indian-private-hospitals-making-profits-up-1737-drugs-dr-mahboob-gqkaf

8 Lok Sabha, 'Unstarred question no. 898, To be answered on 16 July 2024', *Ministry of Health and Family Welfare*, https://sansad.in/getFile/loksabhaquestions/annex/182/AU898_m8klTn.pdf?source=pqals
9 National Digital Health Mission, https://www.niti.gov.in/sites/default/files/2023-02/ndhm_strategy_overview.pdf
10 'How early diagnosis can transform health care', *EY Global*, 14 June 2023, https://www.ey.com/en_gl/insights/life-sciences/how-early-diagnosis-can-transform-health-care
11 'Mapping trends in health research and medical innovation', *Nature Portfolio*, https://www.nature.com/articles/d42473-023-00161-1#:~:text=Big%20data%20and%20artificial%20intelligence,services%20will%20be%20further%20improved
12 U. Venkatesh, Akash Sharma, V.A. Anathan, P. Subbiah, and R. Durga, *Journal of Nutrition Science*, 2021;10:e110. https://pmc.ncbi.nlm.nih.gov/articles/PMC8727714/
13 List of health insurers, Insurance Regulatory and Development Authority of India, https://irdai.gov.in/list-of-health-insurers
14 'Health insurance premiums cross Rs. 1 lakh crore in 10 months, growth slows to 10%', *The Economic Times*, 28 February 2025, https://economictimes.indiatimes.com/industry/banking/finance/insure/health-insurance-premiums-cross-rs-1-lakh-crore-in-10-months-growth-slows-to-10/articleshow/118624113.cms?from=mdr
15 'Growth of health insurance sector enabling healthcare access across India', *YourStory*, 3 January 2025, https://yourstory.com/2025/01/growth-health-insurance-sector-enabling-healthcare-access-across-india
16 Rema Nagarajan, 'Refer a patient, get a cut: Commission game is back in a murkier avatar', *Times of India*, 30 January 2025, https://timesofindia.indiatimes.com/toi-plus/health/refer-a-patient-get-a-cut-commission-game-is-back-in-a-murkier-avatar/articleshow/117723242.cms
17 'I-T covers doctor-lab referral nexus in Bangaluru', *Times of India*, 30 December 2017, https://timesofindia.indiatimes.com/india/i-t-uncovers-doctor-lab-referral-nexus-in-bengaluru/articleshow/61899203.cms
18 Samuel Lovett, Nandi Theint, and Nicola Smith, 'Revealed: Global private hospital group embroiled in "cash for kidneys" racket', *The Telegraph*, 3 December 2023, https://www.telegraph.co.uk/global-health/science-and-disease/kidney-organ-trafficking-scandal-private-healthcare-india-myanmar/
19 IMA Code of Conduct, Indian Medical Association, https://www.ima-india.org/ima/left-side-bar.php?pid=462
20 'First of its kind: Maharashtra Bill to stop doctors' commissions cuts both ways', *Institute of Medicine and Law*, 26 October 2017, https://imlindia.com/blog/first-of-its-kind-maharashtra-bill-to-stop-doctors'-commissions-cuts-both-ways
21 'Unbundled charges by private hospitals to push healthcare costs', *Medical Buyer*, https://medicalbuyer.co.in/unbundled-charges-by-private-hospitals-to-push-healthcare-costs/
22 'Inequality report 2021: India's unequal healthcare story', *Oxfam India*, 19 July 2021, https://www.oxfamindia.org/knowledgehub/workingpaper/inequality-report-2021-indias-unequal-healthcare-story
23 R.S. Nilakantan, India's health report (chapter 1), *South vs North: India's Great Divide* (Juggernaut, 2022).
24 K. Srinath Reddy, *Make Health in India: Reaching a Billion Plus* (Orient Blackswan, 2019).
25 The number of health centres is given in this report. 'Health Ministry releases "Health Dynamics of India (Infrastructure and Human Resources) 2022–23"', 9 September 2024, https://pib.gov.in/PressReleasePage.aspx?PRID=2053070

26 Universal health coverage, World Health Organization, https://www.who.int/health-topics/universal-health-coverage
27 'Over 70% innovation in Indian MedTech startups driven by digital integration; several factors propel industry growth: EY Parthenon report', press release, EY India, https://www.ey.com/en_in/newsroom/2024/11/over-70-percent-innovation-in-indian-medtech-startups-driven-by-digital-integration-several-factors-propel-industry-growth-ey-parthenon-report
28 'India among five countries with largest number of people living in poverty: UN report', *The Economic Times*, 18 October 2024, https://economictimes.indiatimes.com/news/india/india-among-five-countries-with-largest-number-of-people-living-in-poverty-un-report/articleshow/114355591.cms?utm_source=contentofinterest&utm_medium=text&utm_campaign=cppst
29 'Indian middle class will nearly double to 61% by 2046-47: PRICE Report', *Business Standard*, 5 July 2023, https://www.business-standard.com/economy/news/indian-middle-class-will-nearly-double-to-61-by-2046-47-price-report-123070500864_1.html
30 'Top 20 hospitals in value-based purchasing', *Definitive Healthcare*, 6 September 2022, https://www.definitivehc.com/resources/healthcare-insights/hospital-value-based-purchasing-score
31 https://abdm.gov.in:8081/uploads/VBHC_Policy_Document_For_Upload_a20f871a55.pdf
32 'Quality measures and standards for transitioning to value-based health care in India', *Pricewaterhouse Cooper*, https://www.pwc.in/assets/pdfs/quality-measures-and-standards-for-transitioning-to-value-based-healthcare-in-india.pdf
33 Lok Sabha, unstarred question, Ministry of Health and Family Welfare, https://sansad.in/getFile/loksabhaquestions/annex/182/AU898_m8klTn.pdf?source=pqals
34 'Study on the not-for-profit hospital: Model in India', NITI Aayog, https://www.niti.gov.in/sites/default/files/2023-03/Study-on-Not-for-Profit-Hospital-model-in-India.pdf
35 M. Khalifa and M. Albadawy, 'Artificial intelligence for clinical prediction: Exploring key domains and essential functions', *Computer Methods and Programs in Biomedicine Update,* 2024;5:100148. https://www.sciencedirect.com/science/article/pii/S2666990024000156#:~:text=This%20process%20involves%20the%20use,diagnoses%2C%20and%20improving%20treatment%20planning
36 'Internet of Medial Things (IoMT) for healthcare IoT', *TechTarget*, https://www.techtarget.com/iotagenda/definition/IoMT-Internet-of-Medical-Things
37 'The Internet of Medical Things (IoMT): A brief introduction', *Splunk*, https://www.splunk.com/en_us/blog/learn/the-internet-of-medical-things-iomt.html
38 'Top healthcare technology trends in 2025 to elevate your medical business', *Acropolium*, https://acropolium.com/blog/top-healthcare-technology-trends/
39 'Top 17 healthcare technology trends in 2025', *Tateeda*, https://tateeda.com/blog/healthcare-technology-trends
40 *IDF Diabetes Atlas*, 10th ed., Brussels: International Diabetes Foundation, https://www.ncbi.nlm.nih.gov/books/NBK581934/
41 K. Sathishkumar, M. Chaturvedi, P. Das, S. Stephen, and P. Mathur, *Indian Journal of Medical Research* 2022;156:598–607, https://pubmed.ncbi.nlm.nih.gov/36510887/
42 'A study of how rural people are using digital channels', https://ascentgroupindia.com/wp-content/uploads/2021/09/How-rural-people-are-using-Digital-Channels-3.pdf

Index

Note: Page numbers in *Italics* refer to figures; page numbers in **Bold** refer to tables

For Product Safety Concerns and Information please contact our EU representative GPSR@taylorandfrancis.com Taylor & Francis Verlag GmbH, Kaufingerstraße 24, 80331 München, Germany